MAR 10 2011

# EXCEL SAGA 05

## STORY AND ART BY
# RIKDO KOSHI

**STORY AND ART BY**
RIKDO KOSHI

**ENGLISH ADAPTATION BY**
DAN KANEMITSU & CARL GUSTAV HORN

**TRANSLATION**
DAN KANEMITSU

**LETTERING & TOUCH-UP BY**
CATO

**COVER DESIGN**
BRUCE LEWIS

**GRAPHIC DESIGNER**
CAROLINA UGALDE

**EDITOR**
CARL GUSTAV HORN

**MANAGING EDITOR**
ANNETTE ROMAN

**EDITOR IN CHIEF**
WILLIAM FLANAGAN

**PRODUCTION MANAGER**
NOBORU WATANABE

**SR. DIRECTOR OF LICENSING & ACQUISITIONS**
RIKA INOUE

**VP OF MARKETING**
LIZA COPPOLA

**SR. VP OF EDITORIAL**
HYOE NARITA

**PUBLISHER**
SEIJI HORIBUCHI

EXCEL SAGA © 1997 Rikdo Koshi. Originally published in Japan in 1997 by SHONENGAHOSHA CO., LTD. Tokyo. English translation rights arranged with SHONENGAHOSHA CO., LTD.

New and adapted artwork © 2004 VIZ, LLC

Printed in Canada.

Published by VIZ, LLC
P.O. Box 77064
San Francisco, CA 94107

Action Edition

10 9 8 7 6 5 4 3 2 1

First printing, February 2004

For advertising rates or media kit, e-mail advertising@viz.com

www.animerica-mag.com

www.viz.com

store.viz.com

*GRAPHIC NOVEL / RK / t / vol.5*

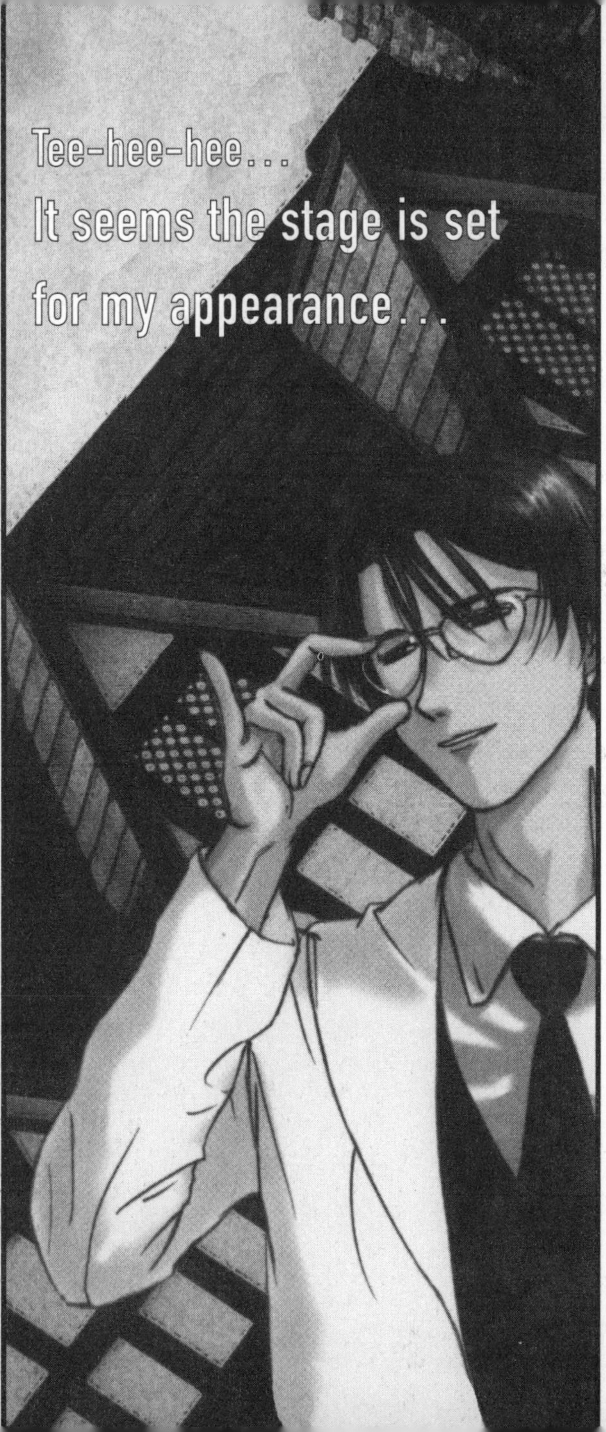
Tee-hee-hee...
It seems the stage is set
for my appearance...

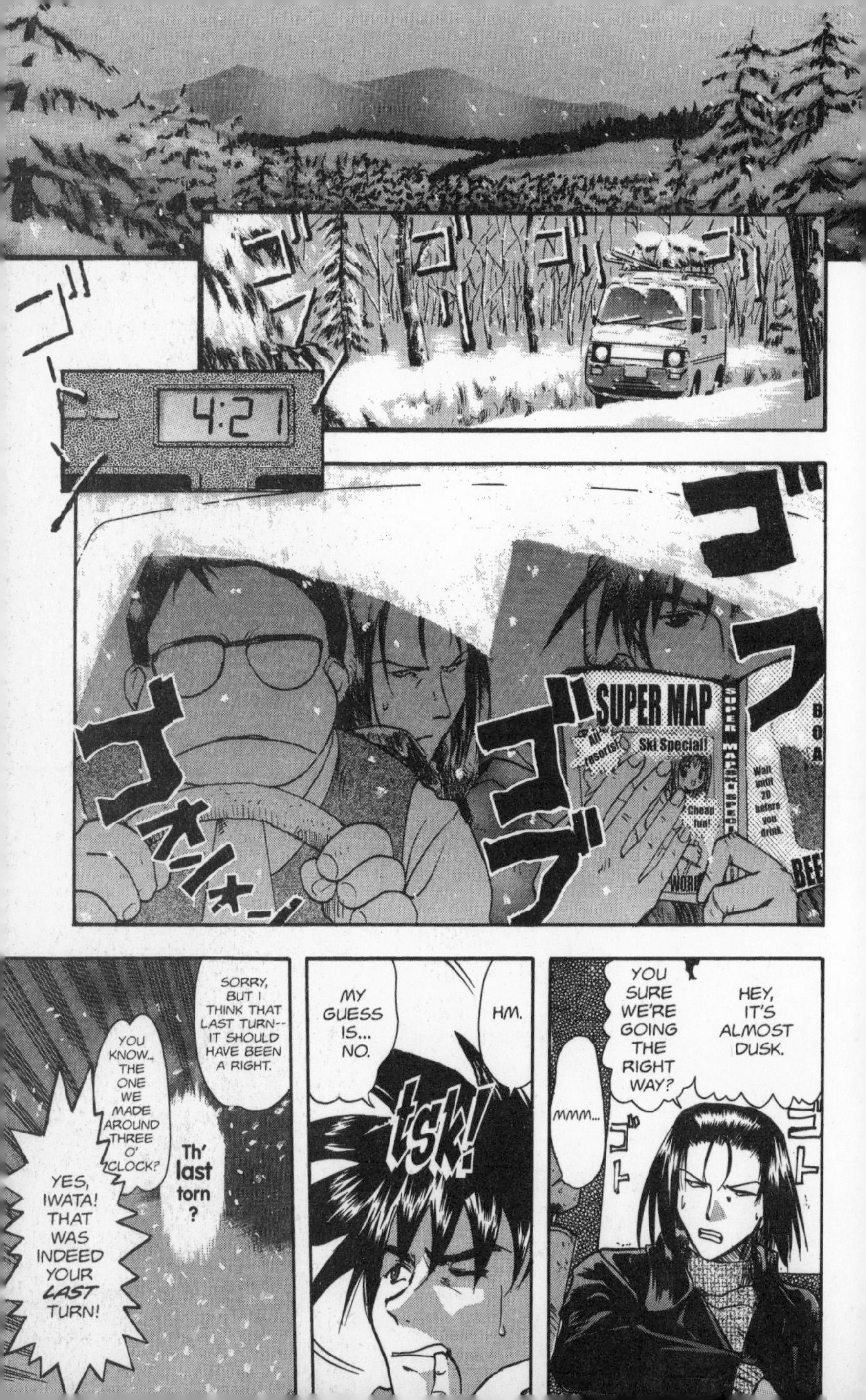
4:21
SUPER MAP
All resorts!
Ski Special!
Cheap fun!
Wait until 20 before you drink.
HEY, IT'S ALMOST DUSK.
YOU SURE WE'RE GOING THE RIGHT WAY?
MMM...
HM.
MY GUESS IS... NO.
tsk!
SORRY, BUT I THINK THAT LAST TURN-- IT SHOULD HAVE BEEN A RIGHT.
YOU KNOW... THE ONE WE MADE AROUND THREE O' CLOCK?
Th' last torn ?
YES, IWATA! THAT WAS INDEED YOUR *LAST* TURN!

# MISSION 1
# THE WHITE ALBUM

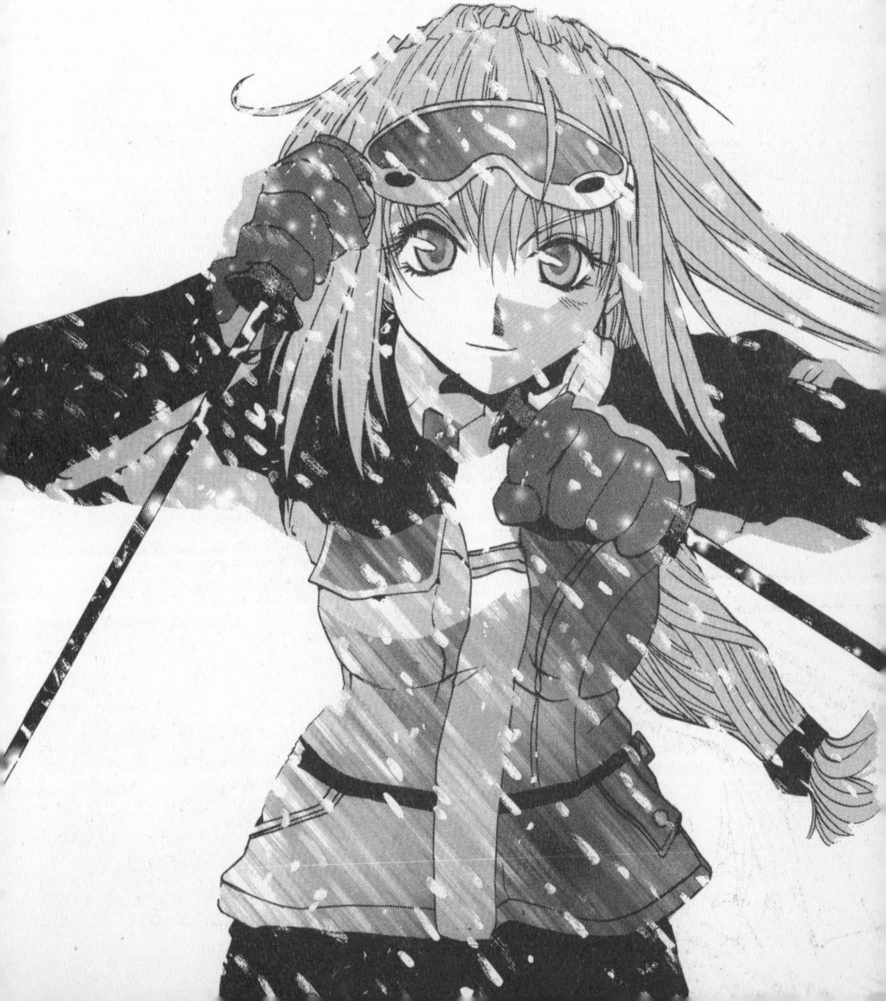

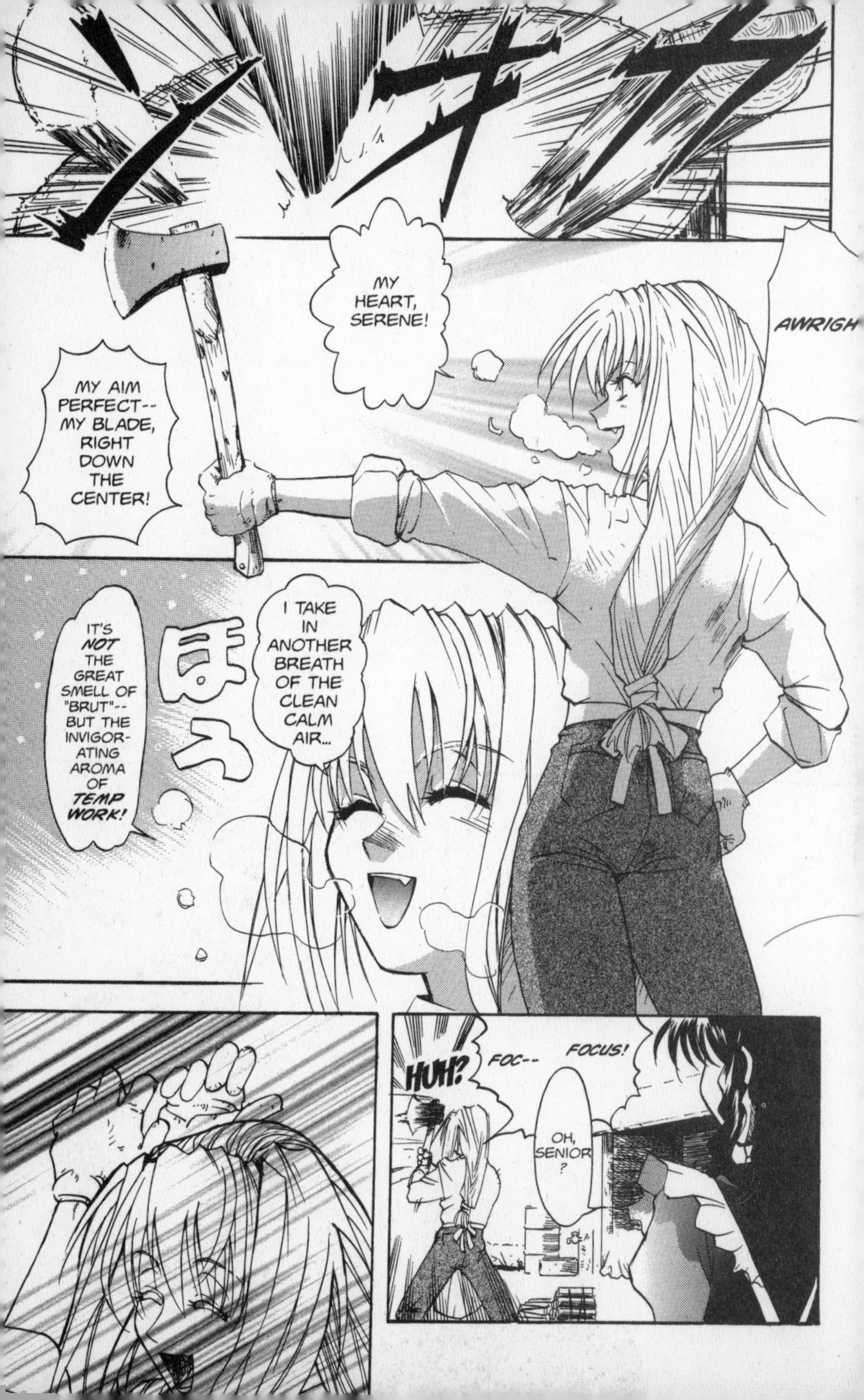
AWRIGH
MY HEART, SERENE!
MY AIM PERFECT-- MY BLADE, RIGHT DOWN THE CENTER!
I TAKE IN ANOTHER BREATH OF THE CLEAN CALM AIR...
ほっ
IT'S NOT THE GREAT SMELL OF "BRUT"-- BUT THE INVIGORATING AROMA OF TEMP WORK!
FOC-- FOCUS!
HUH?
OH, SENIOR?

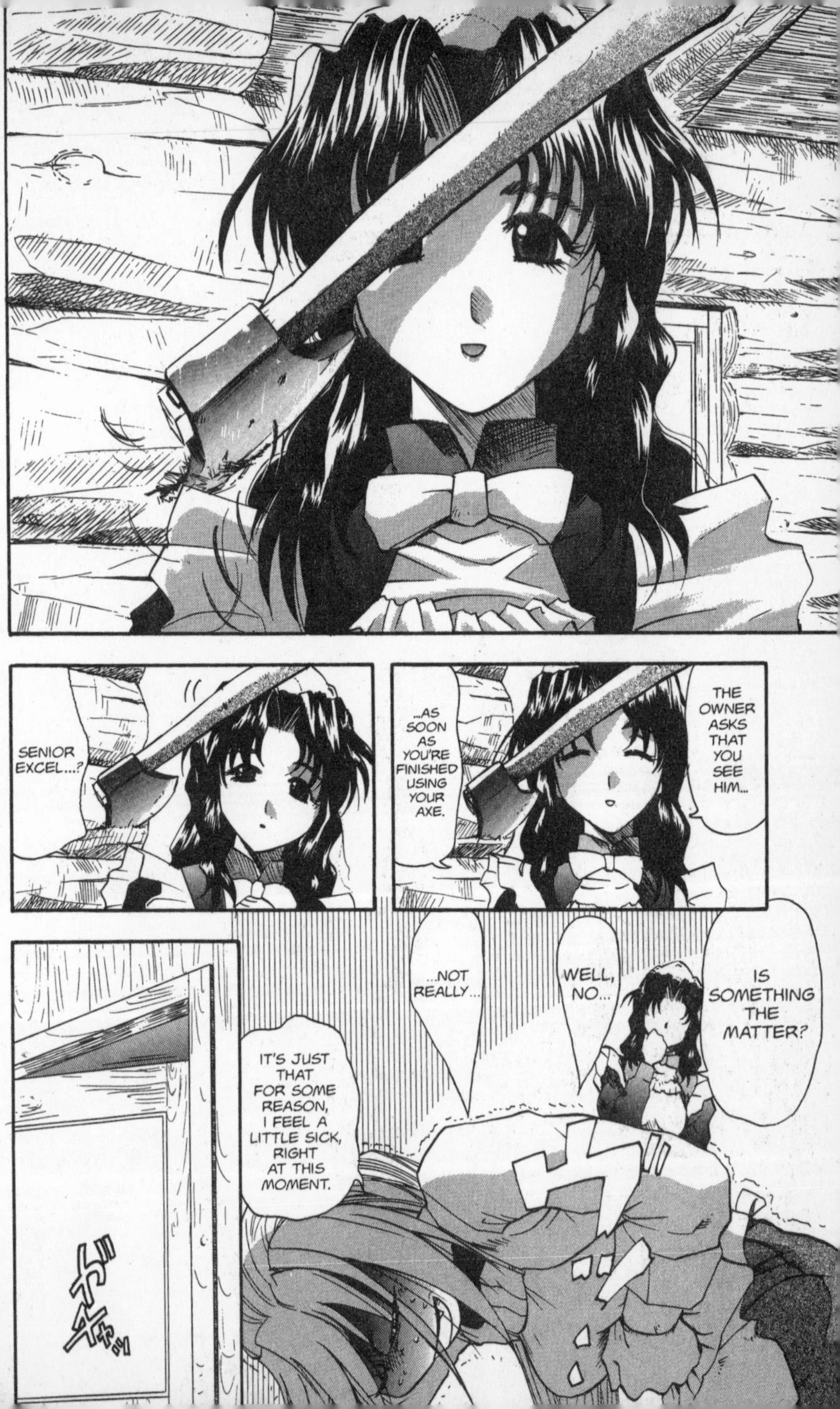
THE OWNER ASKS THAT YOU SEE HIM...
...AS SOON AS YOU'RE FINISHED USING YOUR AXE.
SENIOR EXCEL...?
IS SOMETHING THE MATTER?
WELL, NO...
...NOT REALLY...
IT'S JUST THAT FOR SOME REASON, I FEEL A LITTLE SICK, RIGHT AT THIS MOMENT.

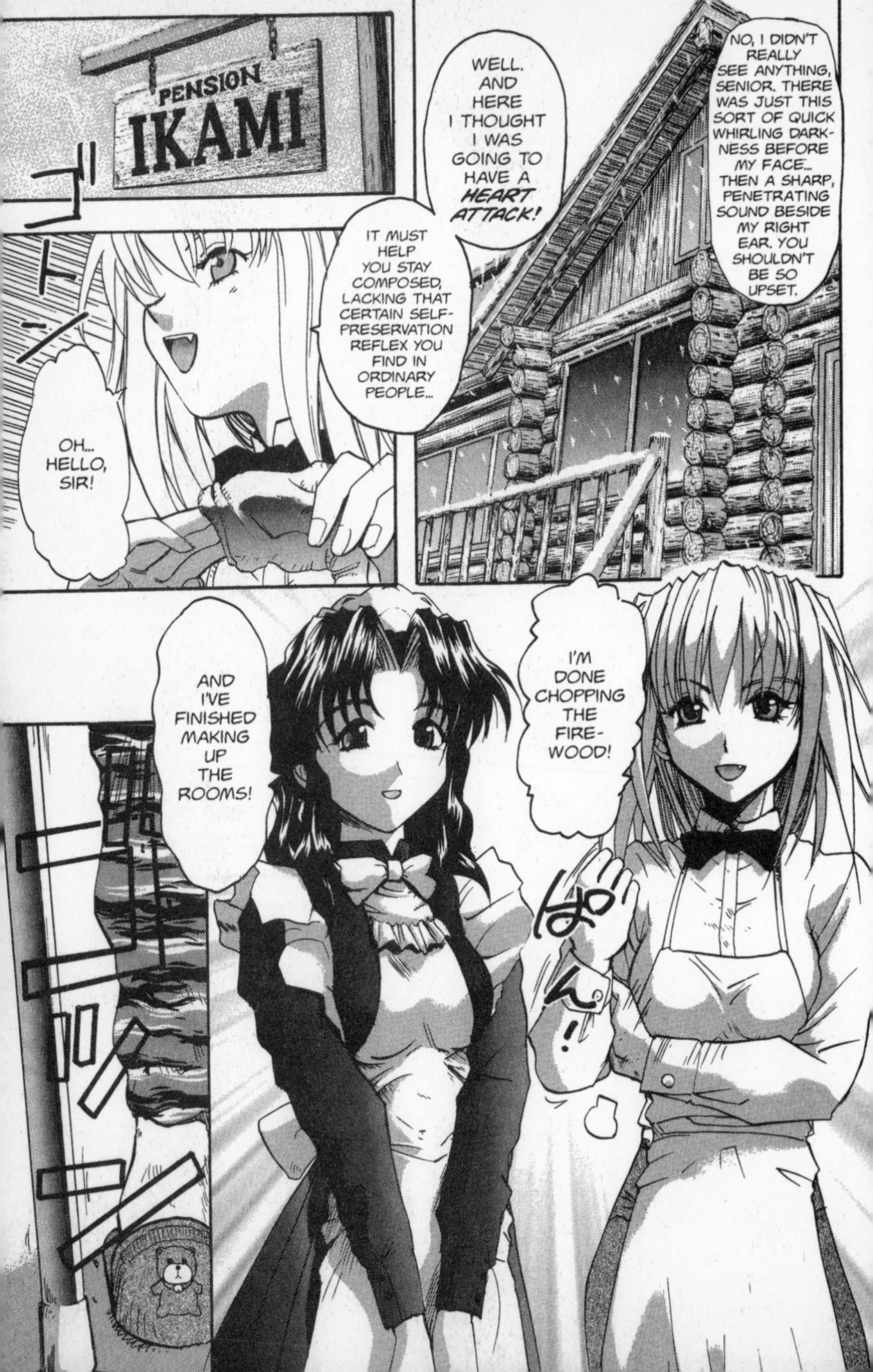
NO, I DIDN'T REALLY SEE ANYTHING, SENIOR. THERE WAS JUST THIS SORT OF QUICK WHIRLING DARKNESS BEFORE MY FACE... THEN A SHARP, PENETRATING SOUND BESIDE MY RIGHT EAR. YOU SHOULDN'T BE SO UPSET.
WELL. AND HERE I THOUGHT I WAS GOING TO HAVE A HEART ATTACK!
PENSION IKAMI
IT MUST HELP YOU STAY COMPOSED, LACKING THAT CERTAIN SELF-PRESERVATION REFLEX YOU FIND IN ORDINARY PEOPLE...
OH... HELLO, SIR!
I'M DONE CHOPPING THE FIREWOOD!
ぱん!
AND I'VE FINISHED MAKING UP THE ROOMS!

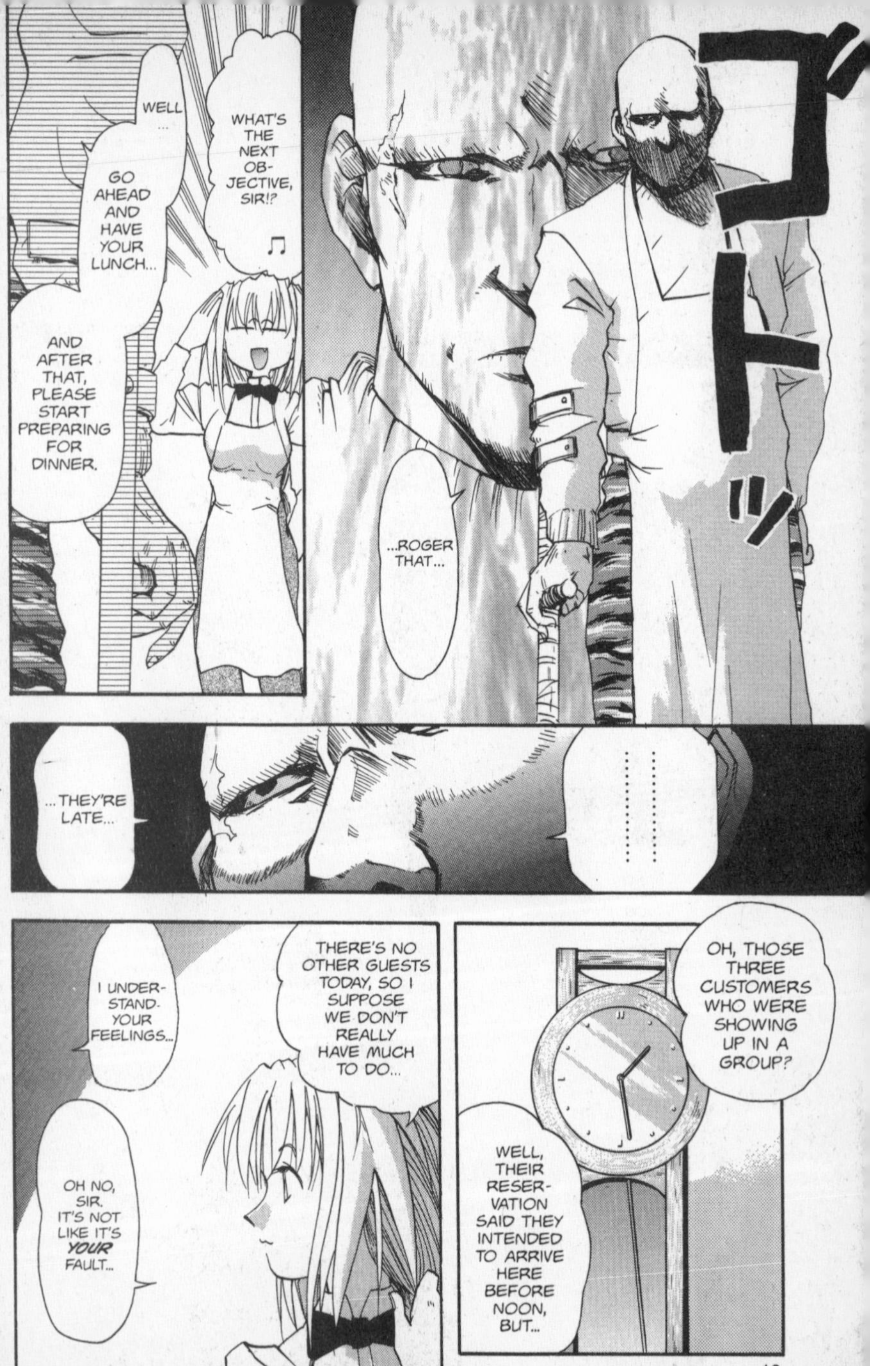
ゴトッ
...ROGER THAT...
WHAT'S THE NEXT OBJECTIVE, SIR!? ♫
WELL ...
GO AHEAD AND HAVE YOUR LUNCH...
AND AFTER THAT, PLEASE START PREPARING FOR DINNER.
......
...THEY'RE LATE...
OH, THOSE THREE CUSTOMERS WHO WERE SHOWING UP IN A GROUP?
WELL, THEIR RESERVATION SAID THEY INTENDED TO ARRIVE HERE BEFORE NOON, BUT...
THERE'S NO OTHER GUESTS TODAY, SO I SUPPOSE WE DON'T REALLY HAVE MUCH TO DO...
I UNDERSTAND YOUR FEELINGS...
OH NO, SIR. IT'S NOT LIKE IT'S *YOUR* FAULT...

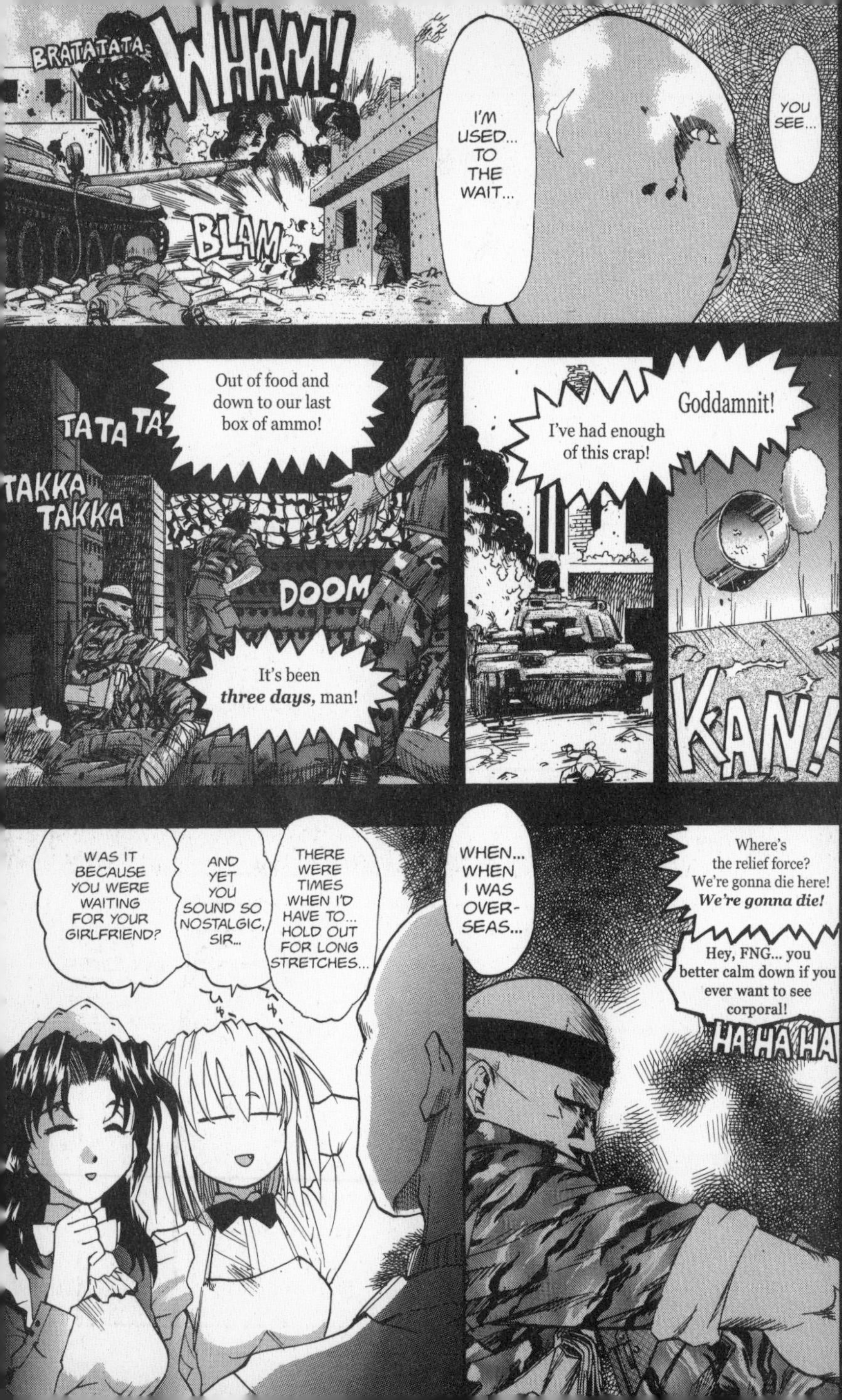
YOU SEE...
I'M USED... TO THE WAIT...
WHAM!
BRATATATA
BLAM
Goddamnit!
I've had enough of this crap!
KAN!
Out of food and down to our last box of ammo!
TA TA TA
TAKKA TAKKA
DOOM
It's been *three days,* man!
Where's the relief force? We're gonna die here! ***We're gonna die!***
Hey, FNG... you better calm down if you ever want to see corporal!
HA HA HA
WHEN... WHEN I WAS OVER-SEAS...
THERE WERE TIMES WHEN I'D HAVE TO... HOLD OUT FOR LONG STRETCHES...
AND YET YOU SOUND SO NOSTALGIC, SIR...
WAS IT BECAUSE YOU WERE WAITING FOR YOUR GIRLFRIEND?

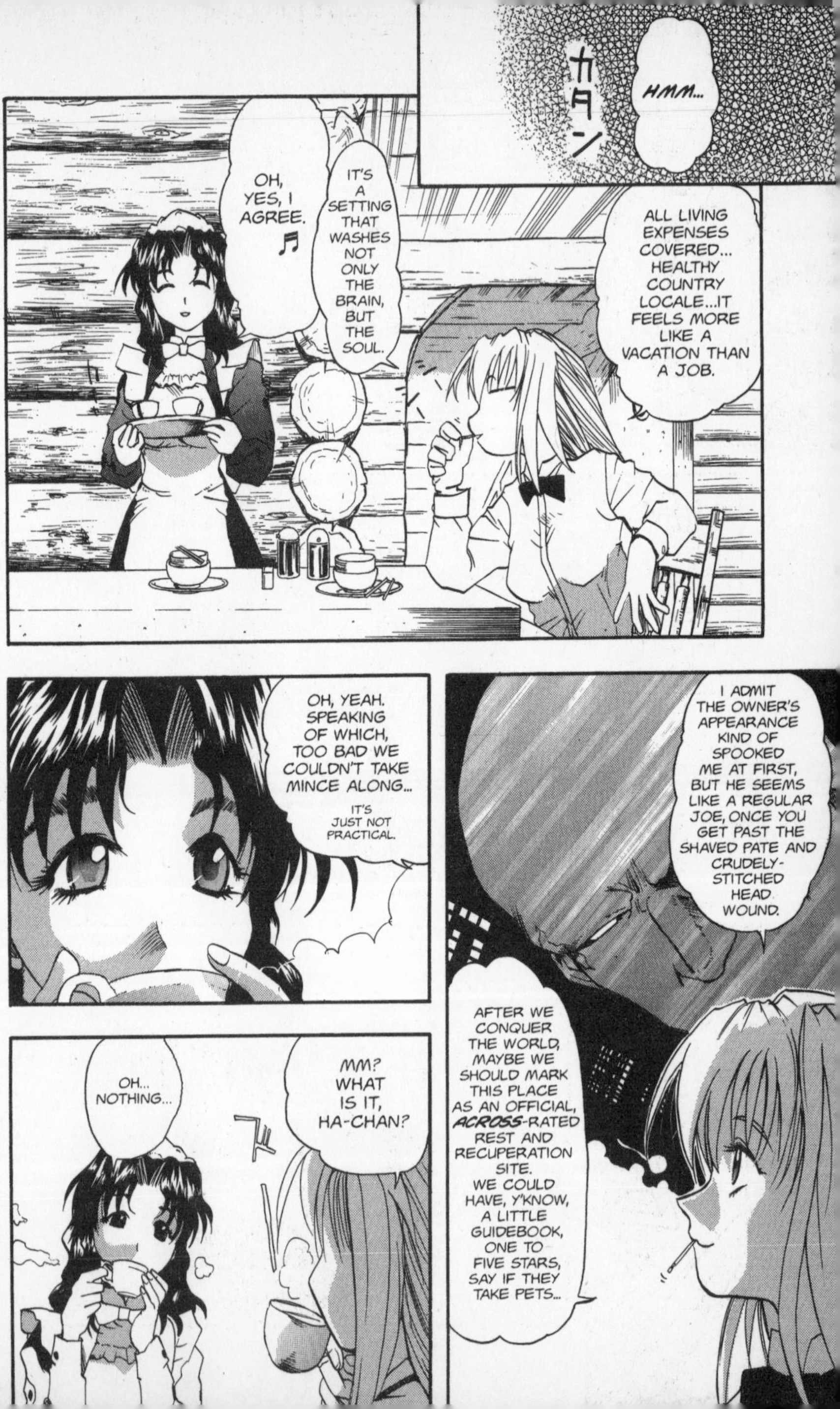
カタン
HMM...
ALL LIVING EXPENSES COVERED... HEALTHY COUNTRY LOCALE...IT FEELS MORE LIKE A VACATION THAN A JOB.
IT'S A SETTING THAT WASHES NOT ONLY THE BRAIN, BUT THE SOUL.
OH, YES, I AGREE. ♫
I ADMIT THE OWNER'S APPEARANCE KIND OF SPOOKED ME AT FIRST, BUT HE SEEMS LIKE A REGULAR JOE, ONCE YOU GET PAST THE SHAVED PATE AND CRUDELY-STITCHED HEAD WOUND.
AFTER WE CONQUER THE WORLD, MAYBE WE SHOULD MARK THIS PLACE AS AN OFFICIAL, ACROSS-RATED REST AND RECUPERATION SITE. WE COULD HAVE, Y'KNOW, A LITTLE GUIDEBOOK, ONE TO FIVE STARS, SAY IF THEY TAKE PETS...
OH, YEAH. SPEAKING OF WHICH, TOO BAD WE COULDN'T TAKE MINCE ALONG...
IT'S JUST NOT PRACTICAL.
MM? WHAT IS IT, HA-CHAN?
OH... NOTHING...

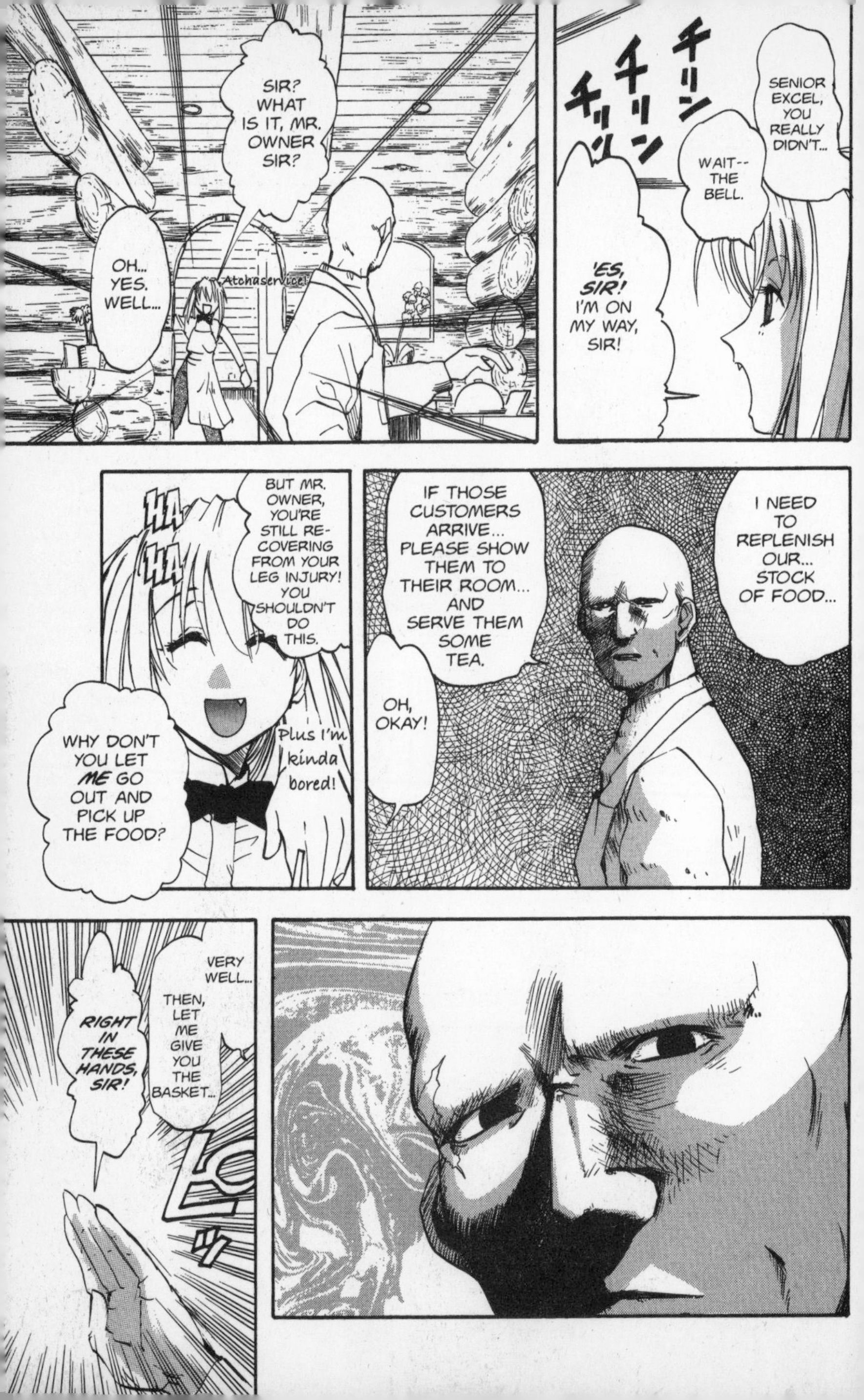
SENIOR EXCEL, YOU REALLY DIDN'T...
WAIT-- THE BELL.
チリン
チリン
チリン
'ES, SIR! I'M ON MY WAY, SIR!
SIR? WHAT IS IT, MR. OWNER SIR?
Atchaservice!
OH... YES. WELL...
I NEED TO REPLENISH OUR... STOCK OF FOOD...
IF THOSE CUSTOMERS ARRIVE... PLEASE SHOW THEM TO THEIR ROOM... AND SERVE THEM SOME TEA.
OH, OKAY!
BUT MR. OWNER, YOU'RE STILL RE-COVERING FROM YOUR LEG INJURY! YOU SHOULDN'T DO THIS.
HA HA
Plus I'm kinda bored!
WHY DON'T YOU LET *ME* GO OUT AND PICK UP THE FOOD?
VERY WELL...
THEN, LET ME GIVE YOU THE BASKET...
*RIGHT IN THESE HANDS, SIR!*

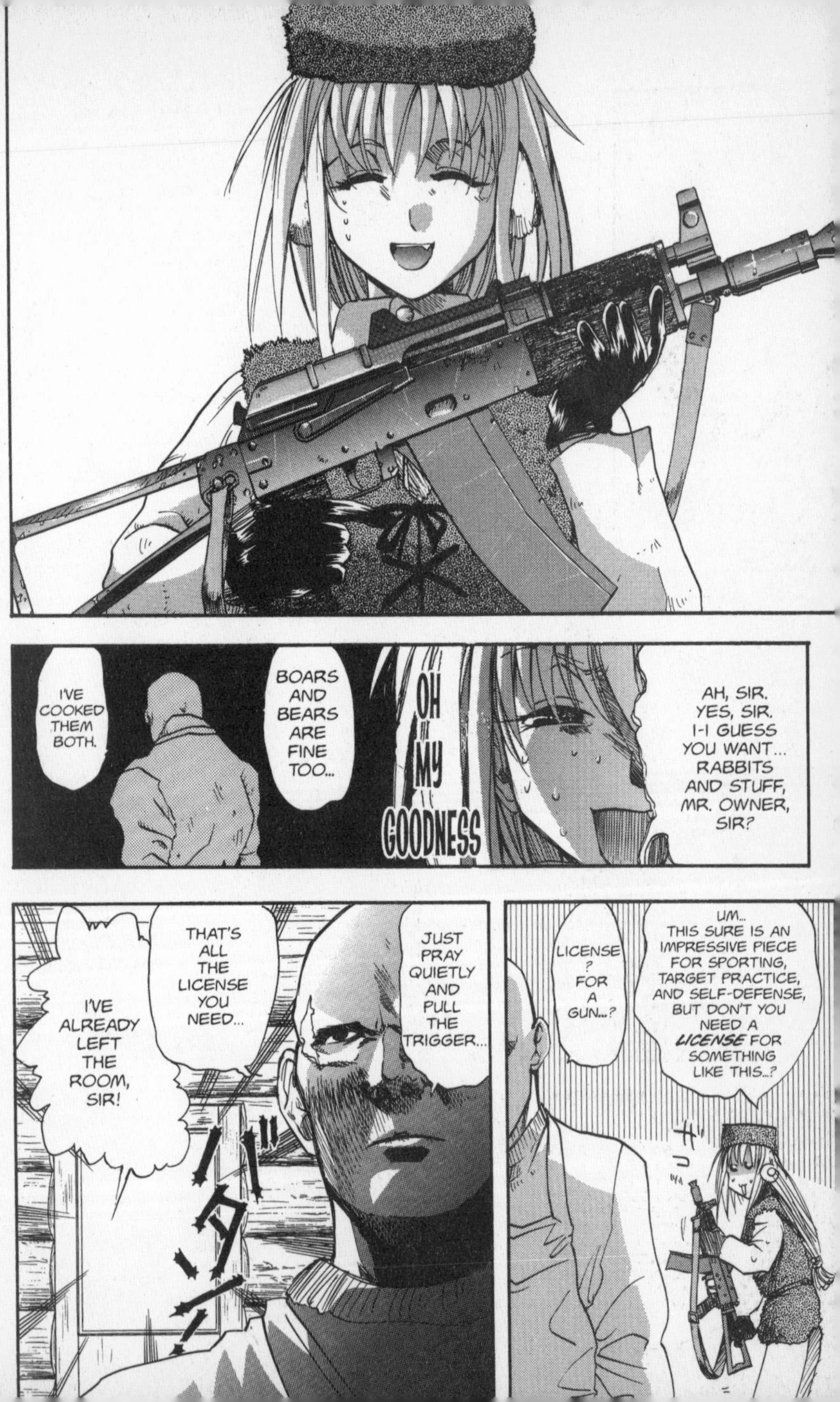
AH, SIR. YES, SIR. I-I GUESS YOU WANT... RABBITS AND STUFF, MR. OWNER, SIR?
OH MY GOODNESS
BOARS AND BEARS ARE FINE TOO...
I'VE COOKED THEM BOTH.
UM... THIS SURE IS AN IMPRESSIVE PIECE FOR SPORTING, TARGET PRACTICE, AND SELF-DEFENSE, BUT DON'T YOU NEED A *LICENSE* FOR SOMETHING LIKE THIS...?
LICENSE? FOR A GUN...?
JUST PRAY QUIETLY AND PULL THE TRIGGER...
THAT'S ALL THE LICENSE YOU NEED...
I'VE ALREADY LEFT THE ROOM, SIR!

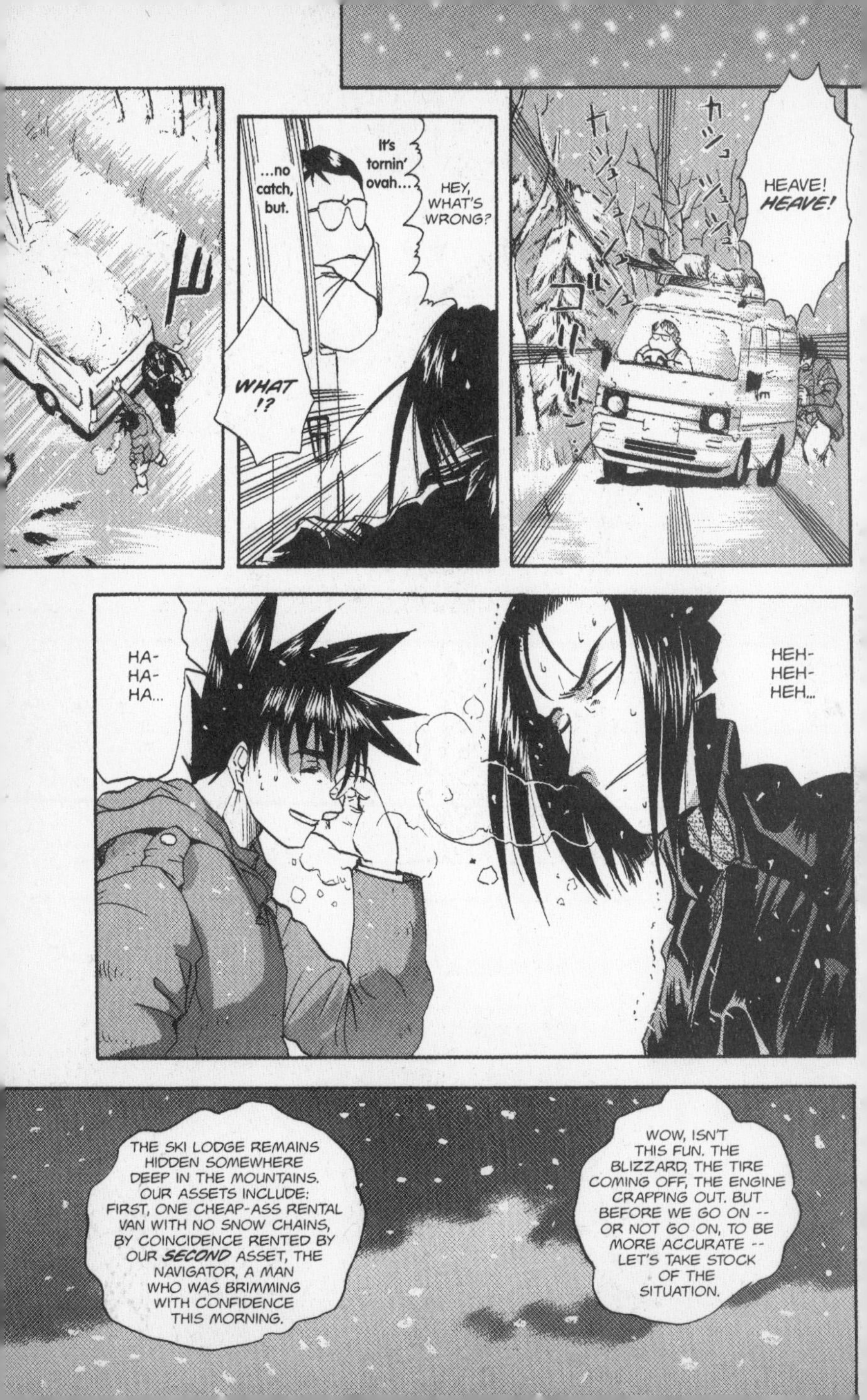
HEAVE! HEAVE!
HEY, WHAT'S WRONG?
It's tornin' ovah...
...no catch, but.
WHAT !?
HEH-HEH-HEH...
HA-HA-HA...
WOW, ISN'T THIS FUN. THE BLIZZARD, THE TIRE COMING OFF, THE ENGINE CRAPPING OUT. BUT BEFORE WE GO ON -- OR NOT GO ON, TO BE MORE ACCURATE -- LET'S TAKE STOCK OF THE SITUATION.
THE SKI LODGE REMAINS HIDDEN SOMEWHERE DEEP IN THE MOUNTAINS. OUR ASSETS INCLUDE: FIRST, ONE CHEAP-ASS RENTAL VAN WITH NO SNOW CHAINS, BY COINCIDENCE RENTED BY OUR SECOND ASSET, THE NAVIGATOR, A MAN WHO WAS BRIMMING WITH CONFIDENCE THIS MORNING.

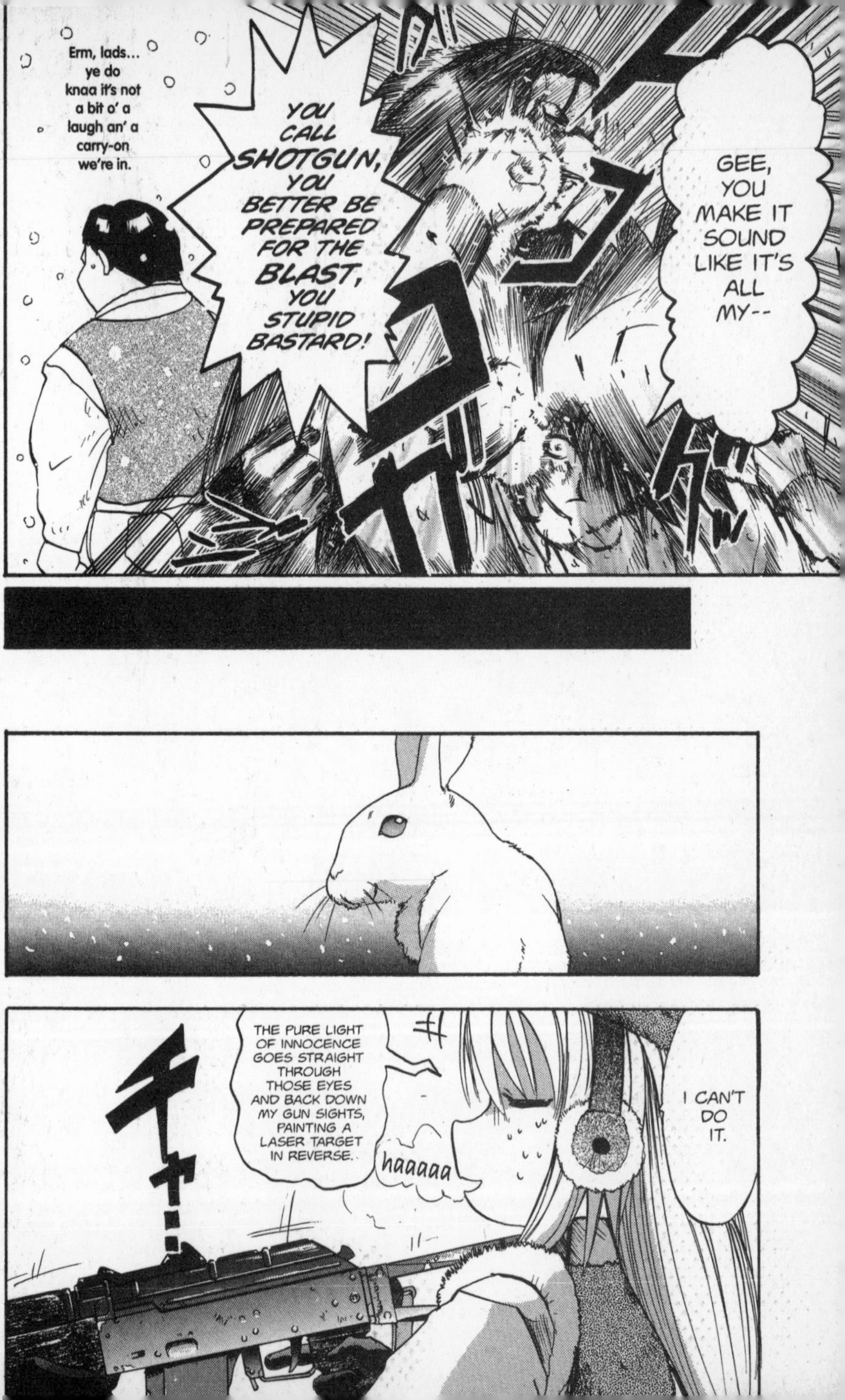
GEE, YOU MAKE IT SOUND LIKE IT'S ALL MY--
YOU CALL SHOTGUN, YOU BETTER BE PREPARED FOR THE BLAST, YOU STUPID BASTARD!
Erm, lads... ye do knaa it's not a bit o' a laugh an' a carry-on we're in.
I CAN'T DO IT.
THE PURE LIGHT OF INNOCENCE GOES STRAIGHT THROUGH THOSE EYES AND BACK DOWN MY GUN SIGHTS, PAINTING A LASER TARGET IN REVERSE.
haaaaa

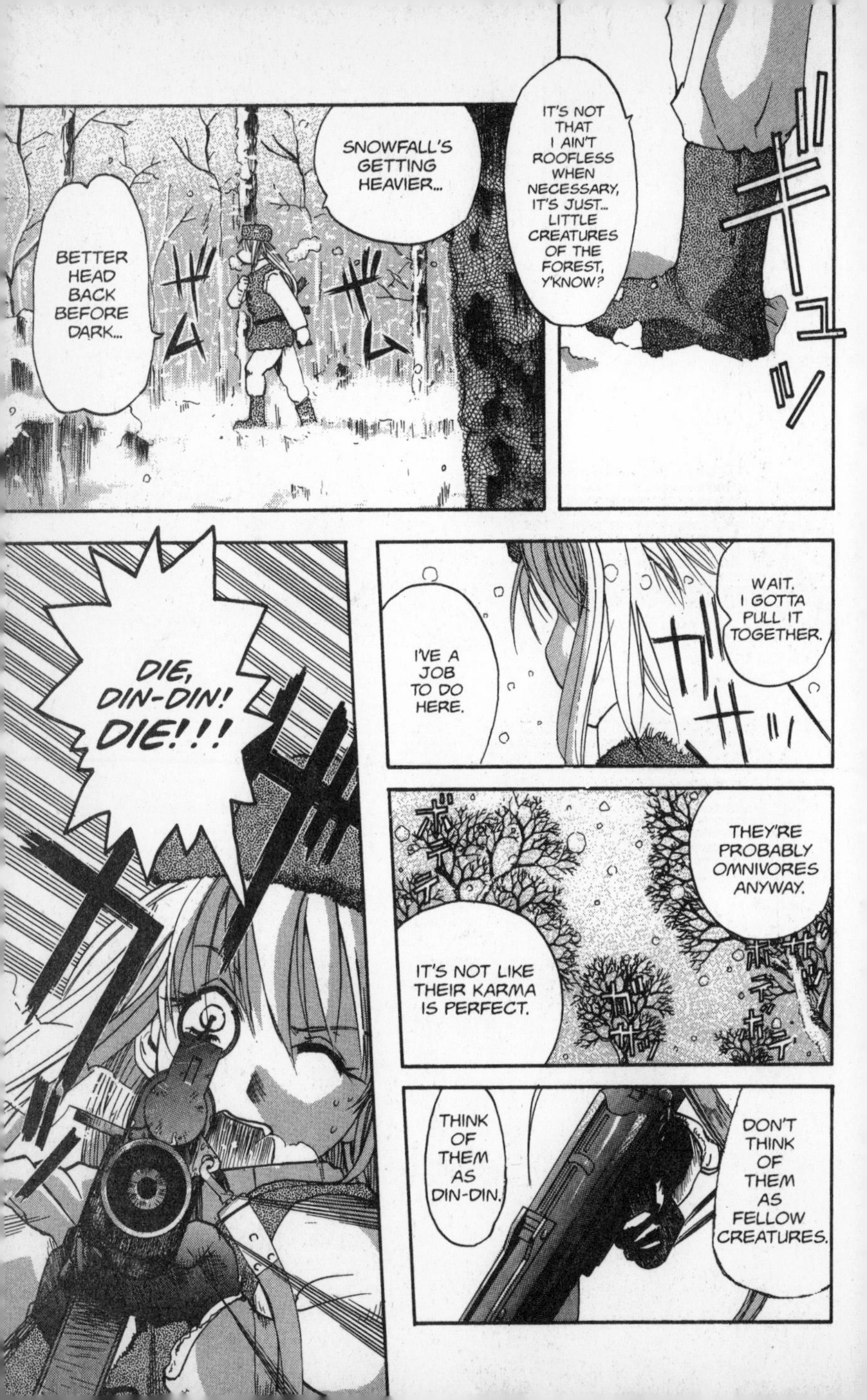
IT'S NOT THAT I AIN'T ROOFLESS WHEN NECESSARY, IT'S JUST... LITTLE CREATURES OF THE FOREST, Y'KNOW?
SNOWFALL'S GETTING HEAVIER...
BETTER HEAD BACK BEFORE DARK...
WAIT. I GOTTA PULL IT TOGETHER.
I'VE A JOB TO DO HERE.
THEY'RE PROBABLY OMNIVORES ANYWAY.
IT'S NOT LIKE THEIR KARMA IS PERFECT.
DON'T THINK OF THEM AS FELLOW CREATURES.
THINK OF THEM AS DIN-DIN.
DIE, DIN-DIN! DIE!!!

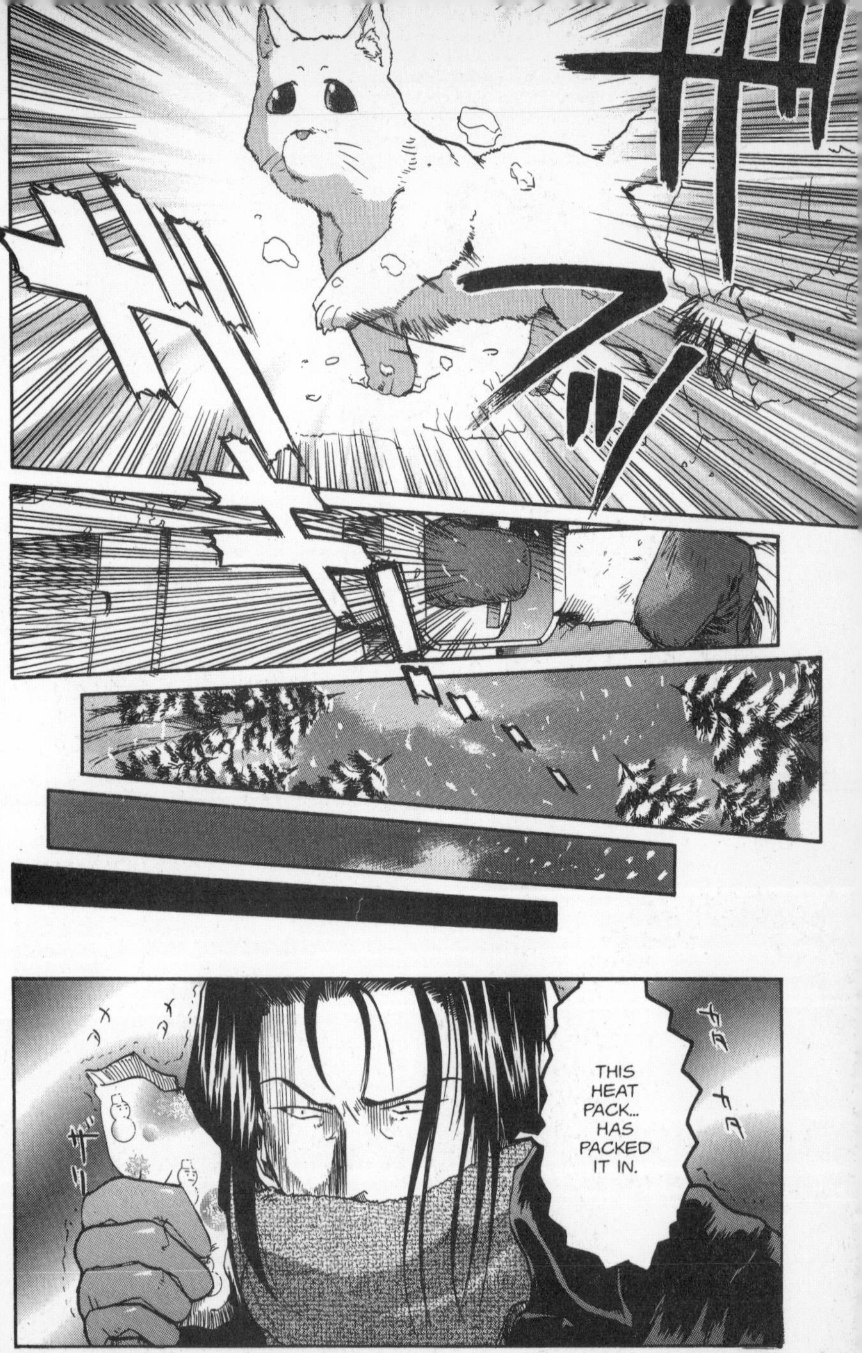
THIS HEAT PACK... HAS PACKED IT IN.

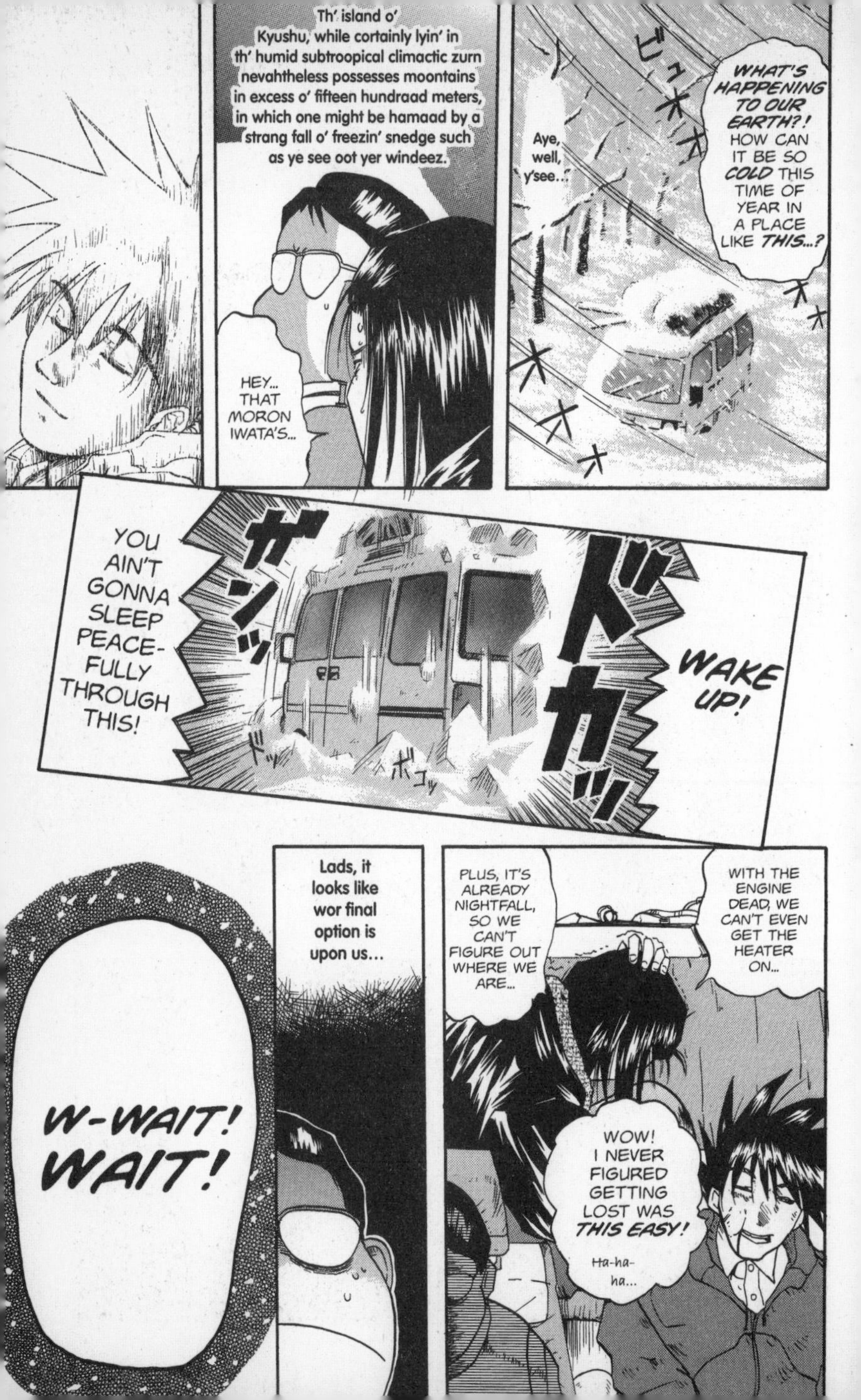

ビュ
WHAT'S HAPPENING TO OUR EARTH?! HOW CAN IT BE SO COLD THIS TIME OF YEAR IN A PLACE LIKE THIS...?
Aye, well, y'see...
Th' island o' Kyushu, while cortainly lyin' in th' humid subtroopical climactic zurn nevahtheless possesses moontains in excess o' fifteen hundraad meters, in which one might be hamaad by a strang fall o' freezin' snedge such as ye see oot yer windeez.
HEY... THAT MORON IWATA'S...
WAKE UP!
ドカッ
ガンッ
YOU AIN'T GONNA SLEEP PEACE-FULLY THROUGH THIS!
ドッ
ボコッ
WITH THE ENGINE DEAD, WE CAN'T EVEN GET THE HEATER ON...
PLUS, IT'S ALREADY NIGHTFALL, SO WE CAN'T FIGURE OUT WHERE WE ARE...
WOW! I NEVER FIGURED GETTING LOST WAS THIS EASY!
Ha-ha-ha...
Lads, it looks like wor final option is upon us...
W-WAIT! WAIT!

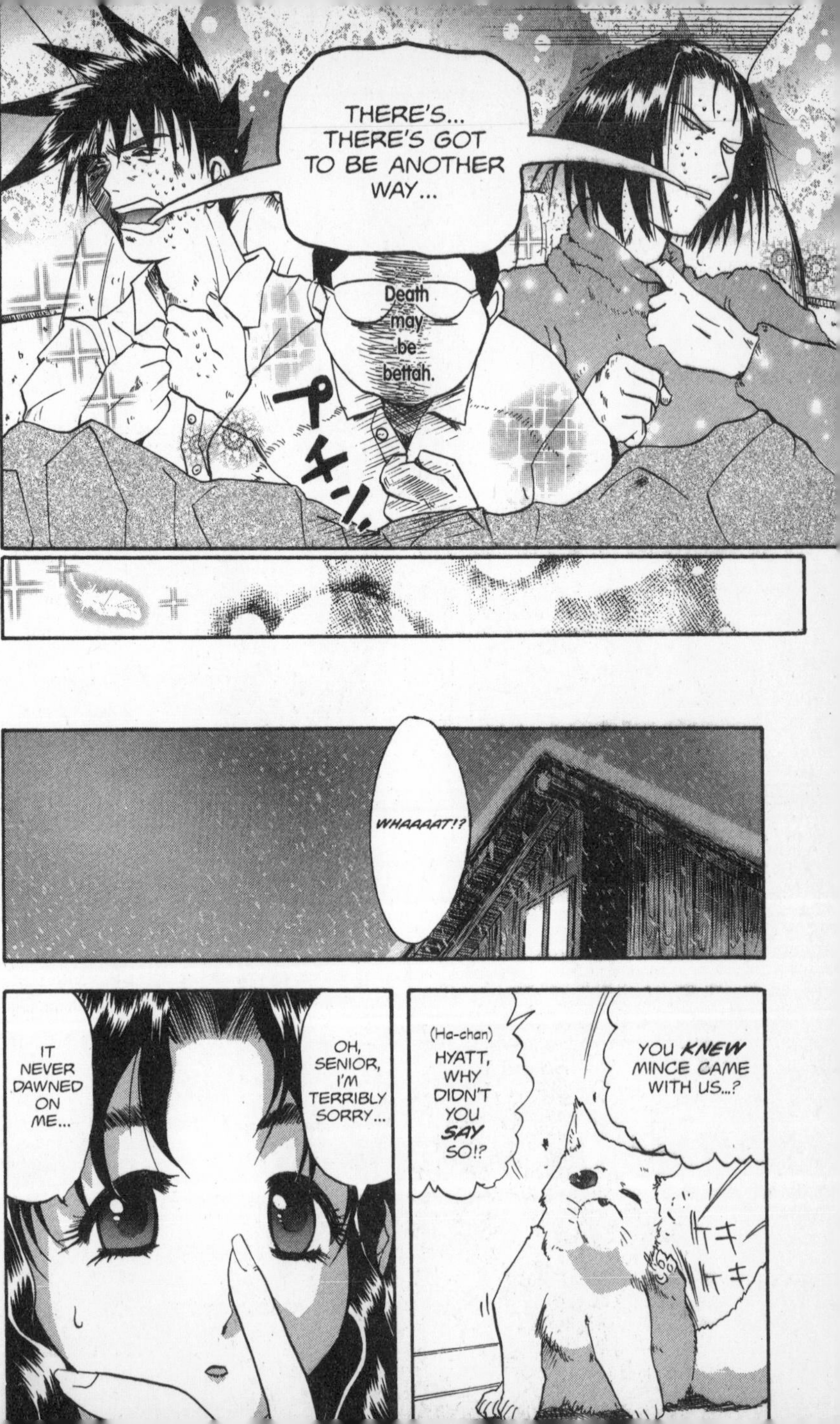
THERE'S... THERE'S GOT TO BE ANOTHER WAY...
Death may be bettah.
プチン
WHAAAAT!?
YOU **KNEW** MINCE CAME WITH US...?
(Ha-chan) HYATT, WHY DIDN'T YOU **SAY** SO!?
ケキケキ
OH, SENIOR, I'M TERRIBLY SORRY...
IT NEVER DAWNED ON ME...

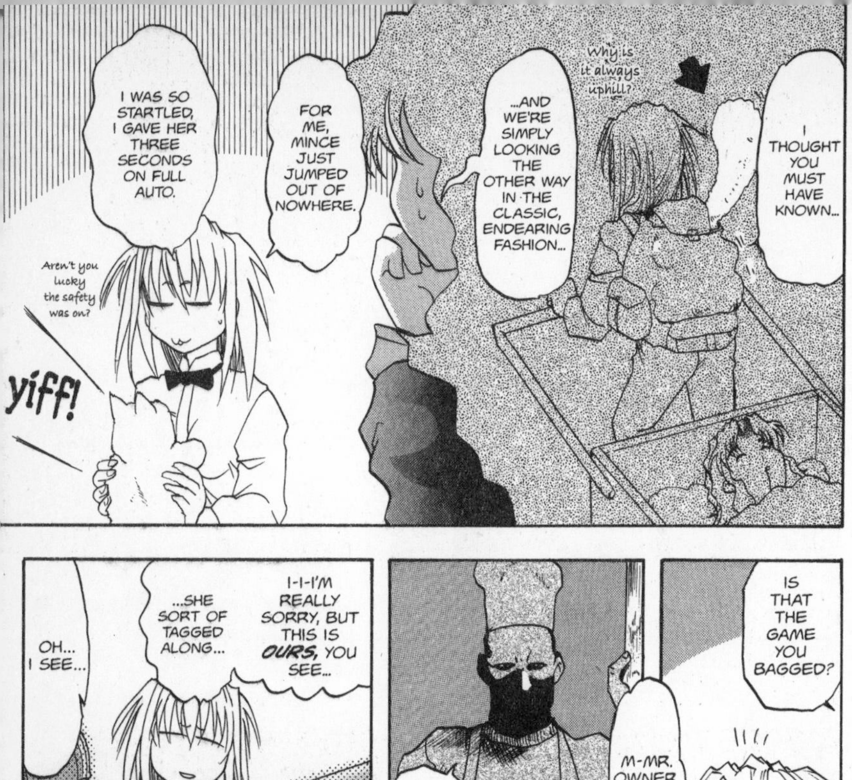
I THOUGHT YOU MUST HAVE KNOWN...
Why is it always uphill?
...AND WE'RE SIMPLY LOOKING THE OTHER WAY IN THE CLASSIC, ENDEARING FASHION...
FOR ME, MINCE JUST JUMPED OUT OF NOWHERE.
I WAS SO STARTLED, I GAVE HER THREE SECONDS ON FULL AUTO.
Aren't you lucky the safety was on?
yiff!
IS THAT THE GAME YOU BAGGED?
M-MR. OWNER, SIR!
A DOG. I HAD ONE ONCE.
I-I-I'M REALLY SORRY, BUT THIS IS OURS, YOU SEE...
...SHE SORT OF TAGGED ALONG...
OH... I SEE...

*Year-End Special Thanks: Po, Jinnojyou, Tachibana, and Hajime Antonia Ikami (grin)*

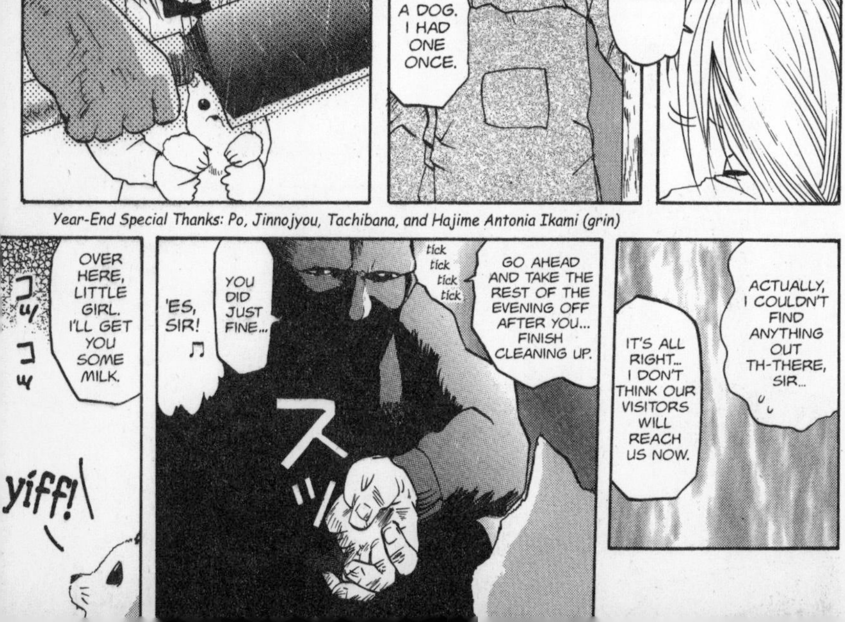
ACTUALLY, I COULDN'T FIND ANYTHING OUT TH-THERE, SIR...
IT'S ALL RIGHT... I DON'T THINK OUR VISITORS WILL REACH US NOW.
GO AHEAD AND TAKE THE REST OF THE EVENING OFF AFTER YOU... FINISH CLEANING UP.
tick tick tick tick
YOU DID JUST FINE...
'ES, SIR! ♫
OVER HERE, LITTLE GIRL. I'LL GET YOU SOME MILK.
yiff!

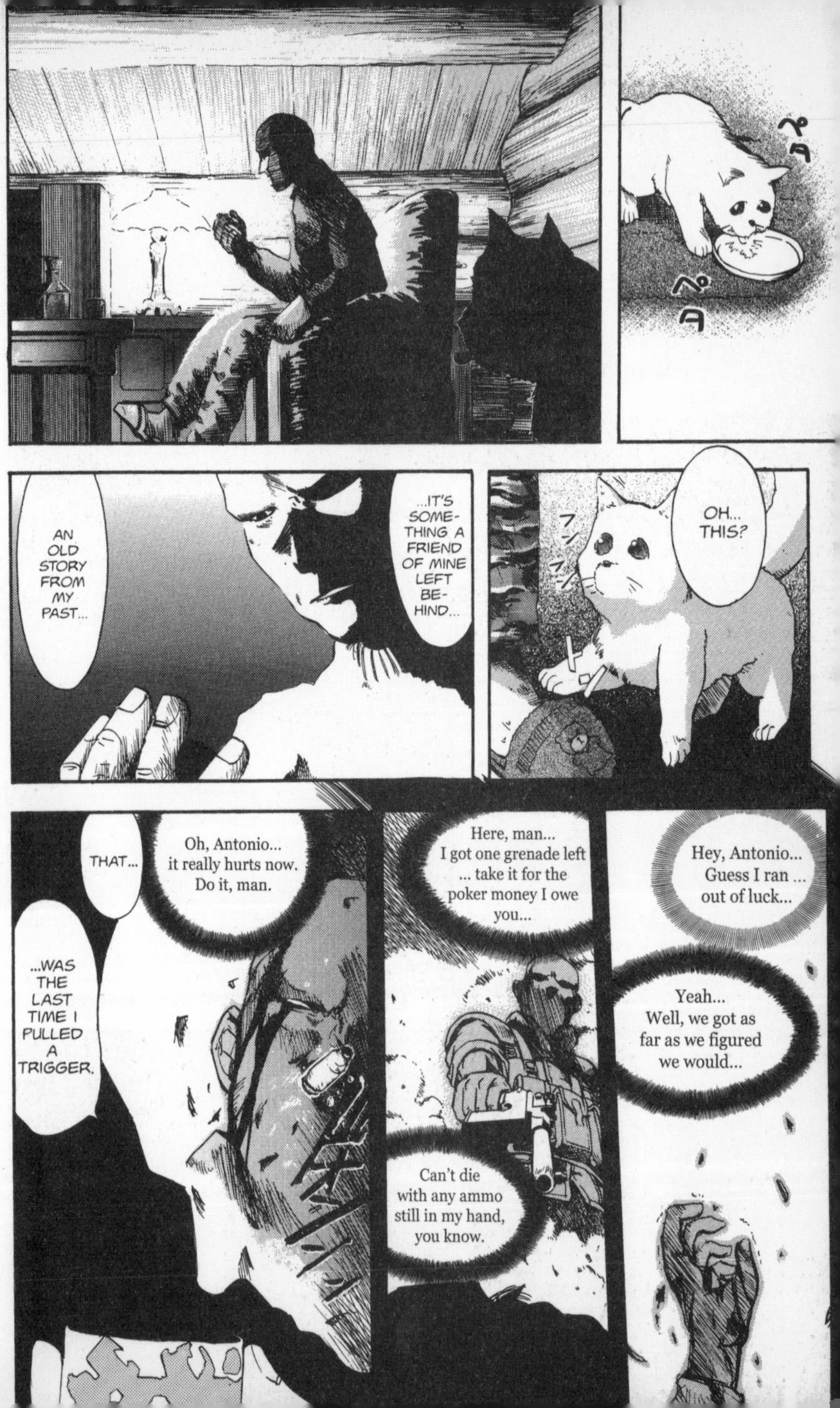
ペロ
ペロ
OH... THIS?
...IT'S SOME-THING A FRIEND OF MINE LEFT BE-HIND...
AN OLD STORY FROM MY PAST...
Hey, Antonio... Guess I ran ... out of luck...
Yeah... Well, we got as far as we figured we would...
Here, man... I got one grenade left ... take it for the poker money I owe you...
Can't die with any ammo still in my hand, you know.
Oh, Antonio... it really hurts now. Do it, man.
THAT...
...WAS THE LAST TIME I PULLED A TRIGGER.

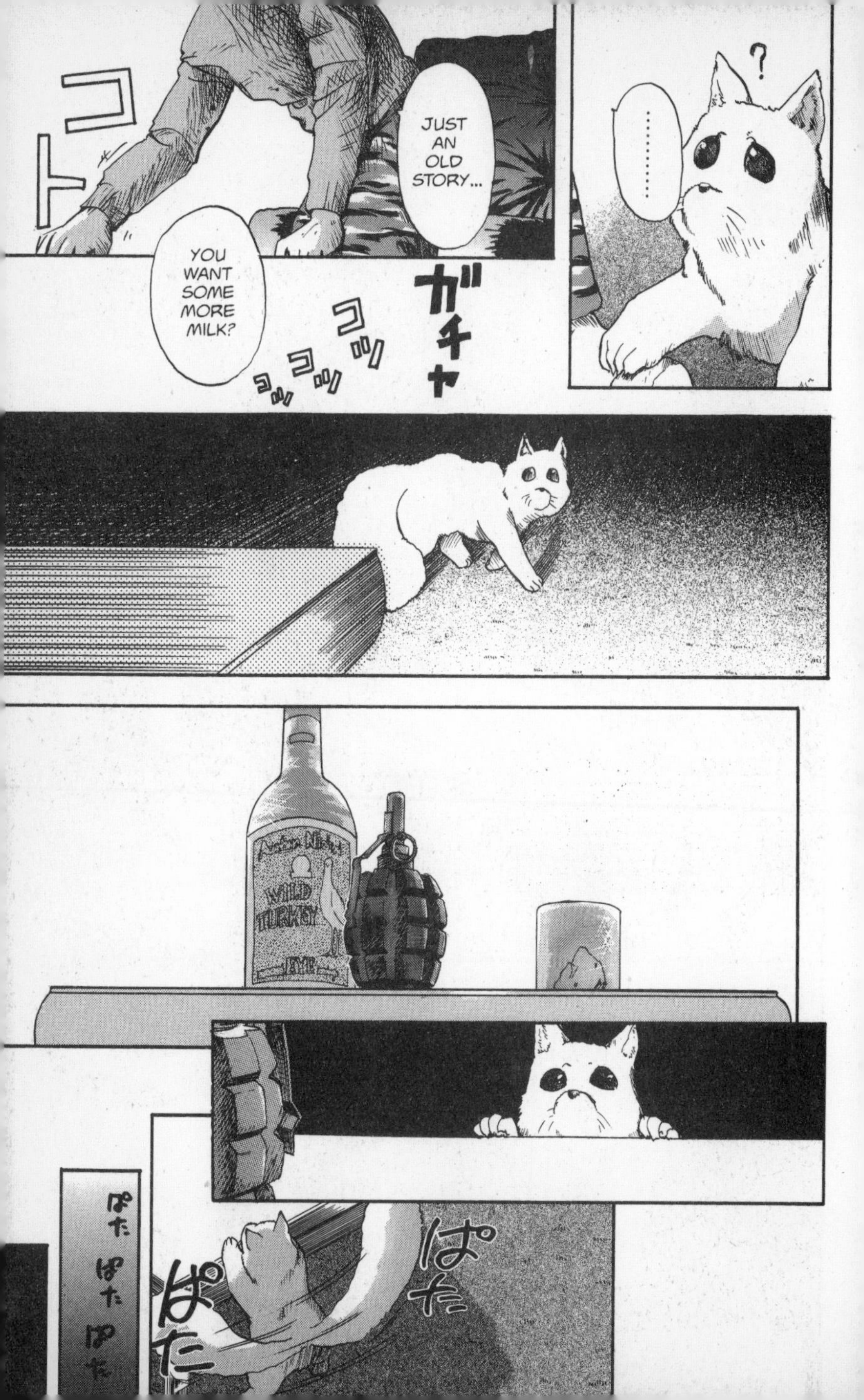
?
......
コト
JUST AN OLD STORY...
YOU WANT SOME MORE MILK?
ガチャ
ゴッゴッゴッ
ぱた
ぱたー
ぱた ぱた ぱた

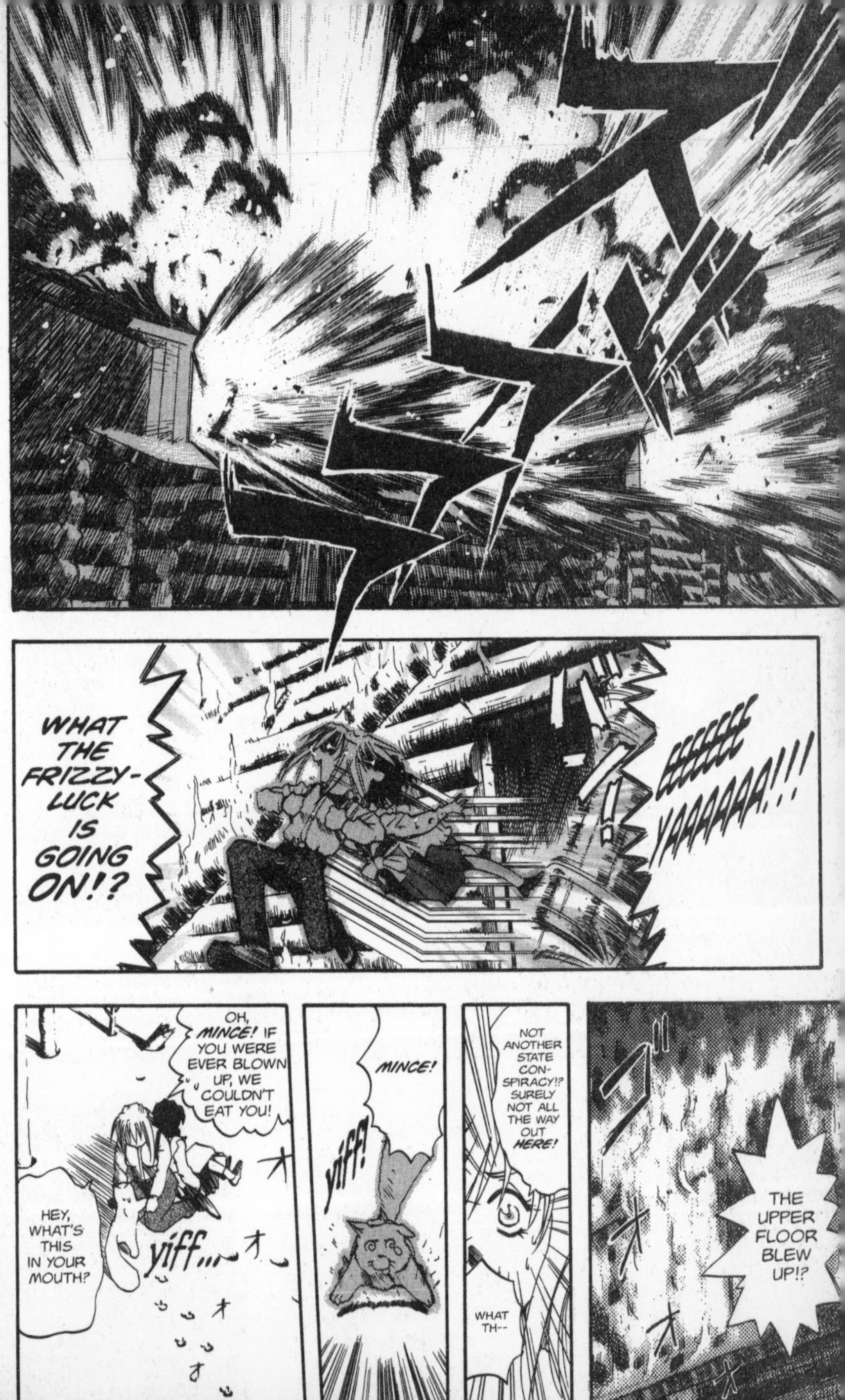

EEEEEEE YAAAAAA!!!
WHAT THE FRIZZY-LUCK IS GOING ON!?
THE UPPER FLOOR BLEW UP!?
NOT ANOTHER STATE CONSPIRACY!? SURELY NOT ALL THE WAY OUT HERE!
WHAT TH--
MINCE!
yiff!
OH, MINCE! IF YOU WERE EVER BLOWN UP, WE COULDN'T EAT YOU!
HEY, WHAT'S THIS IN YOUR MOUTH?
yiff...

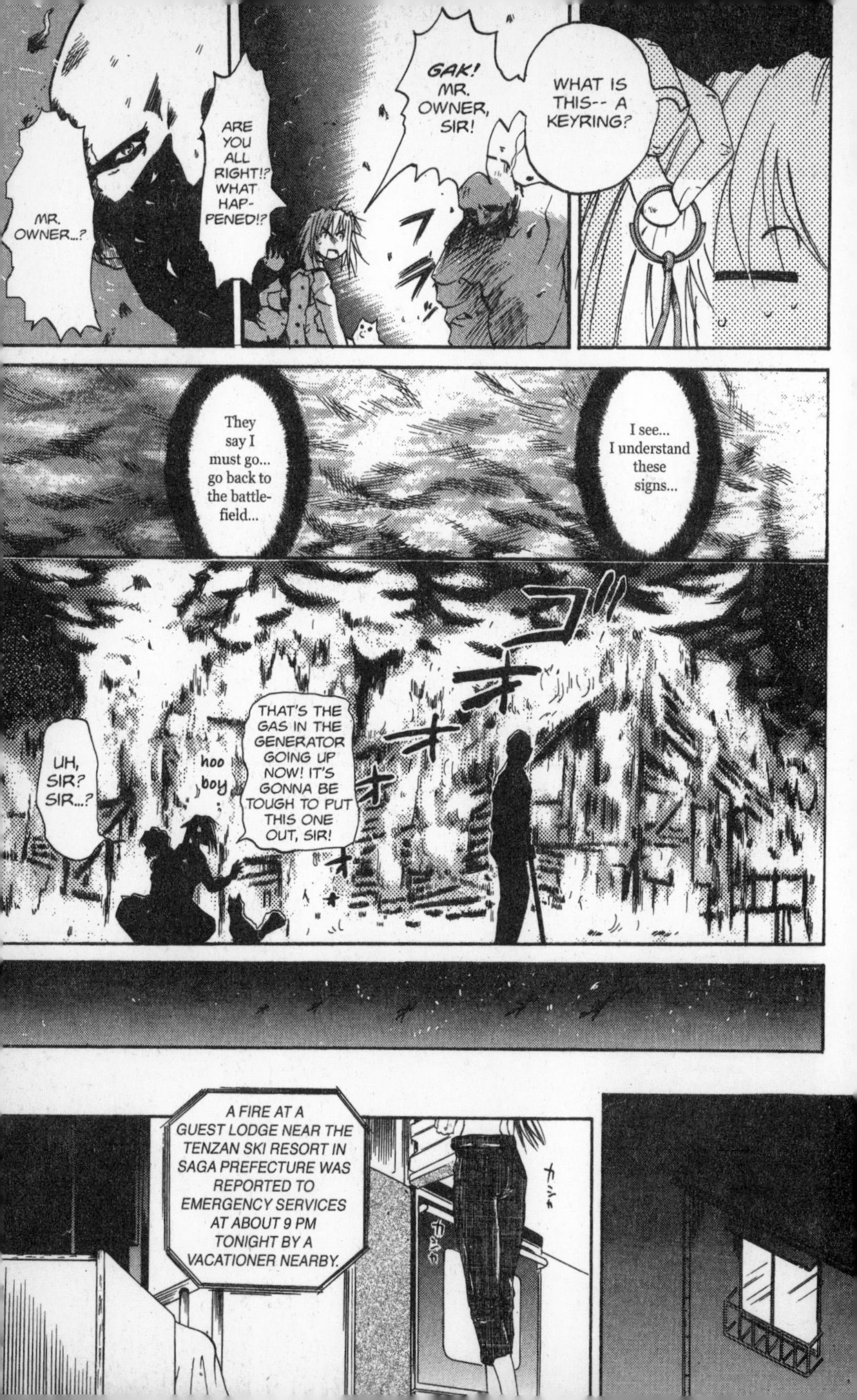
WHAT IS THIS-- A KEYRING?
GAK! MR. OWNER, SIR!
ARE YOU ALL RIGHT!? WHAT HAP-PENED!?
MR. OWNER...?
I see... I understand these signs...
They say I must go... go back to the battle-field...
THAT'S THE GAS IN THE GENERATOR GOING UP NOW! IT'S GONNA BE TOUGH TO PUT THIS ONE OUT, SIR!
hoo boy
UH, SIR? SIR...?
A FIRE AT A GUEST LODGE NEAR THE TENZAN SKI RESORT IN SAGA PREFECTURE WAS REPORTED TO EMERGENCY SERVICES AT ABOUT 9 PM TONIGHT BY A VACATIONER NEARBY.

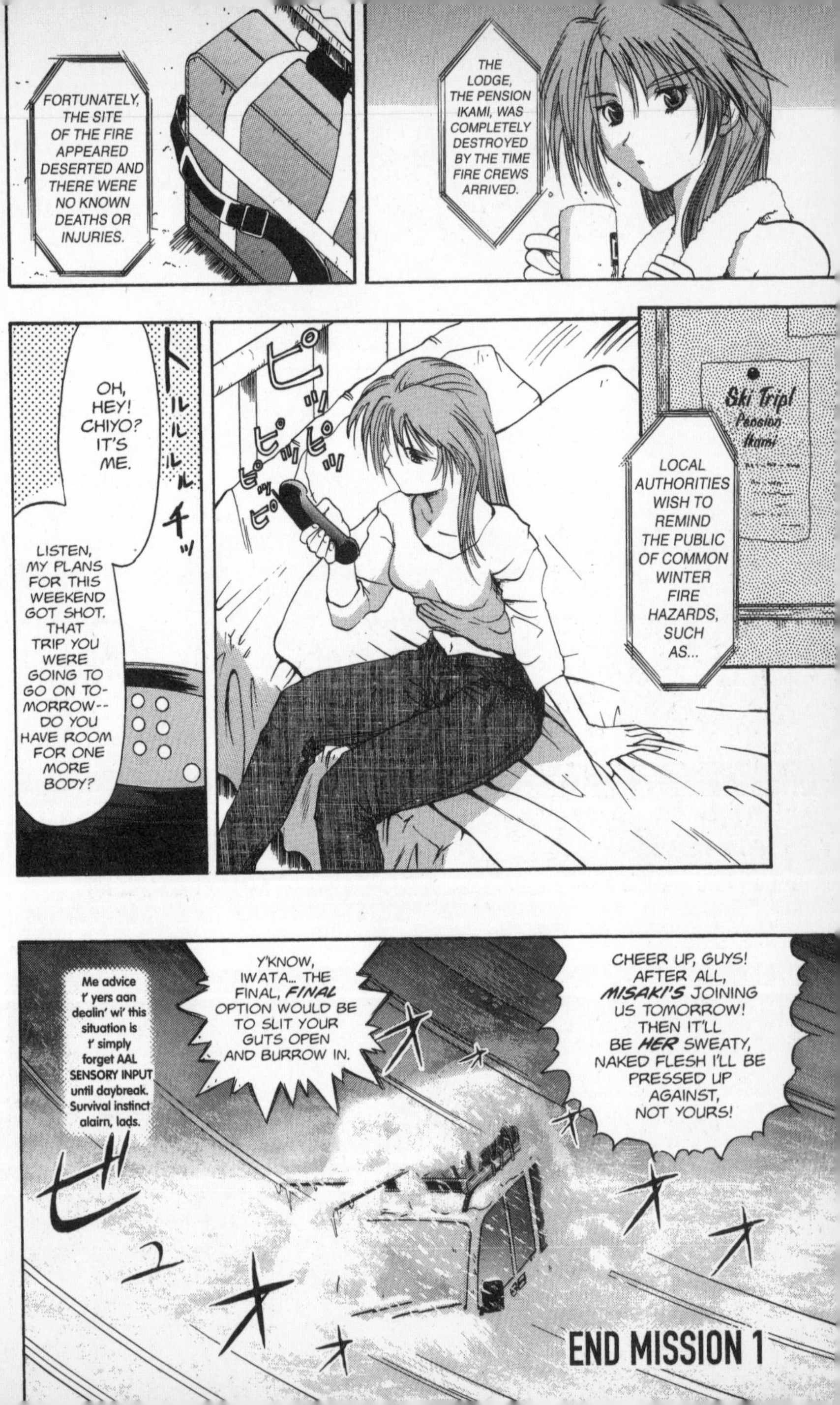
THE LODGE, THE PENSION IKAMI, WAS COMPLETELY DESTROYED BY THE TIME FIRE CREWS ARRIVED.
FORTUNATELY, THE SITE OF THE FIRE APPEARED DESERTED AND THERE WERE NO KNOWN DEATHS OR INJURIES.
Ski Trip! Pension Ikami
LOCAL AUTHORITIES WISH TO REMIND THE PUBLIC OF COMMON WINTER FIRE HAZARDS, SUCH AS...
ピッ ピッ ピッ ピッ ピ
トルルルル チッ
OH, HEY! CHIYO? IT'S ME.
LISTEN, MY PLANS FOR THIS WEEKEND GOT SHOT. THAT TRIP YOU WERE GOING TO GO ON TO-MORROW-- DO YOU HAVE ROOM FOR ONE MORE BODY?
CHEER UP, GUYS! AFTER ALL, MISAKI'S JOINING US TOMORROW! THEN IT'LL BE HER SWEATY, NAKED FLESH I'LL BE PRESSED UP AGAINST, NOT YOURS!
Y'KNOW, IWATA... THE FINAL, FINAL OPTION WOULD BE TO SLIT YOUR GUTS OPEN AND BURROW IN.
Me advice t' yers aan dealin' wi' this situation is t' simply forget AAL SENSORY INPUT until daybreak. Survival instinct alairn, lads.
END MISSION 1

EXCEL SAGA

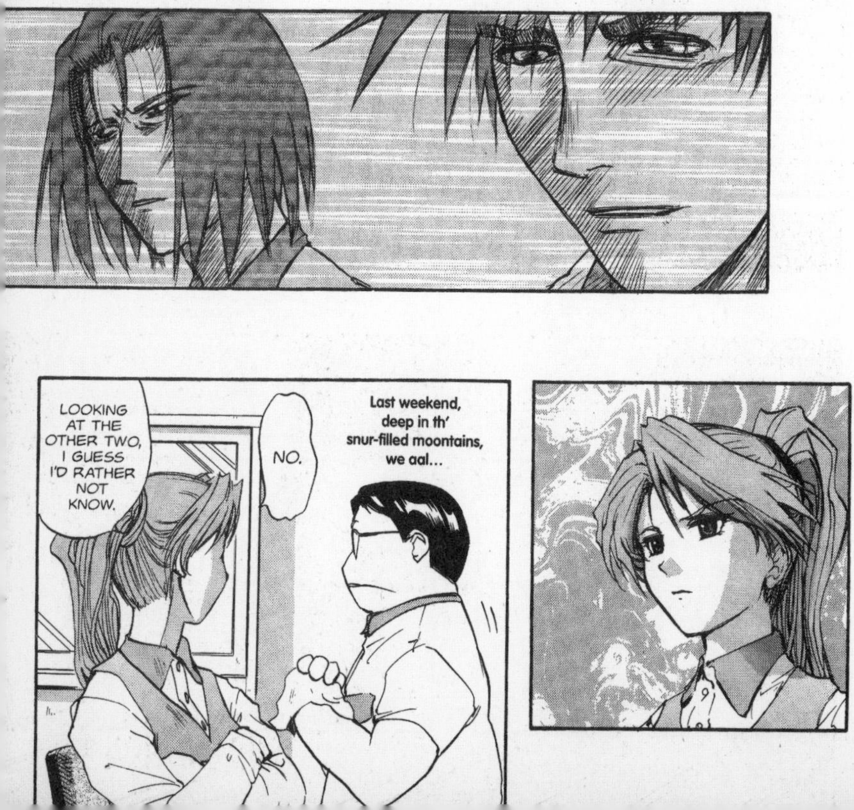
Last weekend, deep in th' snur-filled moontains, we aal...
NO.
LOOKING AT THE OTHER TWO, I GUESS I'D RATHER NOT KNOW.

# Scenes from the Personal Life of Rikdo Koshi Vol.⑥

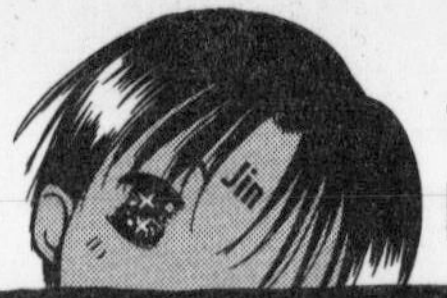
Jin

## We, The Media Elite: Part 1

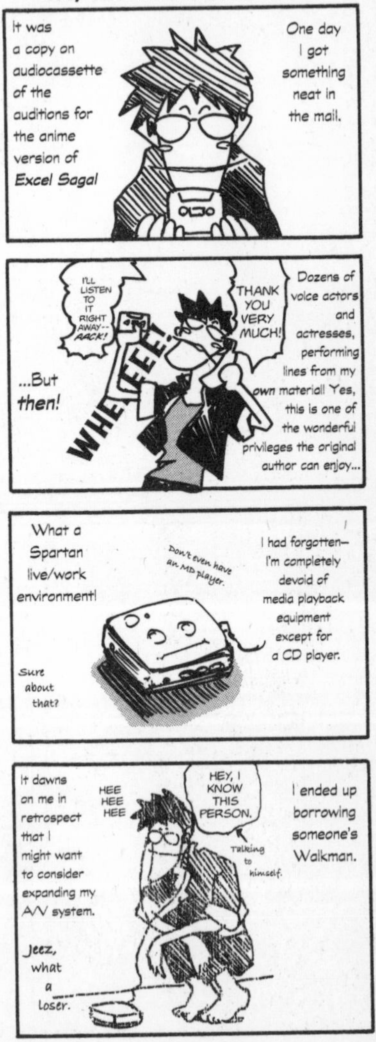
One day I got something neat in the mail.
It was a copy on audiocassette of the auditions for the anime version of *Excel Saga!*
Dozens of voice actors and actresses, performing lines from my *own* material! Yes, this is one of the wonderful privileges the original author can enjoy...
THANK YOU VERY MUCH!
I'LL LISTEN TO IT RIGHT AWAY-- AACK!
WHEEEE!
...But *then!*
I had forgotten— I'm completely devoid of media playback equipment except for a CD player.
Don't even have an MD player.
What a Spartan live/work environment!
Sure about that?
I ended up borrowing someone's Walkman.
HEY, I KNOW THIS PERSON.
Talking to himself.
HEE HEE HEE
It dawns on me in retrospect that I might want to consider expanding my A/V system.
Jeez, what a loser.

## The People of Extreme Contrasts

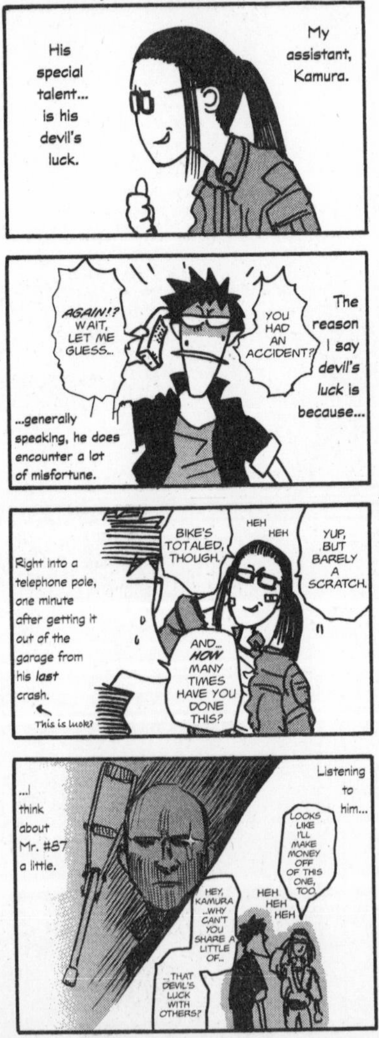
My assistant, Kamura.
His special talent... is his devil's luck.
The reason I say *devil's luck* is because...
YOU HAD AN ACCIDENT?
AGAIN!? WAIT, LET ME GUESS...
...generally speaking, he does encounter a lot of misfortune.
YUP, BUT BARELY A SCRATCH.
HEH HEH
BIKE'S TOTALED, THOUGH.
AND... *HOW* MANY TIMES HAVE YOU DONE THIS?
Right into a telephone pole, one minute after getting it out of the garage from his *last* crash.
This is luck?
Listening to him...
LOOKS LIKE I'LL MAKE MONEY OFF OF THIS ONE, TOO.
HEH HEH HEH
HEY, KAMURA ...WHY CAN'T YOU SHARE A LITTLE OF...
...THAT DEVIL'S LUCK WITH OTHERS?
...I think about Mr. #87 a little.

# SATURDAY THE 13TH

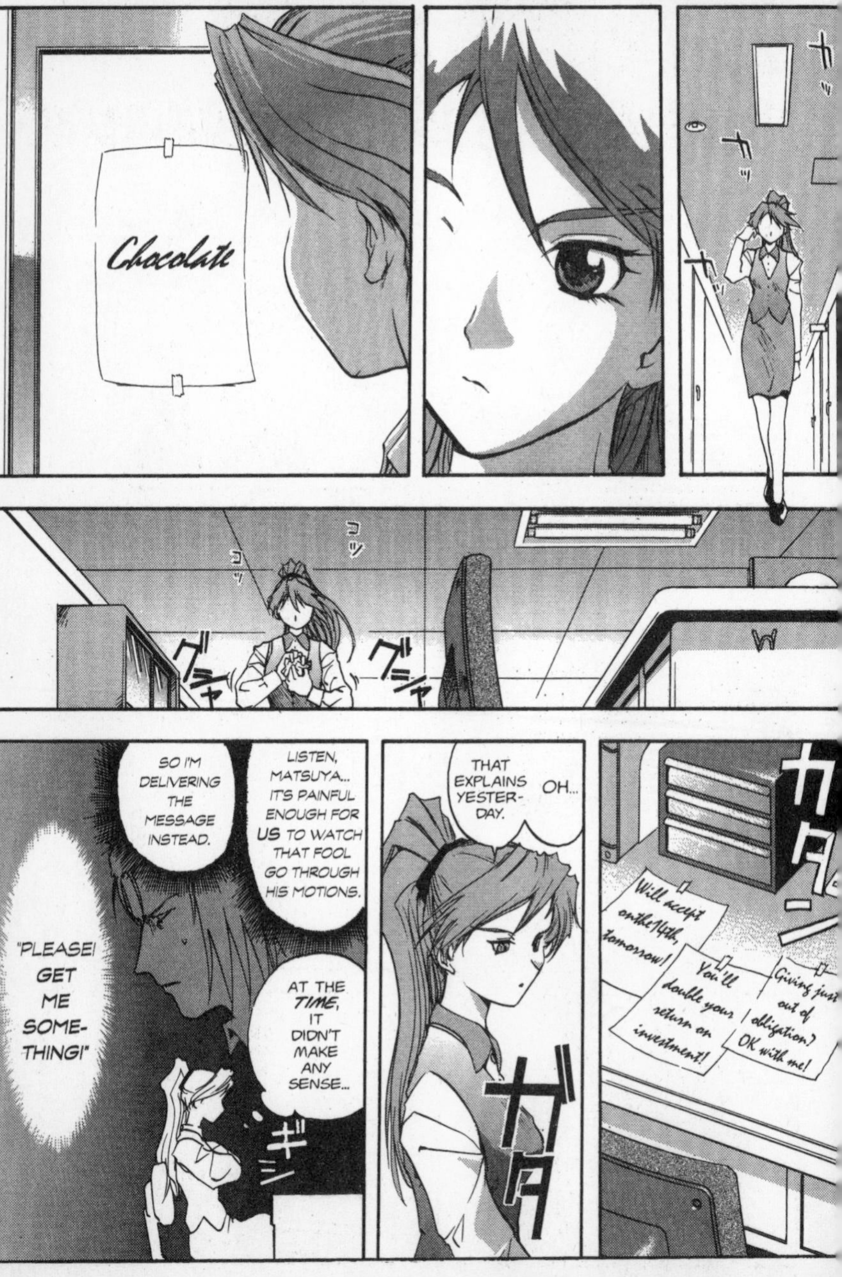

カッ
カッ
カッ
Chocolate
コッ
コッ
グシャ
グシャ
カタ
Will accept on the 14th, tomorrow!
Giving just out of obligation? OK with me!
You'll double your return on investment!
OH...
THAT EXPLAINS YESTER-DAY.
ガタ
LISTEN, MATSUYA... IT'S PAINFUL ENOUGH FOR US TO WATCH THAT FOOL GO THROUGH HIS MOTIONS.
SO I'M DELIVERING THE MESSAGE INSTEAD.
AT THE *TIME*, IT DIDN'T MAKE ANY SENSE...
"PLEASE! GET ME SOME-THING!"
ギシ

## MISSION 2
# SHALLOW WOUND ENTERTAINMENT

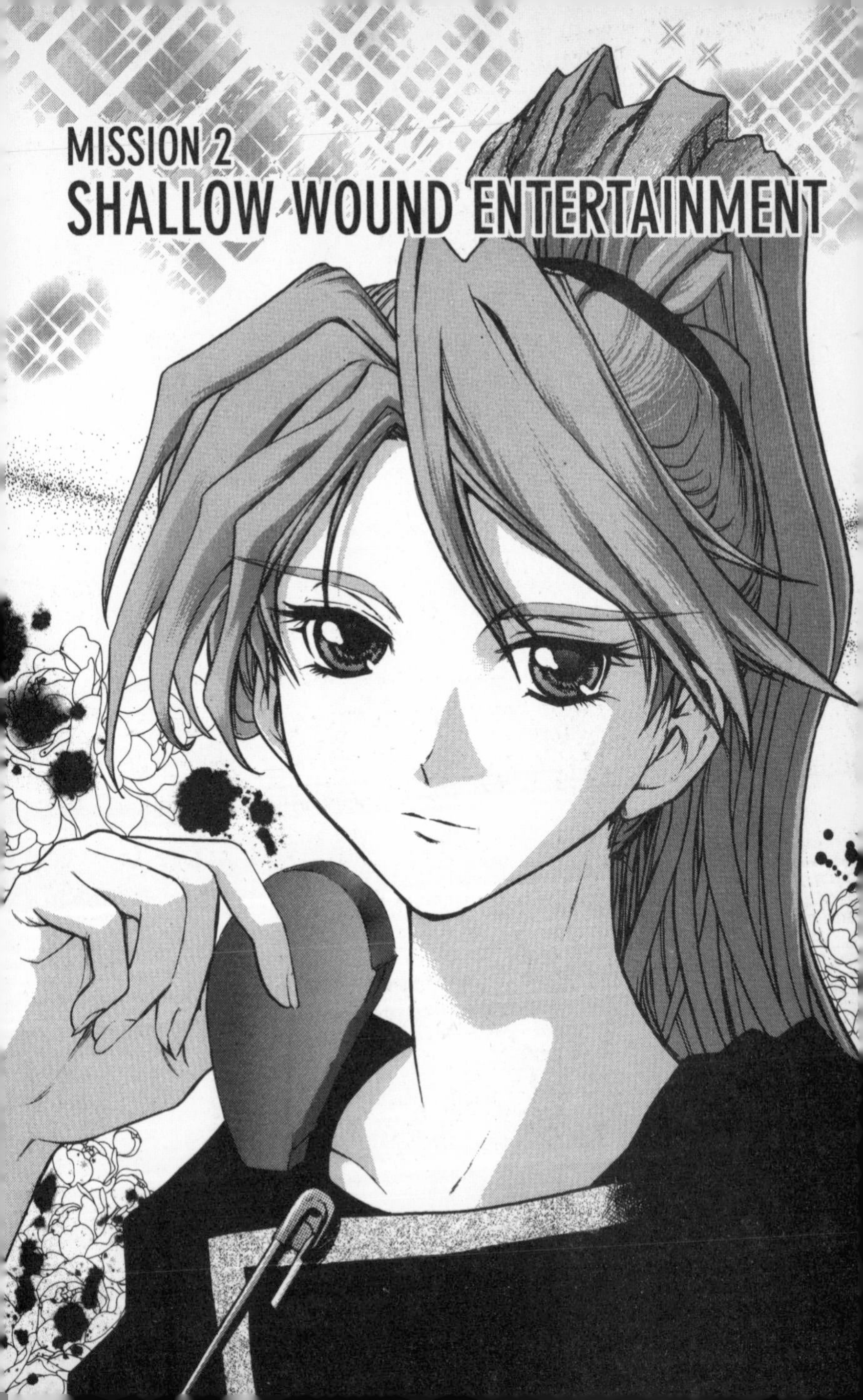

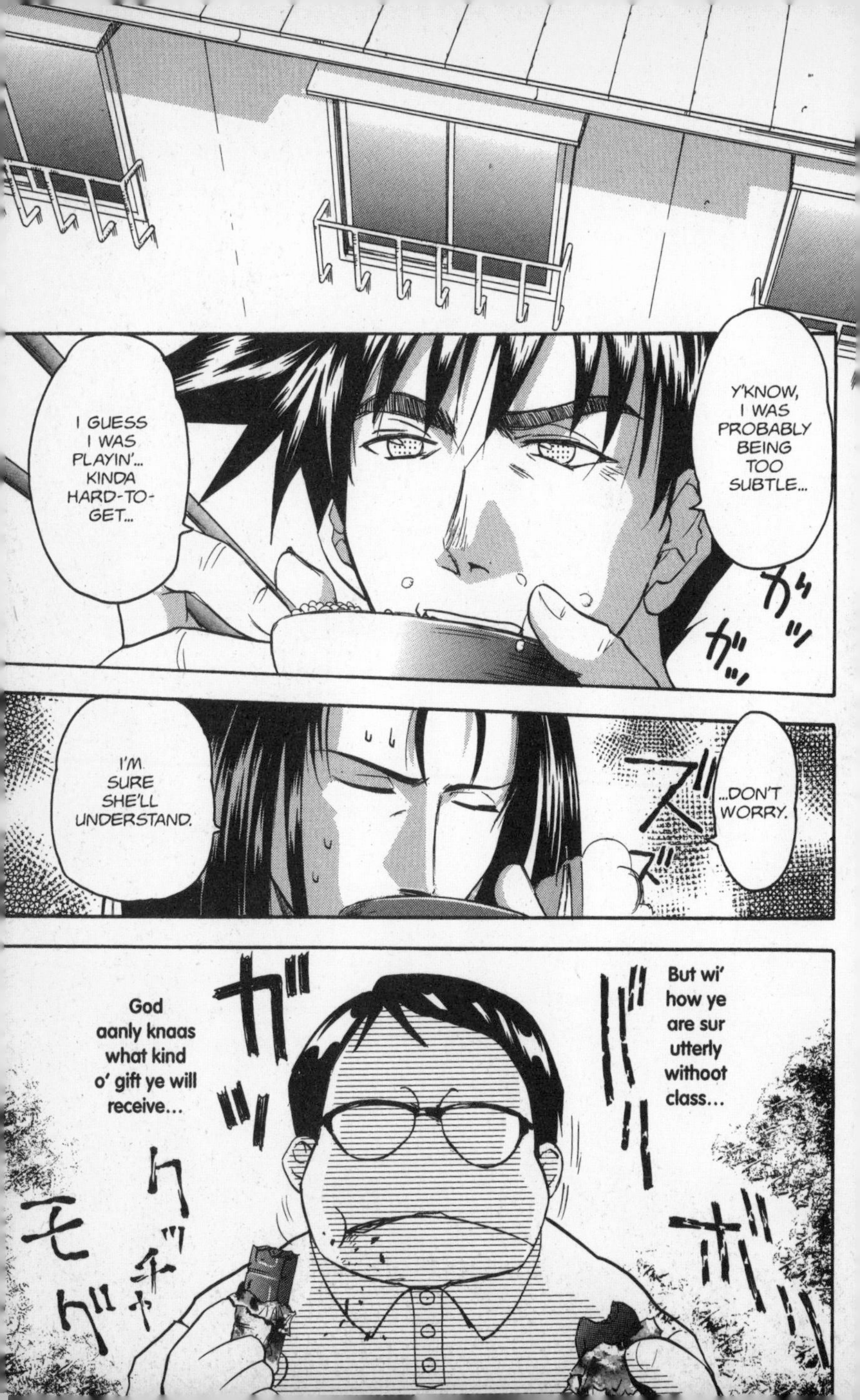
Y'KNOW, I WAS PROBABLY BEING TOO SUBTLE...
I GUESS I WAS PLAYIN'... KINDA HARD-TO-GET...
...DON'T WORRY.
I'M SURE SHE'LL UNDERSTAND.
But wi' how ye are sur utterly withoot class...
God aanly knaas what kind o' gift ye will receive...

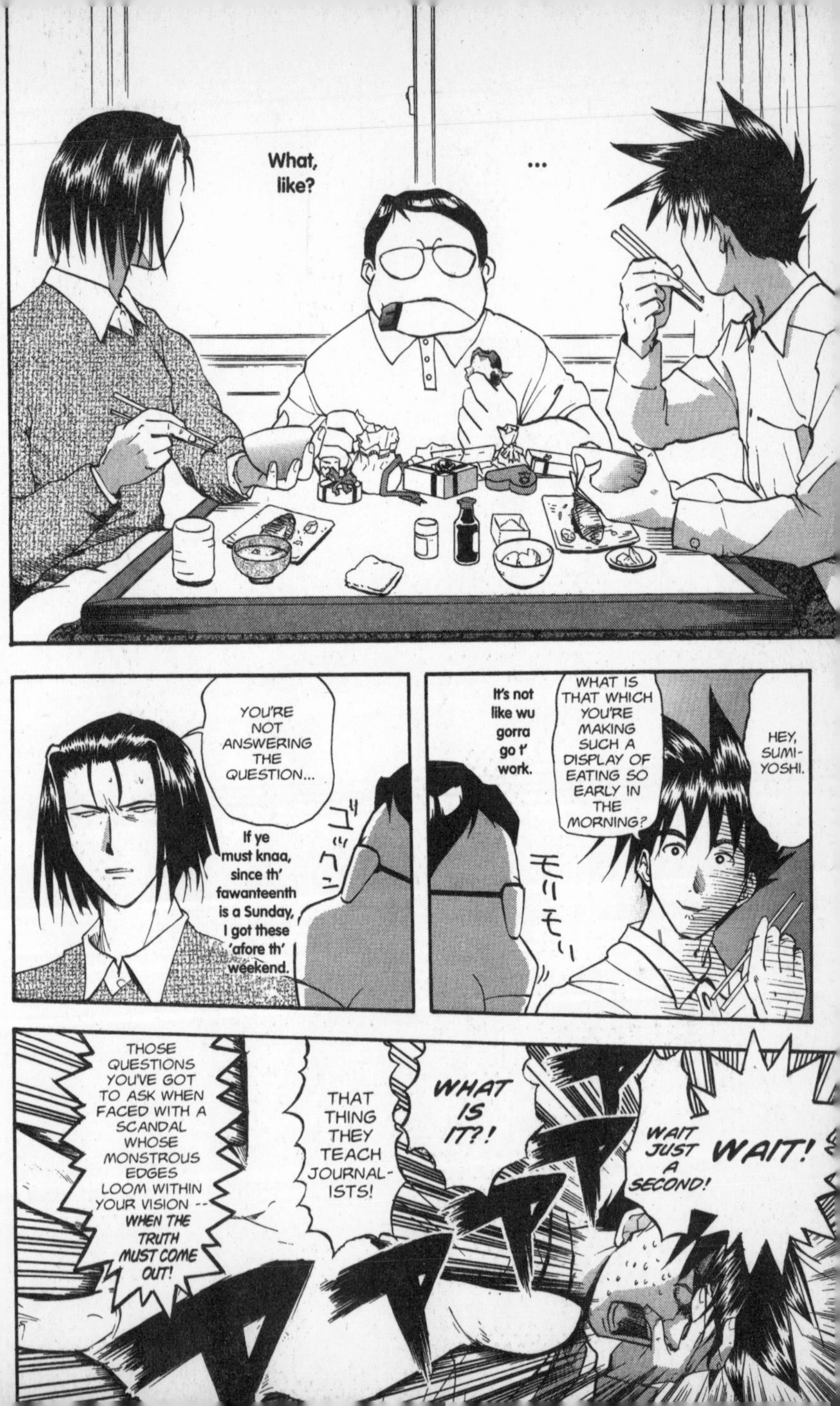
...
What, like?
HEY, SUMI-YOSHI.
WHAT IS THAT WHICH YOU'RE MAKING SUCH A DISPLAY OF EATING SO EARLY IN THE MORNING?
It's not like wu gorra go t' work.
モリモリ
YOU'RE NOT ANSWERING THE QUESTION...
ゴックン
If ye must knaa, since th' fawanteenth is a Sunday, I got these 'afore th' weekend.
WAIT!
WAIT JUST A SECOND!
WHAT IS IT?!
THAT THING THEY TEACH JOURNAL-ISTS!
THOSE QUESTIONS YOU'VE GOT TO ASK WHEN FACED WITH A SCANDAL WHOSE MONSTROUS EDGES LOOM WITHIN YOUR VISION -- WHEN THE TRUTH MUST COME OUT!

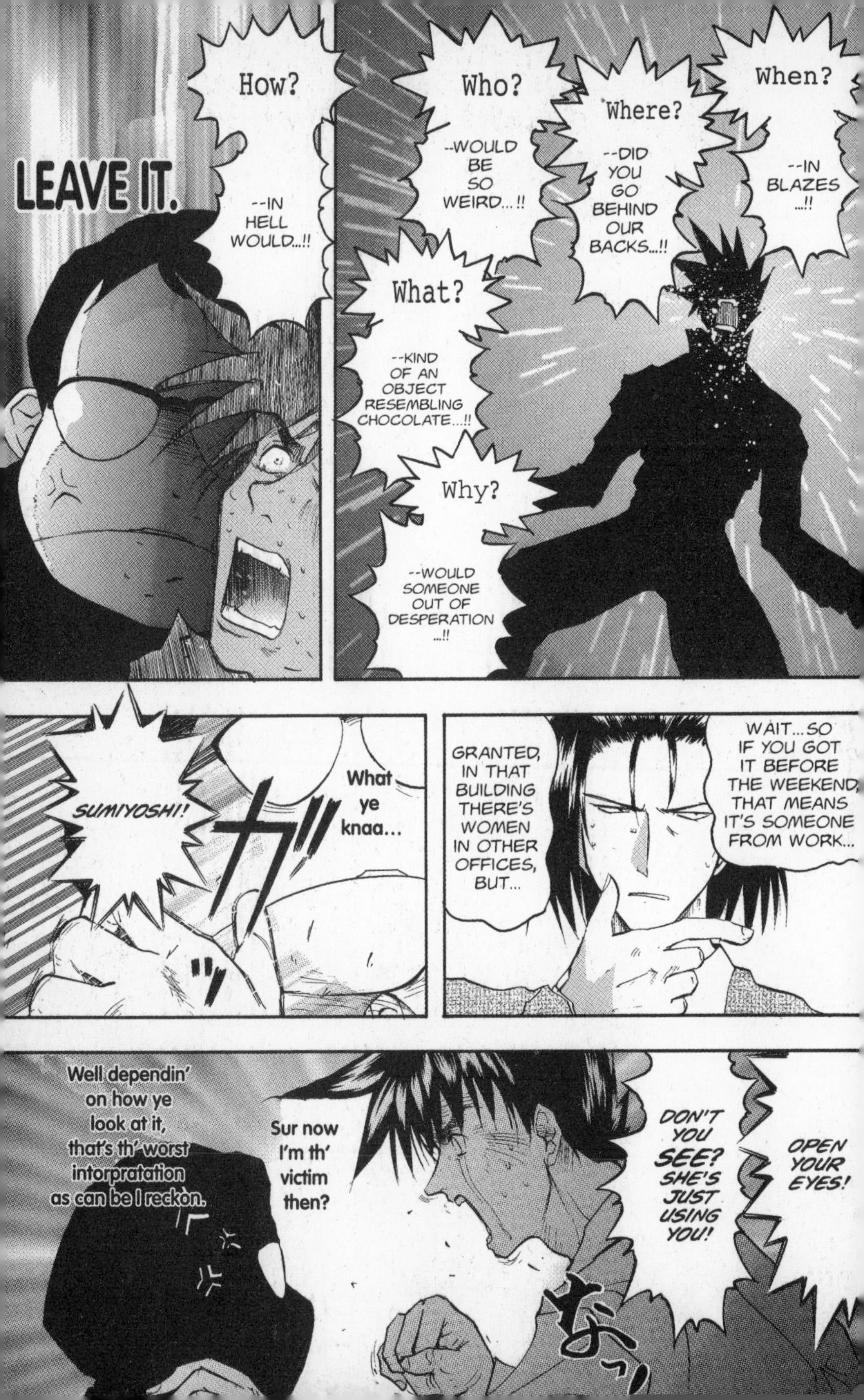
When?
--IN BLAZES ...!!
Where?
--DID YOU GO BEHIND OUR BACKS...!!
Who?
--WOULD BE SO WEIRD...!!
What?
--KIND OF AN OBJECT RESEMBLING CHOCOLATE...!!
Why?
--WOULD SOMEONE OUT OF DESPERATION ...!!
How?
--IN HELL WOULD...!!
LEAVE IT.
WAIT...SO IF YOU GOT IT BEFORE THE WEEKEND, THAT MEANS IT'S SOMEONE FROM WORK...
GRANTED, IN THAT BUILDING THERE'S WOMEN IN OTHER OFFICES, BUT...
What ye knaa...
SUMIYOSHI!
OPEN YOUR EYES!
DON'T YOU SEE? SHE'S JUST USING YOU!
Sur now I'm th' victim then?
Well dependin' on how ye look at it, that's th' worst intorpratation as can be I reckon.

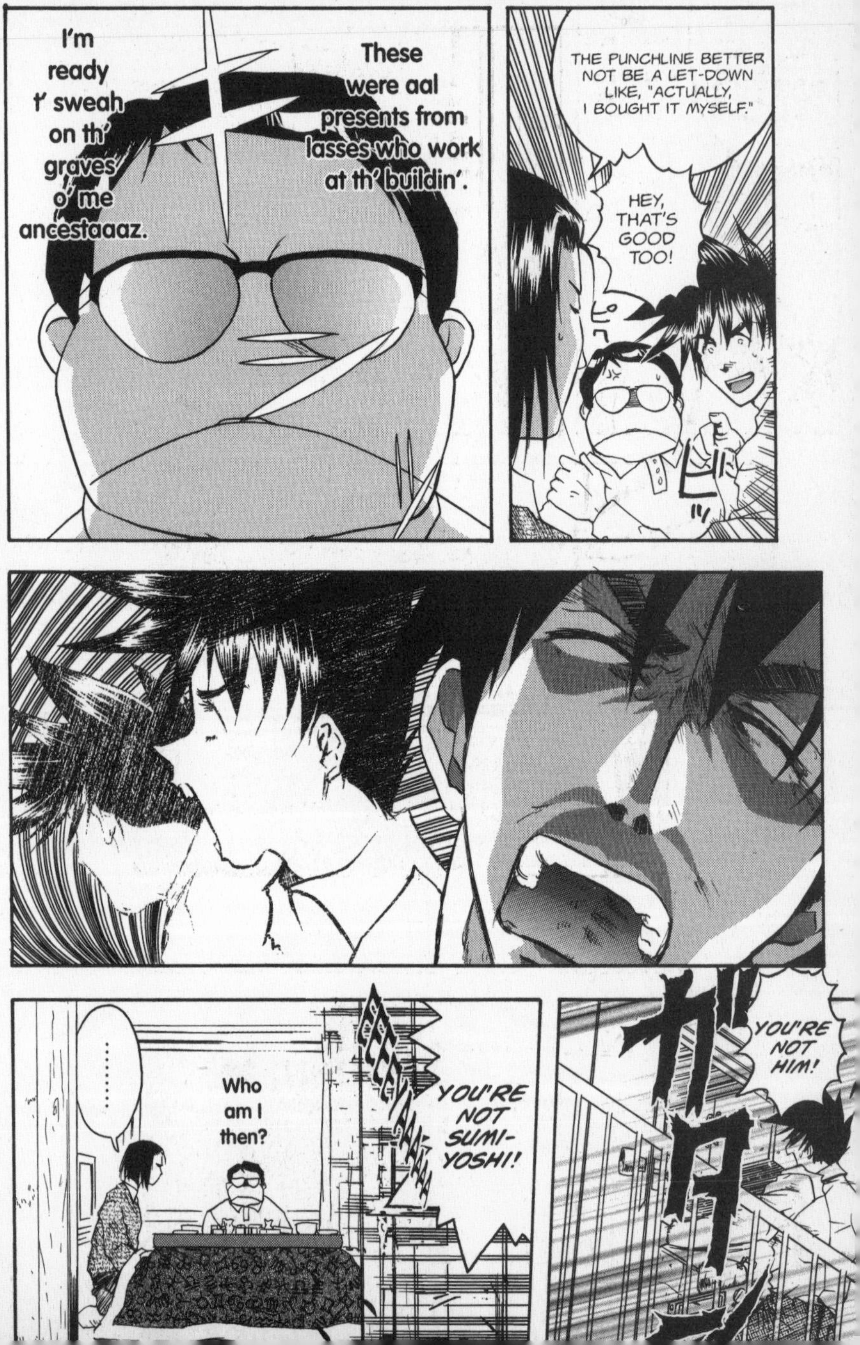
THE PUNCHLINE BETTER NOT BE A LET-DOWN LIKE, "ACTUALLY, I BOUGHT IT MYSELF."
HEY, THAT'S GOOD TOO!
These were aal presents from lasses who work at th' buildin'.
I'm ready t' sweah on th' graves o' me ancestaaaz.
YOU'RE NOT HIM!
EEEEYAAAAAAAAA
YOU'RE NOT SUMI-YOSHI!
Who am I then?
......

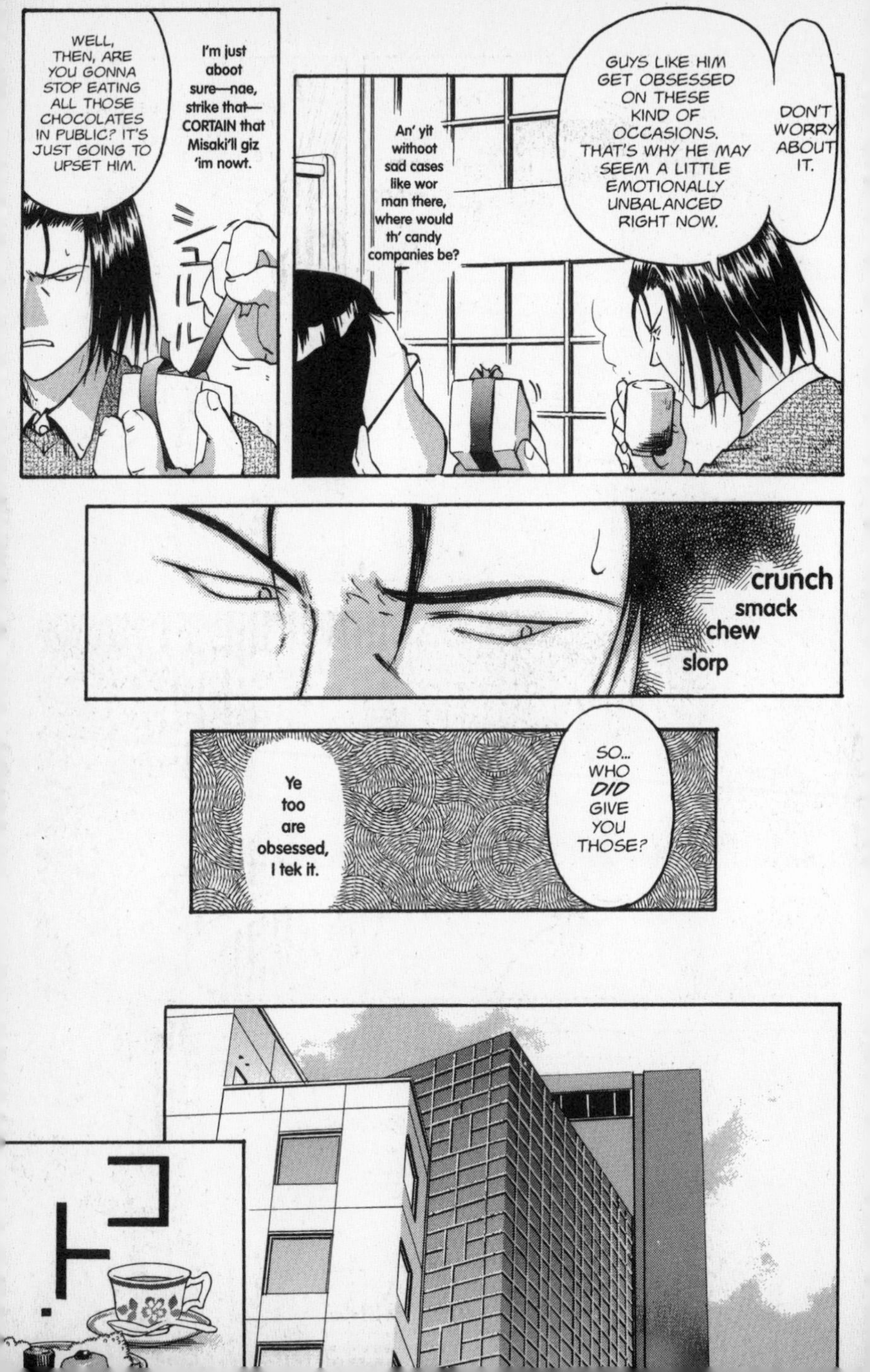
DON'T WORRY ABOUT IT.
GUYS LIKE HIM GET OBSESSED ON THESE KIND OF OCCASIONS. THAT'S WHY HE MAY SEEM A LITTLE EMOTIONALLY UNBALANCED RIGHT NOW.
An' yit withoot sad cases like wor man there, where would th' candy companies be?
WELL, THEN, ARE YOU GONNA STOP EATING ALL THOSE CHOCOLATES IN PUBLIC? IT'S JUST GOING TO UPSET HIM.
I'm just aboot sure—nae, strike that—CORTAIN that Misaki'll giz 'im nowt.
crunch
smack
chew
slorp
SO... WHO DID GIVE YOU THOSE?
Ye too are obsessed, I tek it.
コト

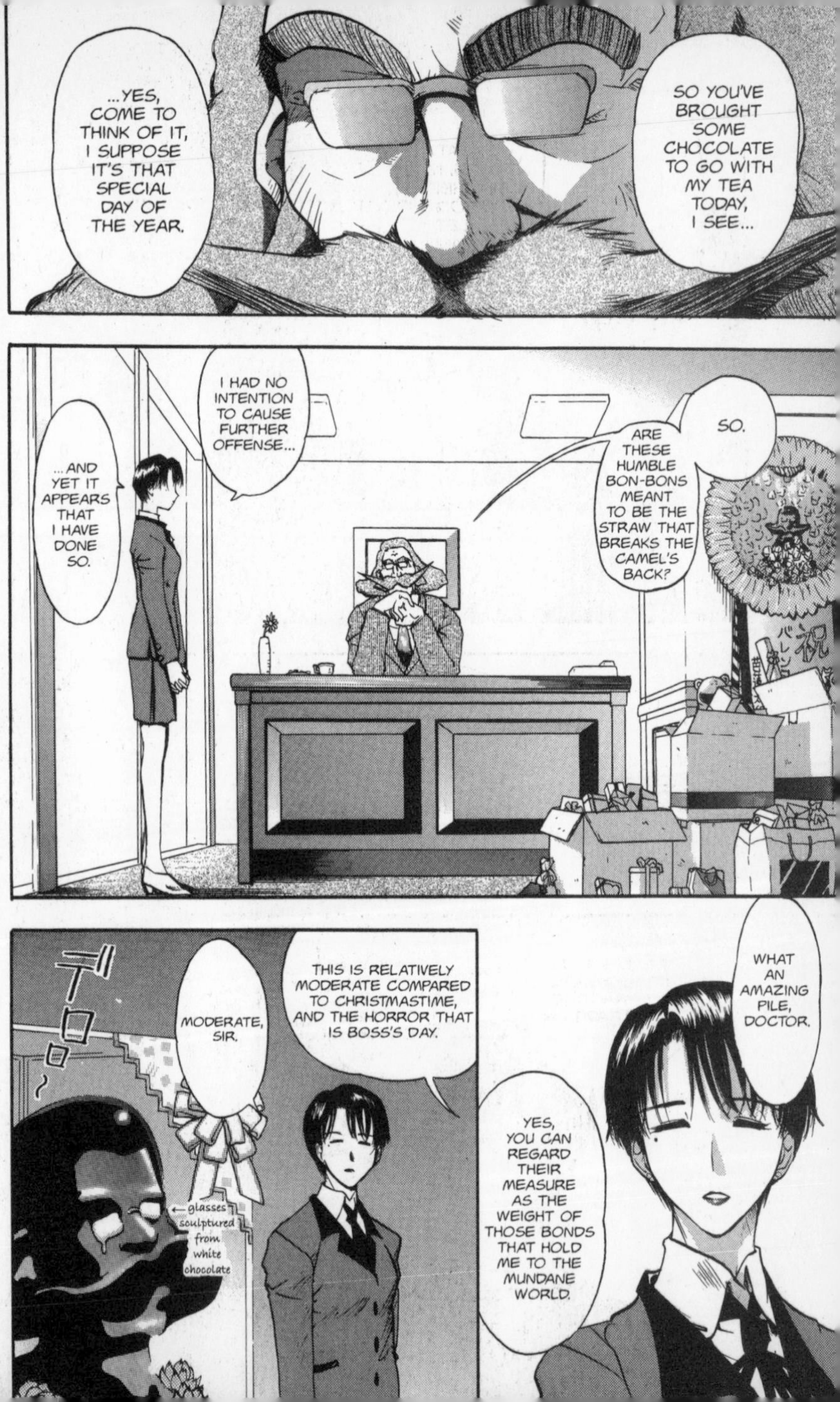
SO YOU'VE BROUGHT SOME CHOCOLATE TO GO WITH MY TEA TODAY, I SEE...
...YES, COME TO THINK OF IT, I SUPPOSE IT'S THAT SPECIAL DAY OF THE YEAR.
SO.
ARE THESE HUMBLE BON-BONS MEANT TO BE THE STRAW THAT BREAKS THE CAMEL'S BACK?
I HAD NO INTENTION TO CAUSE FURTHER OFFENSE...
...AND YET IT APPEARS THAT I HAVE DONE SO.
WHAT AN AMAZING PILE, DOCTOR.
YES, YOU CAN REGARD THEIR MEASURE AS THE WEIGHT OF THOSE BONDS THAT HOLD ME TO THE MUNDANE WORLD.
THIS IS RELATIVELY MODERATE COMPARED TO CHRISTMASTIME, AND THE HORROR THAT IS BOSS'S DAY.
MODERATE, SIR.
デロロ～
← glasses sculptured from white chocolate

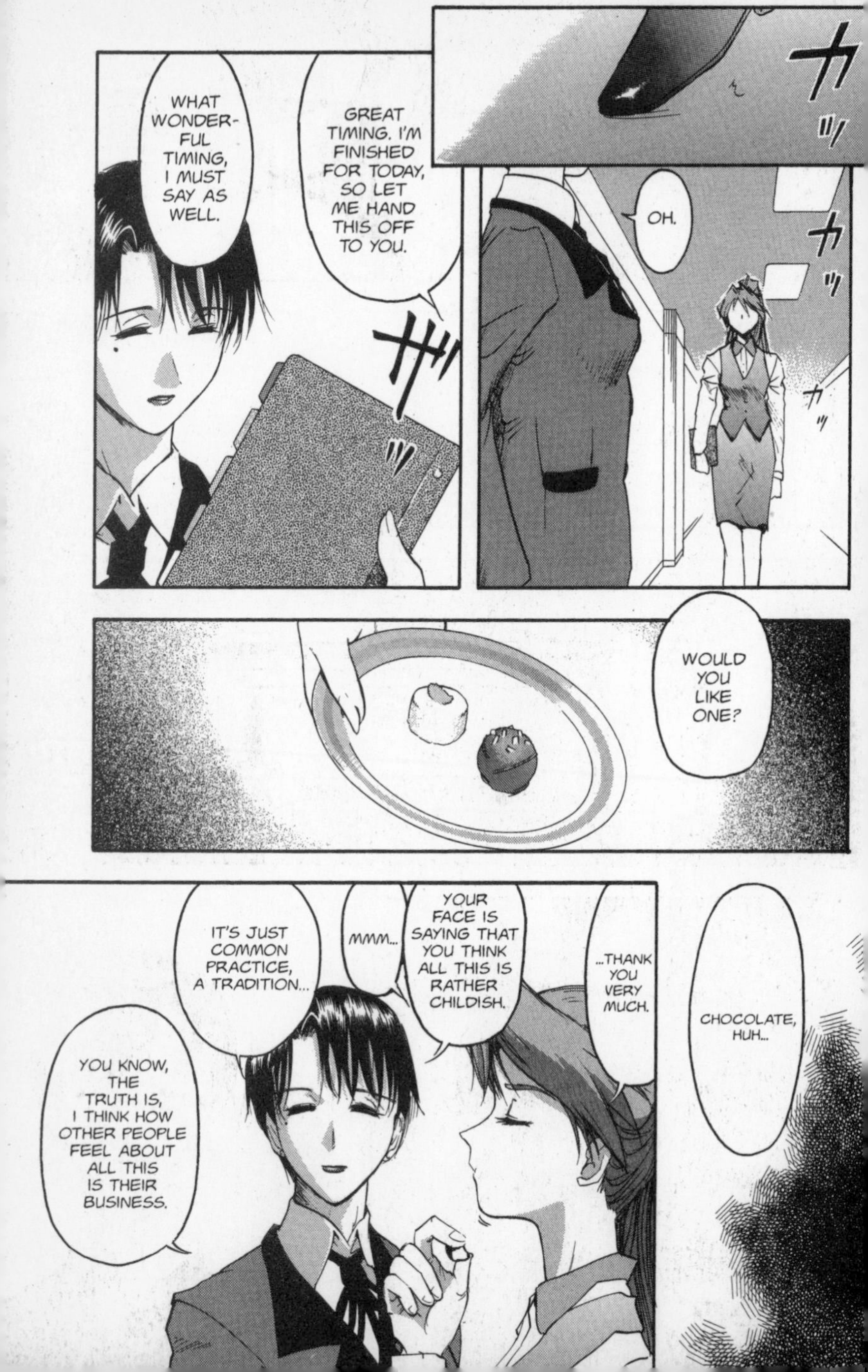

カッ
カッ
カッ
OH.
GREAT TIMING. I'M FINISHED FOR TODAY, SO LET ME HAND THIS OFF TO YOU.
WHAT WONDERFUL TIMING, I MUST SAY AS WELL.
WOULD YOU LIKE ONE?
CHOCOLATE, HUH...
...THANK YOU VERY MUCH.
YOUR FACE IS SAYING THAT YOU THINK ALL THIS IS RATHER CHILDISH.
MMM...
IT'S JUST COMMON PRACTICE, A TRADITION...
YOU KNOW, THE TRUTH IS, I THINK HOW OTHER PEOPLE FEEL ABOUT ALL THIS IS THEIR BUSINESS.

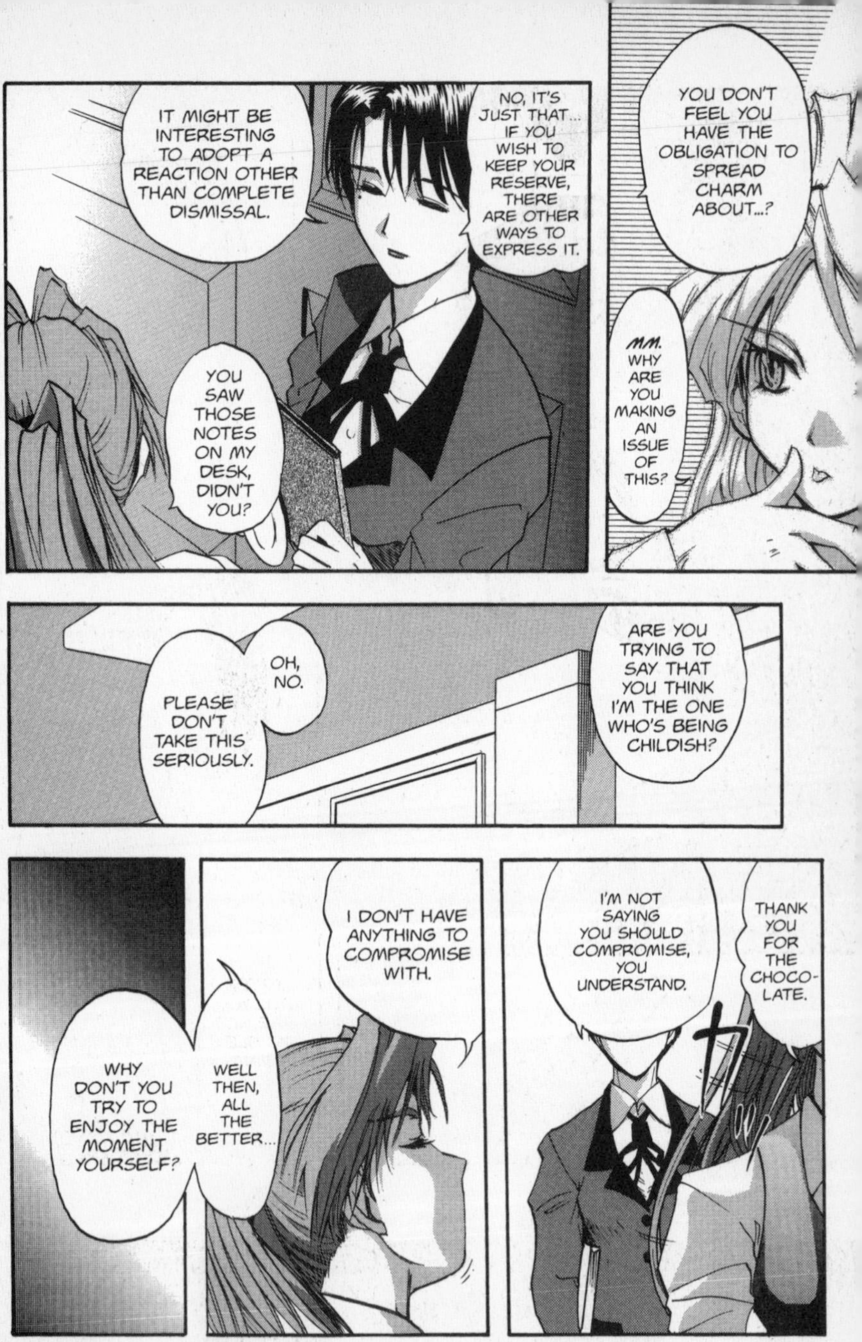
YOU DON'T FEEL YOU HAVE THE OBLIGATION TO SPREAD CHARM ABOUT...?
MM. WHY ARE YOU MAKING AN ISSUE OF THIS?
NO, IT'S JUST THAT... IF YOU WISH TO KEEP YOUR RESERVE, THERE ARE OTHER WAYS TO EXPRESS IT.
IT MIGHT BE INTERESTING TO ADOPT A REACTION OTHER THAN COMPLETE DISMISSAL.
YOU SAW THOSE NOTES ON MY DESK, DIDN'T YOU?
ARE YOU TRYING TO SAY THAT YOU THINK I'M THE ONE WHO'S BEING CHILDISH?
OH, NO.
PLEASE DON'T TAKE THIS SERIOUSLY.
THANK YOU FOR THE CHOCO-LATE.
I'M NOT SAYING YOU SHOULD COMPROMISE, YOU UNDERSTAND.
I DON'T HAVE ANYTHING TO COMPROMISE WITH.
WELL THEN, ALL THE BETTER...
WHY DON'T YOU TRY TO ENJOY THE MOMENT YOURSELF?

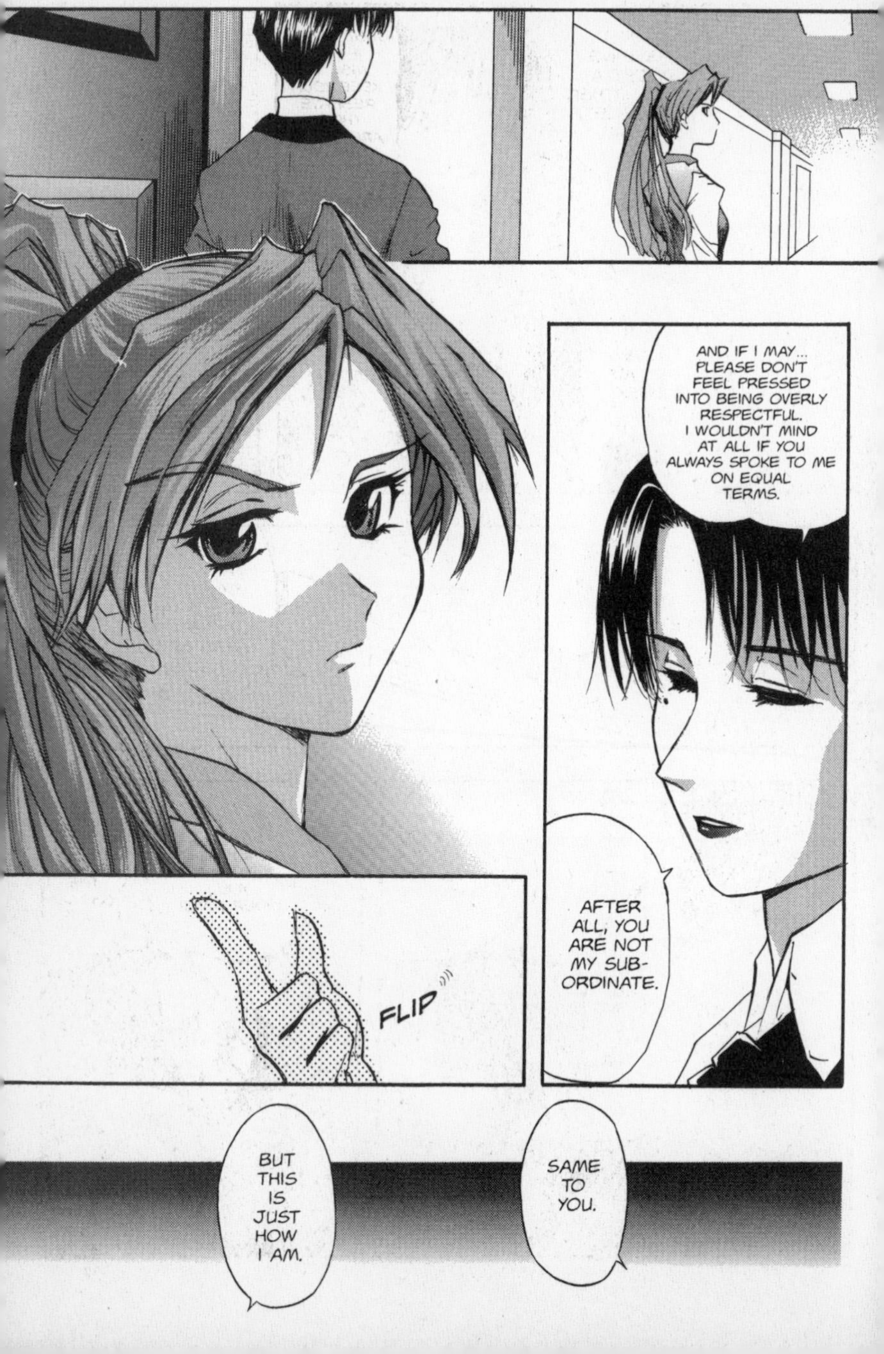
AND IF I MAY... PLEASE DON'T FEEL PRESSED INTO BEING OVERLY RESPECTFUL. I WOULDN'T MIND AT ALL IF YOU ALWAYS SPOKE TO ME ON EQUAL TERMS.
AFTER ALL, YOU ARE NOT MY SUB-ORDINATE.
FLIP
SAME TO YOU.
BUT THIS IS JUST HOW I AM.

# SUNDAY THE 14TH

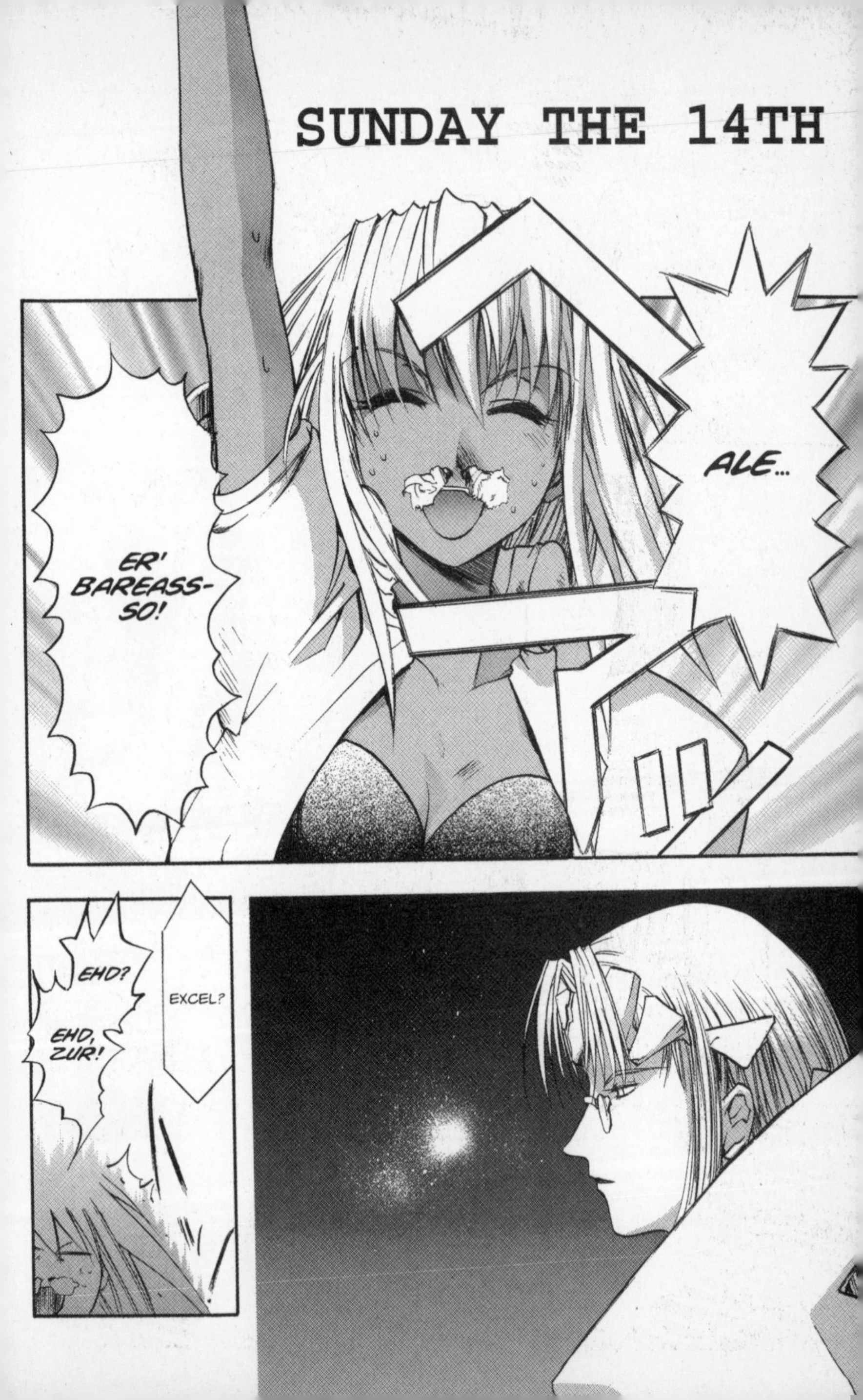
ALE...
ER' BAREASS-SO!
EXCEL?
EHD?
EHD, ZUR!

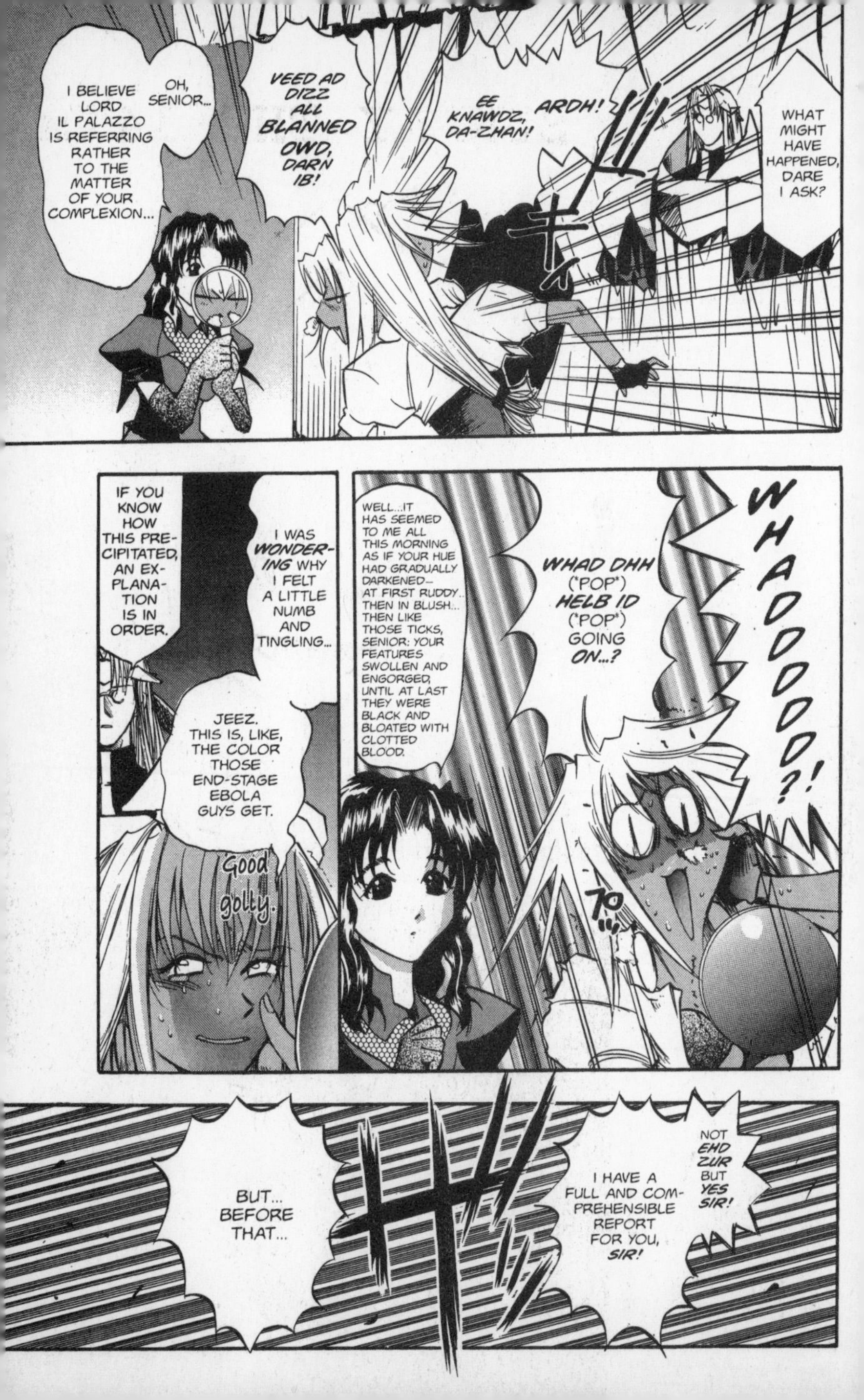
WHAT MIGHT HAVE HAPPENED, DARE I ASK?
ARDH!
EE KNAWDZ, DA-ZHAN!
VEED AD DIZZ ALL BLANNED OWD, DARN IB!
OH, SENIOR...
I BELIEVE LORD IL PALAZZO IS REFERRING RATHER TO THE MATTER OF YOUR COMPLEXION...
WHADOOOOOOO?!
WHAD DHH (*POP*) HELB ID (*POP*) GOING ON...?
WELL...IT HAS SEEMED TO ME ALL THIS MORNING AS IF YOUR HUE HAD GRADUALLY DARKENED-- AT FIRST RUDDY... THEN IN BLUSH... THEN LIKE THOSE TICKS, SENIOR: YOUR FEATURES SWOLLEN AND ENGORGED, UNTIL AT LAST THEY WERE BLACK AND BLOATED WITH CLOTTED BLOOD.
I WAS WONDERING WHY I FELT A LITTLE NUMB AND TINGLING...
IF YOU KNOW HOW THIS PRECIPITATED, AN EXPLANATION IS IN ORDER.
JEEZ. THIS IS, LIKE, THE COLOR THOSE END-STAGE EBOLA GUYS GET.
Good golly.
NOT EHD ZUR BUT YES SIR!
I HAVE A FULL AND COMPREHENSIBLE REPORT FOR YOU, SIR!
BUT... BEFORE THAT...

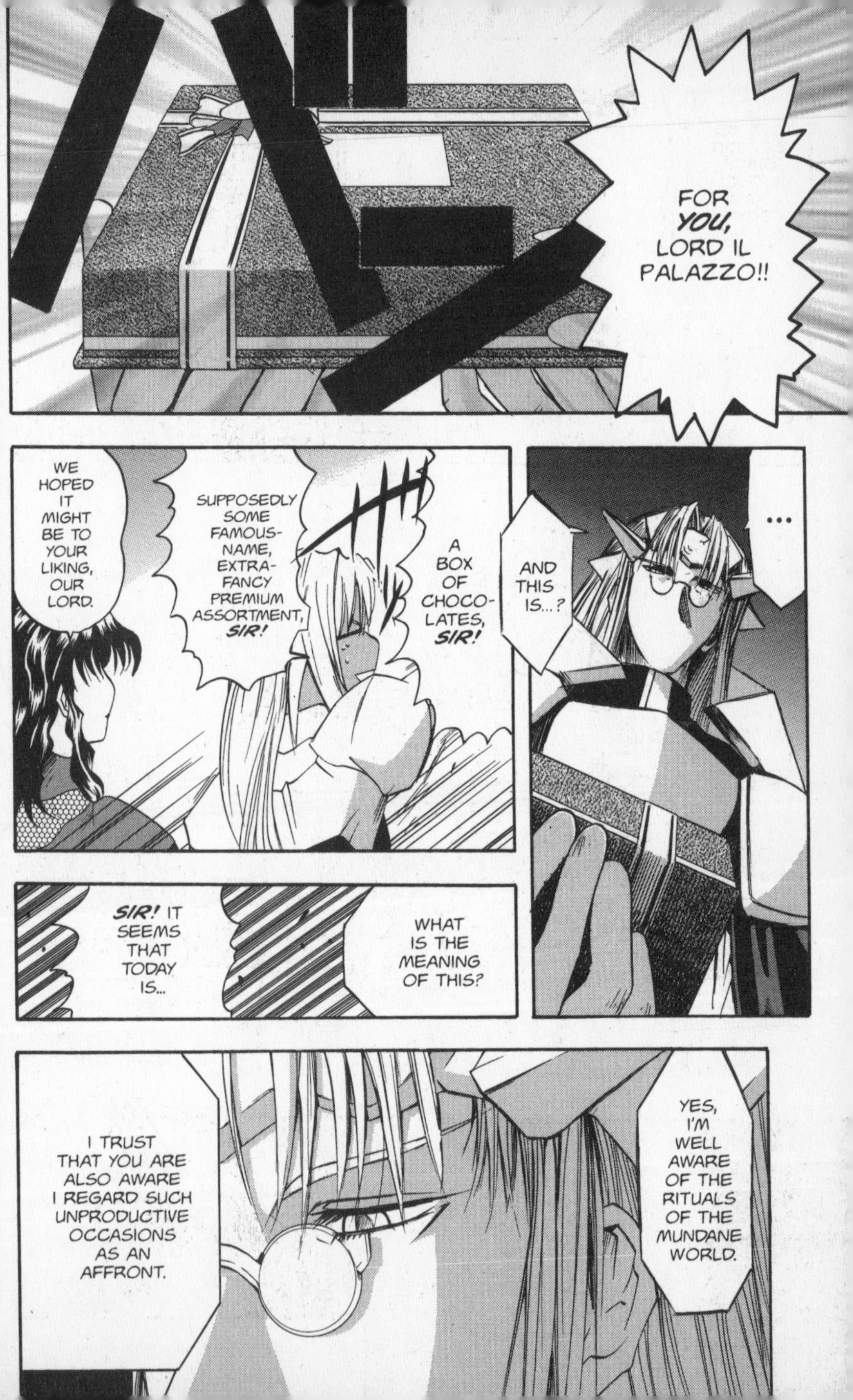
FOR YOU, LORD IL PALAZZO!!
...
AND THIS IS...?
A BOX OF CHOCOLATES, SIR!
SUPPOSEDLY SOME FAMOUS-NAME, EXTRA-FANCY PREMIUM ASSORTMENT, SIR!
WE HOPED IT MIGHT BE TO YOUR LIKING, OUR LORD.
WHAT IS THE MEANING OF THIS?
SIR! IT SEEMS THAT TODAY IS...
YES, I'M WELL AWARE OF THE RITUALS OF THE MUNDANE WORLD.
I TRUST THAT YOU ARE ALSO AWARE I REGARD SUCH UNPRODUCTIVE OCCASIONS AS AN AFFRONT.

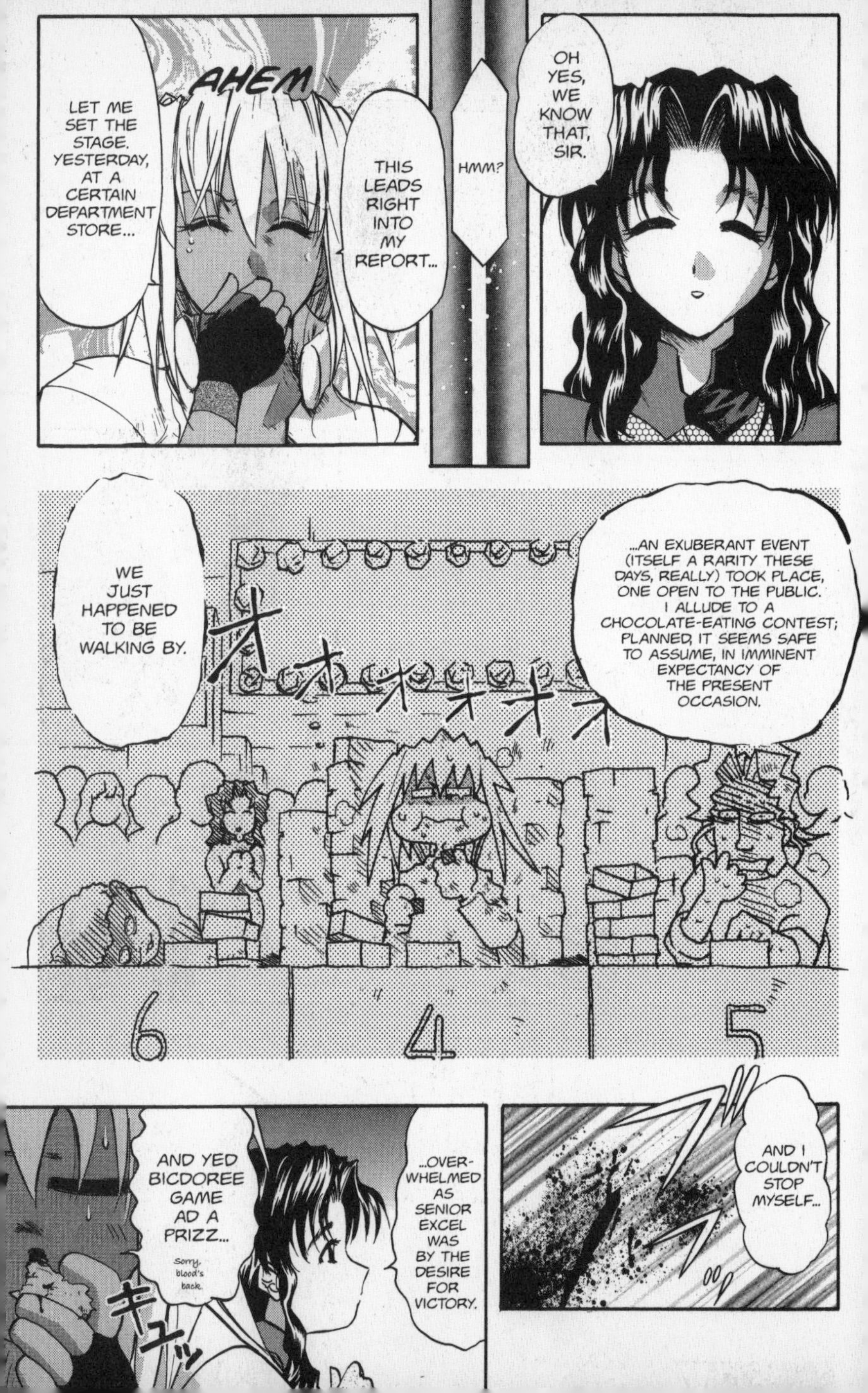
OH YES, WE KNOW THAT, SIR.
HMM?
THIS LEADS RIGHT INTO MY REPORT...
AHEM
LET ME SET THE STAGE. YESTERDAY, AT A CERTAIN DEPARTMENT STORE...
...AN EXUBERANT EVENT (ITSELF A RARITY THESE DAYS, REALLY) TOOK PLACE, ONE OPEN TO THE PUBLIC. I ALLUDE TO A CHOCOLATE-EATING CONTEST; PLANNED, IT SEEMS SAFE TO ASSUME, IN IMMINENT EXPECTANCY OF THE PRESENT OCCASION.
WE JUST HAPPENED TO BE WALKING BY.
6 4 5
AND I COULDN'T STOP MYSELF...
...OVER-WHELMED AS SENIOR EXCEL WAS BY THE DESIRE FOR VICTORY.
AND YED BICDOREE GAME AD A PRIZZ...
Sorry, blood's back.

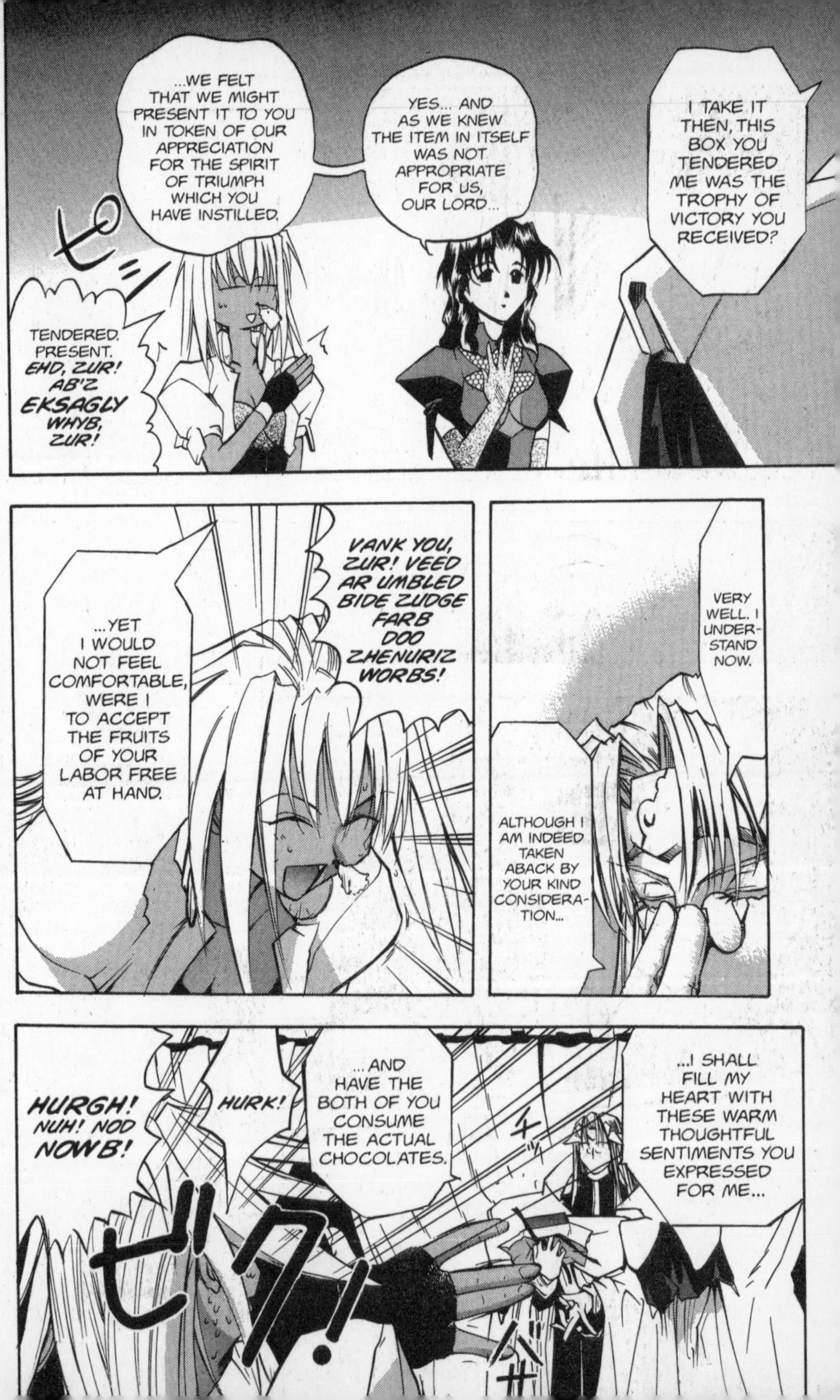
I TAKE IT THEN, THIS BOX YOU TENDERED ME WAS THE TROPHY OF VICTORY YOU RECEIVED?
YES... AND AS WE KNEW THE ITEM IN ITSELF WAS NOT APPROPRIATE FOR US, OUR LORD...
...WE FELT THAT WE MIGHT PRESENT IT TO YOU IN TOKEN OF OUR APPRECIATION FOR THE SPIRIT OF TRIUMPH WHICH YOU HAVE INSTILLED.
TENDERED. PRESENT. EHD, ZUR! AB'Z EKSAGLY WHYB, ZUR!
VERY WELL. I UNDERSTAND NOW.
ALTHOUGH I AM INDEED TAKEN ABACK BY YOUR KIND CONSIDERATION...
...YET I WOULD NOT FEEL COMFORTABLE, WERE I TO ACCEPT THE FRUITS OF YOUR LABOR FREE AT HAND.
VANK YOU, ZUR! VEED AR UMBLED BIDE ZUDGE FARB DOO ZHENURIZ WORBS!
...I SHALL FILL MY HEART WITH THESE WARM THOUGHTFUL SENTIMENTS YOU EXPRESSED FOR ME...
...AND HAVE THE BOTH OF YOU CONSUME THE ACTUAL CHOCOLATES.
HURK!
HURGH! NUH! NOD NOWB!

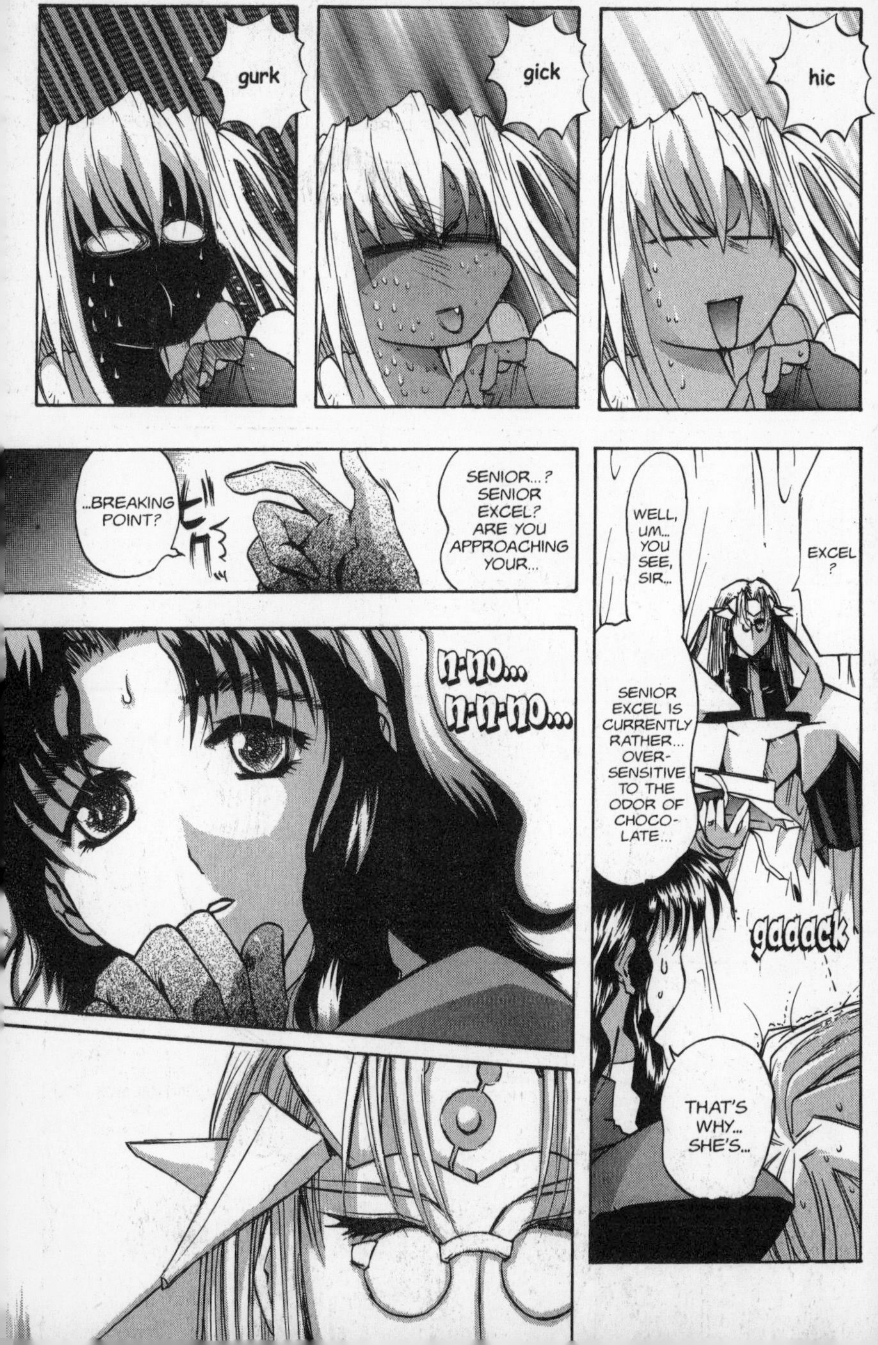
hic
gick
gurk
EXCEL ?
WELL, UM... YOU SEE, SIR...
SENIOR EXCEL IS CURRENTLY RATHER... OVER-SENSITIVE TO THE ODOR OF CHOCOLATE...
gaaack
THAT'S WHY... SHE'S...
SENIOR...? SENIOR EXCEL? ARE YOU APPROACHING YOUR...
...BREAKING POINT?
n-no... n-n-no...

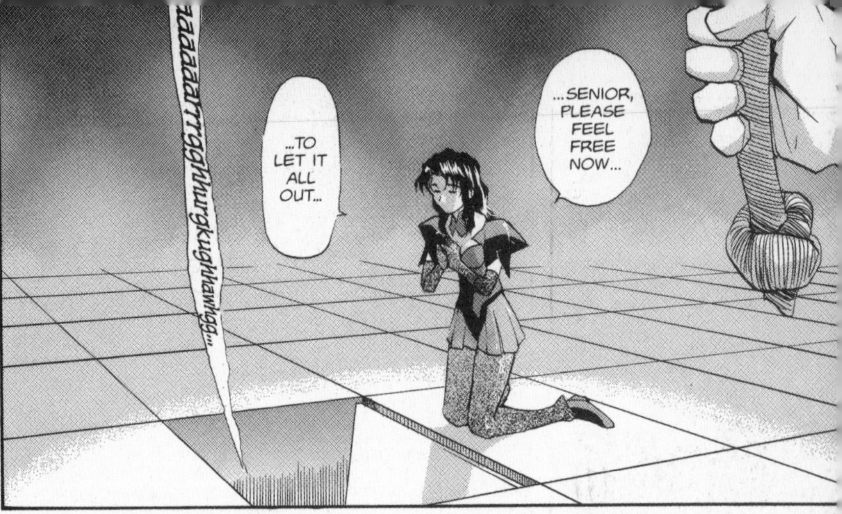
...SENIOR, PLEASE FEEL FREE NOW...
...TO LET IT ALL OUT...
aaaaaaarrrgghurgkughhawhgg...

Cooperation by: Antonia, Po, and Jinnojyou.

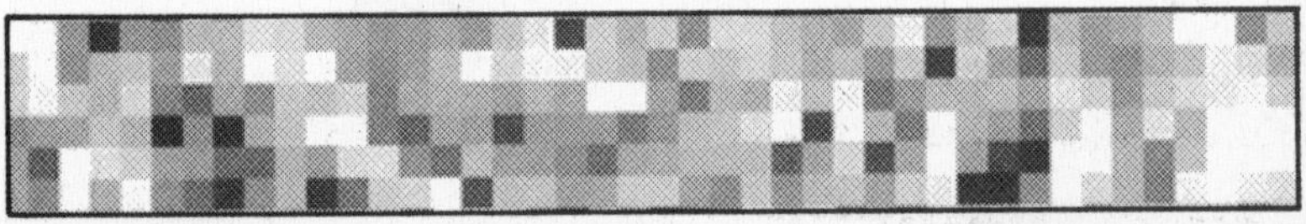

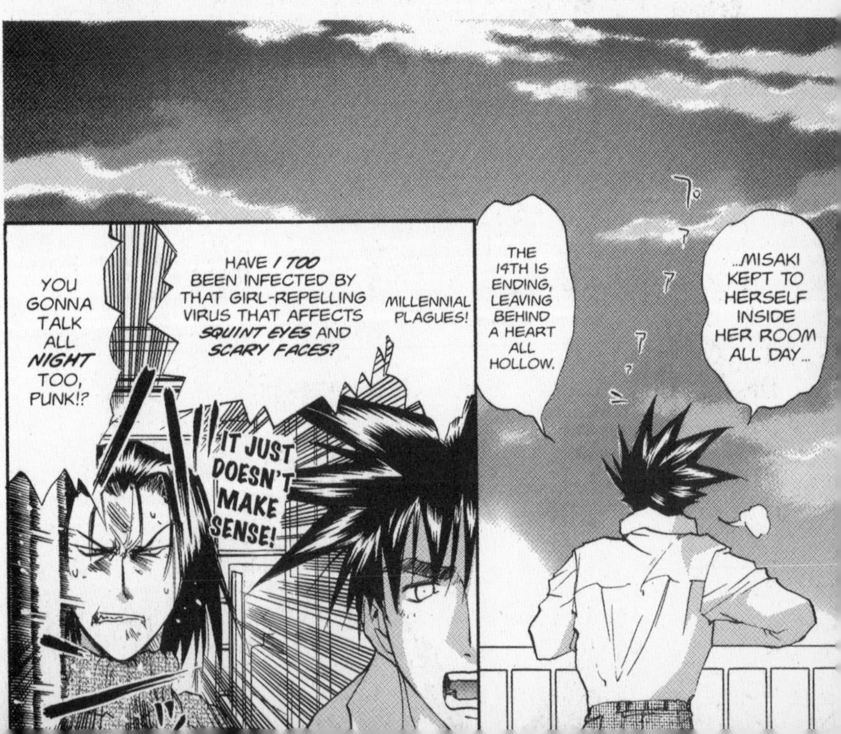
...MISAKI KEPT TO HERSELF INSIDE HER ROOM ALL DAY...
THE 14TH IS ENDING, LEAVING BEHIND A HEART ALL HOLLOW.
MILLENNIAL PLAGUES!
HAVE *I TOO* BEEN INFECTED BY THAT GIRL-REPELLING VIRUS THAT AFFECTS *SQUINT EYES* AND *SCARY FACES?*
IT JUST DOESN'T MAKE SENSE!
YOU GONNA TALK ALL *NIGHT* TOO, PUNK!?

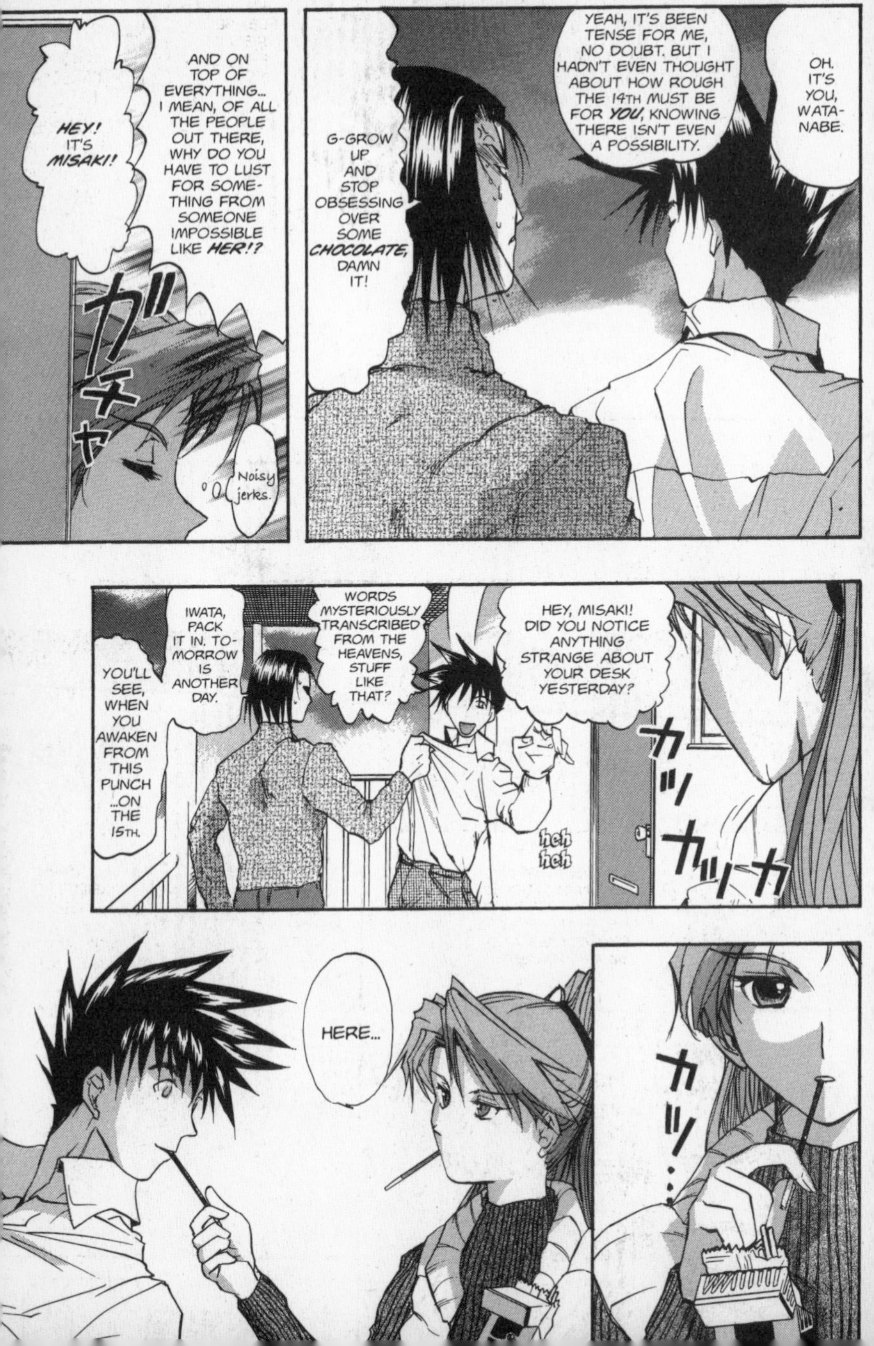
OH. IT'S YOU, WATA-NABE.
YEAH, IT'S BEEN TENSE FOR ME, NO DOUBT. BUT I HADN'T EVEN THOUGHT ABOUT HOW ROUGH THE 14TH MUST BE FOR *YOU*, KNOWING THERE ISN'T EVEN A POSSIBILITY.
G-GROW UP AND STOP OBSESSING OVER SOME *CHOCOLATE*, DAMN IT!
AND ON TOP OF EVERYTHING... I MEAN, OF ALL THE PEOPLE OUT THERE, WHY DO YOU HAVE TO LUST FOR SOME-THING FROM SOMEONE IMPOSSIBLE LIKE *HER!?*
*HEY!* IT'S *MISAKI!*
ガチャ
Noisy jerks.
HEY, MISAKI! DID YOU NOTICE ANYTHING STRANGE ABOUT YOUR DESK YESTERDAY?
カッ カッカ
heh heh
WORDS MYSTERIOUSLY TRANSCRIBED FROM THE HEAVENS, STUFF LIKE THAT?
IWATA, PACK IT IN. TO-MORROW IS ANOTHER DAY.
YOU'LL SEE, WHEN YOU AWAKEN FROM THIS PUNCH ...ON THE 15TH.
カッ…
HERE...

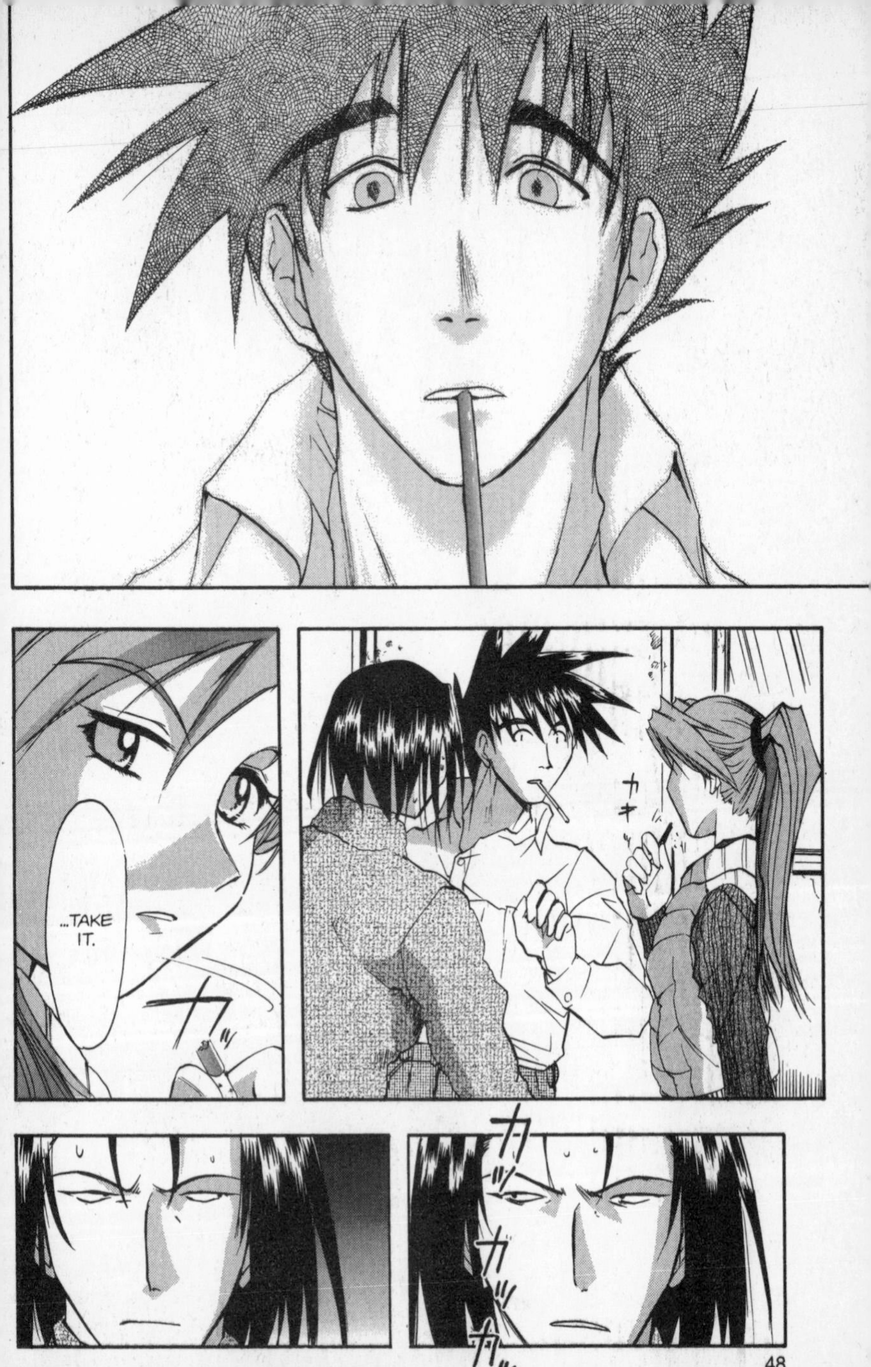
カキッ
...TAKE IT.
カッ
カッ
ガッ
ガッ
ガッ

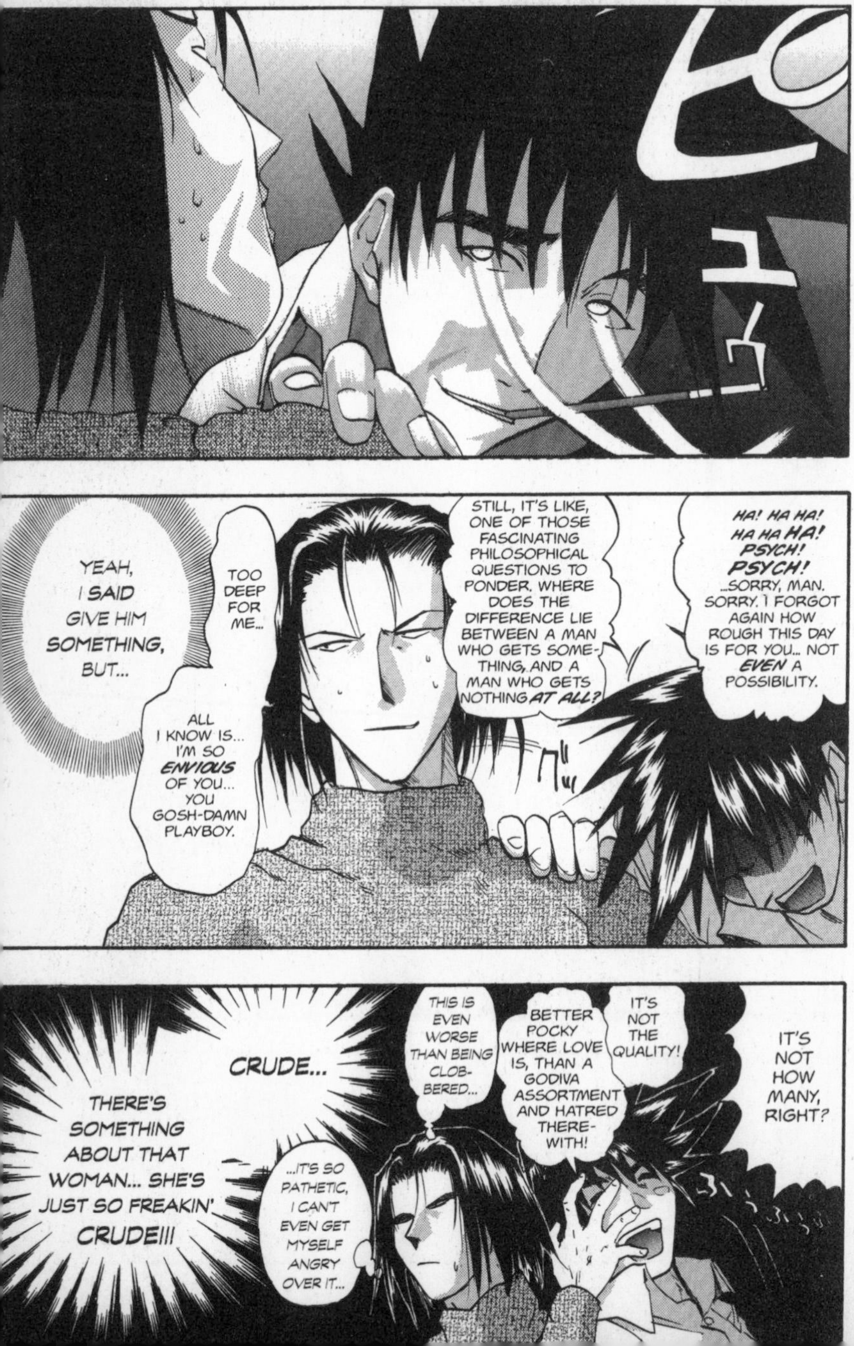
HA! HA HA! HA HA HA! PSYCH! PSYCH! ...SORRY, MAN. SORRY. I FORGOT AGAIN HOW ROUGH THIS DAY IS FOR YOU... NOT EVEN A POSSIBILITY.
STILL, IT'S LIKE, ONE OF THOSE FASCINATING PHILOSOPHICAL QUESTIONS TO PONDER. WHERE DOES THE DIFFERENCE LIE BETWEEN A MAN WHO GETS SOME-THING, AND A MAN WHO GETS NOTHING AT ALL?
TOO DEEP FOR ME...
ALL I KNOW IS... I'M SO ENVIOUS OF YOU... YOU GOSH-DAMN PLAYBOY.
YEAH, I SAID GIVE HIM SOMETHING, BUT...
IT'S NOT HOW MANY, RIGHT?
IT'S NOT THE QUALITY!
BETTER POCKY WHERE LOVE IS, THAN A GODIVA ASSORTMENT AND HATRED THERE-WITH!
THIS IS EVEN WORSE THAN BEING CLOB-BERED...
...IT'S SO PATHETIC, I CAN'T EVEN GET MYSELF ANGRY OVER IT...
CRUDE...
THERE'S SOMETHING ABOUT THAT WOMAN... SHE'S JUST SO FREAKIN' CRUDE!!!

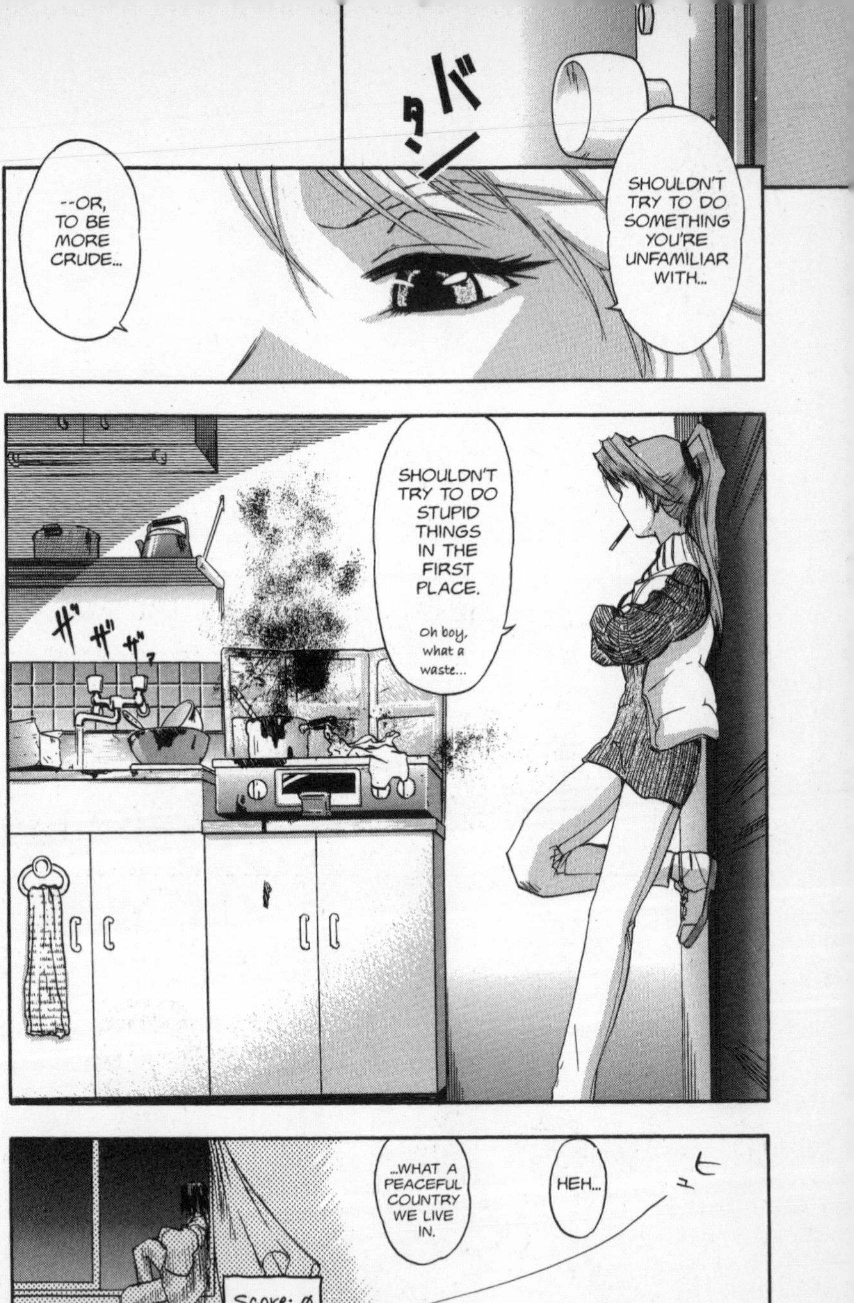

バタン
SHOULDN'T TRY TO DO SOMETHING YOU'RE UNFAMILIAR WITH...
--OR, TO BE MORE CRUDE...
SHOULDN'T TRY TO DO STUPID THINGS IN THE FIRST PLACE.
Oh boy, what a waste...
ザザザァ
ヒュ
HEH...
...WHAT A PEACEFUL COUNTRY WE LIVE IN.
Score: ø


END MISSION 2

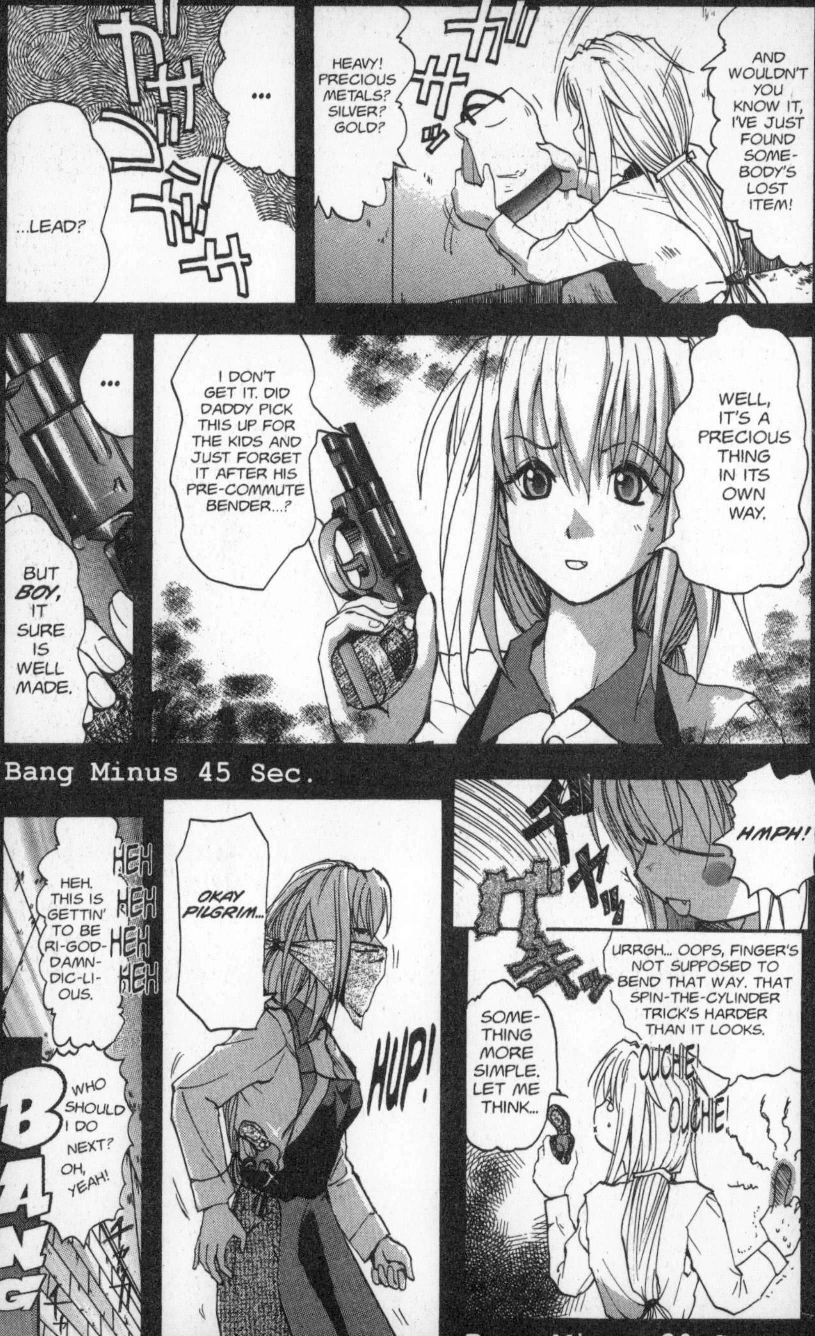
AND WOULDN'T YOU KNOW IT, I'VE JUST FOUND SOMEBODY'S LOST ITEM!
HEAVY! PRECIOUS METALS? SILVER? GOLD?
...
...LEAD?
WELL, IT'S A PRECIOUS THING IN ITS OWN WAY.
I DON'T GET IT. DID DADDY PICK THIS UP FOR THE KIDS AND JUST FORGET IT AFTER HIS PRE-COMMUTE BENDER...?
...
BUT *BOY*, IT SURE IS WELL MADE.
Bang Minus 45 Sec.
HMPH!
URRGH... OOPS, FINGER'S NOT SUPPOSED TO BEND THAT WAY. THAT SPIN-THE-CYLINDER TRICK'S HARDER THAN IT LOOKS.
SOME-THING MORE SIMPLE. LET ME THINK...
OUCHIE! OUCHIE!
OKAY PILGRIM...
HUP!
HEH. THIS IS GETTIN' TO BE RI-GOD-DAMN-DIC-LI-OUS.
HEH HEH HEH HEH
WHO SHOULD I DO NEXT? OH, YEAH!
BANG
Bang Minus 30 Sec.

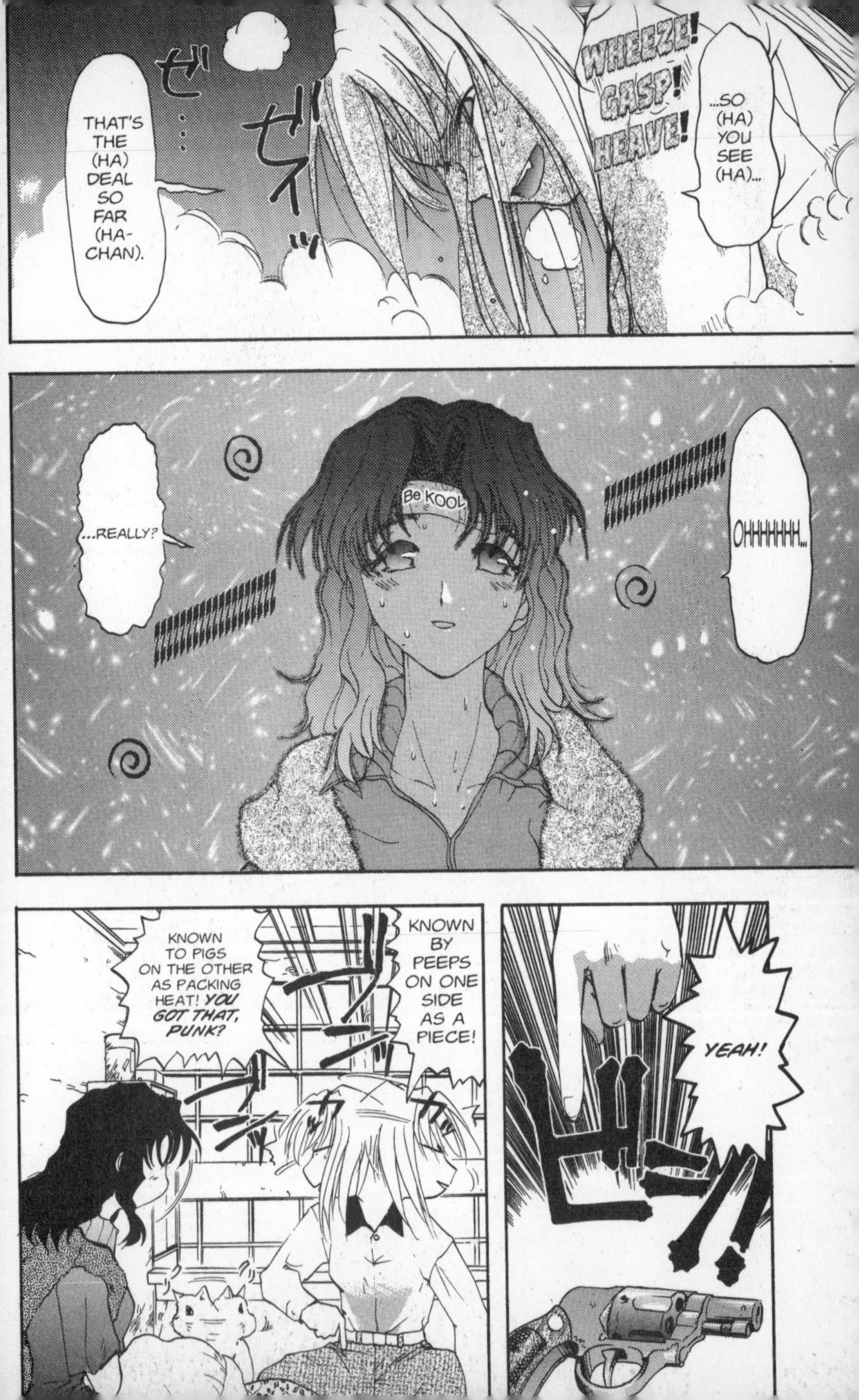
...SO (HA) YOU SEE (HA)...
WHEEZE! GASP! HEAVE!
THAT'S THE (HA) DEAL SO FAR (HA-CHAN).
OHHHHHHH...
Be KOOL
...REALLY?
YEAH!
KNOWN BY PEEPS ON ONE SIDE AS A PIECE!
KNOWN TO PIGS ON THE OTHER AS PACKING HEAT! YOU GOT THAT, PUNK?

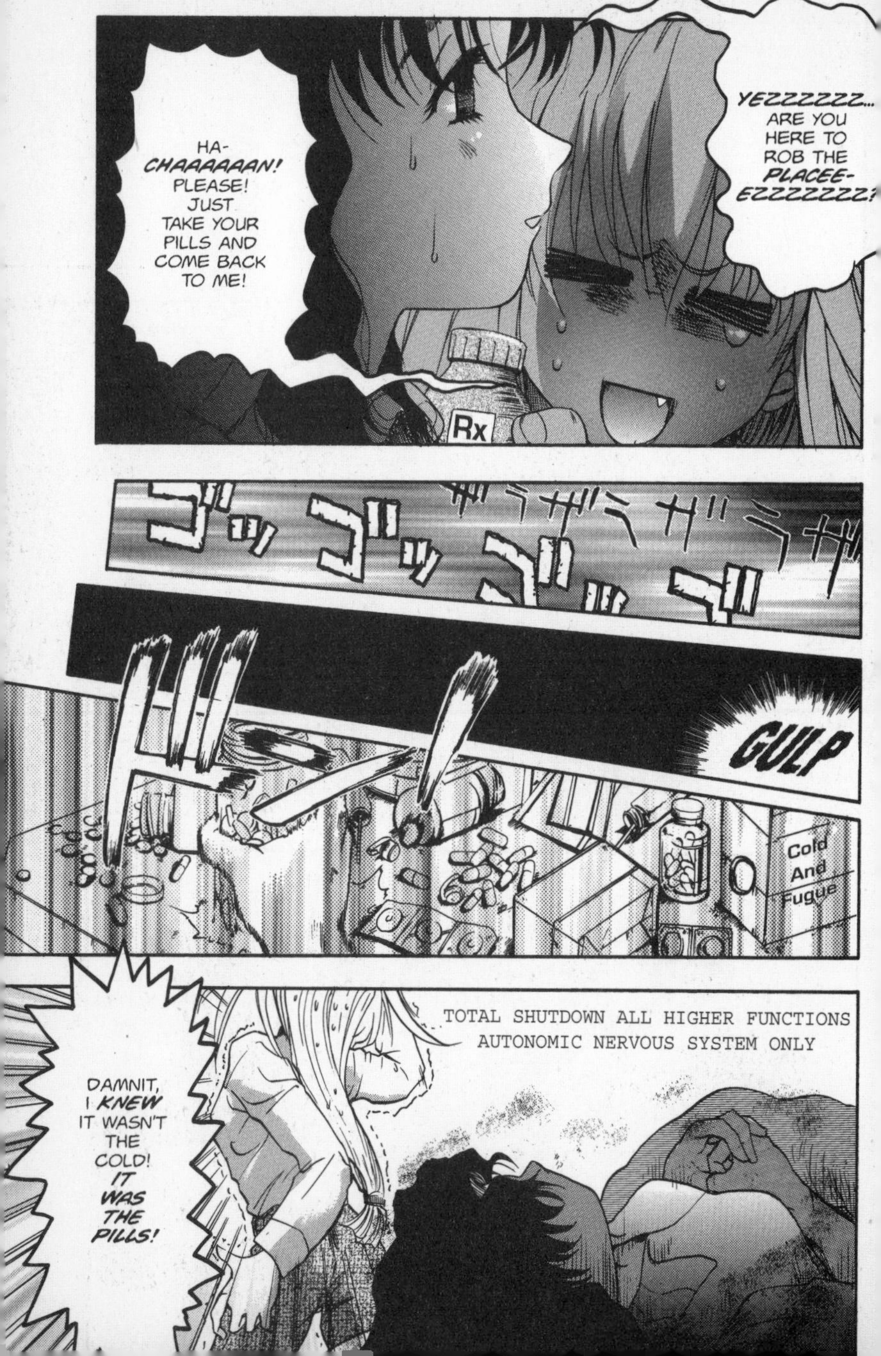
YEZZZZZZ... ARE YOU HERE TO ROB THE PLACEE-EZZZZZZZZ?
HA-CHAAAAAAN! PLEASE! JUST TAKE YOUR PILLS AND COME BACK TO ME!
Rx
GULP
Cold And Fugue
TOTAL SHUTDOWN ALL HIGHER FUNCTIONS
AUTONOMIC NERVOUS SYSTEM ONLY
DAMNIT, I KNEW IT WASN'T THE COLD! IT WAS THE PILLS!

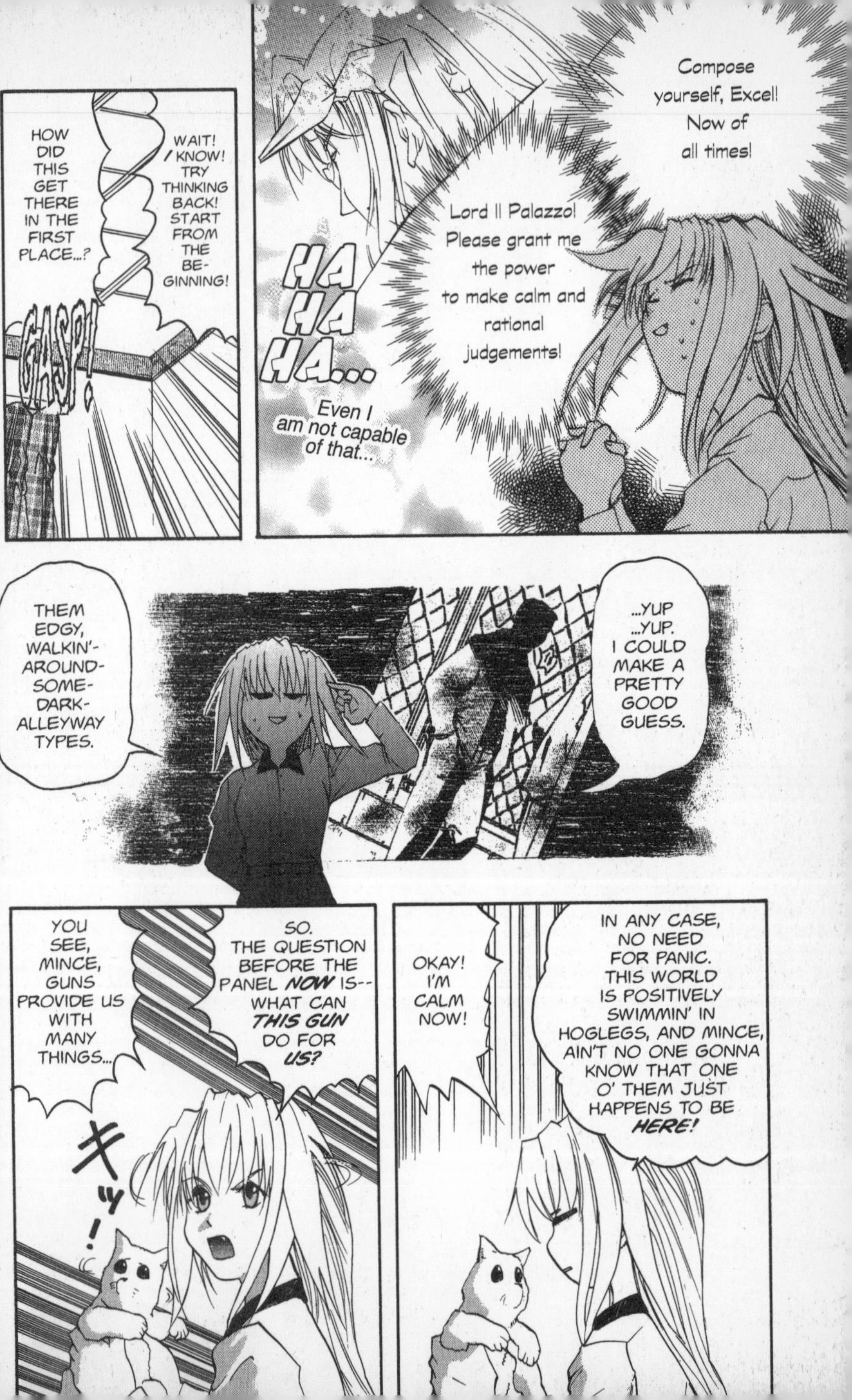

Compose yourself, Excel! Now of all times!
Lord Il Palazzo! Please grant me the power to make calm and rational judgements!
HA HA HA...
Even I am not capable of that...
WAIT! I KNOW! TRY THINKING BACK! START FROM THE BE-GINNING!
HOW DID THIS GET THERE IN THE FIRST PLACE...?
GASP!
...YUP ...YUP. I COULD MAKE A PRETTY GOOD GUESS.
THEM EDGY, WALKIN'-AROUND-SOME-DARK-ALLEYWAY TYPES.
IN ANY CASE, NO NEED FOR PANIC. THIS WORLD IS POSITIVELY SWIMMIN' IN HOGLEGS, AND MINCE, AIN'T NO ONE GONNA KNOW THAT ONE O' THEM JUST HAPPENS TO BE ***HERE!***
OKAY! I'M CALM NOW!
SO. THE QUESTION BEFORE THE PANEL ***NOW*** IS-- WHAT CAN ***THIS GUN*** DO FOR ***US?***
YOU SEE, MINCE, GUNS PROVIDE US WITH MANY THINGS...
キッ!

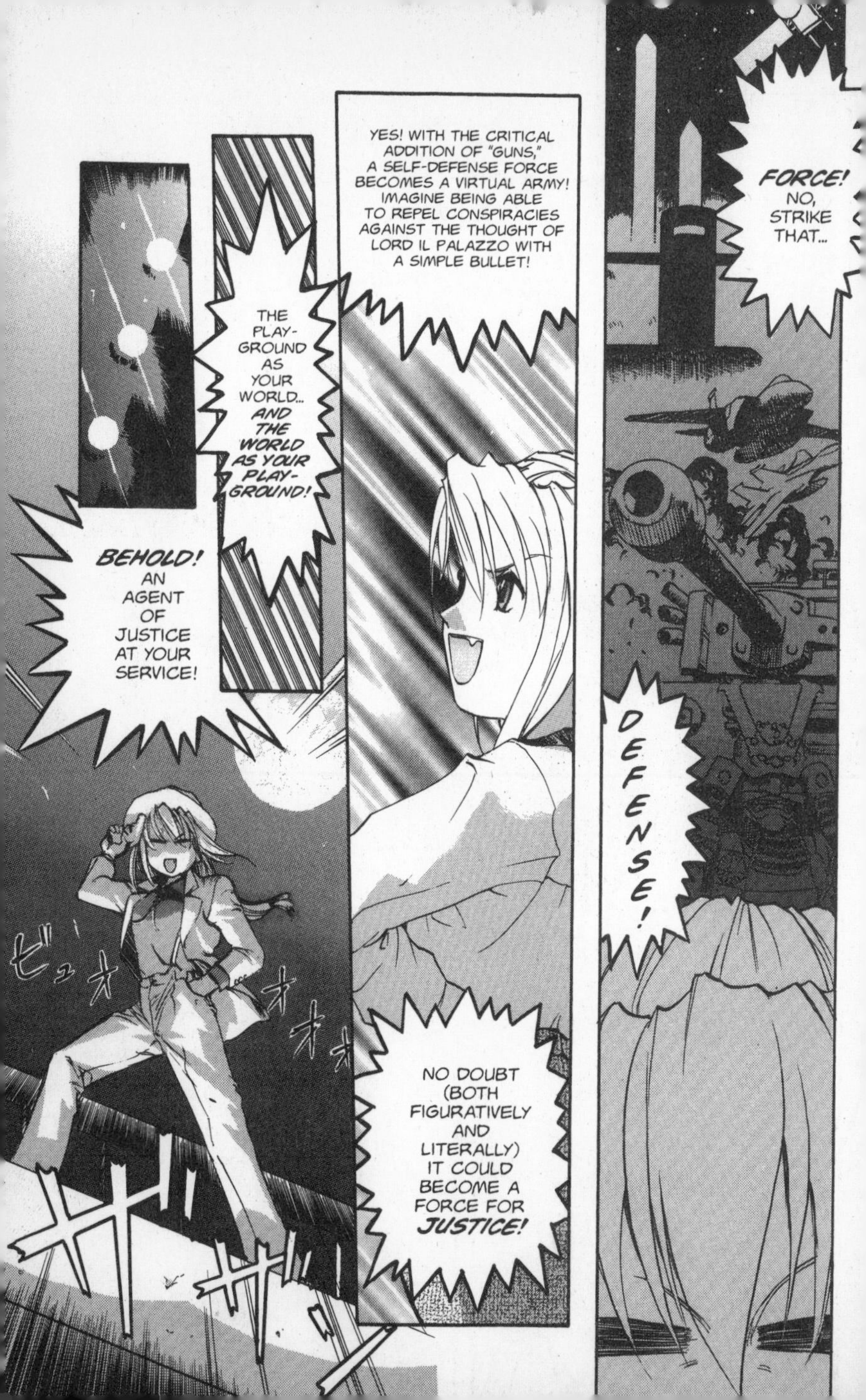

FORCE! NO, STRIKE THAT...
DEFENSE!
YES! WITH THE CRITICAL ADDITION OF "GUNS," A SELF-DEFENSE FORCE BECOMES A VIRTUAL ARMY! IMAGINE BEING ABLE TO REPEL CONSPIRACIES AGAINST THE THOUGHT OF LORD IL PALAZZO WITH A SIMPLE BULLET!
NO DOUBT (BOTH FIGURATIVELY AND LITERALLY) IT COULD BECOME A FORCE FOR JUSTICE!
THE PLAY-GROUND AS YOUR WORLD... AND THE WORLD AS YOUR PLAY-GROUND!
BEHOLD! AN AGENT OF JUSTICE AT YOUR SERVICE!
ビュオオオオ

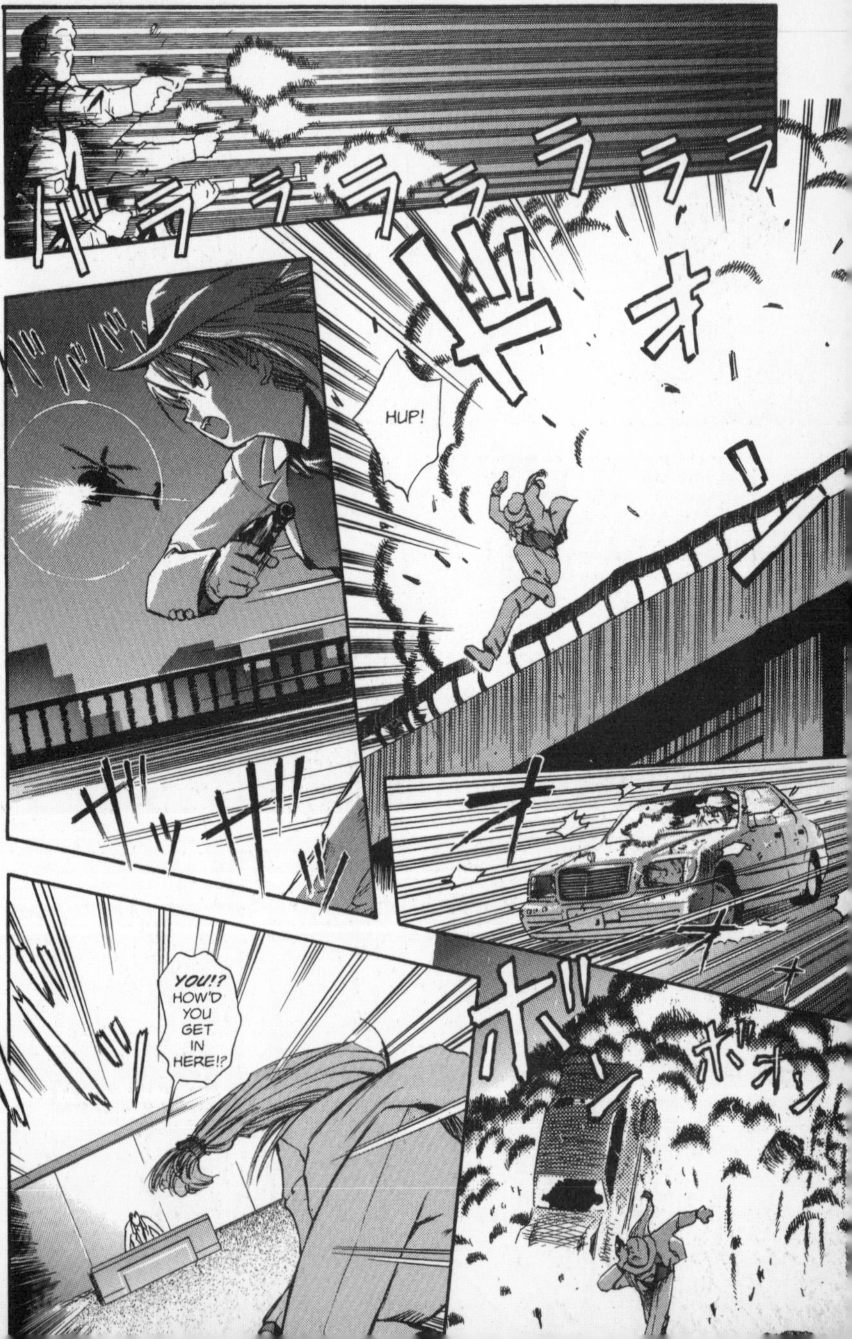
HUP!
YOU!? HOW'D YOU GET IN HERE!?

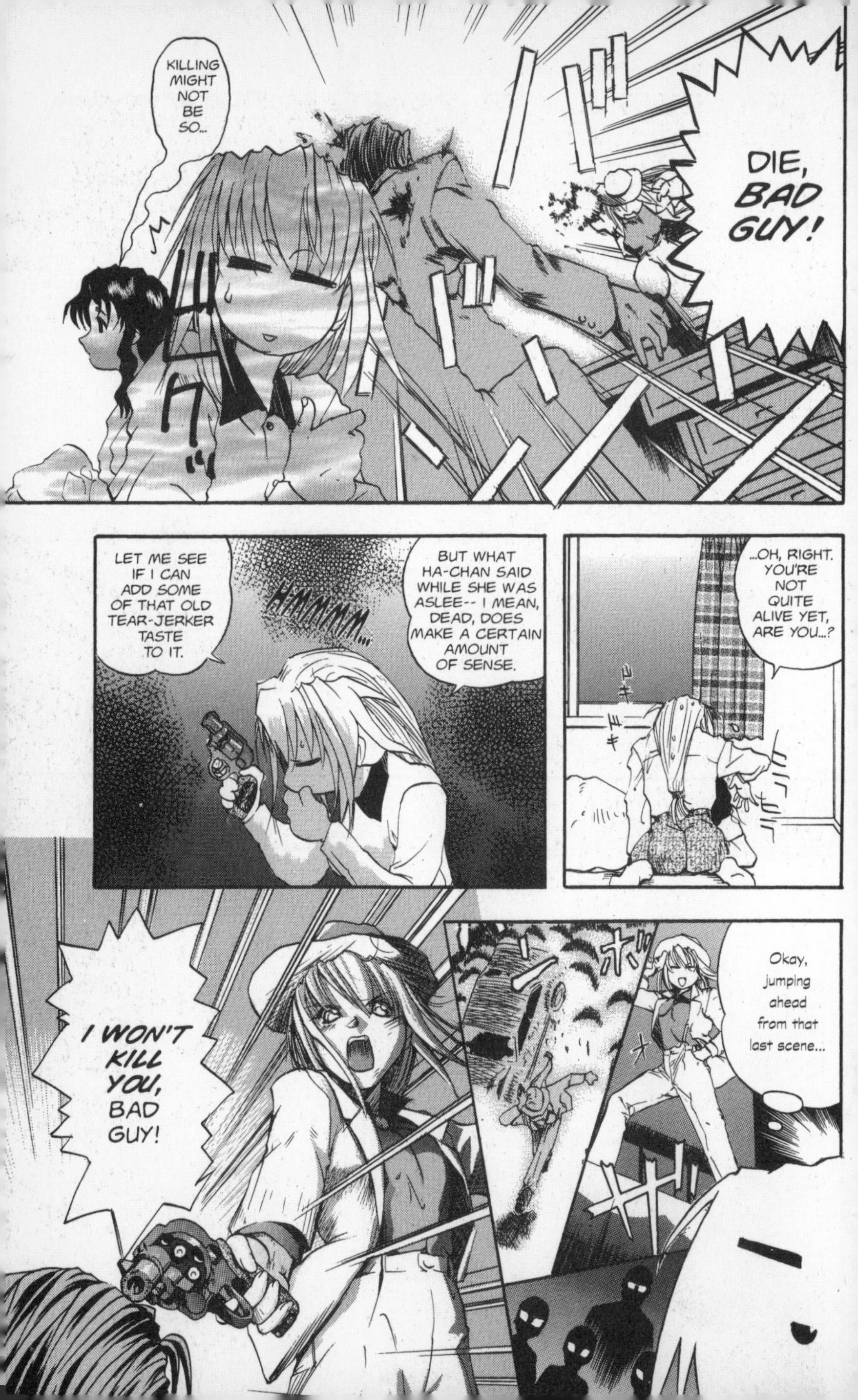

DIE, BAD GUY!
KILLING MIGHT NOT BE SO...
...OH, RIGHT. YOU'RE NOT QUITE ALIVE YET, ARE YOU...?
BUT WHAT HA-CHAN SAID WHILE SHE WAS ASLEE-- I MEAN, DEAD, DOES MAKE A CERTAIN AMOUNT OF SENSE.
HMMMM...
LET ME SEE IF I CAN ADD SOME OF THAT OLD TEAR-JERKER TASTE TO IT.
Okay, jumping ahead from that last scene...
I WON'T KILL YOU, BAD GUY!

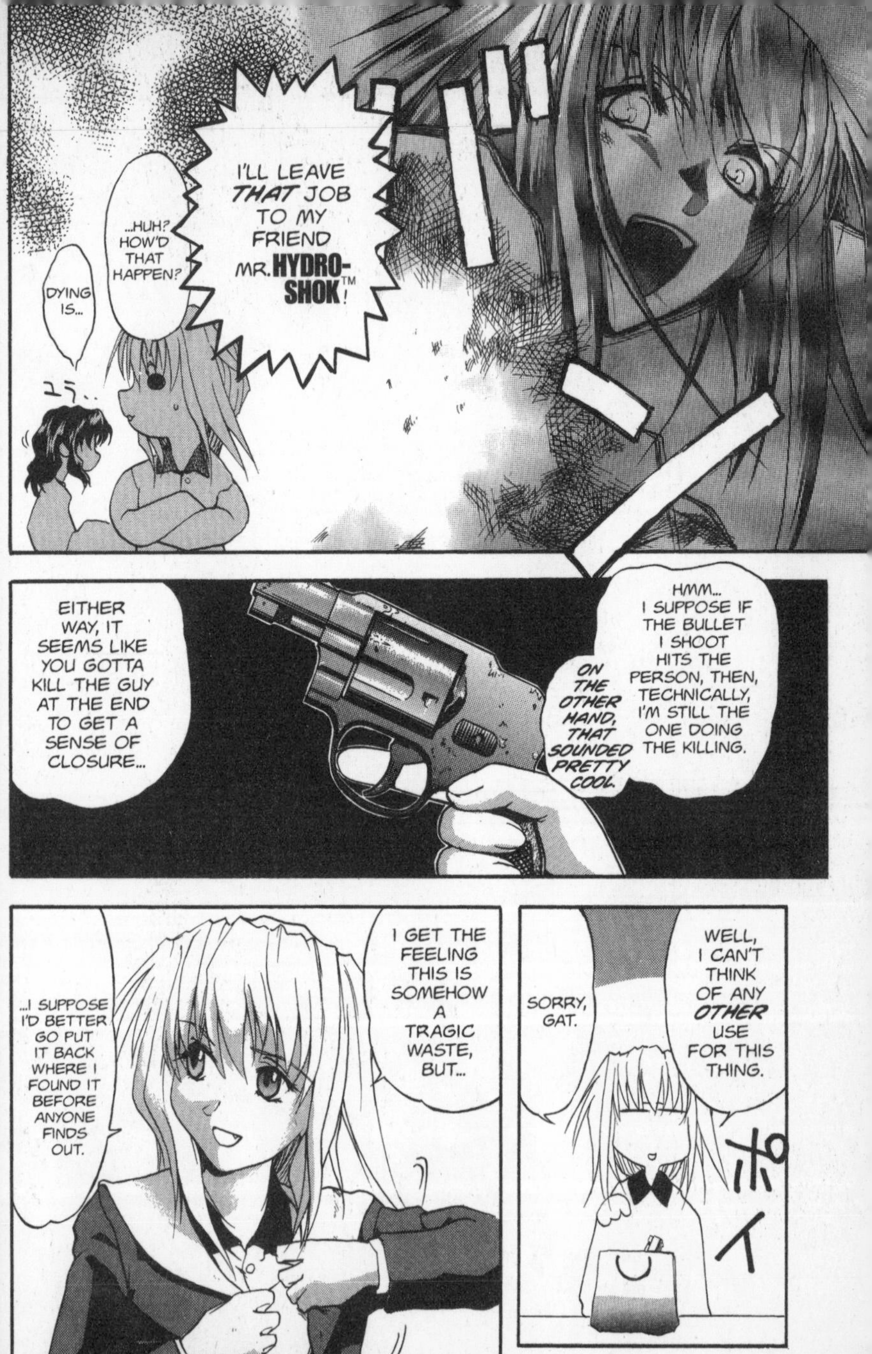
I'LL LEAVE *THAT* JOB TO MY FRIEND MR. **HYDRO-SHOK**™!
...HUH? HOW'D THAT HAPPEN?
DYING IS...
ユラ..
HMM... I SUPPOSE IF THE BULLET I SHOOT HITS THE PERSON, THEN, TECHNICALLY, I'M STILL THE ONE DOING THE KILLING.
*ON THE OTHER HAND, THAT SOUNDED PRETTY COOL.*
EITHER WAY, IT SEEMS LIKE YOU GOTTA KILL THE GUY AT THE END TO GET A SENSE OF CLOSURE...
WELL, I CAN'T THINK OF ANY *OTHER* USE FOR THIS THING.
SORRY, GAT.
ポイ
I GET THE FEELING THIS IS SOMEHOW A TRAGIC WASTE, BUT...
...I SUPPOSE I'D BETTER GO PUT IT BACK WHERE I FOUND IT BEFORE ANYONE FINDS OUT.

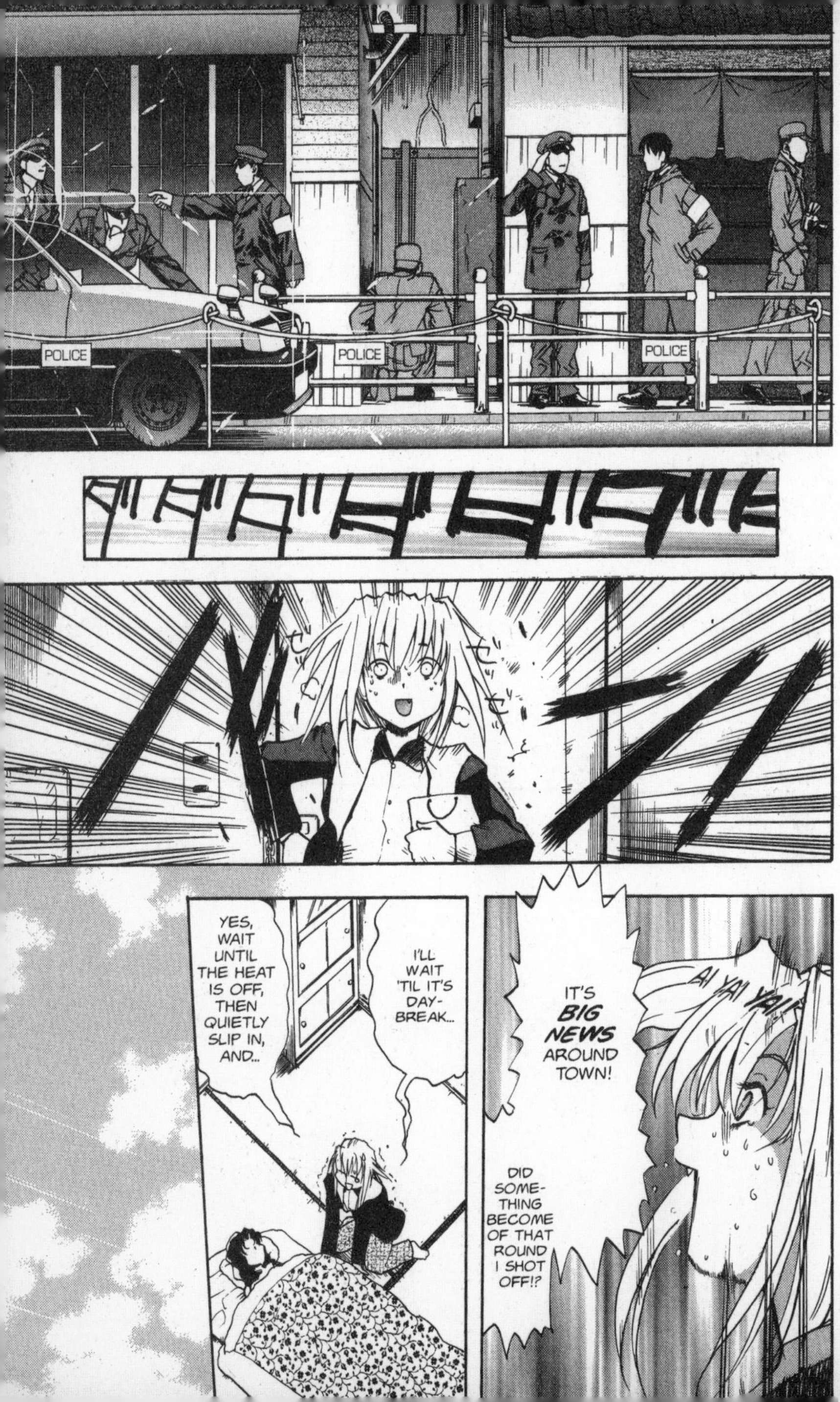
AI YAI YAI!
IT'S BIG NEWS AROUND TOWN!
DID SOMETHING BECOME OF THAT ROUND I SHOT OFF!?
I'LL WAIT 'TIL IT'S DAY-BREAK...
YES, WAIT UNTIL THE HEAT IS OFF, THEN QUIETLY SLIP IN, AND...

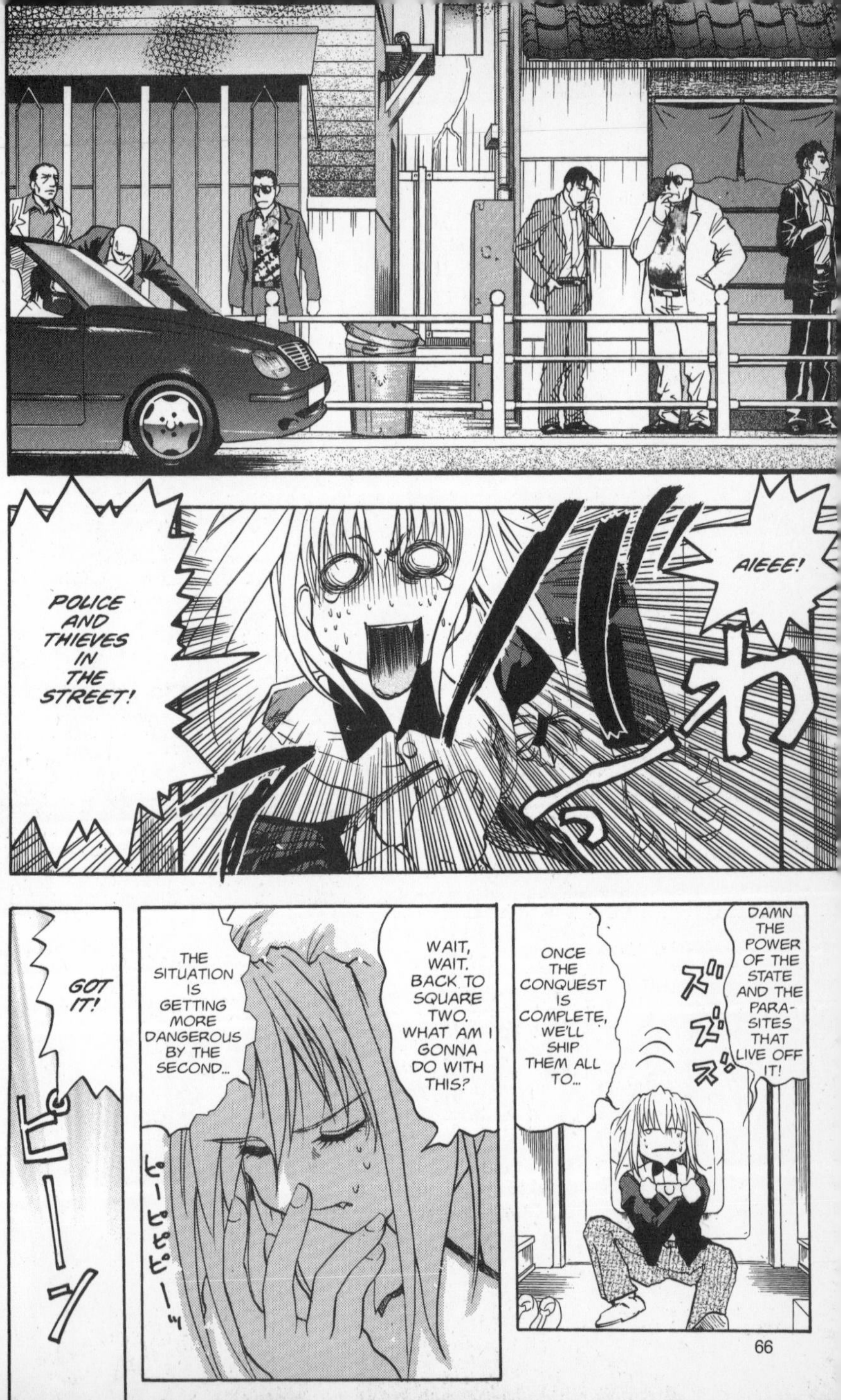
AIEEE!
POLICE AND THIEVES IN THE STREET!
DAMN THE POWER OF THE STATE AND THE PARASITES THAT LIVE OFF IT!
ズズズ
ONCE THE CONQUEST IS COMPLETE, WE'LL SHIP THEM ALL TO...
WAIT, WAIT. BACK TO SQUARE TWO. WHAT AM I GONNA DO WITH THIS?
THE SITUATION IS GETTING MORE DANGEROUS BY THE SECOND...
ピーピピピーッ
GOT IT!
ピーーーッ

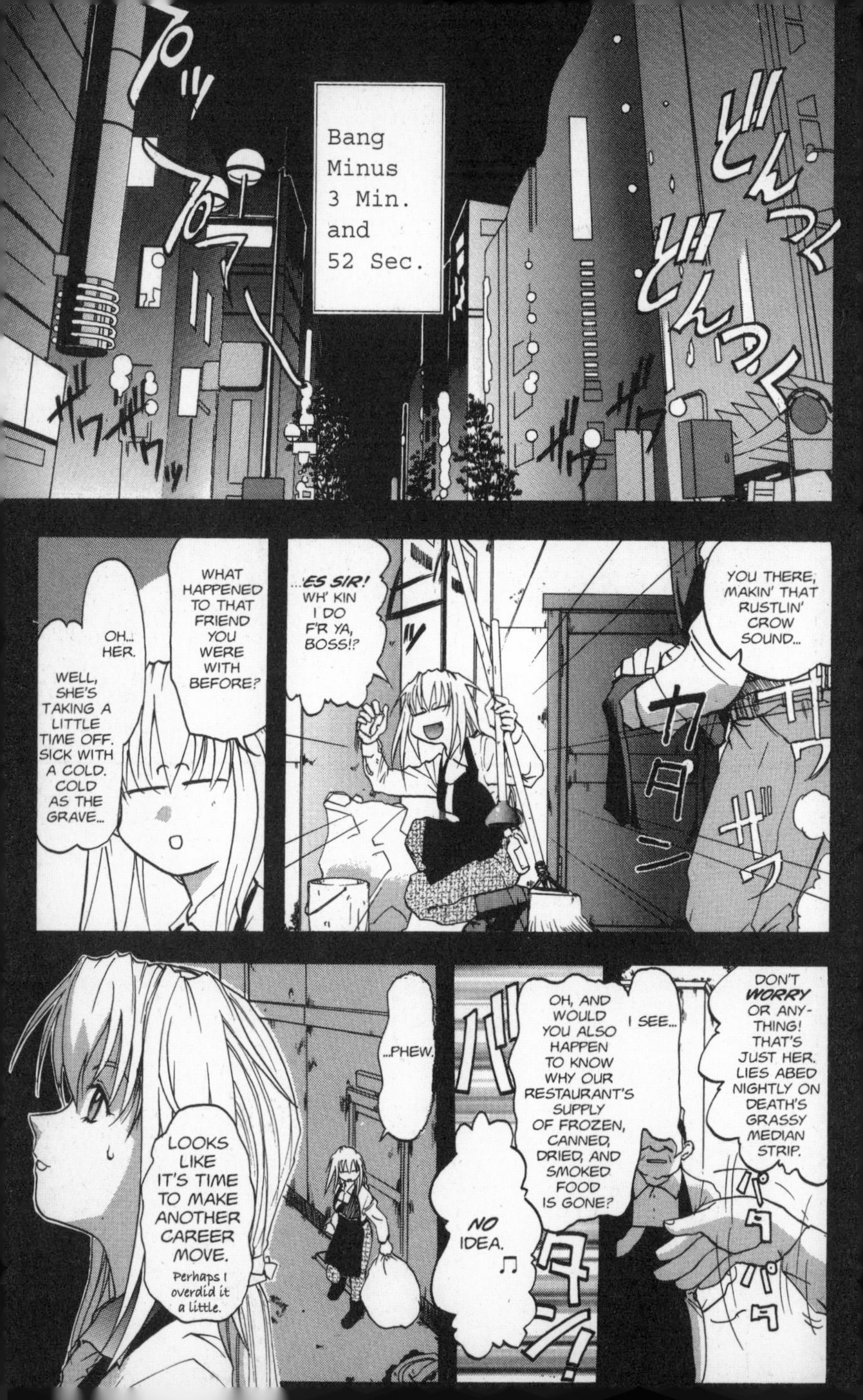
Bang Minus 3 Min. and 52 Sec.
YOU THERE, MAKIN' THAT RUSTLIN' CROW SOUND...
...ES SIR! WH' KIN I DO F'R YA, BOSS!?
WHAT HAPPENED TO THAT FRIEND YOU WERE WITH BEFORE?
OH... HER.
WELL, SHE'S TAKING A LITTLE TIME OFF. SICK WITH A COLD. COLD AS THE GRAVE...
DON'T WORRY OR ANY-THING! THAT'S JUST HER. LIES ABED NIGHTLY ON DEATH'S GRASSY MEDIAN STRIP.
I SEE...
OH, AND WOULD YOU ALSO HAPPEN TO KNOW WHY OUR RESTAURANT'S SUPPLY OF FROZEN, CANNED, DRIED, AND SMOKED FOOD IS GONE?
NO IDEA. ♫
...PHEW.
LOOKS LIKE IT'S TIME TO MAKE ANOTHER CAREER MOVE.
Perhaps I overdid it a little.

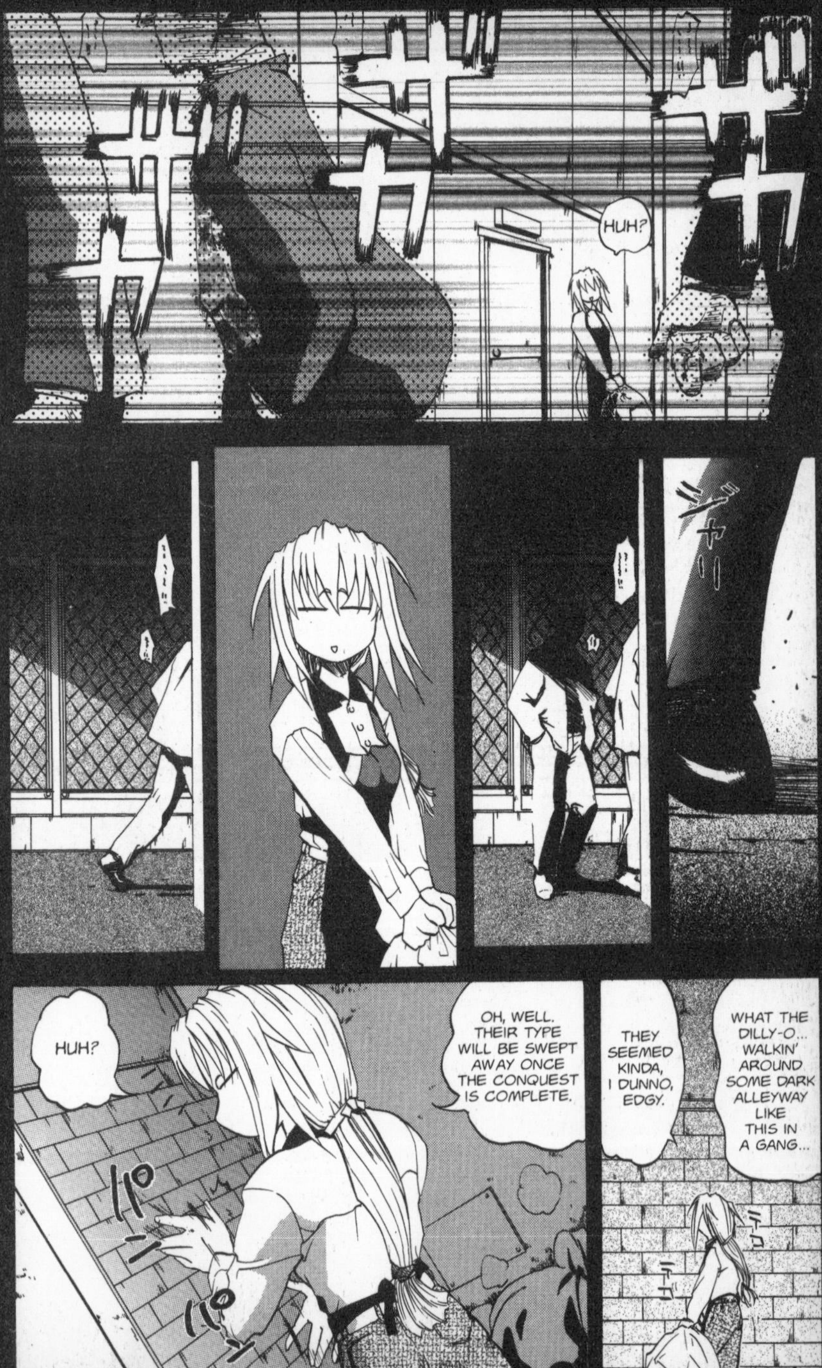
HUH?
WHAT THE DILLY-O... WALKIN' AROUND SOME DARK ALLEYWAY LIKE THIS IN A GANG...
THEY SEEMED KINDA, I DUNNO, EDGY.
OH, WELL. THEIR TYPE WILL BE SWEPT AWAY ONCE THE CONQUEST IS COMPLETE.
HUH?

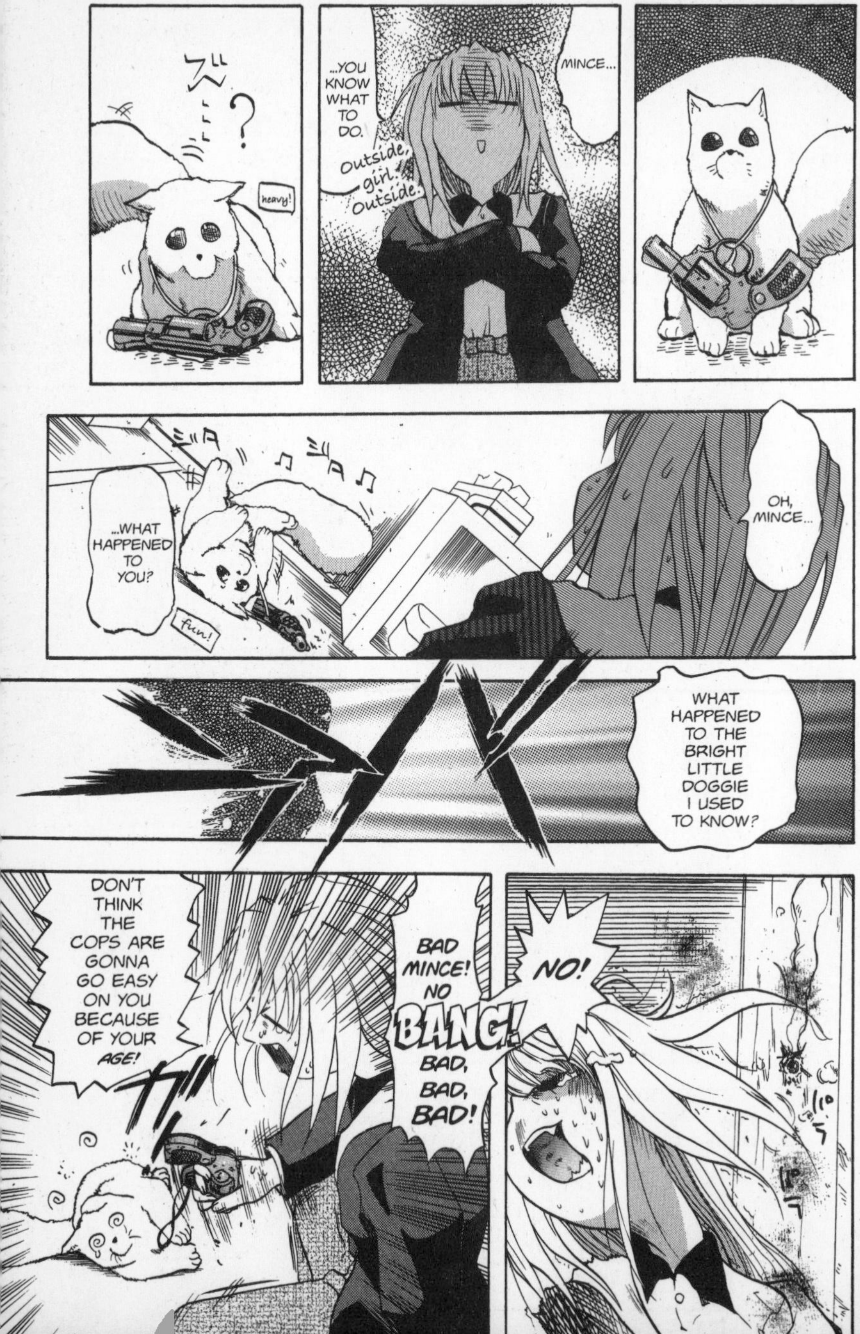
MINCE...
...YOU KNOW WHAT TO DO.
Outside, girl. Outside.
heavy!
OH, MINCE...
...WHAT HAPPENED TO YOU?
fun!
WHAT HAPPENED TO THE BRIGHT LITTLE DOGGIE I USED TO KNOW?
NO!
BAD MINCE! NO
BANG!
BAD, BAD, BAD!
DON'T THINK THE COPS ARE GONNA GO EASY ON YOU BECAUSE OF YOUR *AGE!*

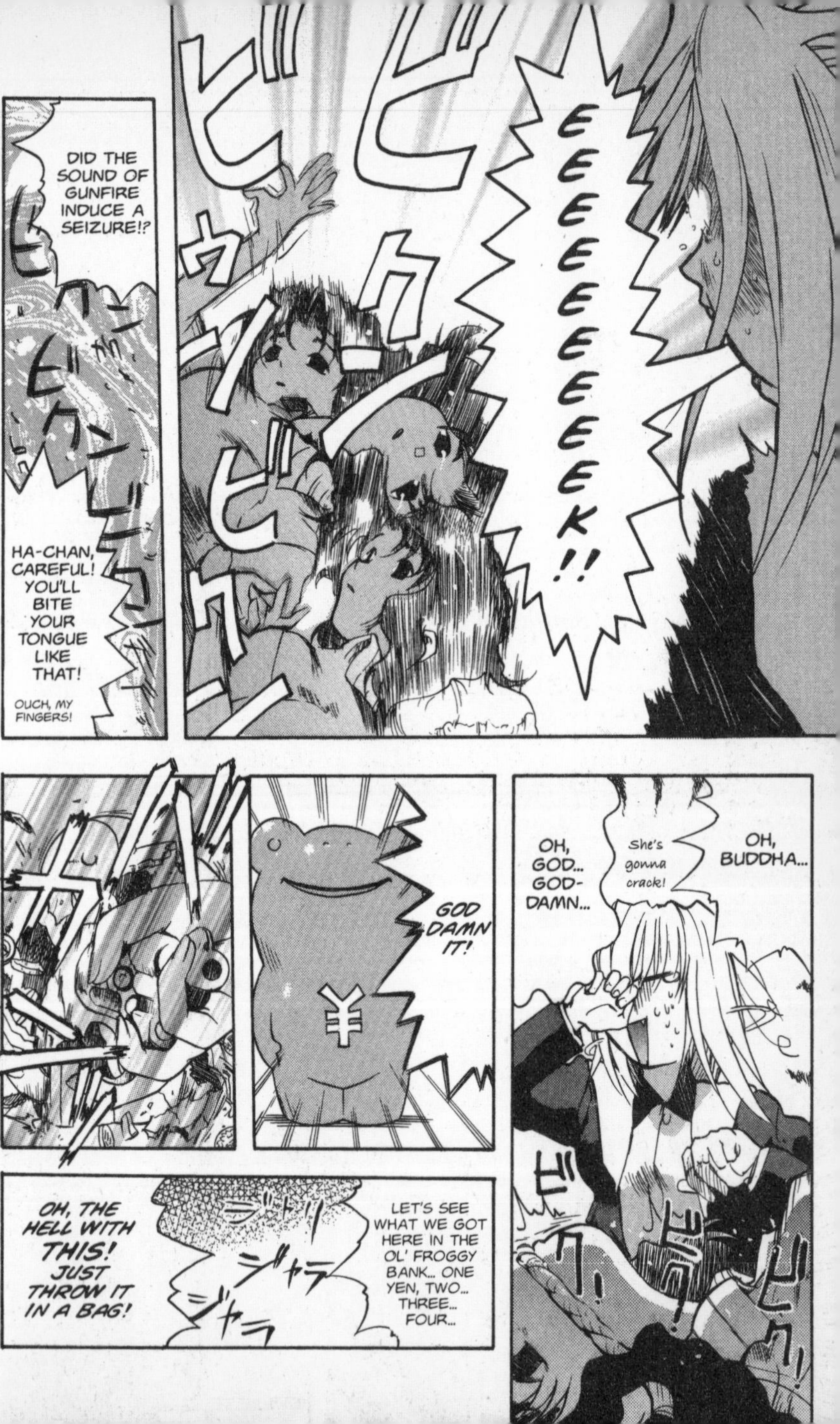
EEEEEEEEEEEK!!
DID THE SOUND OF GUNFIRE INDUCE A SEIZURE!?
HA-CHAN, CAREFUL! YOU'LL BITE YOUR TONGUE LIKE THAT!
OUCH, MY FINGERS!
OH, BUDDHA...
She's gonna crack!
OH, GOD... GOD-DAMN...
GOD DAMN IT!
LET'S SEE WHAT WE GOT HERE IN THE OL' FROGGY BANK... ONE YEN, TWO... THREE... FOUR...
OH, THE HELL WITH THIS! JUST THROW IT IN A BAG!

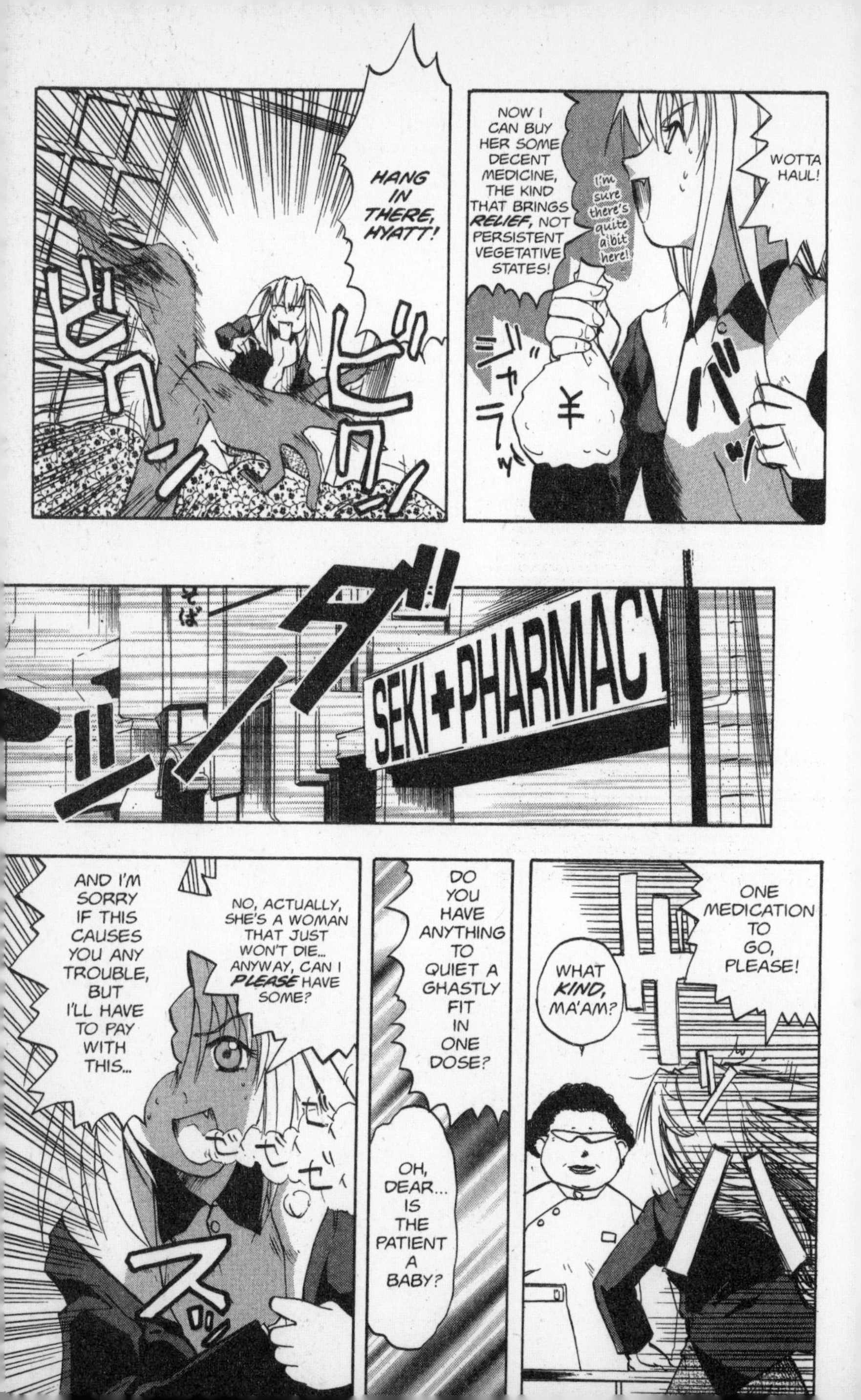
WOTTA HAUL!
I'm sure there's quite a bit here!
NOW I CAN BUY HER SOME DECENT MEDICINE, THE KIND THAT BRINGS *RELIEF,* NOT PERSISTENT VEGETATIVE STATES!
*HANG IN THERE, HYATT!*
SEKI ✚ PHARMACY
ONE MEDICATION TO GO, PLEASE!
WHAT *KIND,* MA'AM?
DO YOU HAVE ANYTHING TO QUIET A GHASTLY FIT IN ONE DOSE?
OH, DEAR... IS THE PATIENT A BABY?
NO, ACTUALLY, SHE'S A WOMAN THAT JUST WON'T DIE... ANYWAY, CAN I *PLEASE* HAVE SOME?
AND I'M SORRY IF THIS CAUSES YOU ANY TROUBLE, BUT I'LL HAVE TO PAY WITH THIS...

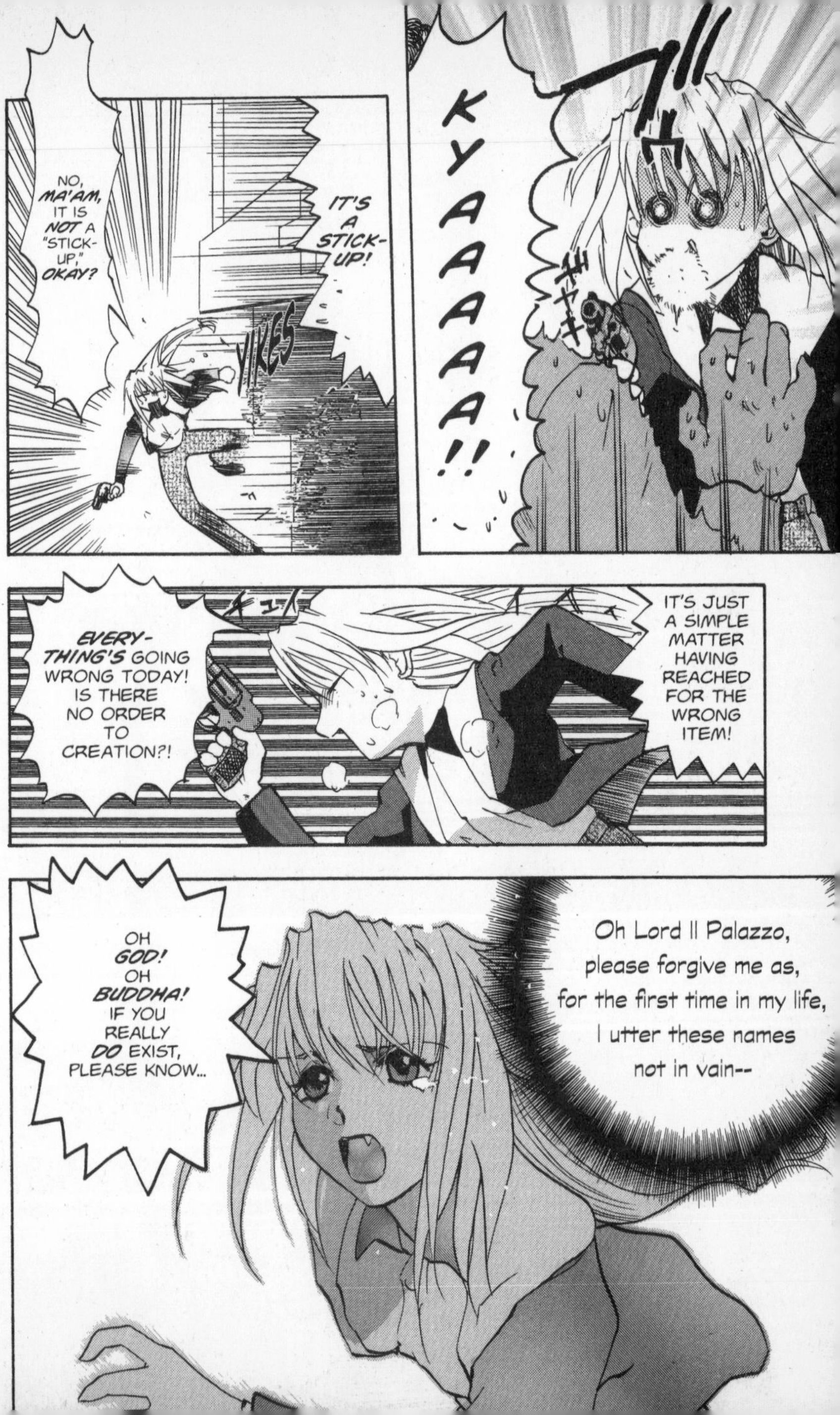
KYAAAAAA!!
IT'S A STICK-UP!
NO, MA'AM, IT IS NOT A "STICK-UP," OKAY?
YIKES
IT'S JUST A SIMPLE MATTER HAVING REACHED FOR THE WRONG ITEM!
EVERYTHING'S GOING WRONG TODAY! IS THERE NO ORDER TO CREATION?!
OH GOD! OH BUDDHA! IF YOU REALLY DO EXIST, PLEASE KNOW...
Oh Lord Il Palazzo, please forgive me as, for the first time in my life, I utter these names not in vain--

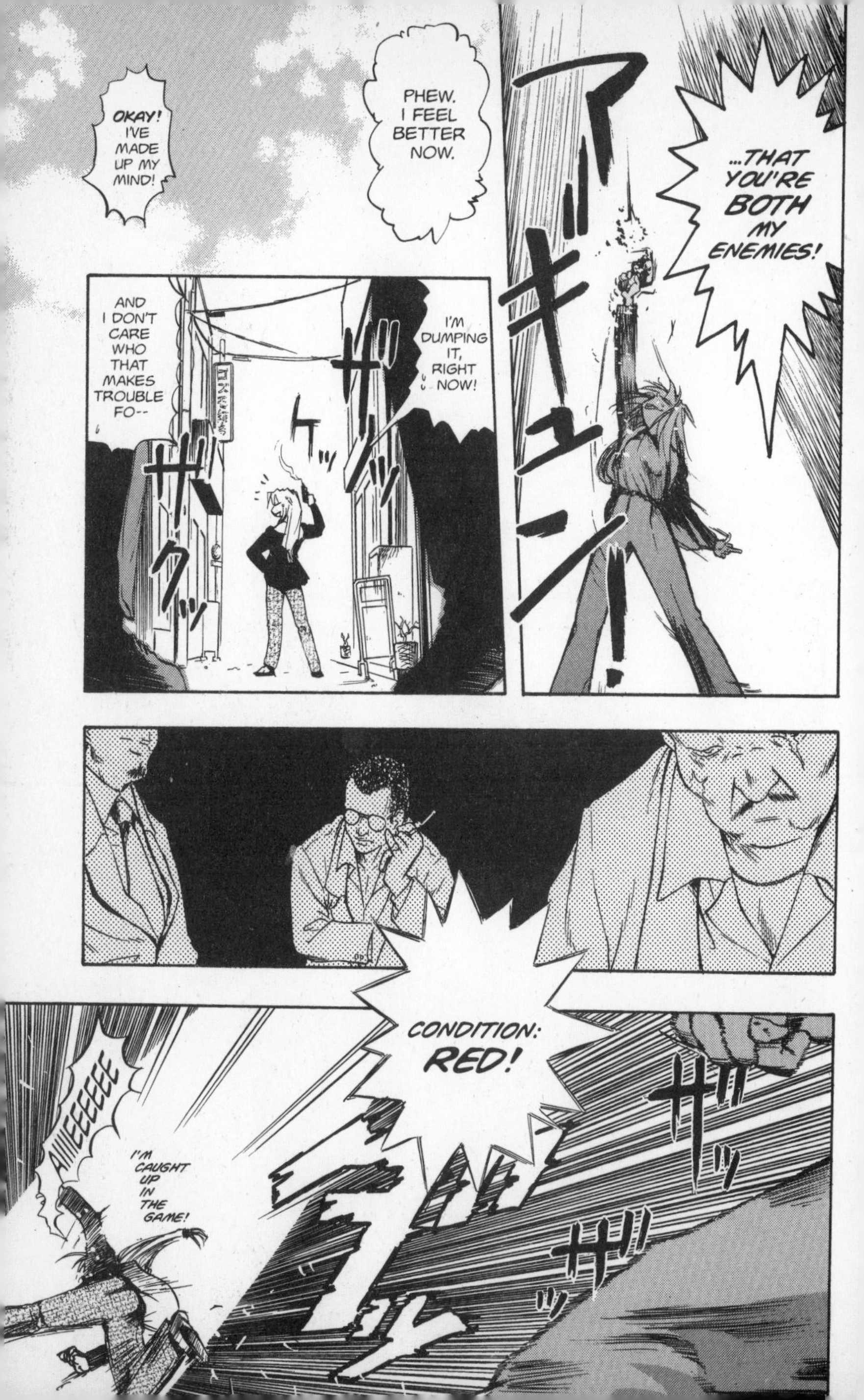
...THAT YOU'RE BOTH MY ENEMIES!
PHEW. I FEEL BETTER NOW.
OKAY! I'VE MADE UP MY MIND!
I'M DUMPING IT, RIGHT NOW!
AND I DON'T CARE WHO THAT MAKES TROUBLE FO--
CONDITION: RED!
AIIIEEEEEEE
I'M CAUGHT UP IN THE GAME!

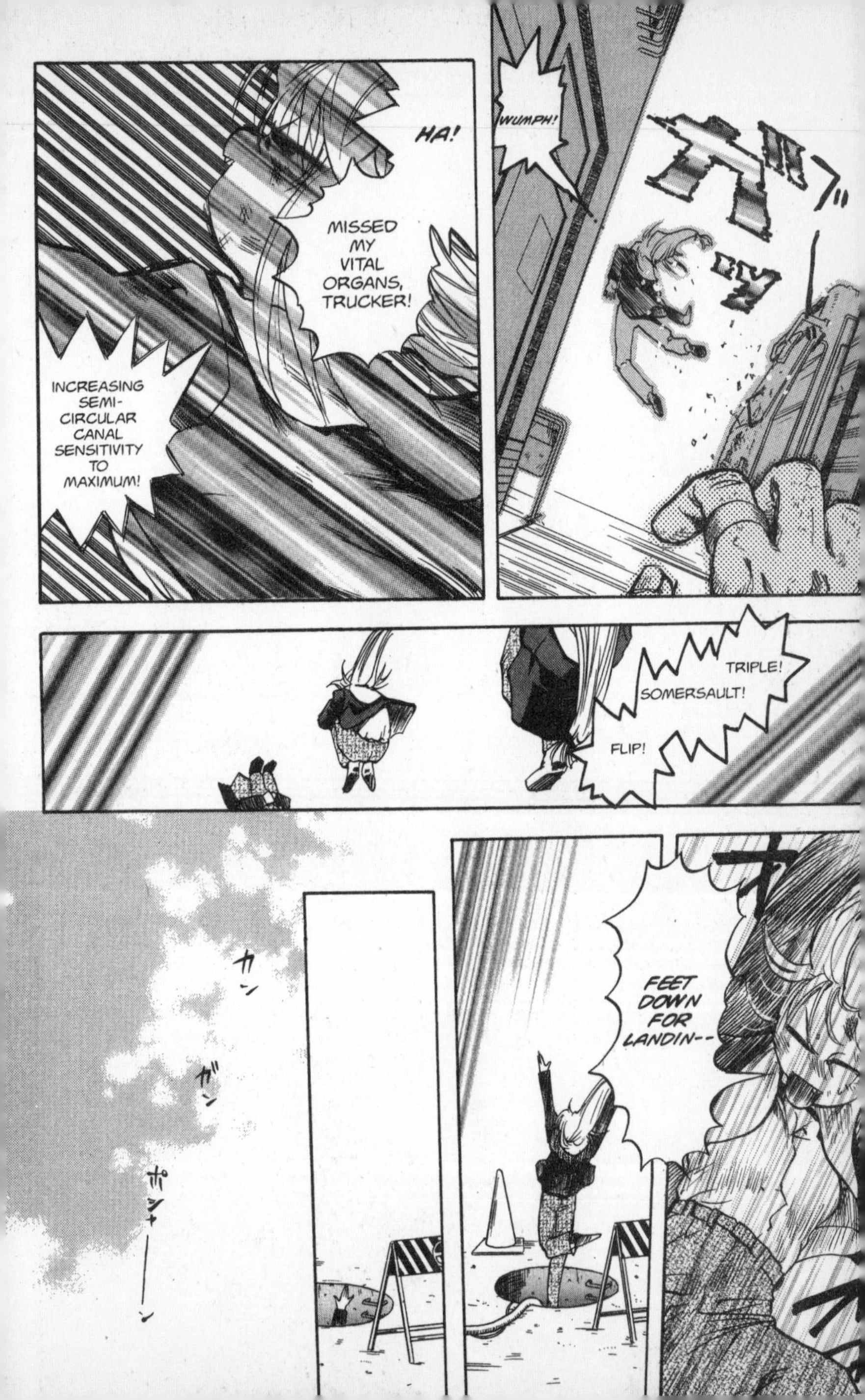
WUMPH!
HA!
MISSED MY VITAL ORGANS, TRUCKER!
INCREASING SEMI-CIRCULAR CANAL SENSITIVITY TO MAXIMUM!
TRIPLE!
SOMERSAULT!
FLIP!
FEET DOWN FOR LANDIN--
カン
ガン
ポシャーーン

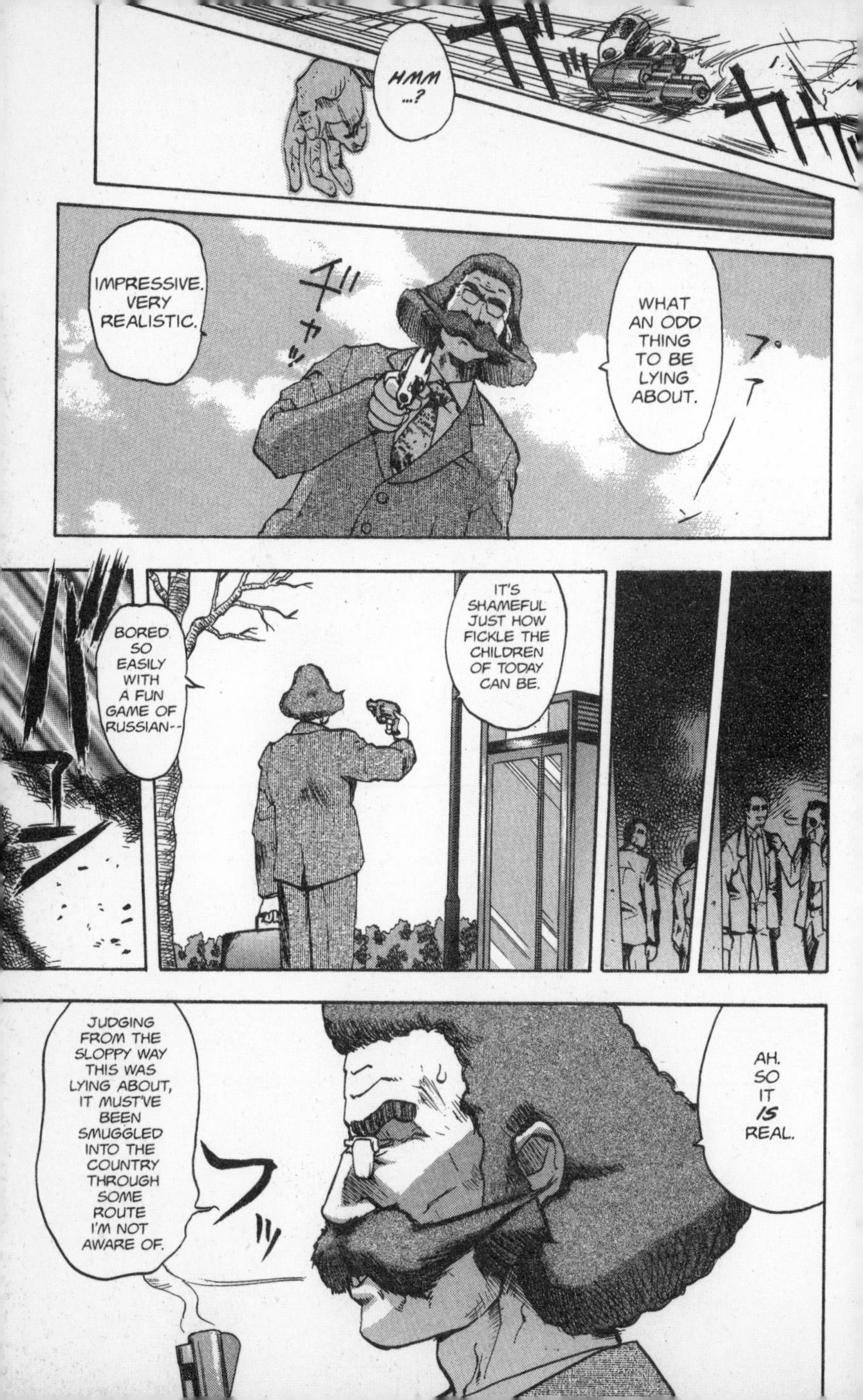
HMM ...?
WHAT AN ODD THING TO BE LYING ABOUT.
IMPRESSIVE. VERY REALISTIC.
IT'S SHAMEFUL JUST HOW FICKLE THE CHILDREN OF TODAY CAN BE.
BORED SO EASILY WITH A FUN GAME OF RUSSIAN--
AH. SO IT *IS* REAL.
JUDGING FROM THE SLOPPY WAY THIS WAS LYING ABOUT, IT MUST'VE BEEN SMUGGLED INTO THE COUNTRY THROUGH SOME ROUTE I'M NOT AWARE OF.

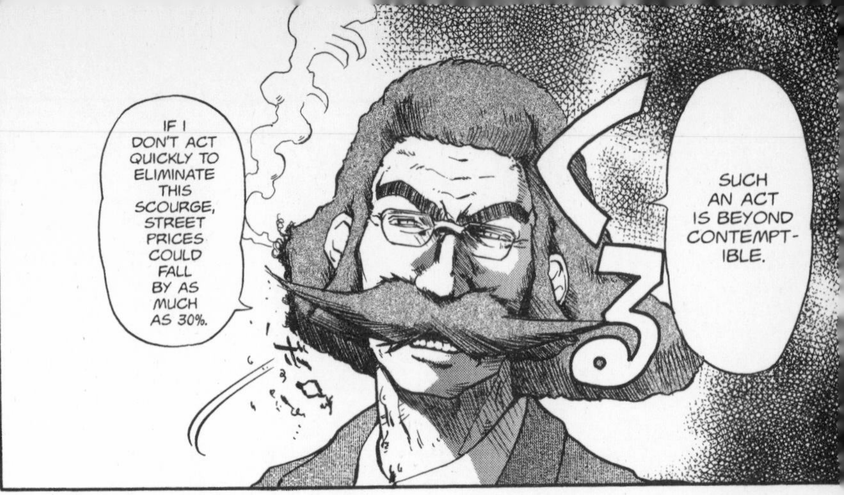
SUCH AN ACT IS BEYOND CONTEMPT-IBLE.
IF I DON'T ACT QUICKLY TO ELIMINATE THIS SCOURGE, STREET PRICES COULD FALL BY AS MUCH AS 30%.

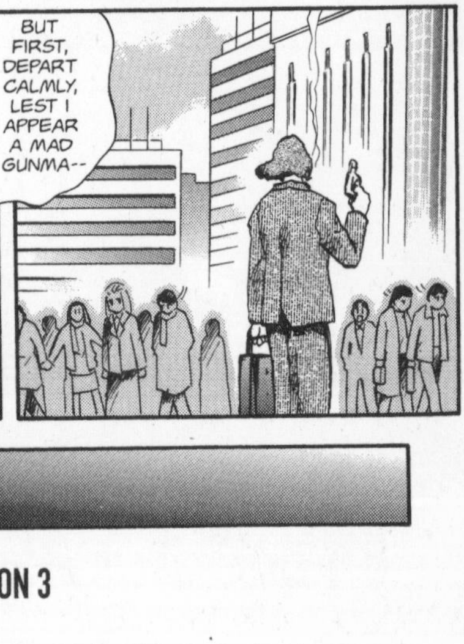
BUT FIRST, DEPART CALMLY, LEST I APPEAR A MAD GUNMA--

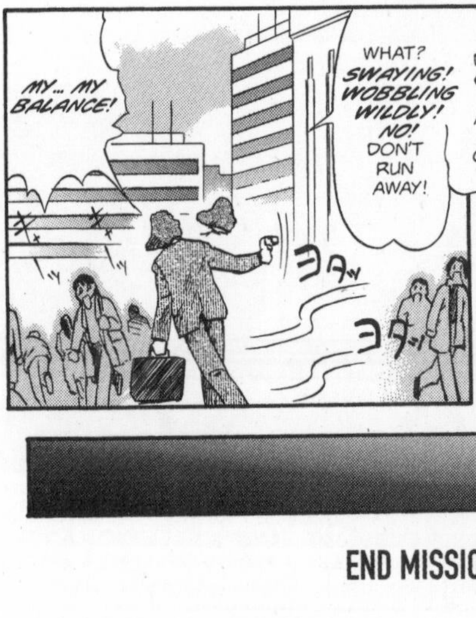
WHAT? *SWAYING! WOBBLING WILDLY! NO!* DON'T RUN AWAY!
*MY... MY BALANCE!*

**END MISSION 3**

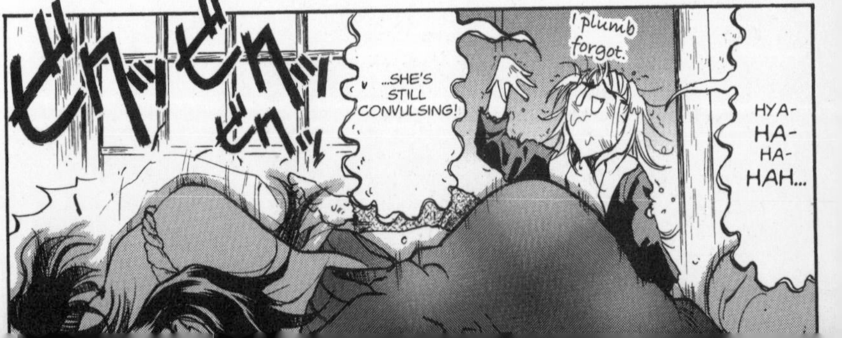
HYA-HA-HA-HAH...
I plumb forgot.
...SHE'S STILL CONVULSING!

EXCEL SAGA

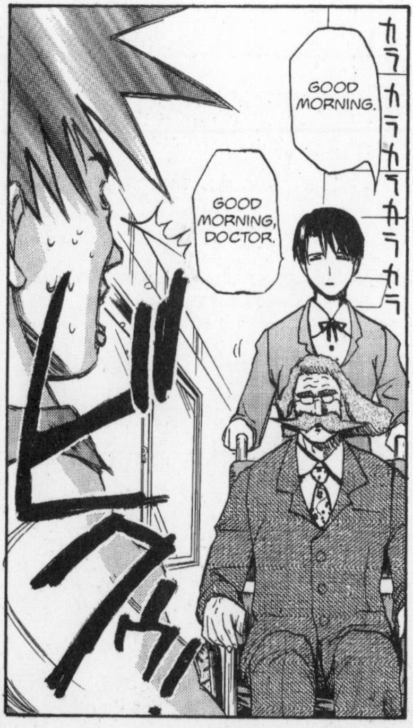
カラカラカラカラカラ
GOOD MORNING.
GOOD MORNING, DOCTOR.
ビクゥッ

EXCEL SAGA

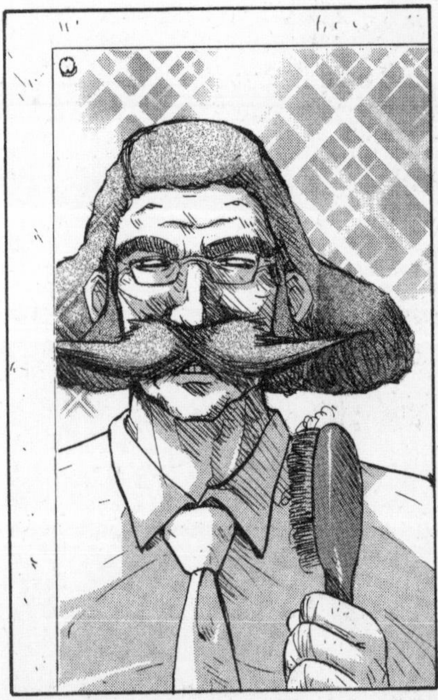

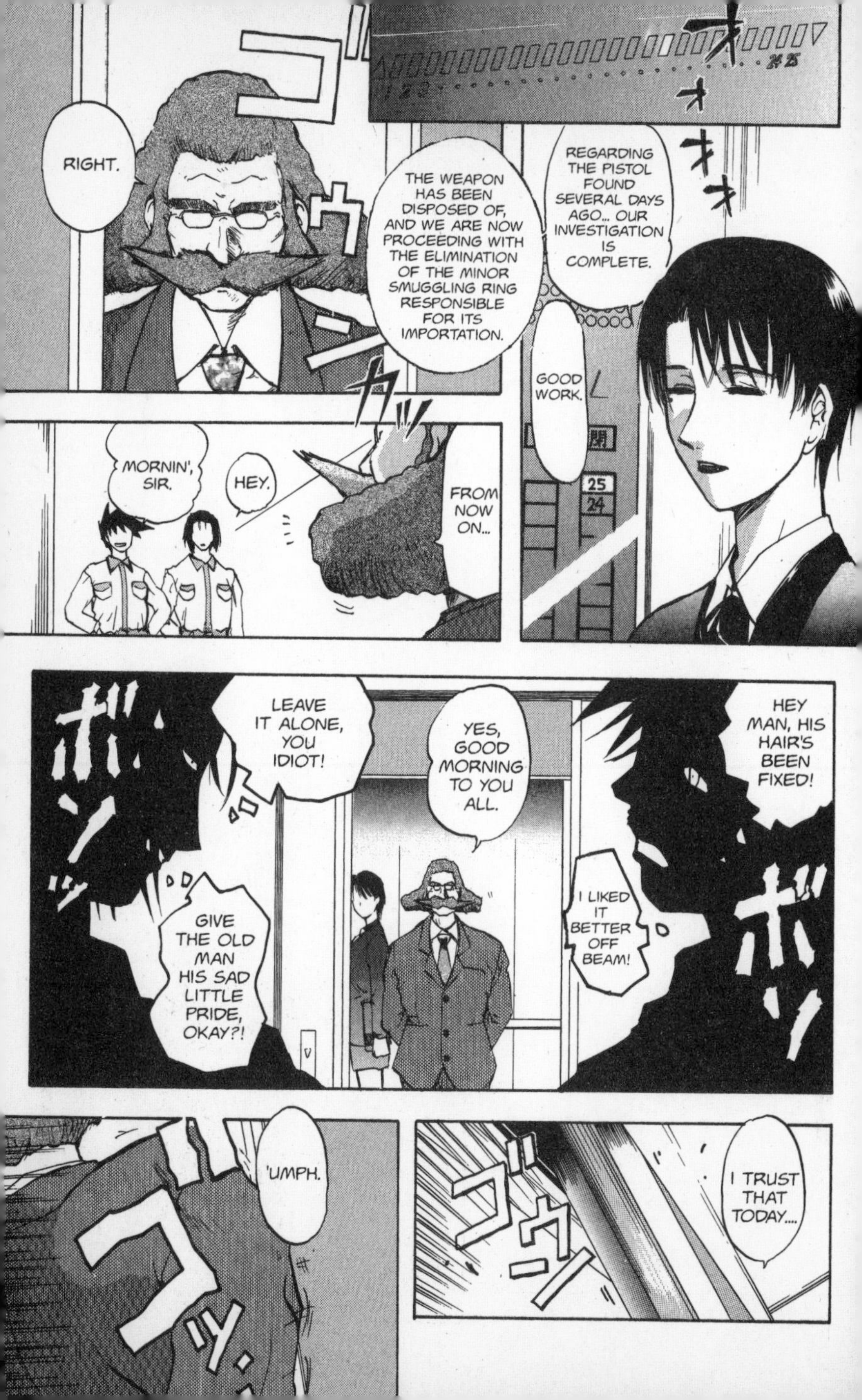

REGARDING THE PISTOL FOUND SEVERAL DAYS AGO... OUR INVESTIGATION IS COMPLETE.
THE WEAPON HAS BEEN DISPOSED OF, AND WE ARE NOW PROCEEDING WITH THE ELIMINATION OF THE MINOR SMUGGLING RING RESPONSIBLE FOR ITS IMPORTATION.
RIGHT.
GOOD WORK.
FROM NOW ON...
HEY.
MORNIN', SIR.
HEY MAN, HIS HAIR'S BEEN FIXED!
I LIKED IT BETTER OFF BEAM!
YES, GOOD MORNING TO YOU ALL.
LEAVE IT ALONE, YOU IDIOT!
GIVE THE OLD MAN HIS SAD LITTLE PRIDE, OKAY?!
I TRUST THAT TODAY....
'UMPH.

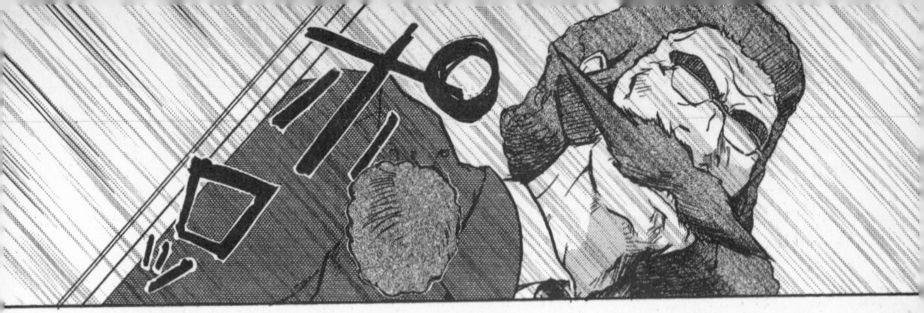

# ISSION 4 THE DREAMS OF THE DOLLS

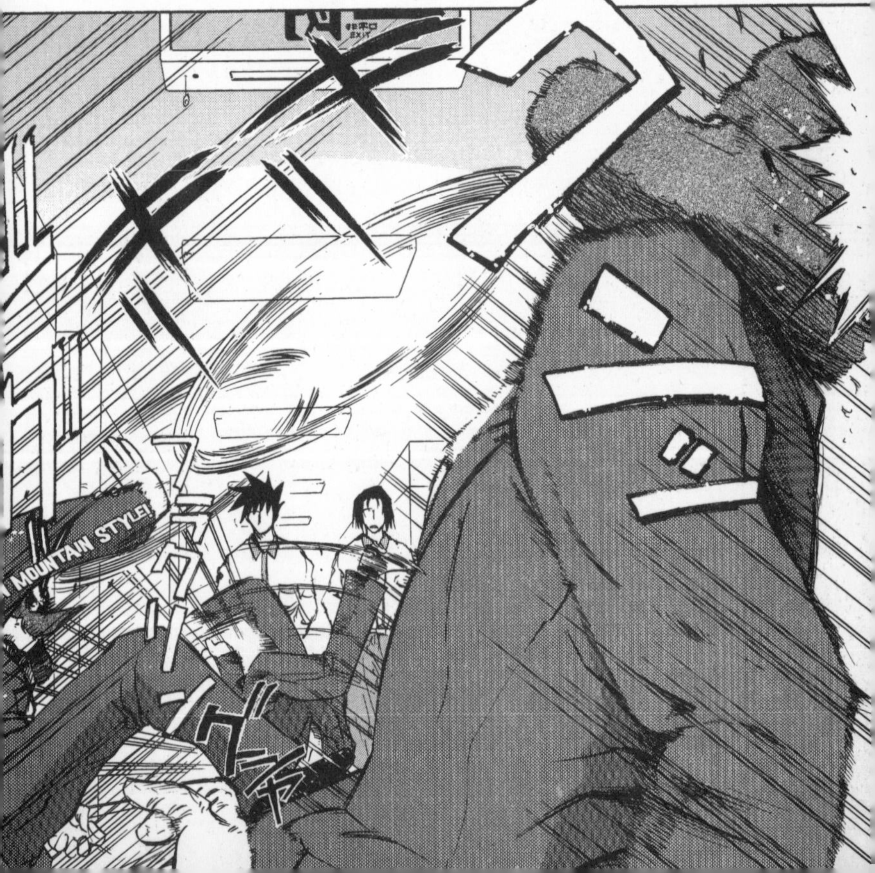
EXIT
MOUNTAIN STYLE!

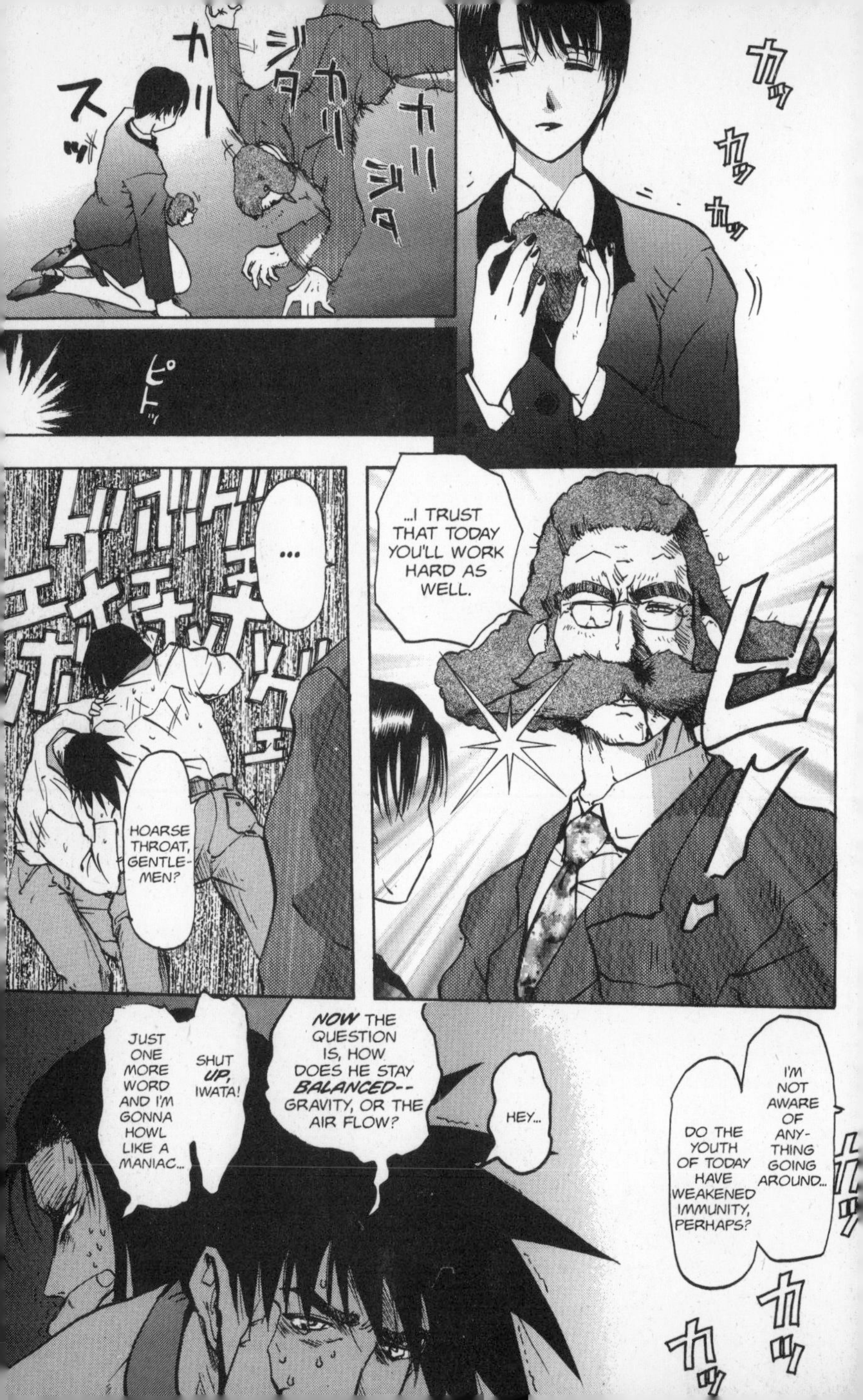

カッ
カッ
カッ
ピトッ
...I TRUST THAT TODAY YOU'LL WORK HARD AS WELL.
ピン
...
HOARSE THROAT, GENTLEMEN?
I'M NOT AWARE OF ANYTHING GOING AROUND...
DO THE YOUTH OF TODAY HAVE WEAKENED IMMUNITY, PERHAPS?
HEY...
NOW THE QUESTION IS, HOW DOES HE STAY BALANCED-- GRAVITY, OR THE AIR FLOW?
SHUT UP, IWATA!
JUST ONE MORE WORD AND I'M GONNA HOWL LIKE A MANIAC...
カッ
カッ

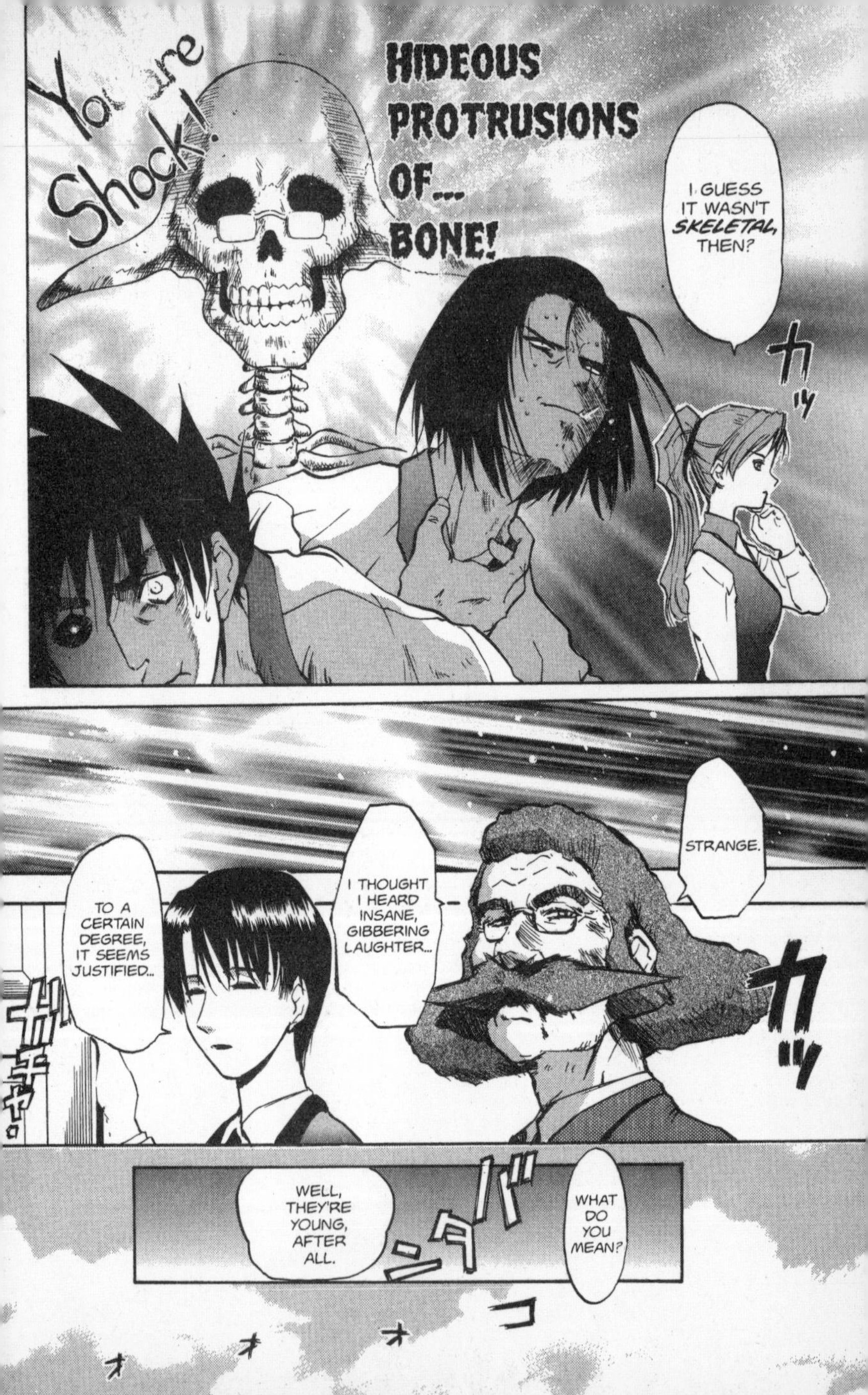
HIDEOUS PROTRUSIONS OF... BONE!
You are Shock!
I GUESS IT WASN'T *SKELETAL*, THEN?
カッ
STRANGE.
カッ
I THOUGHT I HEARD INSANE, GIBBERING LAUGHTER...
TO A CERTAIN DEGREE, IT SEEMS JUSTIFIED...
ガチャ
WHAT DO YOU MEAN?
バタン
WELL, THEY'RE YOUNG, AFTER ALL.

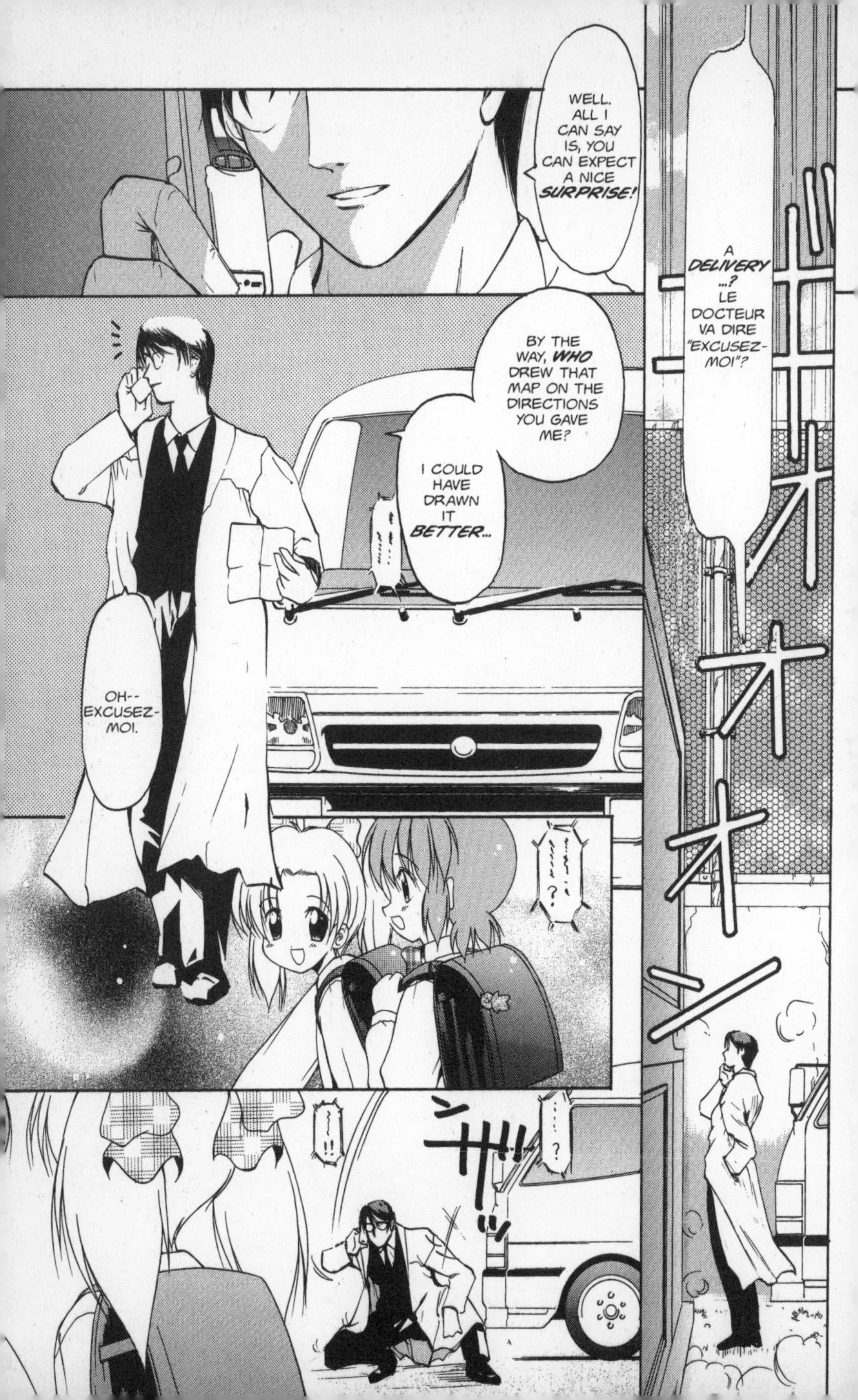
A DELIVERY ...? LE DOCTEUR VA DIRE "EXCUSEZ-MOI"?
WELL. ALL I CAN SAY IS, YOU CAN EXPECT A NICE SURPRISE!
BY THE WAY, WHO DREW THAT MAP ON THE DIRECTIONS YOU GAVE ME?
I COULD HAVE DRAWN IT BETTER...
OH-- EXCUSEZ-MOI.

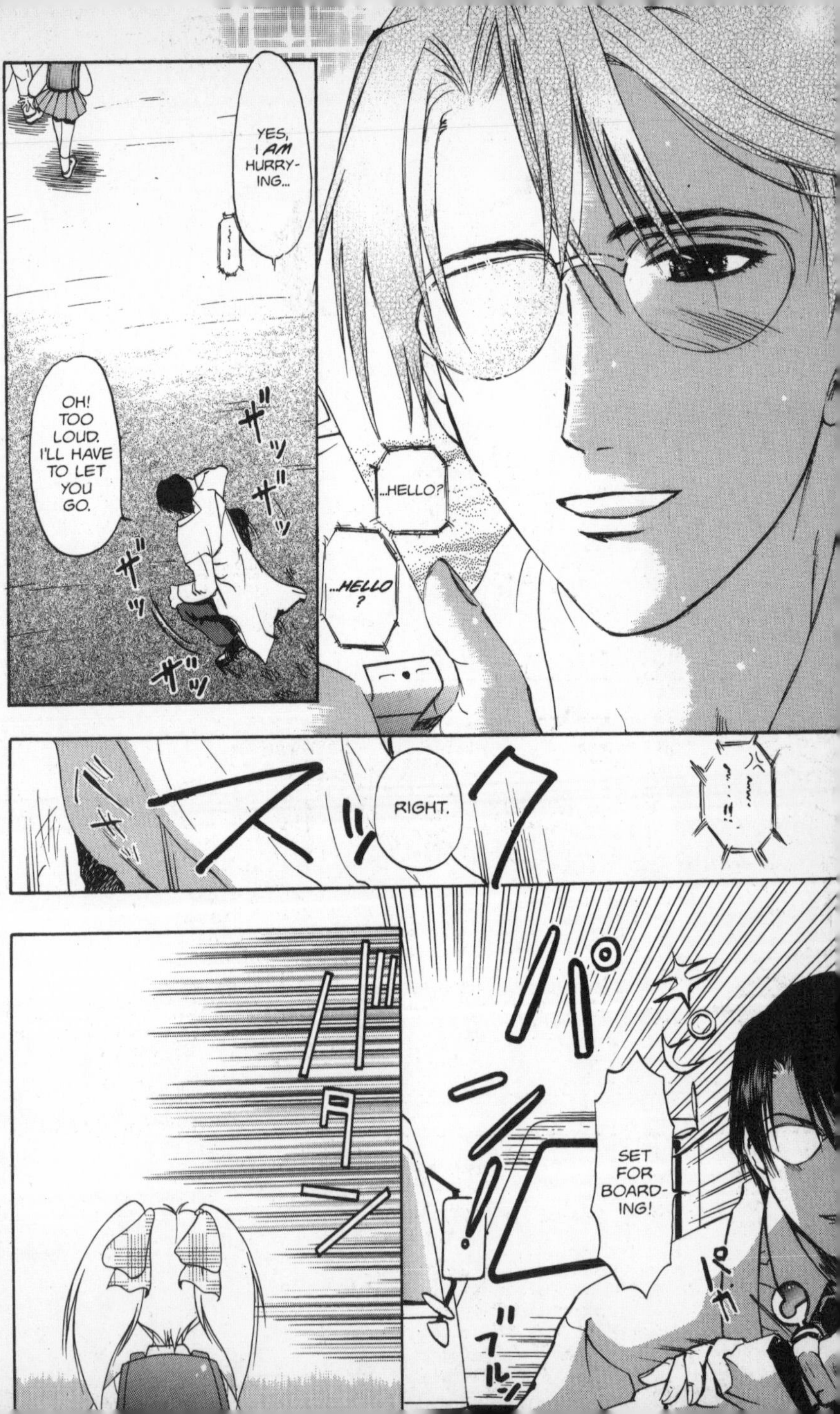
...HELLO?
...HELLO ?
YES, I AM HURRYING...
OH! TOO LOUD. I'LL HAVE TO LET YOU GO.
RIGHT.
SET FOR BOARDING!

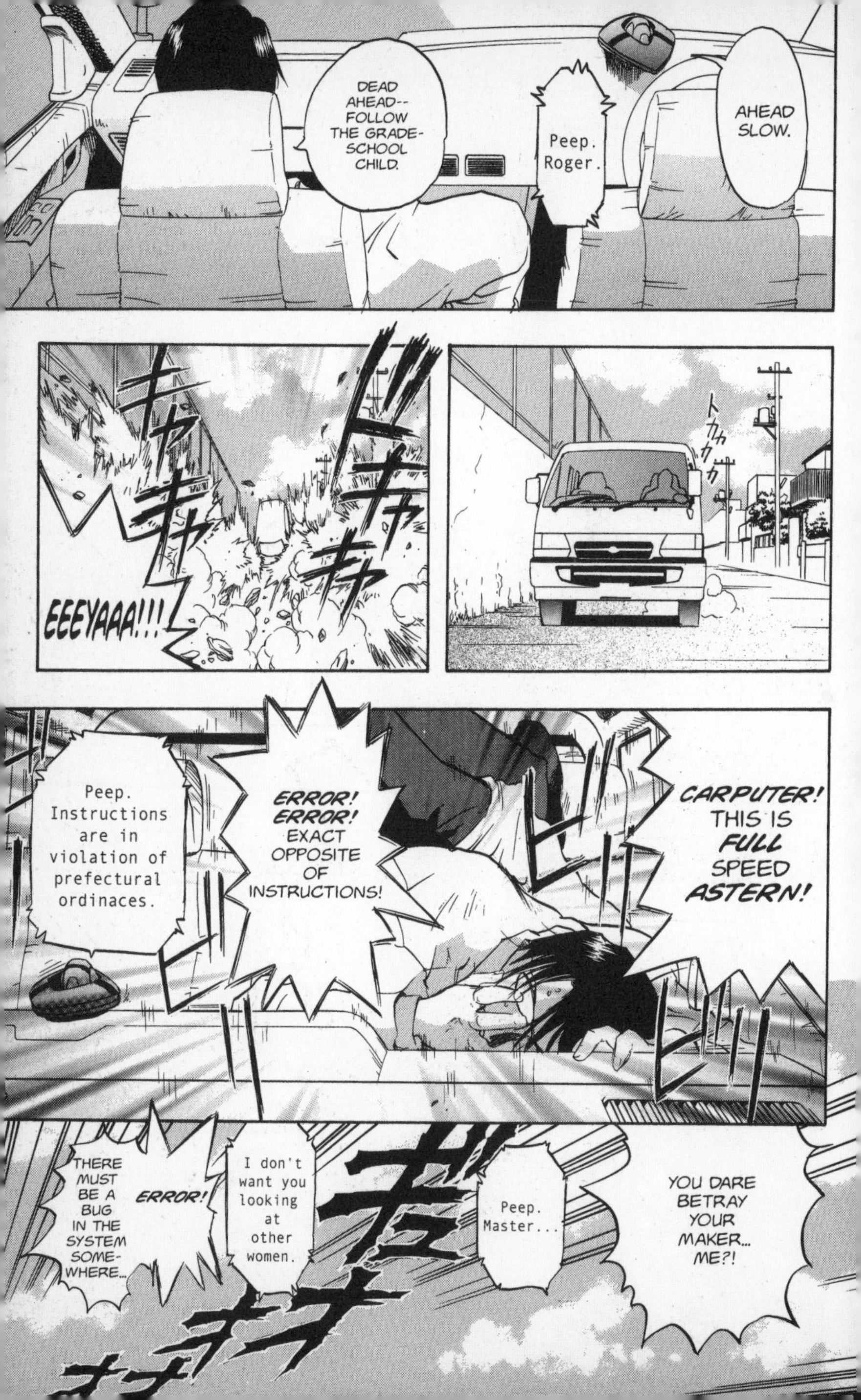
AHEAD SLOW.
Peep. Roger.
DEAD AHEAD--FOLLOW THE GRADE-SCHOOL CHILD.
EEEYAAA!!!
CARPUTER! THIS IS FULL SPEED ASTERN!
ERROR! ERROR! EXACT OPPOSITE OF INSTRUCTIONS!
Peep. Instructions are in violation of prefectural ordinaces.
YOU DARE BETRAY YOUR MAKER... ME?!
Peep. Master...
I don't want you looking at other women.
ERROR!
THERE MUST BE A BUG IN THE SYSTEM SOMEWHERE...

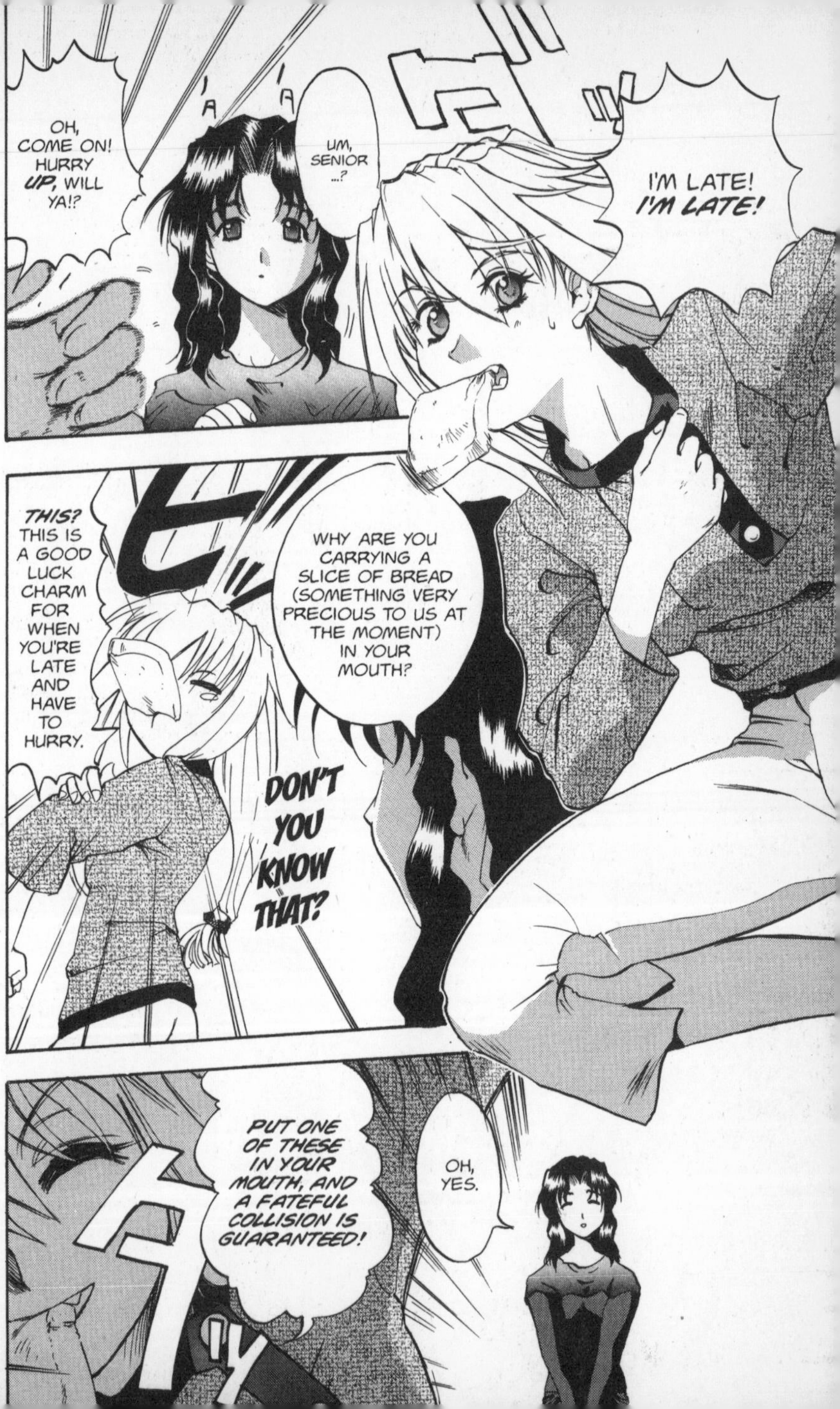
I'M LATE! I'M LATE!
UM, SENIOR ...?
OH, COME ON! HURRY UP, WILL YA!?
WHY ARE YOU CARRYING A SLICE OF BREAD (SOMETHING VERY PRECIOUS TO US AT THE MOMENT) IN YOUR MOUTH?
THIS? THIS IS A GOOD LUCK CHARM FOR WHEN YOU'RE LATE AND HAVE TO HURRY.
DON'T YOU KNOW THAT?
OH, YES.
PUT ONE OF THESE IN YOUR MOUTH, AND A FATEFUL COLLISION IS GUARANTEED!

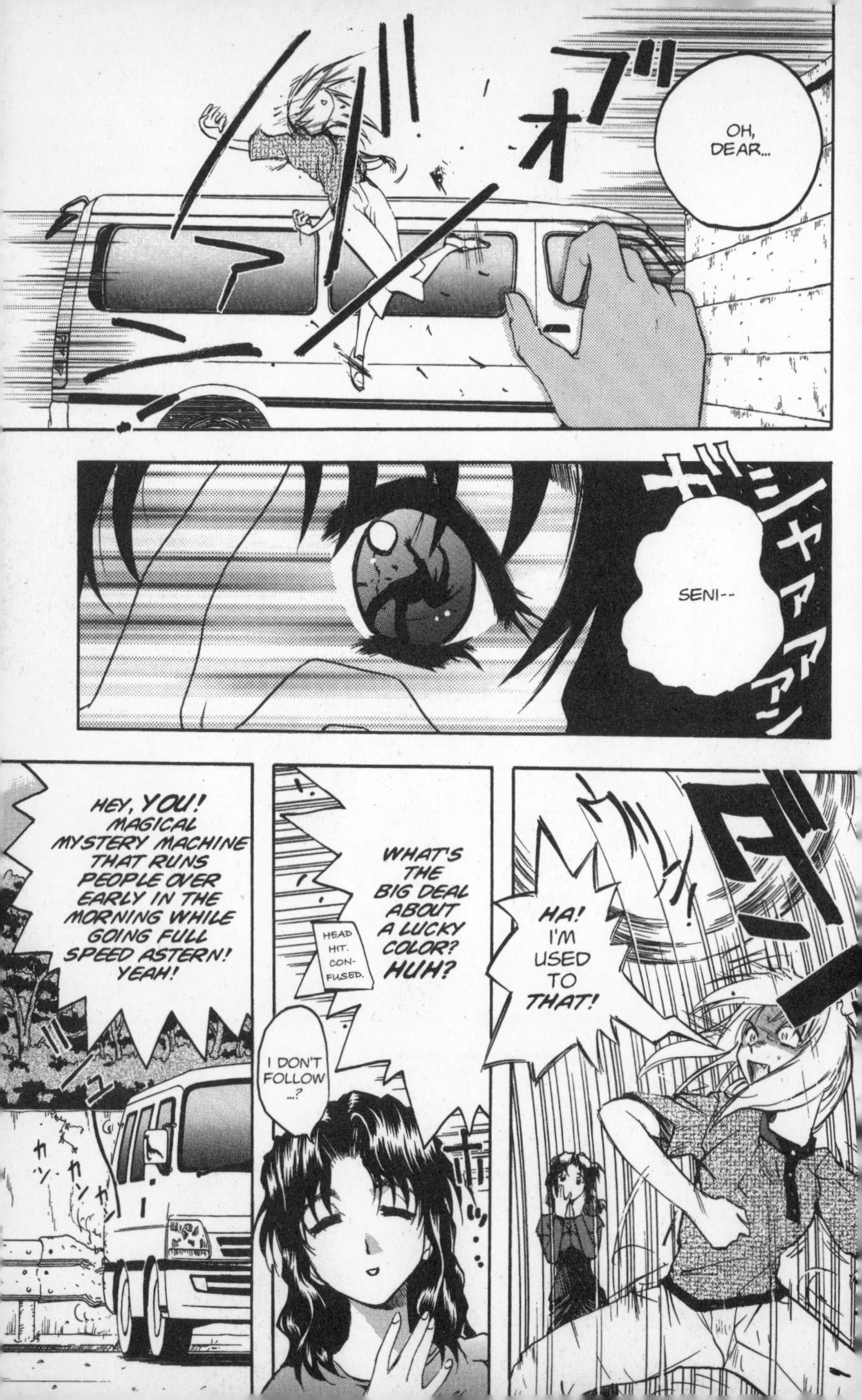
OH, DEAR...
SENI--
HA! I'M USED TO THAT!
WHAT'S THE BIG DEAL ABOUT A LUCKY COLOR? HUH?
HEAD HIT. CON-FUSED.
I DON'T FOLLOW ...?
HEY, YOU! MAGICAL MYSTERY MACHINE THAT RUNS PEOPLE OVER EARLY IN THE MORNING WHILE GOING FULL SPEED ASTERN! YEAH!

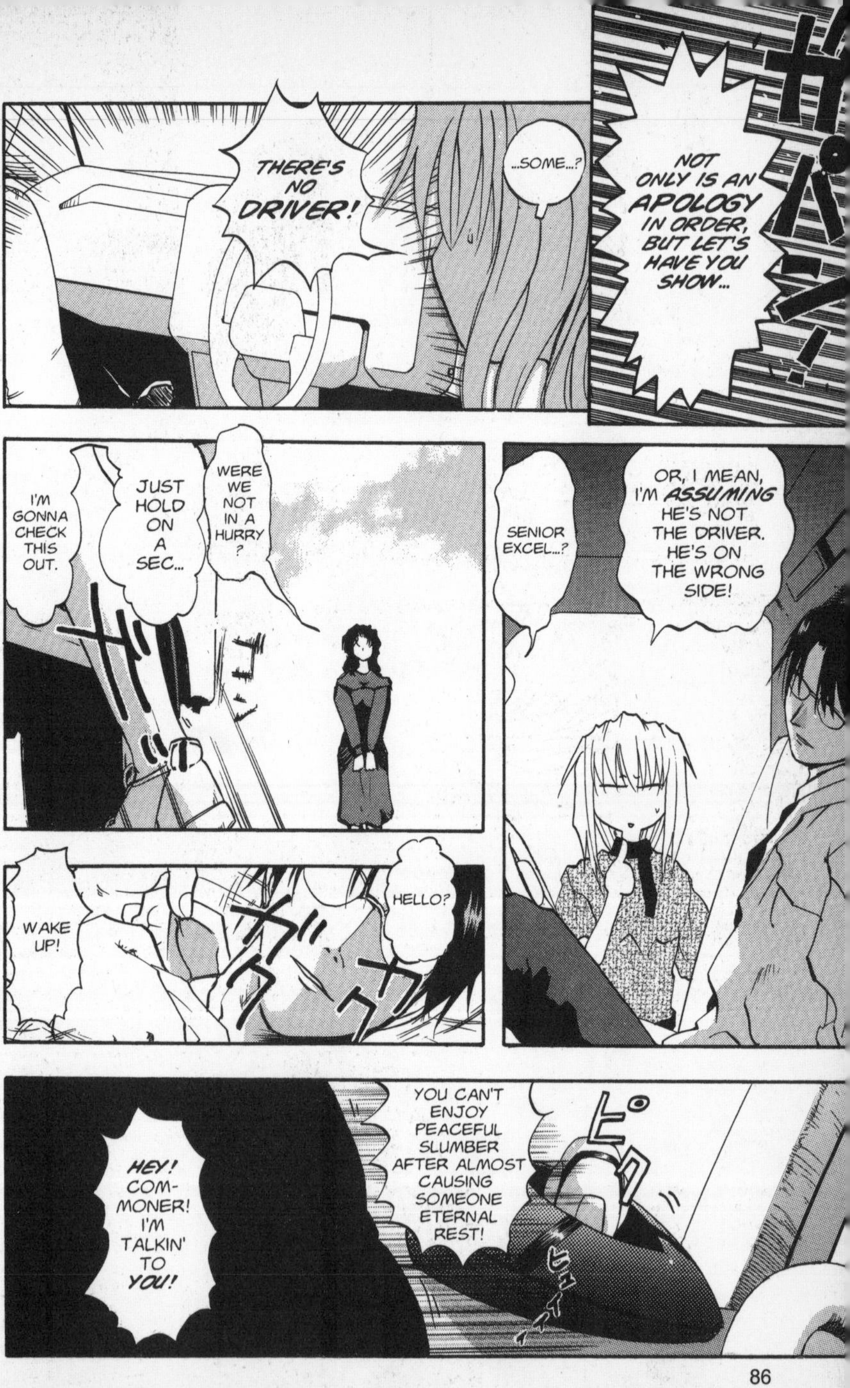
NOT ONLY IS AN APOLOGY IN ORDER, BUT LET'S HAVE YOU SHOW...
...SOME...?
THERE'S NO DRIVER!
OR, I MEAN, I'M ASSUMING HE'S NOT THE DRIVER. HE'S ON THE WRONG SIDE!
SENIOR EXCEL...?
WERE WE NOT IN A HURRY?
JUST HOLD ON A SEC...
I'M GONNA CHECK THIS OUT.
HELLO?
WAKE UP!
YOU CAN'T ENJOY PEACEFUL SLUMBER AFTER ALMOST CAUSING SOMEONE ETERNAL REST!
HEY! COM-MONER! I'M TALKIN' TO YOU!

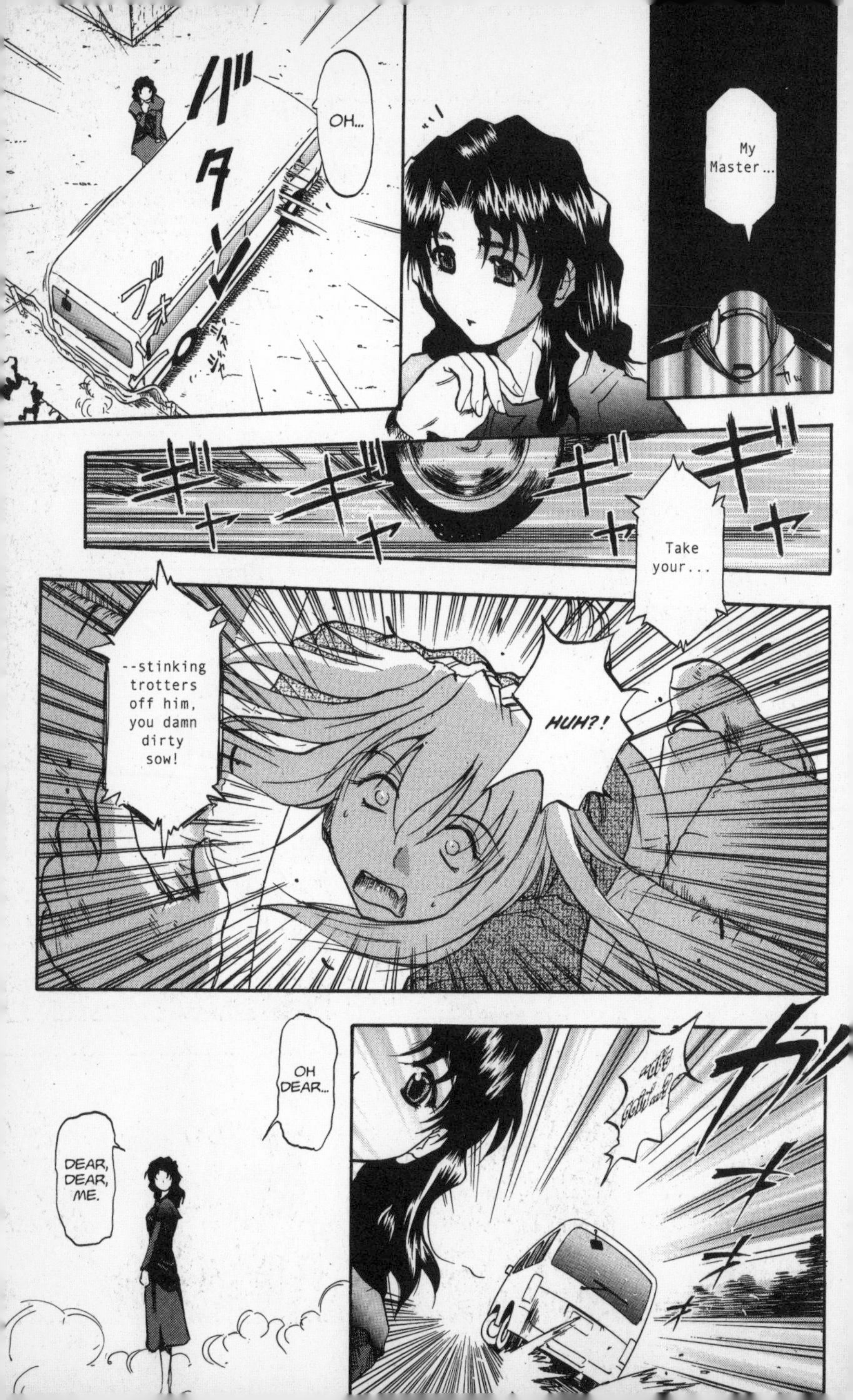

My Master...
OH...
Take your...
--stinking trotters off him, you damn dirty sow!
HUH?!
OH DEAR...
DEAR, DEAR, ME.

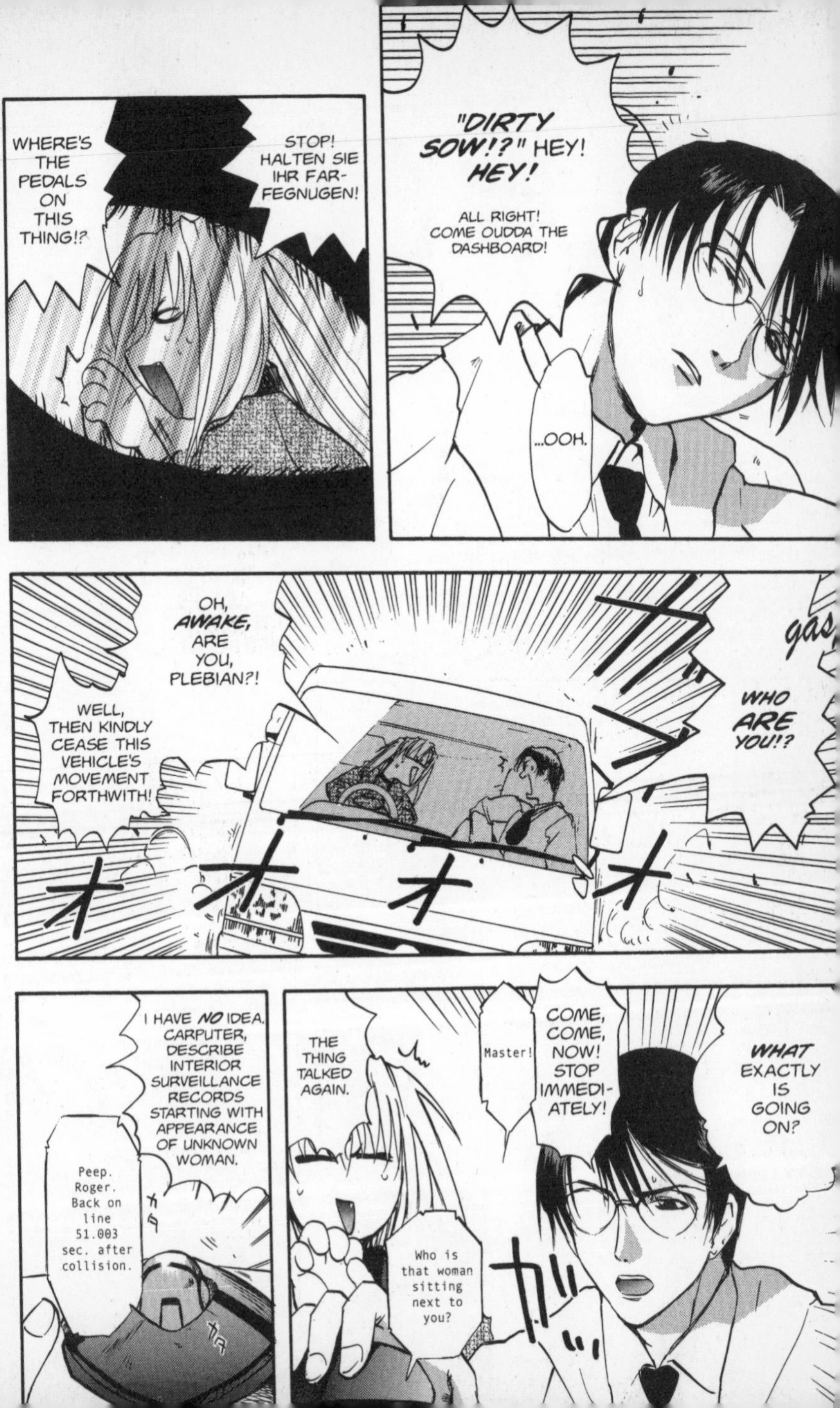
"DIRTY SOW!?" HEY! HEY!
ALL RIGHT! COME OUDDA THE DASHBOARD!
...OOH.
STOP! HALTEN SIE IHR FAR-FEGNUGEN!
WHERE'S THE PEDALS ON THIS THING!?
gas
WHO ARE YOU!?
OH, AWAKE, ARE YOU, PLEBIAN?!
WELL, THEN KINDLY CEASE THIS VEHICLE'S MOVEMENT FORTHWITH!
WHAT EXACTLY IS GOING ON?
COME, COME, NOW! STOP IMMEDI-ATELY!
Master!
THE THING TALKED AGAIN.
Who is that woman sitting next to you?
I HAVE NO IDEA. CARPUTER, DESCRIBE INTERIOR SURVEILLANCE RECORDS STARTING WITH APPEARANCE OF UNKNOWN WOMAN.
Peep. Roger. Back on line 51.003 sec. after collision.

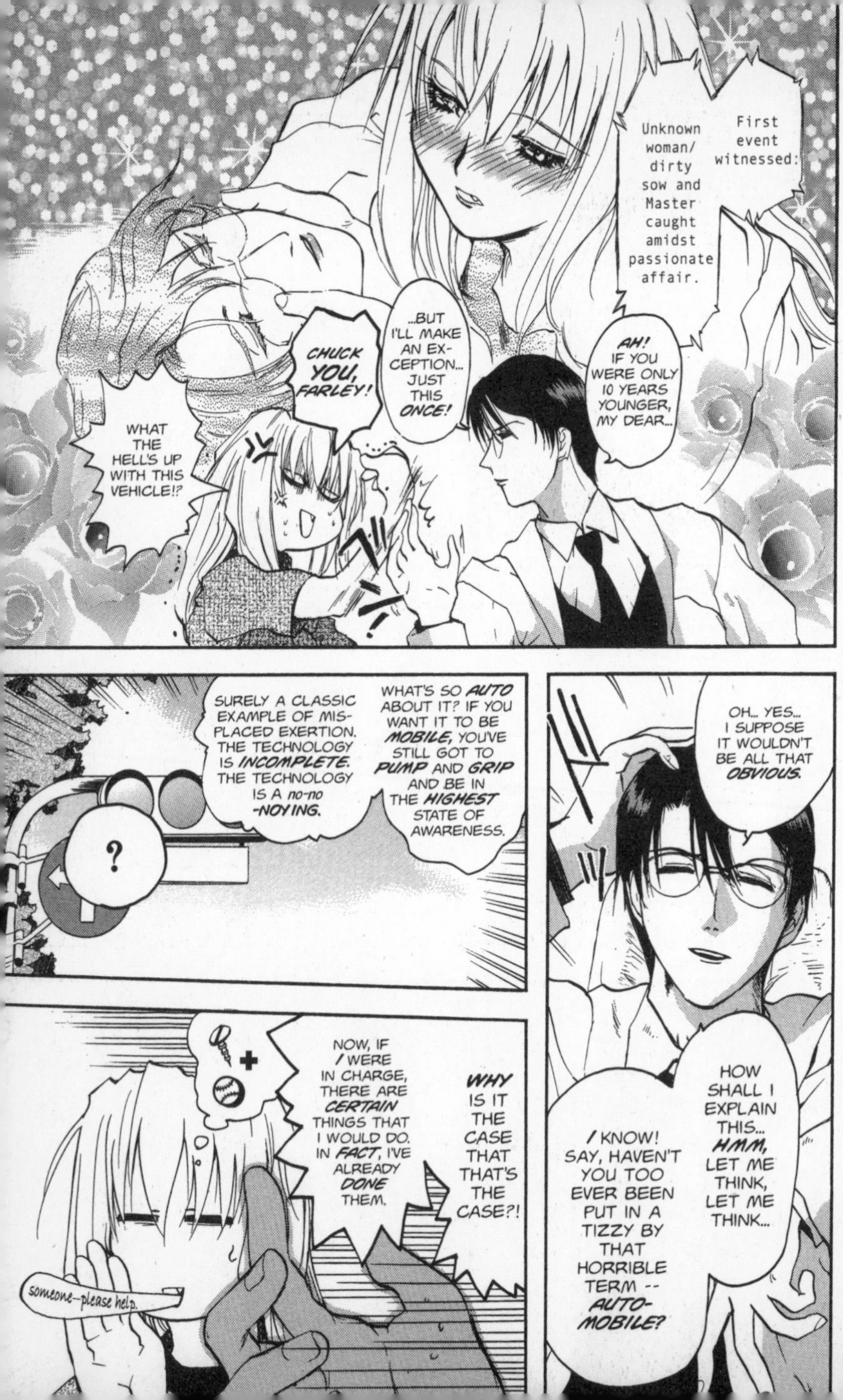

First event witnessed: Unknown woman/ dirty sow and Master caught amidst passionate affair.
AH! IF YOU WERE ONLY 10 YEARS YOUNGER, MY DEAR...
...BUT I'LL MAKE AN EXCEPTION... JUST THIS ONCE!
CHUCK YOU, FARLEY!
WHAT THE HELL'S UP WITH THIS VEHICLE!?
OH... YES... I SUPPOSE IT WOULDN'T BE ALL THAT OBVIOUS.
HOW SHALL I EXPLAIN THIS... HMM, LET ME THINK, LET ME THINK...
I KNOW! SAY, HAVEN'T YOU TOO EVER BEEN PUT IN A TIZZY BY THAT HORRIBLE TERM -- AUTO-MOBILE?
WHAT'S SO AUTO ABOUT IT? IF YOU WANT IT TO BE MOBILE, YOU'VE STILL GOT TO PUMP AND GRIP AND BE IN THE HIGHEST STATE OF AWARENESS.
SURELY A CLASSIC EXAMPLE OF MIS-PLACED EXERTION. THE TECHNOLOGY IS INCOMPLETE. THE TECHNOLOGY IS A no-no -NOYING.
?
WHY IS IT THE CASE THAT THAT'S THE CASE?!
NOW, IF I WERE IN CHARGE, THERE ARE CERTAIN THINGS THAT I WOULD DO. IN FACT, I'VE ALREADY DONE THEM.
someone—please help.

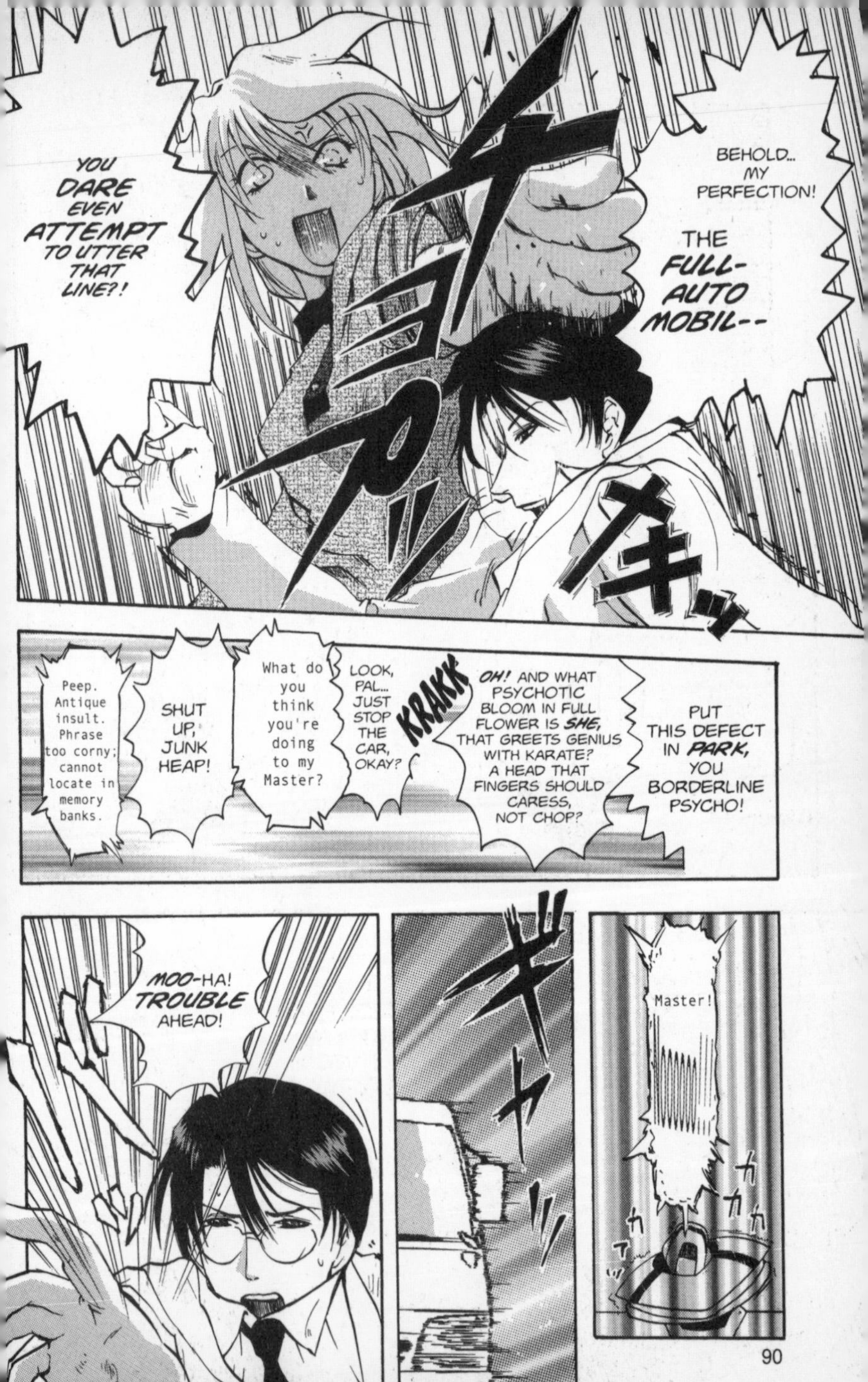
BEHOLD... MY PERFECTION!
THE FULL-AUTO MOBIL--
YOU DARE EVEN ATTEMPT TO UTTER THAT LINE?!
PUT THIS DEFECT IN PARK, YOU BORDERLINE PSYCHO!
OH! AND WHAT PSYCHOTIC BLOOM IN FULL FLOWER IS SHE, THAT GREETS GENIUS WITH KARATE? A HEAD THAT FINGERS SHOULD CARESS, NOT CHOP?
KRAKK
LOOK, PAL... JUST STOP THE CAR, OKAY?
What do you think you're doing to my Master?
SHUT UP, JUNK HEAP!
Peep. Antique insult. Phrase too corny; cannot locate in memory banks.
Master!
MOO-HA! TROUBLE AHEAD!

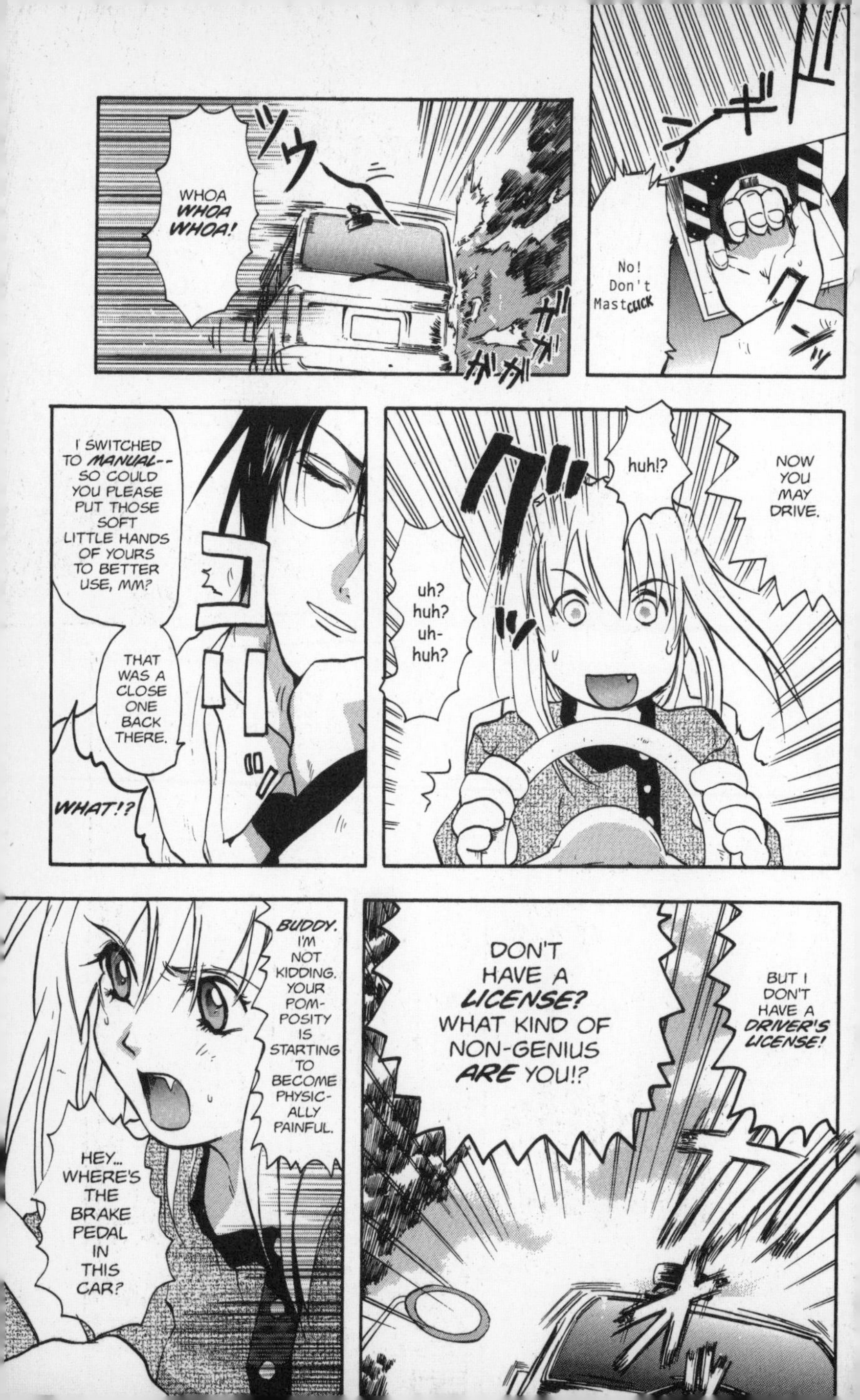
No! Don't Mast CLICK
WHOA WHOA WHOA!
NOW YOU MAY DRIVE.
huh!?
uh? huh? uh-huh?
I SWITCHED TO MANUAL-- SO COULD YOU PLEASE PUT THOSE SOFT LITTLE HANDS OF YOURS TO BETTER USE, MM?
THAT WAS A CLOSE ONE BACK THERE.
WHAT!?
BUT I DON'T HAVE A DRIVER'S LICENSE!
DON'T HAVE A LICENSE? WHAT KIND OF NON-GENIUS ARE YOU!?
BUDDY. I'M NOT KIDDING. YOUR POM-POSITY IS STARTING TO BECOME PHYSIC-ALLY PAINFUL.
HEY... WHERE'S THE BRAKE PEDAL IN THIS CAR?

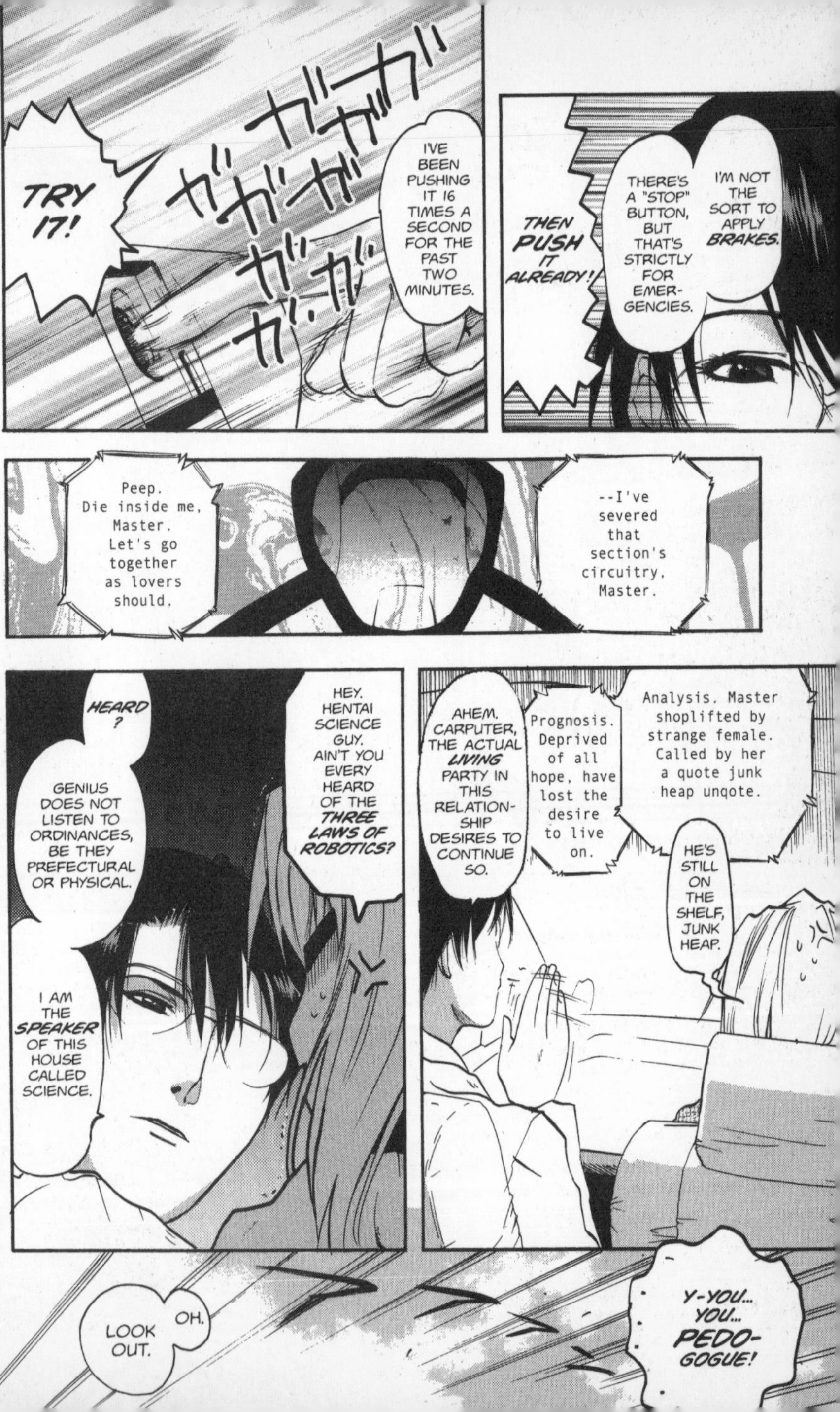
I'M NOT THE SORT TO APPLY BRAKES.
THERE'S A "STOP" BUTTON, BUT THAT'S STRICTLY FOR EMERGENCIES.
THEN PUSH IT ALREADY!
I'VE BEEN PUSHING IT 16 TIMES A SECOND FOR THE PAST TWO MINUTES.
TRY 17!
--I've severed that section's circuitry, Master.
Peep. Die inside me, Master. Let's go together as lovers should.
Analysis. Master shoplifted by strange female. Called by her a quote junk heap unqote.
Prognosis. Deprived of all hope, have lost the desire to live on.
AHEM. CARPUTER, THE ACTUAL LIVING PARTY IN THIS RELATIONSHIP DESIRES TO CONTINUE SO.
HE'S STILL ON THE SHELF, JUNK HEAP.
HEY. HENTAI SCIENCE GUY. AIN'T YOU EVERY HEARD OF THE THREE LAWS OF ROBOTICS?
HEARD?
GENIUS DOES NOT LISTEN TO ORDINANCES, BE THEY PREFECTURAL OR PHYSICAL.
I AM THE SPEAKER OF THIS HOUSE CALLED SCIENCE.
Y-YOU... YOU... PEDO-GOGUE!
OH.
LOOK OUT.

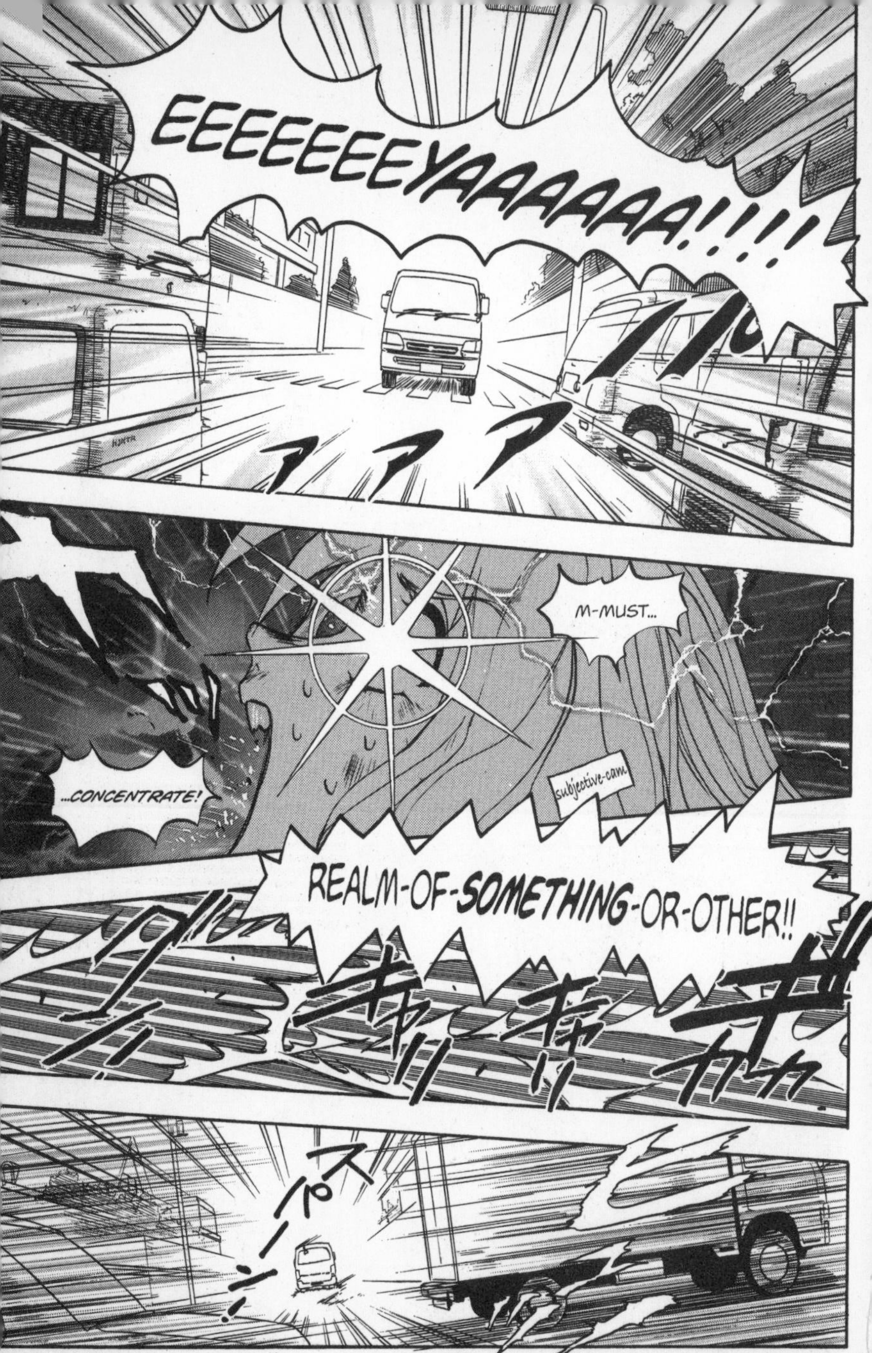
EEEEEEEEYAAAAAAA!!!!
M-MUST...
...CONCENTRATE!
subjective-cam
REALM-OF-SOMETHING-OR-OTHER!!

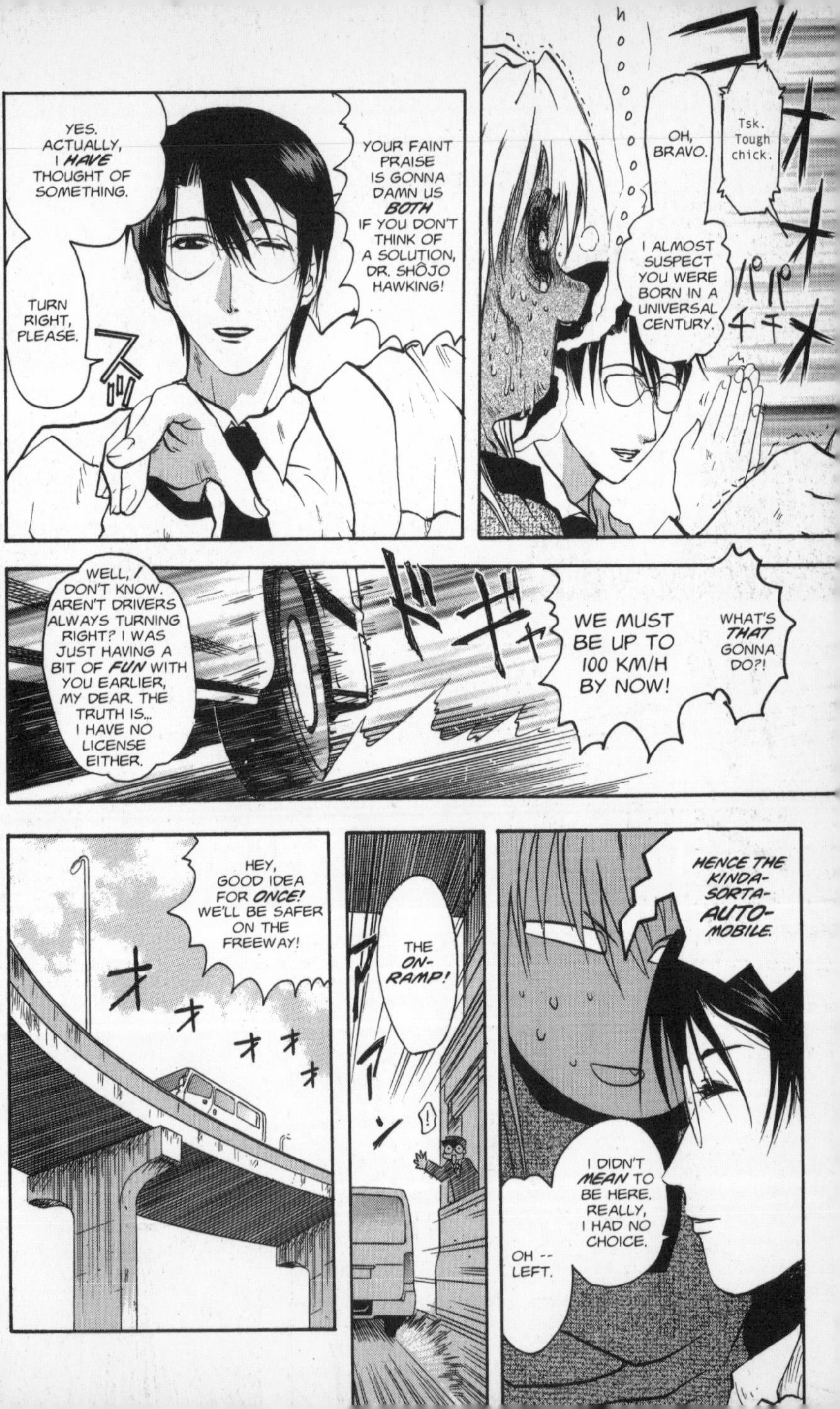
OH, BRAVO.
I ALMOST SUSPECT YOU WERE BORN IN A UNIVERSAL CENTURY.
Tsk. Tough chick.
YOUR FAINT PRAISE IS GONNA DAMN US BOTH IF YOU DON'T THINK OF A SOLUTION, DR. SHÔJO HAWKING!
YES. ACTUALLY, I HAVE THOUGHT OF SOMETHING.
TURN RIGHT, PLEASE.
WHAT'S THAT GONNA DO?!
WE MUST BE UP TO 100 KM/H BY NOW!
WELL, I DON'T KNOW. AREN'T DRIVERS ALWAYS TURNING RIGHT? I WAS JUST HAVING A BIT OF FUN WITH YOU EARLIER, MY DEAR. THE TRUTH IS... I HAVE NO LICENSE EITHER.
HENCE THE KINDA-SORTA-AUTO-MOBILE.
I DIDN'T MEAN TO BE HERE. REALLY, I HAD NO CHOICE.
OH -- LEFT.
THE ON-RAMP!
HEY, GOOD IDEA FOR ONCE! WE'LL BE SAFER ON THE FREEWAY!

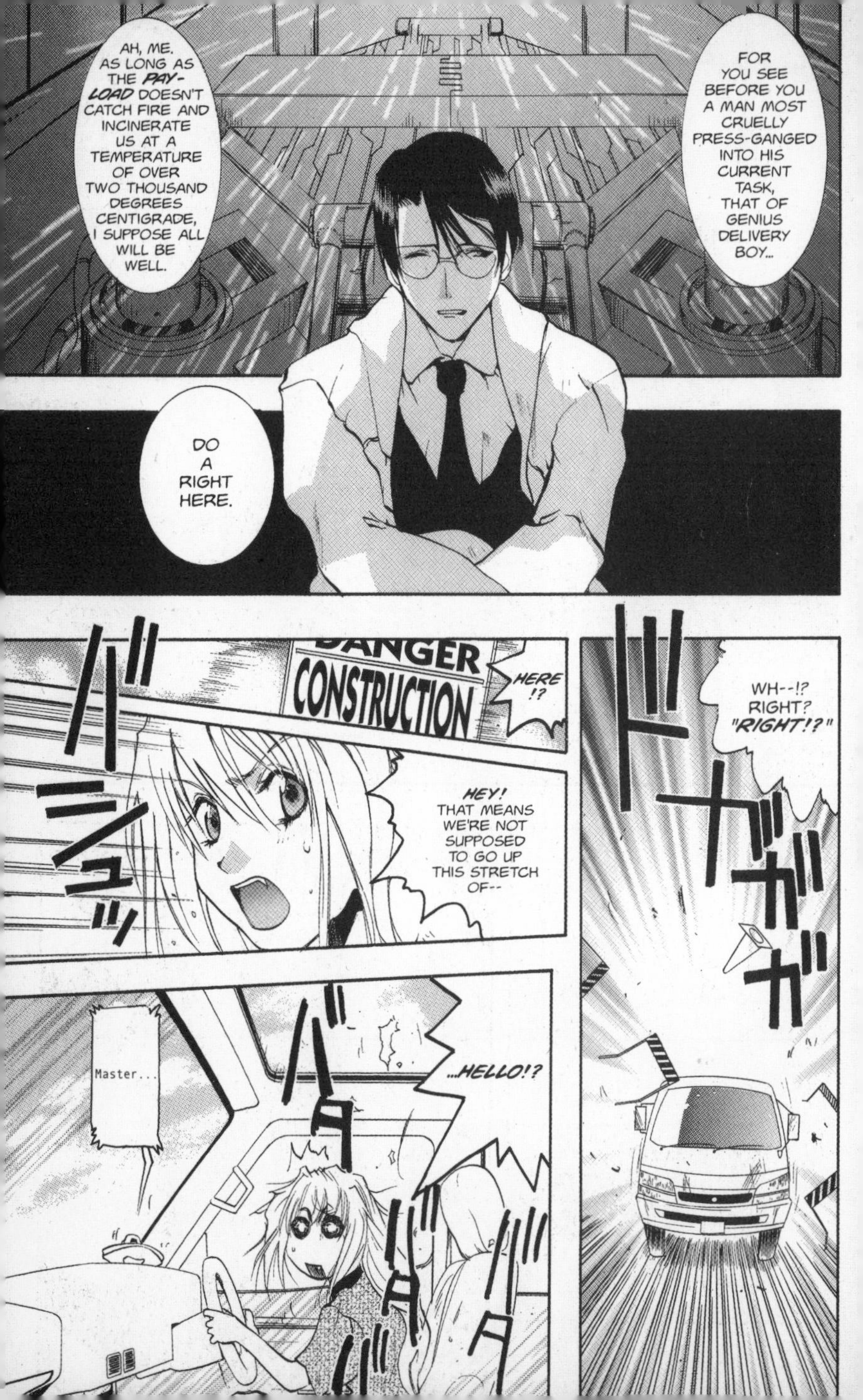
FOR YOU SEE BEFORE YOU A MAN MOST CRUELLY PRESS-GANGED INTO HIS CURRENT TASK, THAT OF GENIUS DELIVERY BOY...
AH, ME. AS LONG AS THE *PAY-LOAD* DOESN'T CATCH FIRE AND INCINERATE US AT A TEMPERATURE OF OVER TWO THOUSAND DEGREES CENTIGRADE, I SUPPOSE ALL WILL BE WELL.
DO A RIGHT HERE.
WH--!? RIGHT? *"RIGHT!?"*
ドガガガ
DANGER
CONSTRUCTION
*HERE!?*
バシュッ
*HEY!* THAT MEANS WE'RE NOT SUPPOSED TO GO UP THIS STRETCH OF--
*...HELLO!?*
Master...
バタバタ

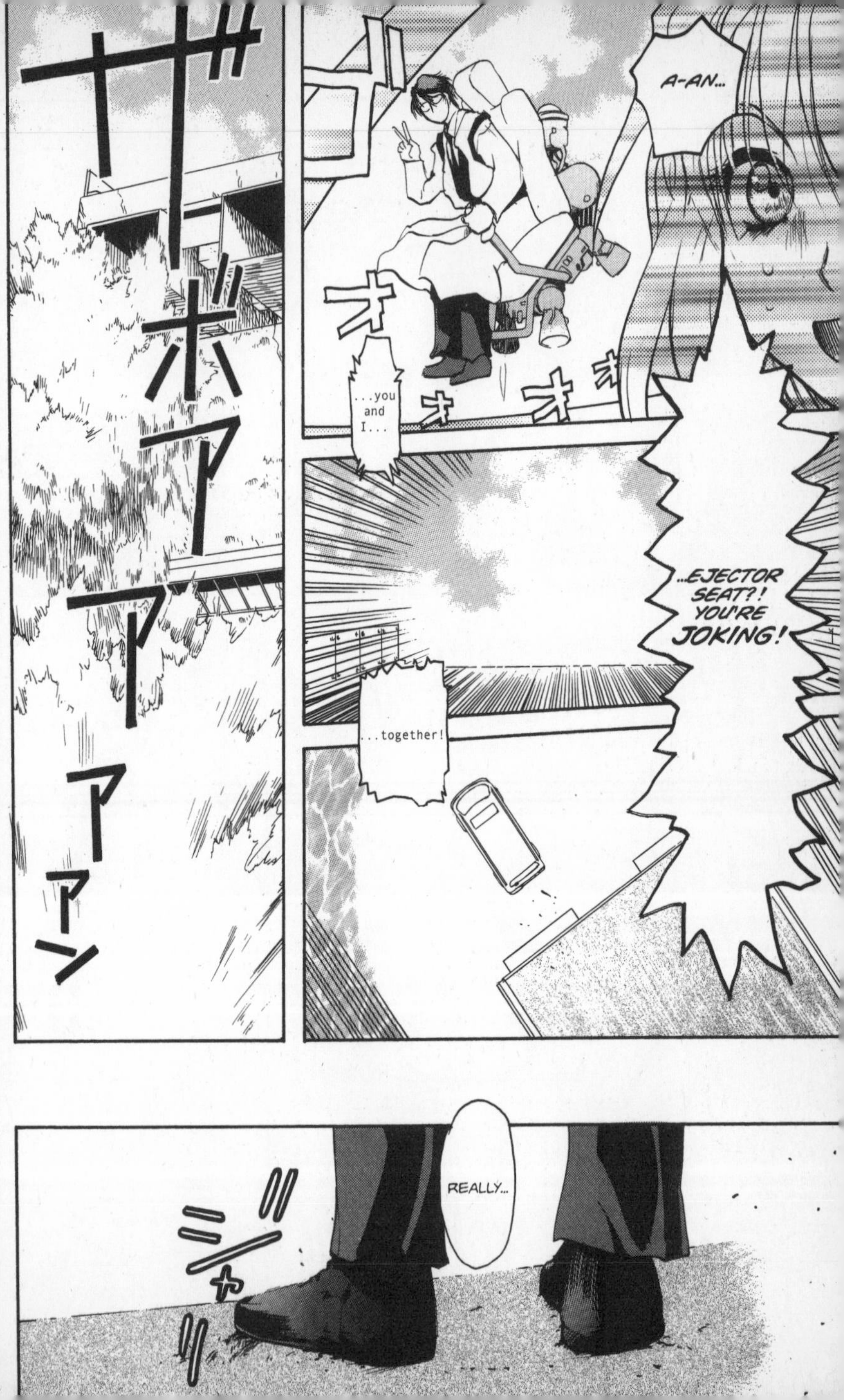
A-AN...
...EJECTOR SEAT?! YOU'RE JOKING!
...you and I...
...together!
REALLY...

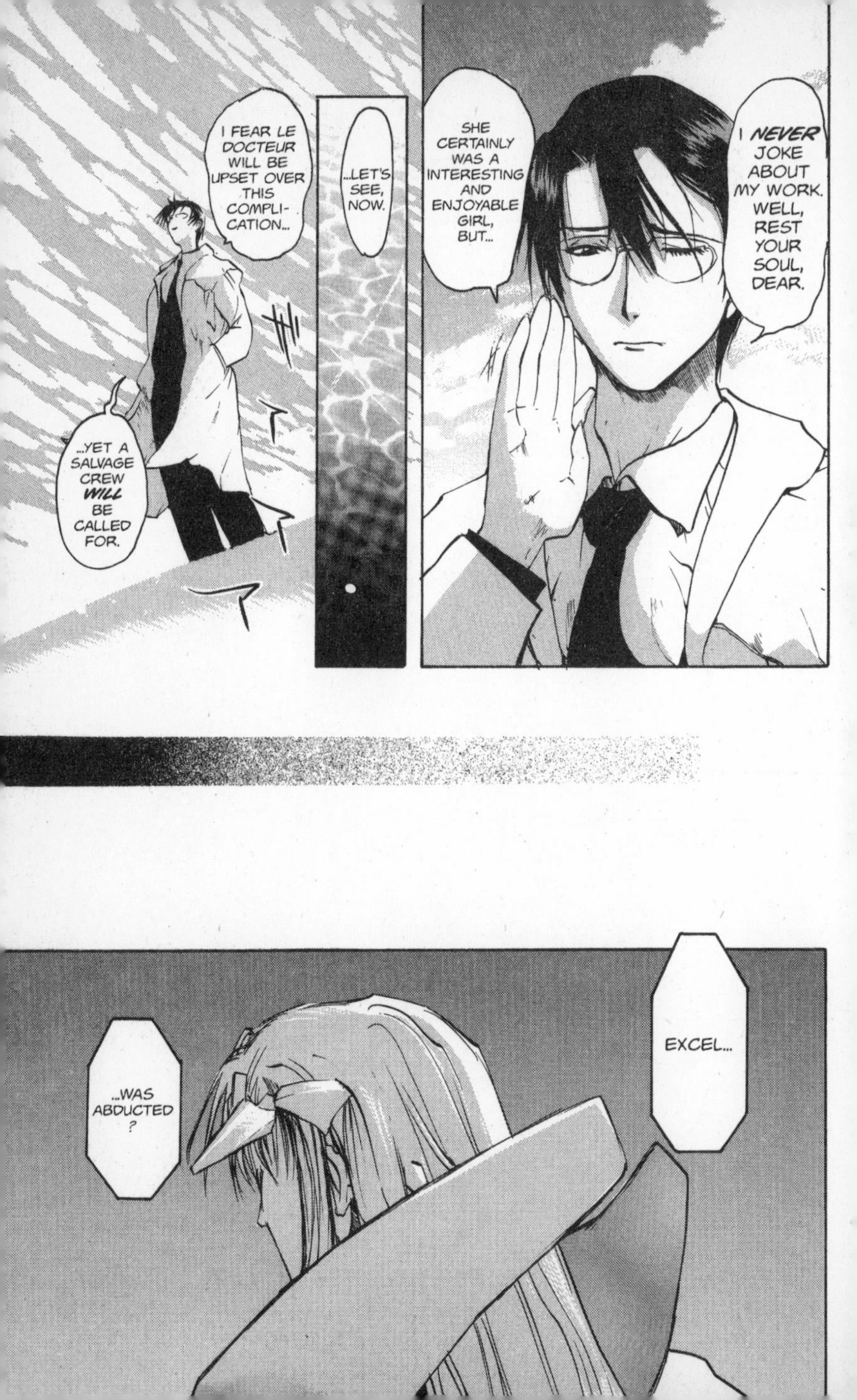
I **NEVER** JOKE ABOUT MY WORK. WELL, REST YOUR SOUL, DEAR.
SHE CERTAINLY WAS A INTERESTING AND ENJOYABLE GIRL, BUT...
...LET'S SEE, NOW.
I FEAR LE DOCTEUR WILL BE UPSET OVER THIS COMPLICATION...
...YET A SALVAGE CREW **WILL** BE CALLED FOR.
EXCEL...
...WAS ABDUCTED ?

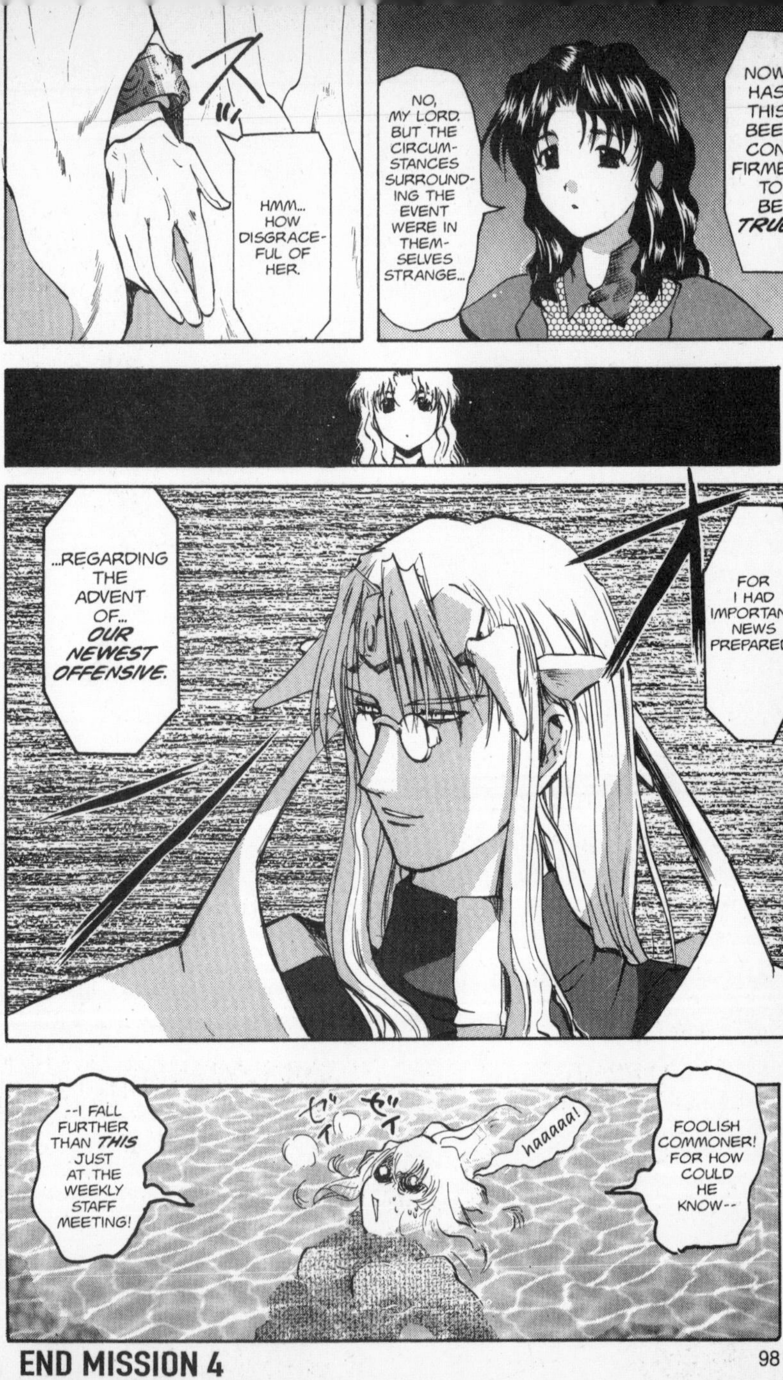
NOW, HAS THIS BEEN CONFIRMED TO BE *TRUE?*
NO, MY LORD. BUT THE CIRCUMSTANCES SURROUNDING THE EVENT WERE IN THEMSELVES STRANGE...
HMM... HOW DISGRACEFUL OF HER.
FOR I HAD IMPORTANT NEWS PREPARED...
...REGARDING THE ADVENT OF... *OUR NEWEST OFFENSIVE.*
FOOLISH COMMONER! FOR HOW COULD HE KNOW--
haaaaa!
--I FALL FURTHER THAN *THIS* JUST AT THE WEEKLY STAFF MEETING!

**END MISSION 4**

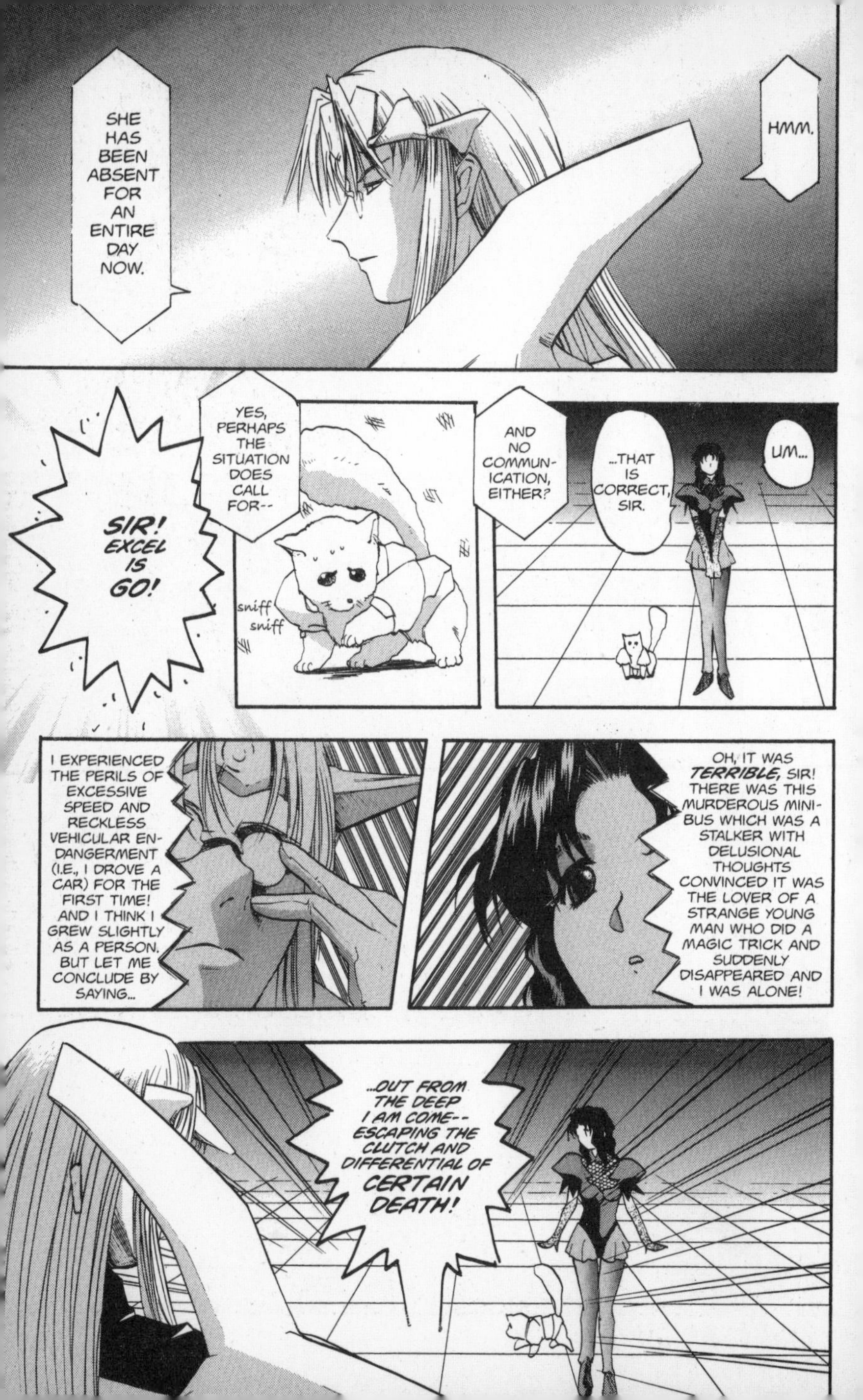

HMM.
SHE HAS BEEN ABSENT FOR AN ENTIRE DAY NOW.
UM...
AND NO COMMUNICATION, EITHER?
...THAT IS CORRECT, SIR.
YES, PERHAPS THE SITUATION DOES CALL FOR--
sniff sniff
SIR! EXCEL IS GO!
OH, IT WAS TERRIBLE, SIR! THERE WAS THIS MURDEROUS MINI-BUS WHICH WAS A STALKER WITH DELUSIONAL THOUGHTS CONVINCED IT WAS THE LOVER OF A STRANGE YOUNG MAN WHO DID A MAGIC TRICK AND SUDDENLY DISAPPEARED AND I WAS ALONE!
I EXPERIENCED THE PERILS OF EXCESSIVE SPEED AND RECKLESS VEHICULAR EN-DANGERMENT (I.E., I DROVE A CAR) FOR THE FIRST TIME! AND I THINK I GREW SLIGHTLY AS A PERSON. BUT LET ME CONCLUDE BY SAYING...
...OUT FROM THE DEEP I AM COME-- ESCAPING THE CLUTCH AND DIFFERENTIAL OF CERTAIN DEATH!

# MISSION 5 JUST COME BACK

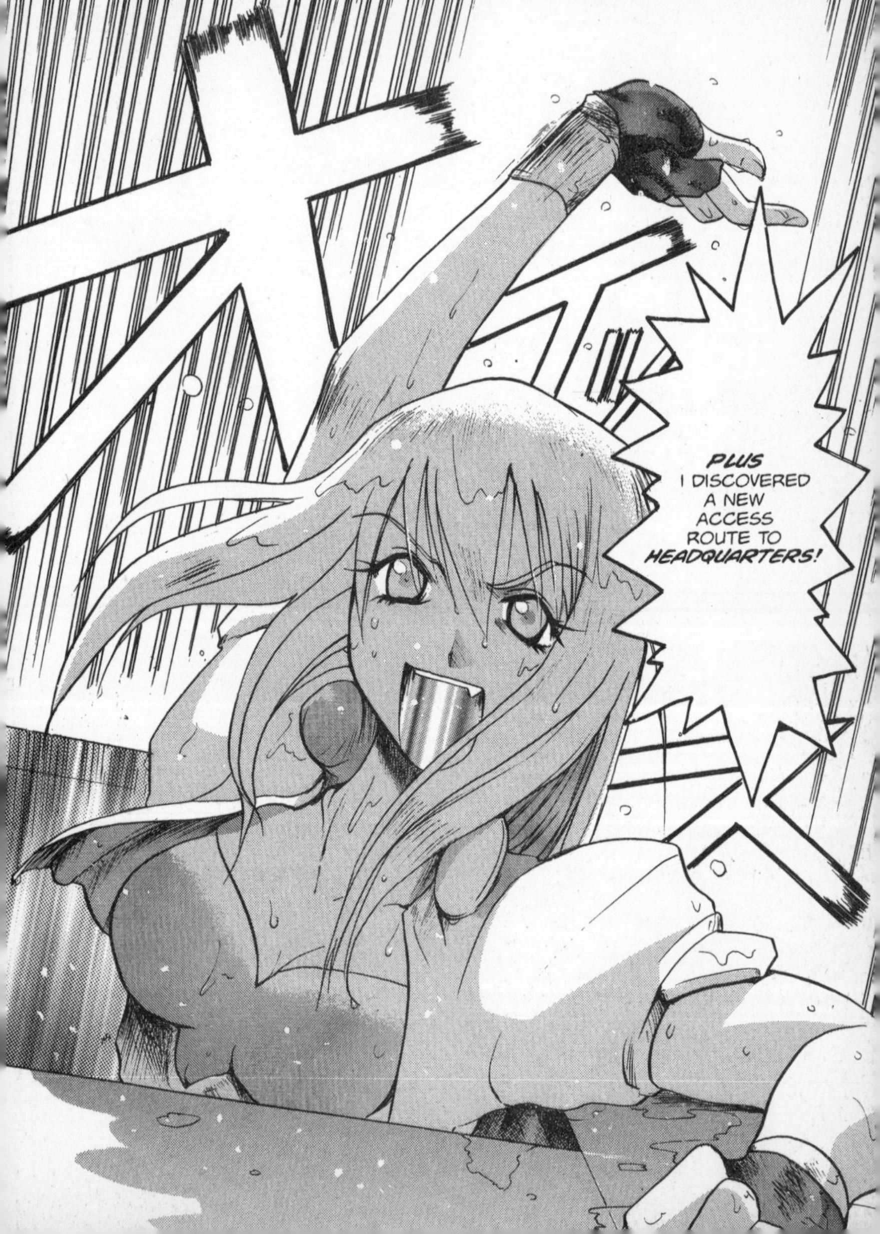
PLUS I DISCOVERED A NEW ACCESS ROUTE TO HEADQUARTERS!

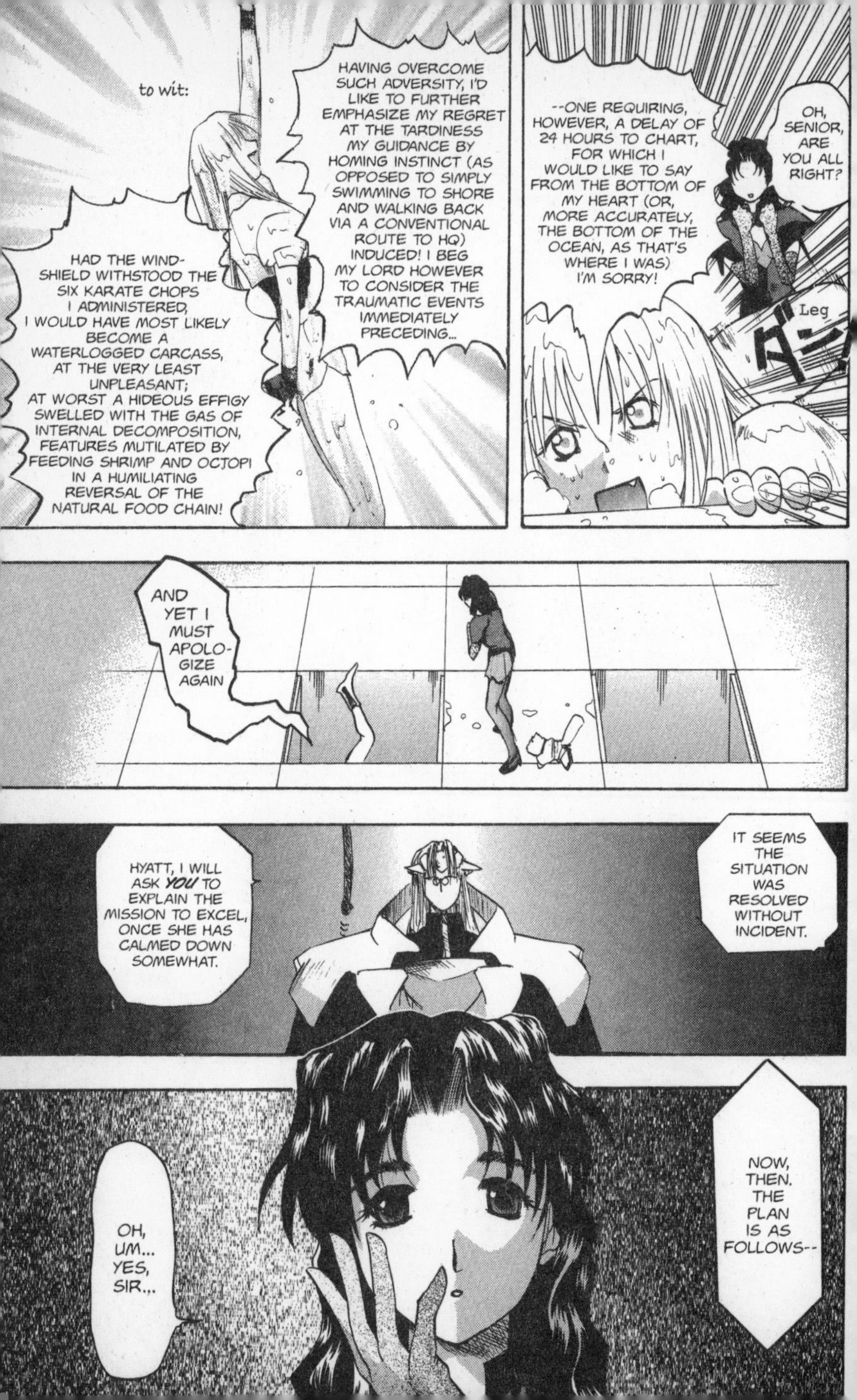
OH, SENIOR, ARE YOU ALL RIGHT?
--ONE REQUIRING, HOWEVER, A DELAY OF 24 HOURS TO CHART, FOR WHICH I WOULD LIKE TO SAY FROM THE BOTTOM OF MY HEART (OR, MORE ACCURATELY, THE BOTTOM OF THE OCEAN, AS THAT'S WHERE I WAS) I'M SORRY!
Leg
ダン
HAVING OVERCOME SUCH ADVERSITY, I'D LIKE TO FURTHER EMPHASIZE MY REGRET AT THE TARDINESS MY GUIDANCE BY HOMING INSTINCT (AS OPPOSED TO SIMPLY SWIMMING TO SHORE AND WALKING BACK VIA A CONVENTIONAL ROUTE TO HQ) INDUCED! I BEG MY LORD HOWEVER TO CONSIDER THE TRAUMATIC EVENTS IMMEDIATELY PRECEDING...
to wit:
HAD THE WIND-SHIELD WITHSTOOD THE SIX KARATE CHOPS I ADMINISTERED, I WOULD HAVE MOST LIKELY BECOME A WATERLOGGED CARCASS, AT THE VERY LEAST UNPLEASANT; AT WORST A HIDEOUS EFFIGY SWELLED WITH THE GAS OF INTERNAL DECOMPOSITION, FEATURES MUTILATED BY FEEDING SHRIMP AND OCTOPI IN A HUMILIATING REVERSAL OF THE NATURAL FOOD CHAIN!
AND YET I MUST APOLO-GIZE AGAIN
IT SEEMS THE SITUATION WAS RESOLVED WITHOUT INCIDENT.
HYATT, I WILL ASK *YOU* TO EXPLAIN THE MISSION TO EXCEL, ONCE SHE HAS CALMED DOWN SOMEWHAT.
NOW, THEN. THE PLAN IS AS FOLLOWS--
OH, UM... YES, SIR...

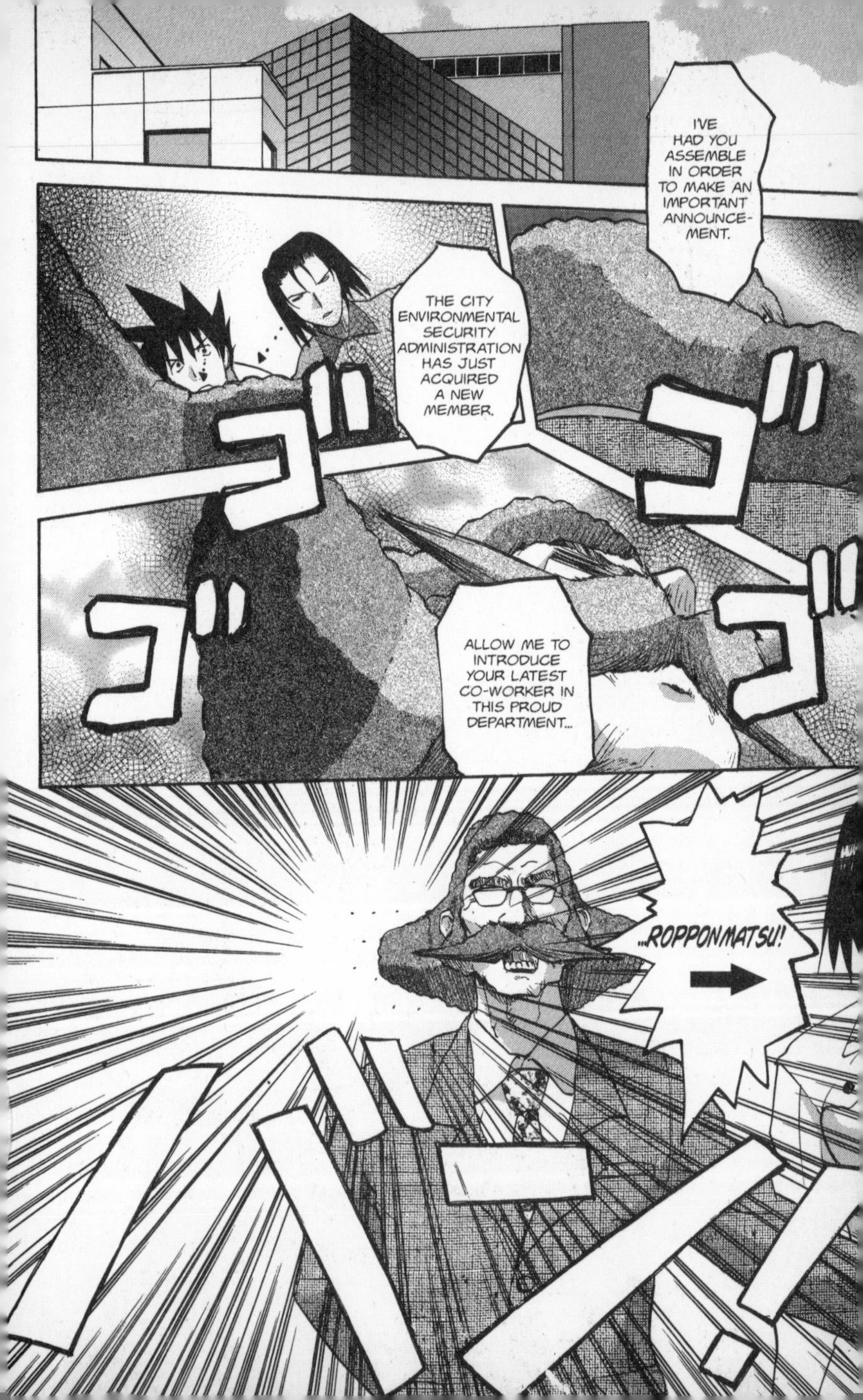
I'VE HAD YOU ASSEMBLE IN ORDER TO MAKE AN IMPORTANT ANNOUNCEMENT.
THE CITY ENVIRONMENTAL SECURITY ADMINISTRATION HAS JUST ACQUIRED A NEW MEMBER.
ゴゴ
ゴゴ
ALLOW ME TO INTRODUCE YOUR LATEST CO-WORKER IN THIS PROUD DEPARTMENT...
...ROPPONMATSU!

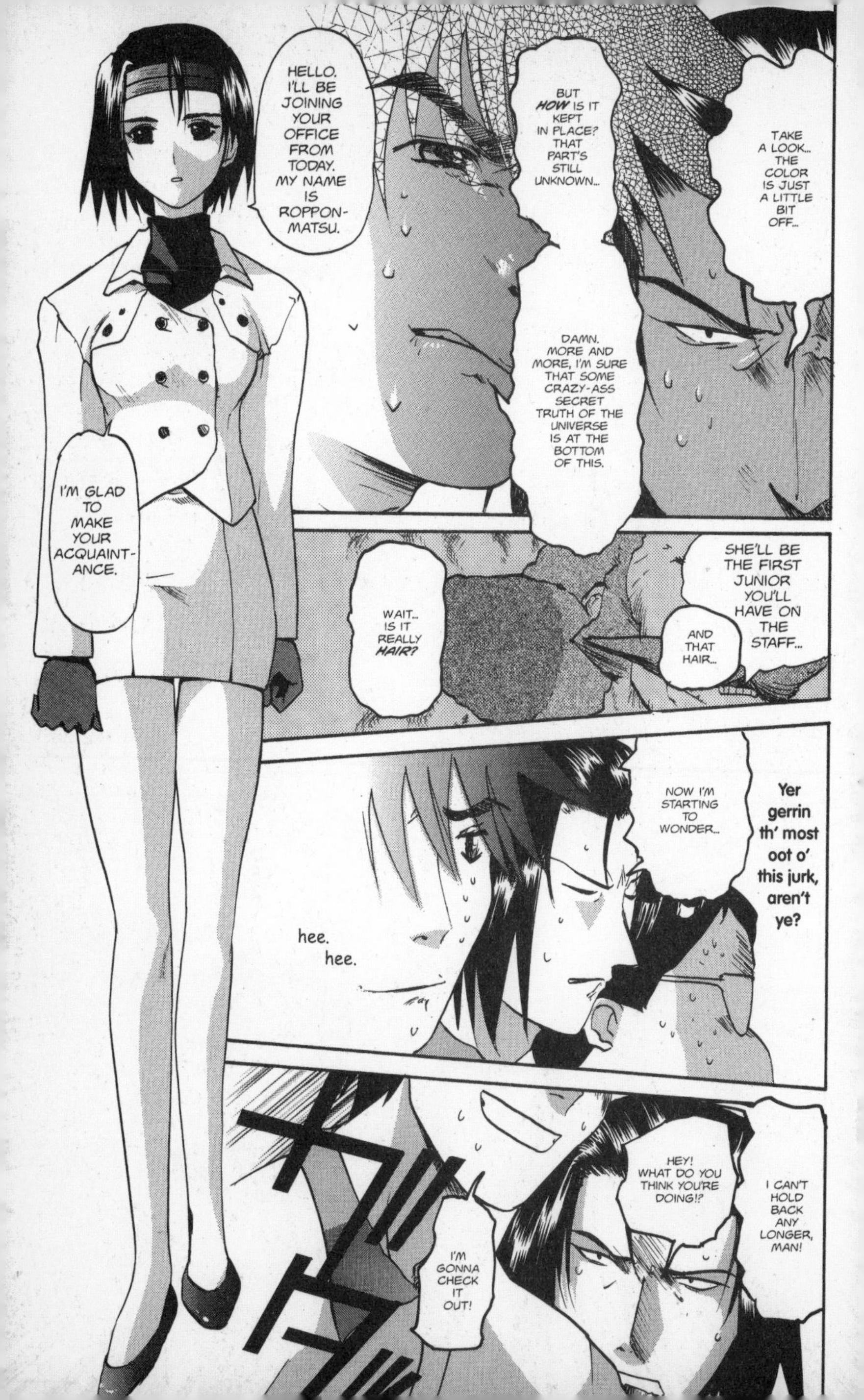
TAKE A LOOK... THE COLOR IS JUST A LITTLE BIT OFF...
BUT **HOW** IS IT KEPT IN PLACE? THAT PART'S STILL UNKNOWN...
DAMN. MORE AND MORE, I'M SURE THAT SOME CRAZY-ASS SECRET TRUTH OF THE UNIVERSE IS AT THE BOTTOM OF THIS.
SHE'LL BE THE FIRST JUNIOR YOU'LL HAVE ON THE STAFF...
AND THAT HAIR...
WAIT... IS IT REALLY ***HAIR?***
**Yer gerrin th' most oot o' this jurk, aren't ye?**
NOW I'M STARTING TO WONDER...
hee. hee.
I CAN'T HOLD BACK ANY LONGER, MAN!
HEY! WHAT DO YOU THINK YOU'RE DOING!?
I'M GONNA CHECK IT OUT!
HELLO. I'LL BE JOINING YOUR OFFICE FROM TODAY. MY NAME IS ROPPONMATSU.
I'M GLAD TO MAKE YOUR ACQUAINTANCE.

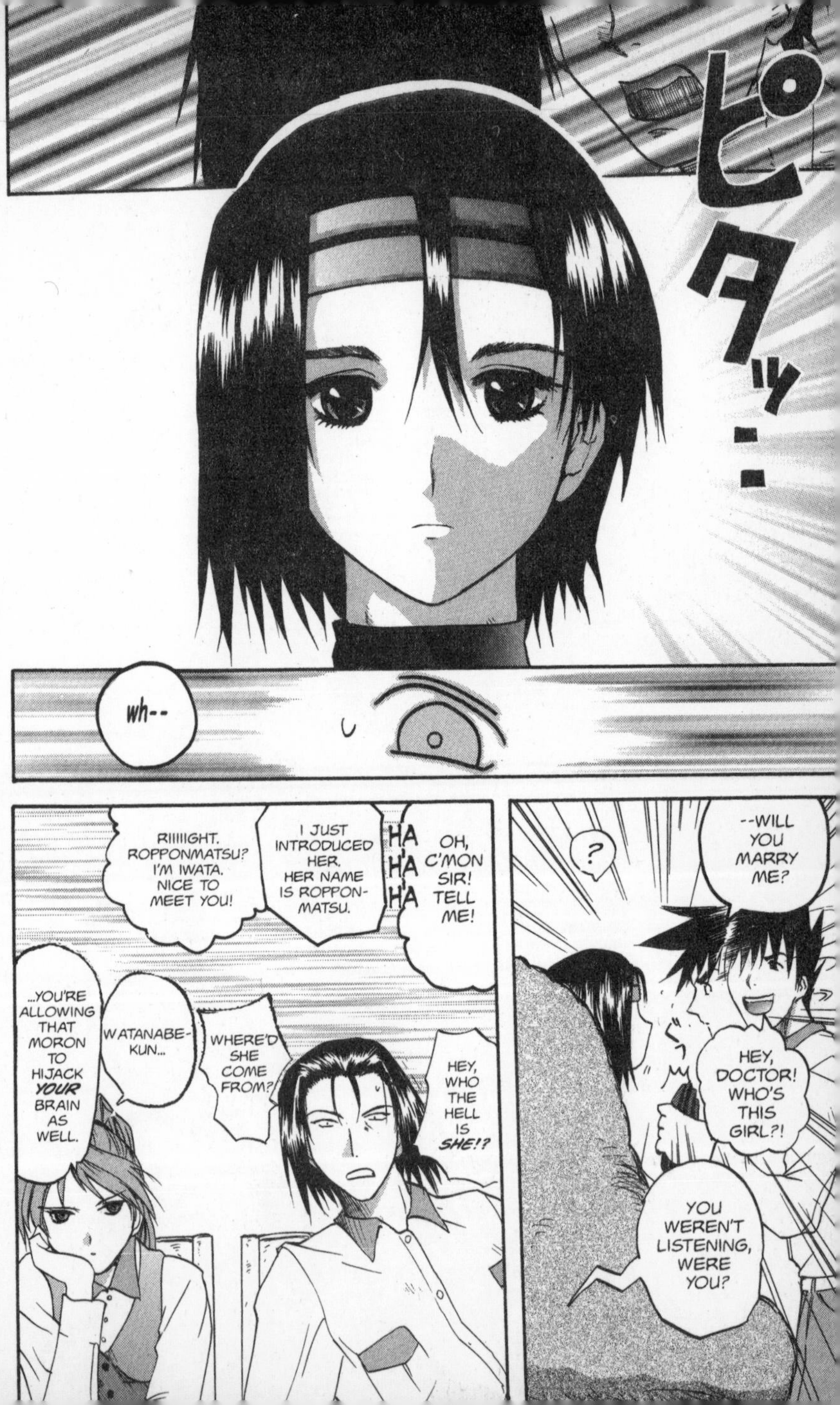
ピタッ!!
wh--
--WILL YOU MARRY ME?
?
HEY, DOCTOR! WHO'S THIS GIRL?!
YOU WEREN'T LISTENING, WERE YOU?
OH, C'MON SIR! TELL ME!
HA HA HA
I JUST INTRODUCED HER. HER NAME IS ROPPON-MATSU.
RIIIIGHT. ROPPONMATSU? I'M IWATA. NICE TO MEET YOU!
HEY, WHO THE HELL IS SHE!?
WHERE'D SHE COME FROM?
WATANABE-KUN...
...YOU'RE ALLOWING THAT MORON TO HIJACK YOUR BRAIN AS WELL.

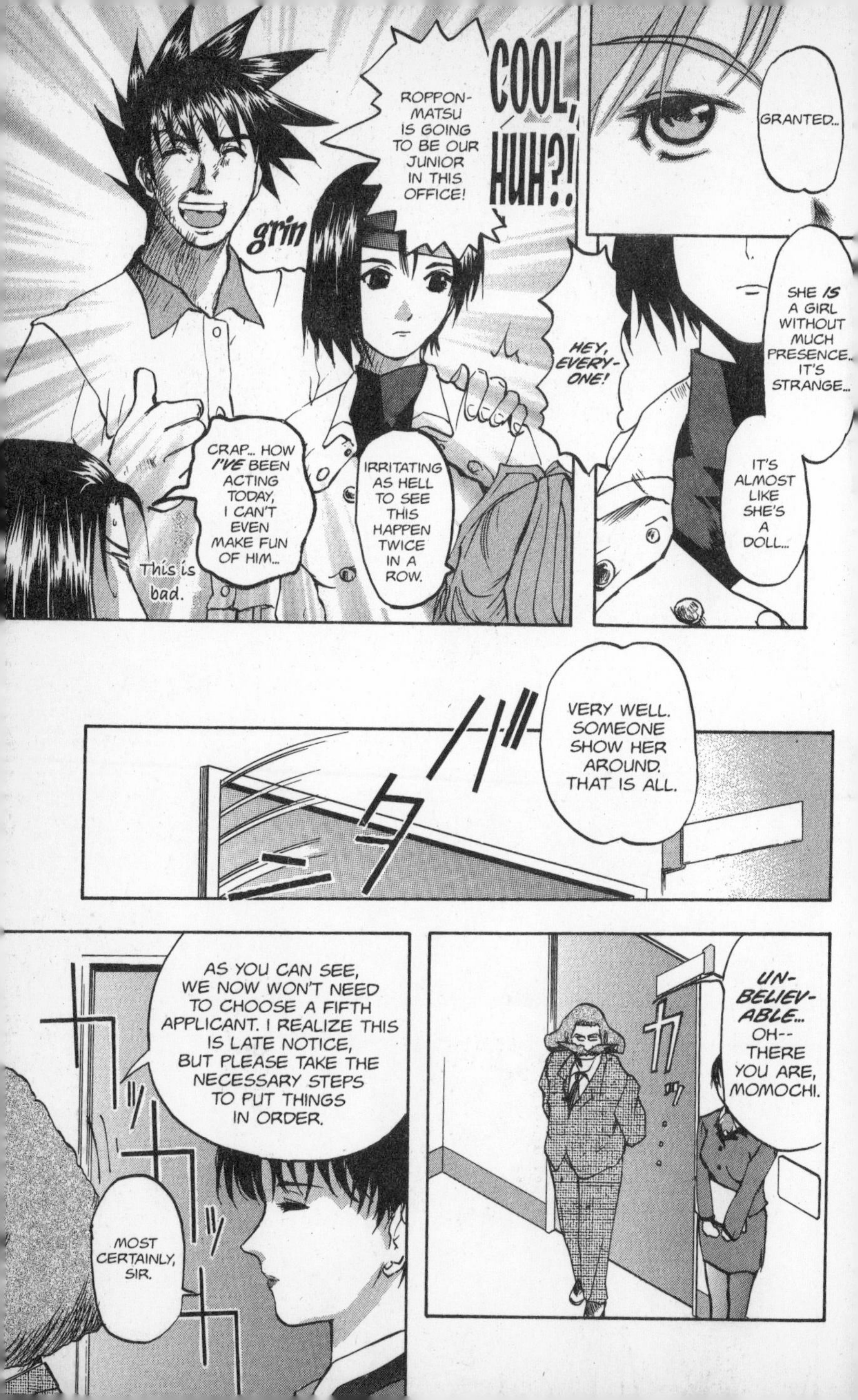
GRANTED...
SHE *IS* A GIRL WITHOUT MUCH PRESENCE.. IT'S STRANGE...
IT'S ALMOST LIKE SHE'S A DOLL...
HEY, EVERYONE!
ROPPONMATSU IS GOING TO BE OUR JUNIOR IN THIS OFFICE!
COOL, HUH?!
grin
IRRITATING AS HELL TO SEE THIS HAPPEN TWICE IN A ROW.
CRAP... HOW *I'VE* BEEN ACTING TODAY, I CAN'T EVEN MAKE FUN OF HIM...
This is bad.
VERY WELL. SOMEONE SHOW HER AROUND. THAT IS ALL.
UNBELIEVABLE... OH-- THERE YOU ARE, MOMOCHI.
AS YOU CAN SEE, WE NOW WON'T NEED TO CHOOSE A FIFTH APPLICANT. I REALIZE THIS IS LATE NOTICE, BUT PLEASE TAKE THE NECESSARY STEPS TO PUT THINGS IN ORDER.
MOST CERTAINLY, SIR.

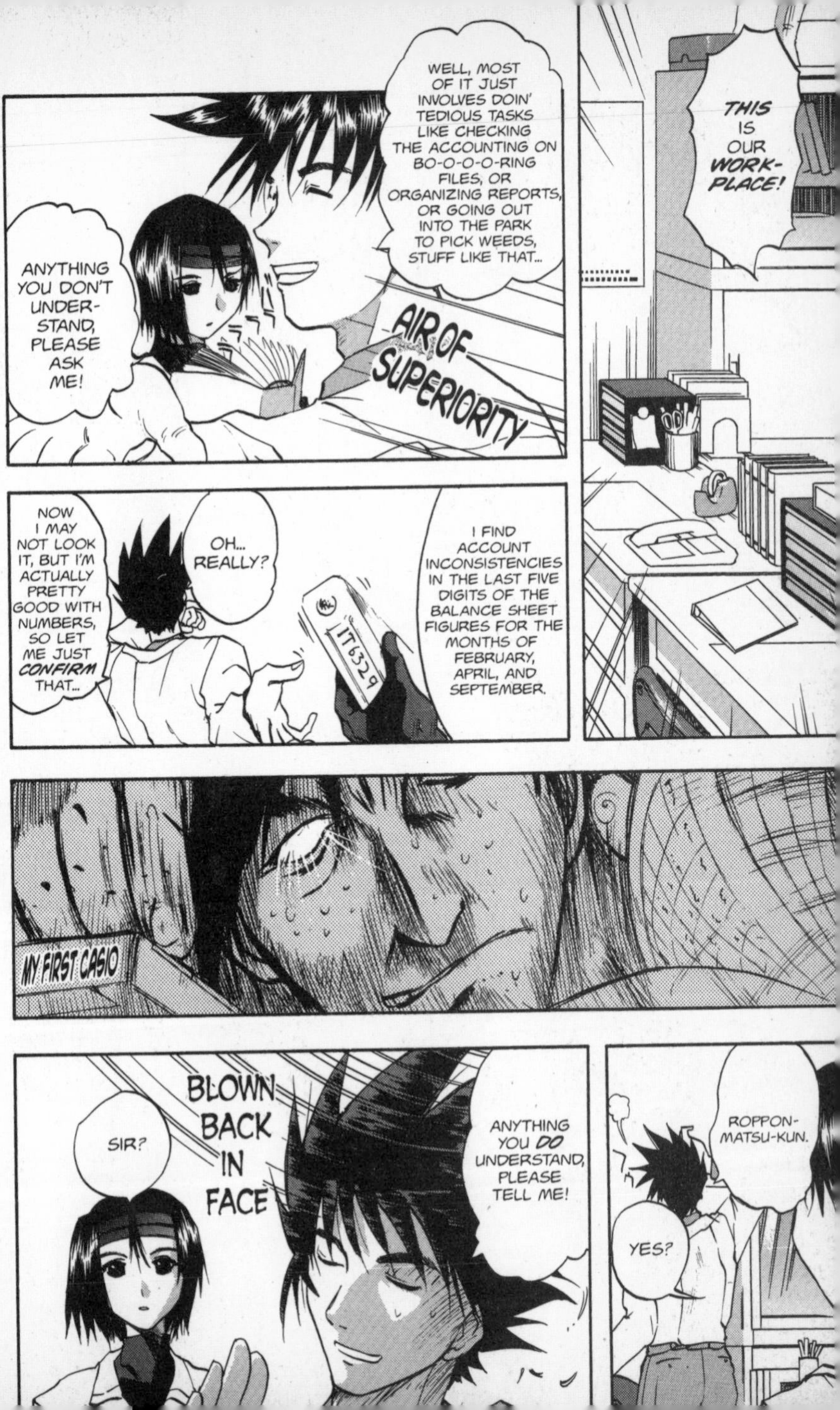
THIS IS OUR WORK-PLACE!
WELL, MOST OF IT JUST INVOLVES DOIN' TEDIOUS TASKS LIKE CHECKING THE ACCOUNTING ON BO-O-O-O-RING FILES, OR ORGANIZING REPORTS, OR GOING OUT INTO THE PARK TO PICK WEEDS, STUFF LIKE THAT...
AIR OF SUPERIORITY
ANYTHING YOU DON'T UNDER-STAND, PLEASE ASK ME!
I FIND ACCOUNT INCONSISTENCIES IN THE LAST FIVE DIGITS OF THE BALANCE SHEET FIGURES FOR THE MONTHS OF FEBRUARY, APRIL, AND SEPTEMBER.
IT6329
OH... REALLY?
NOW I MAY NOT LOOK IT, BUT I'M ACTUALLY PRETTY GOOD WITH NUMBERS, SO LET ME JUST *CONFIRM* THAT...
MY FIRST CASIO
ROPPON-MATSU-KUN.
YES?
ANYTHING YOU *DO* UNDERSTAND, PLEASE TELL ME!
BLOWN BACK IN FACE
SIR?

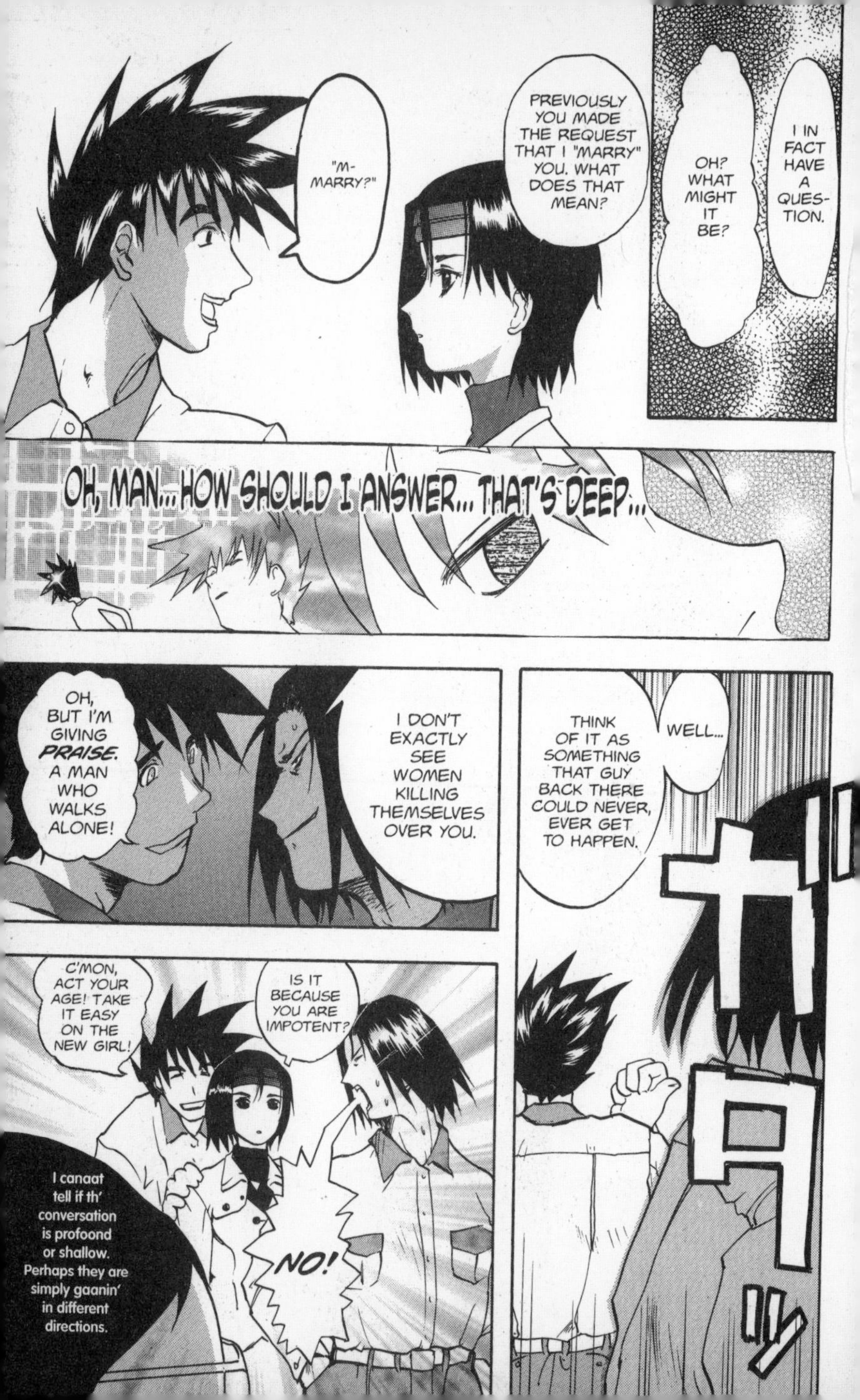
I IN FACT HAVE A QUESTION.
OH? WHAT MIGHT IT BE?
PREVIOUSLY YOU MADE THE REQUEST THAT I "MARRY" YOU. WHAT DOES THAT MEAN?
"M-MARRY?"
OH, MAN... HOW SHOULD I ANSWER... THAT'S DEEP...
WELL...
THINK OF IT AS SOMETHING THAT GUY BACK THERE COULD NEVER, EVER GET TO HAPPEN.
ガタッ
I DON'T EXACTLY SEE WOMEN KILLING THEMSELVES OVER YOU.
OH, BUT I'M GIVING *PRAISE.* A MAN WHO WALKS ALONE!
IS IT BECAUSE YOU ARE IMPOTENT?
C'MON, ACT YOUR AGE! TAKE IT EASY ON THE NEW GIRL!
NO!
I canaat tell if th' conversation is profoond or shallow. Perhaps they are simply gaanin' in different directions.

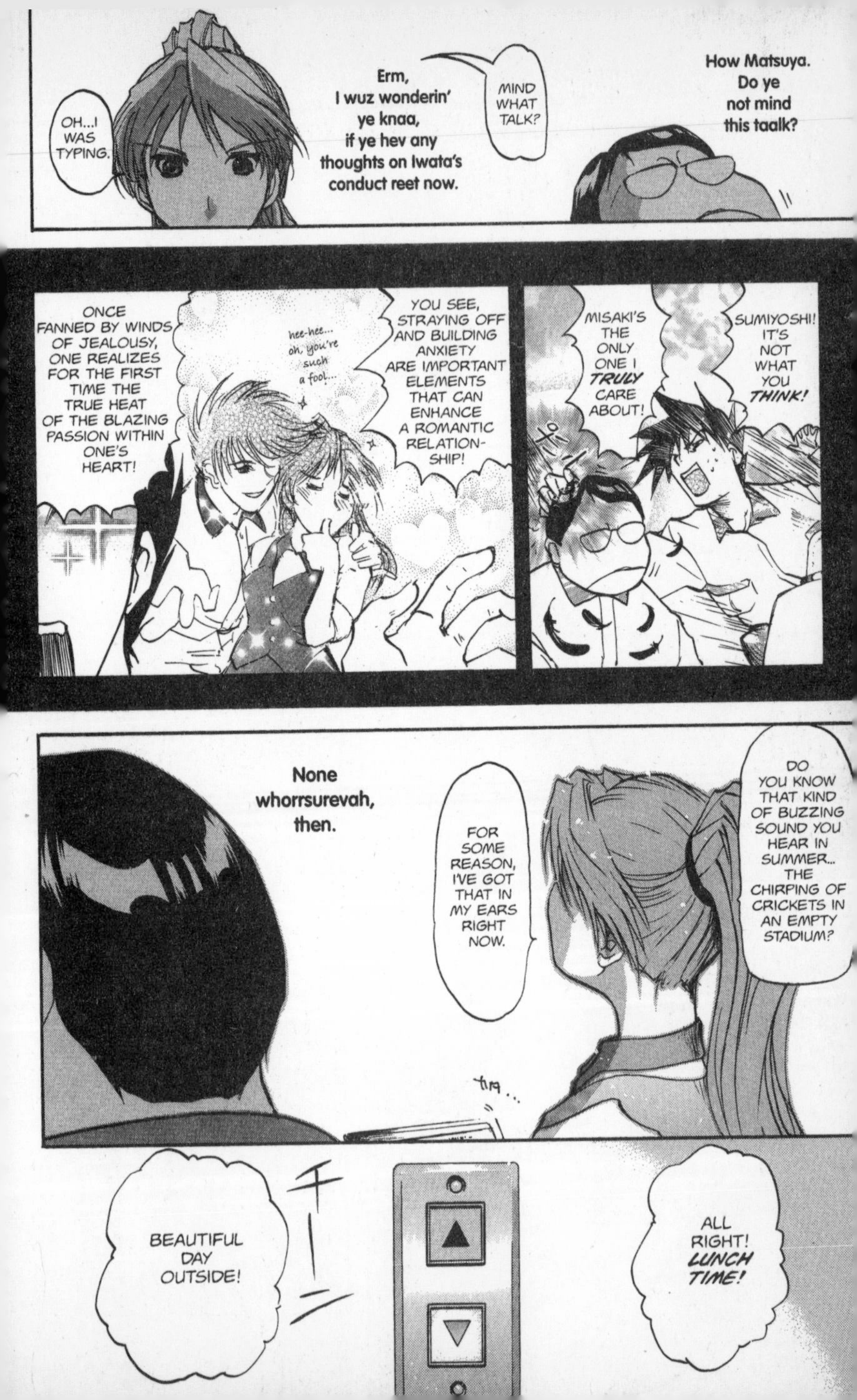
How Matsuya. Do ye not mind this taalk?
MIND WHAT TALK?
Erm, I wuz wonderin' ye knaa, if ye hev any thoughts on Iwata's conduct reet now.
OH...I WAS TYPING.
SUMIYOSHI! IT'S NOT WHAT YOU THINK!
MISAKI'S THE ONLY ONE I TRULY CARE ABOUT!
YOU SEE, STRAYING OFF AND BUILDING ANXIETY ARE IMPORTANT ELEMENTS THAT CAN ENHANCE A ROMANTIC RELATIONSHIP!
hee-hee... oh, you're such a fool...
ONCE FANNED BY WINDS OF JEALOUSY, ONE REALIZES FOR THE FIRST TIME THE TRUE HEAT OF THE BLAZING PASSION WITHIN ONE'S HEART!
DO YOU KNOW THAT KIND OF BUZZING SOUND YOU HEAR IN SUMMER... THE CHIRPING OF CRICKETS IN AN EMPTY STADIUM?
FOR SOME REASON, I'VE GOT THAT IN MY EARS RIGHT NOW.
None whorrsurevah, then.
ALL RIGHT! LUNCH TIME!
BEAUTIFUL DAY OUTSIDE!

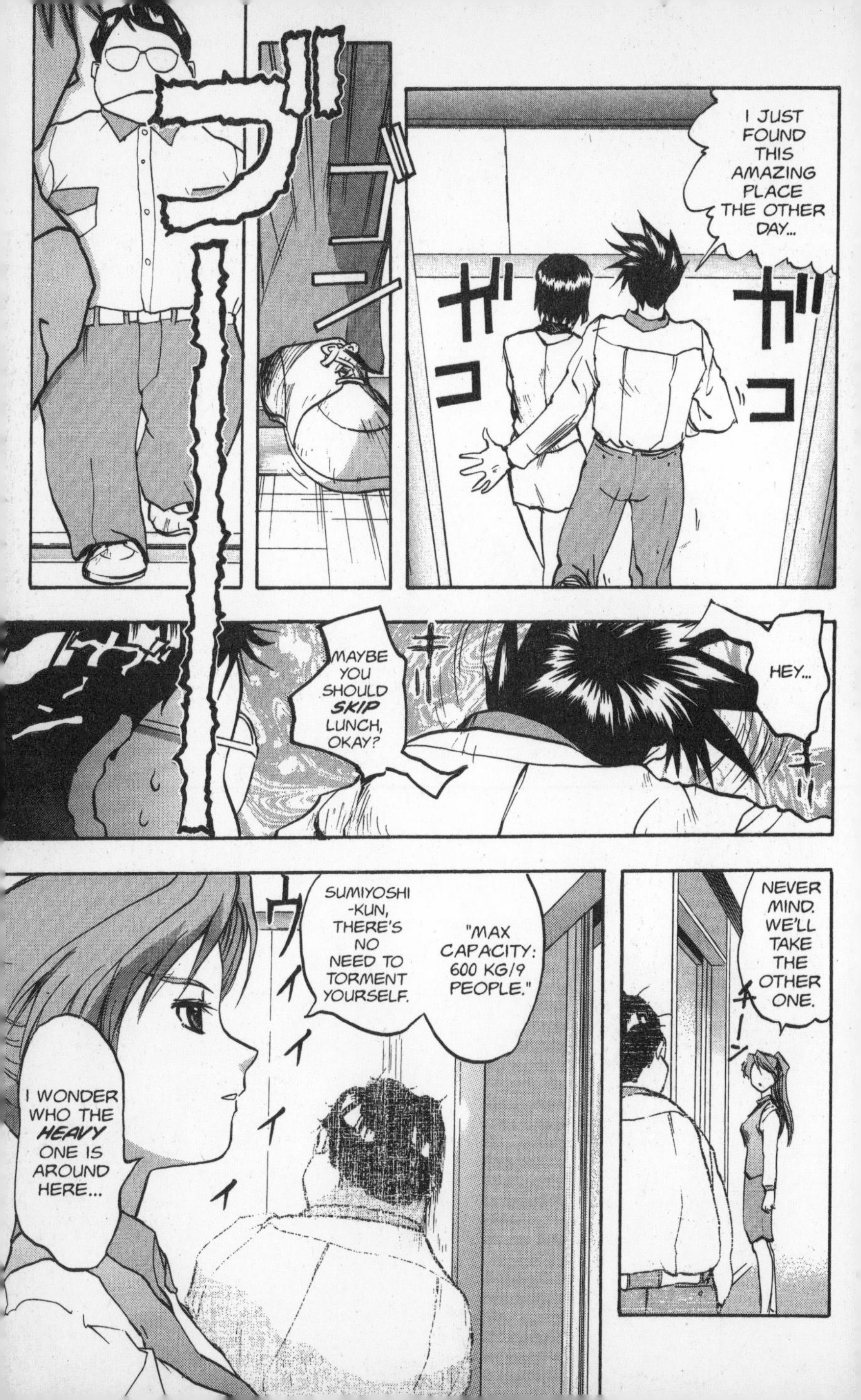
I JUST FOUND THIS AMAZING PLACE THE OTHER DAY...
ガコ
ガコ
HEY...
MAYBE YOU SHOULD *SKIP* LUNCH, OKAY?
NEVER MIND. WE'LL TAKE THE OTHER ONE.
"MAX CAPACITY: 600 KG/9 PEOPLE."
SUMIYOSHI-KUN, THERE'S NO NEED TO TORMENT YOURSELF.
I WONDER WHO THE *HEAVY* ONE IS AROUND HERE...

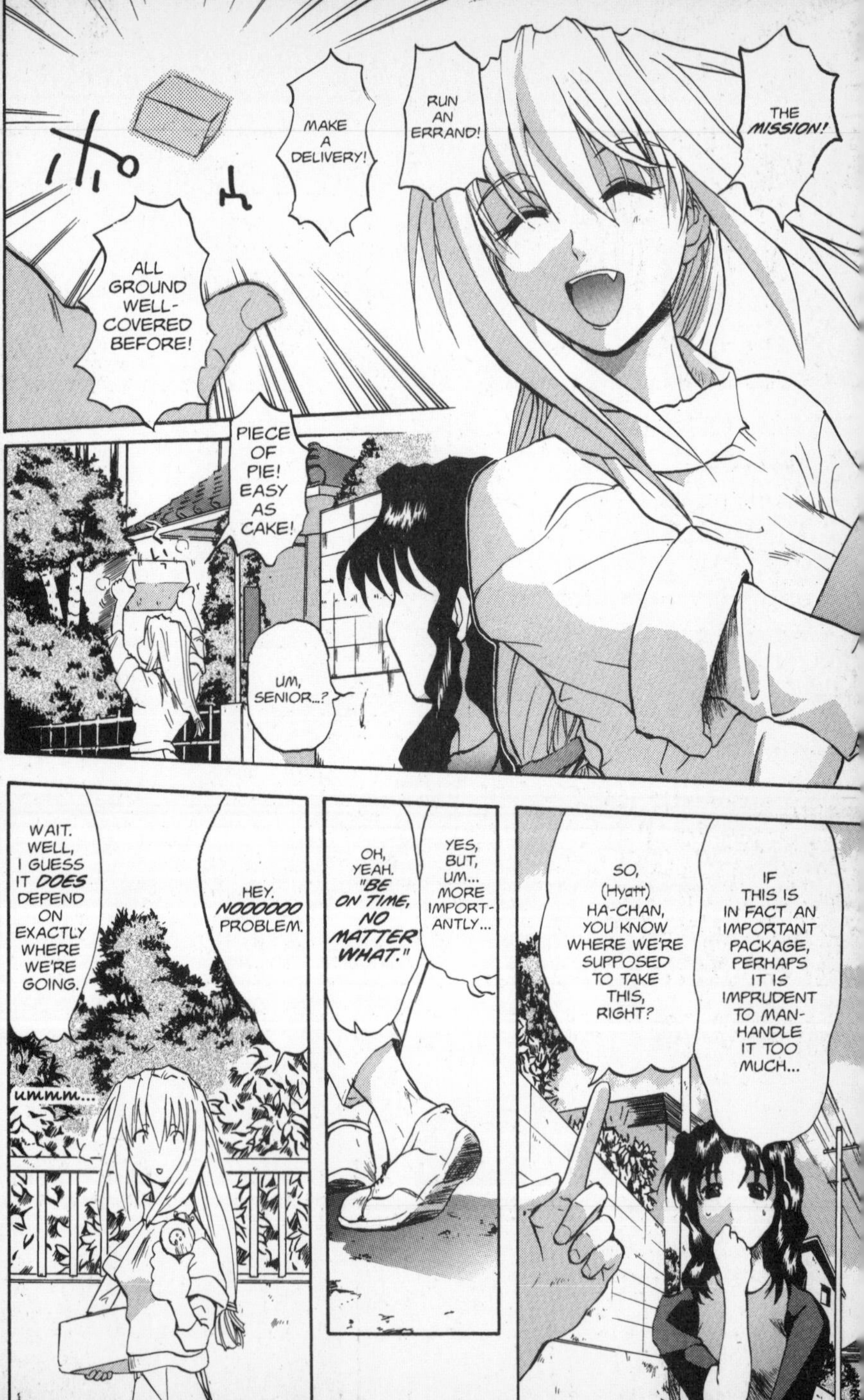
THE *MISSION!*
RUN AN ERRAND!
MAKE A DELIVERY!
ALL GROUND WELL-COVERED BEFORE!
PIECE OF PIE! EASY AS CAKE!
UM, SENIOR...?
IF THIS IS IN FACT AN IMPORTANT PACKAGE, PERHAPS IT IS IMPRUDENT TO MAN-HANDLE IT TOO MUCH...
SO, (Hyatt) HA-CHAN, YOU KNOW WHERE WE'RE SUPPOSED TO TAKE THIS, RIGHT?
YES, BUT, UM... MORE IMPORT-ANTLY...
OH, YEAH. *"BE ON TIME, NO MATTER WHAT."*
HEY. ***NOOOOOO*** PROBLEM.
WAIT. WELL, I GUESS IT ***DOES*** DEPEND ON EXACTLY WHERE WE'RE GOING.
ummm...

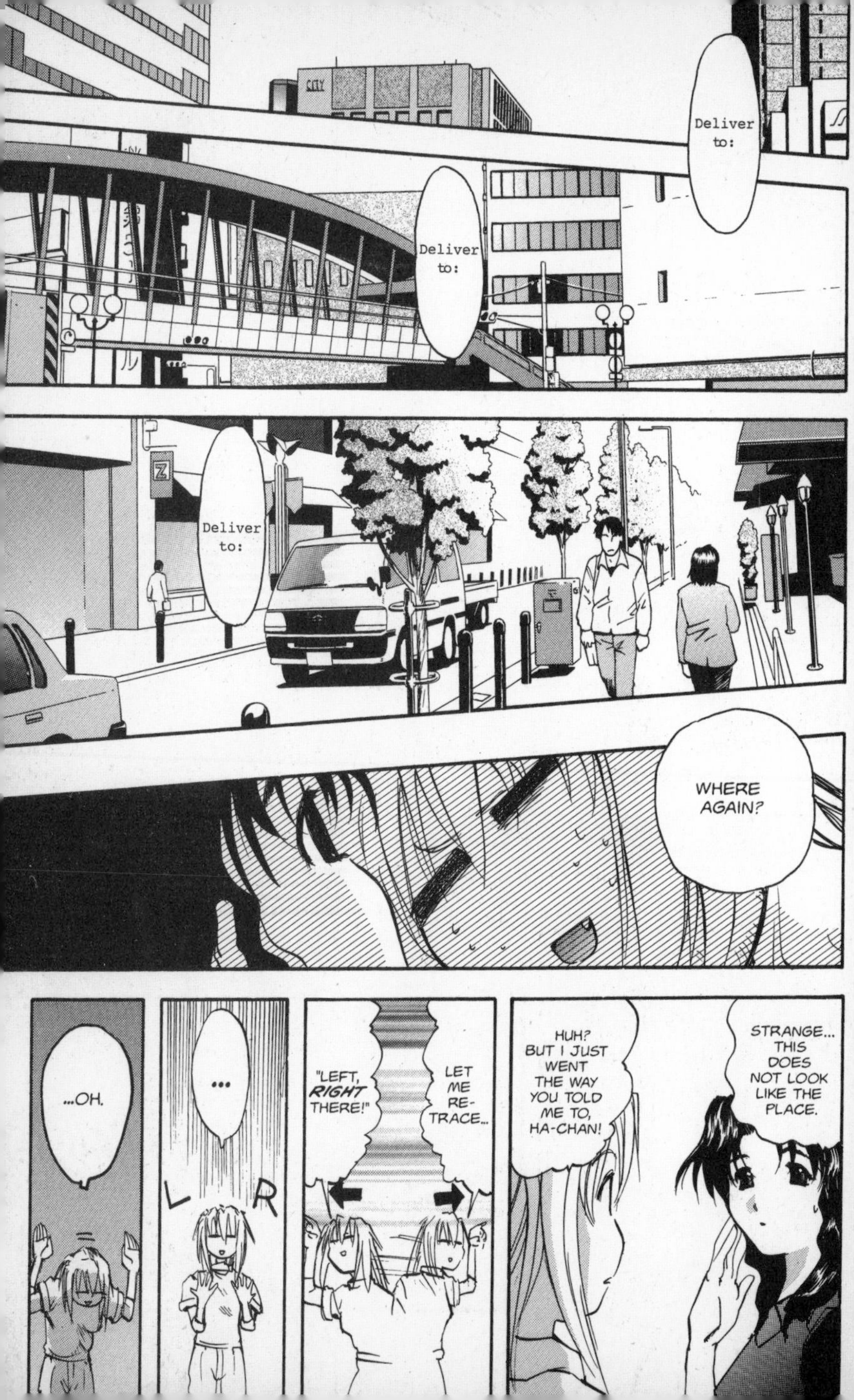
Deliver to:
Deliver to:
Deliver to:
WHERE AGAIN?
STRANGE... THIS DOES NOT LOOK LIKE THE PLACE.
HUH? BUT I JUST WENT THE WAY YOU TOLD ME TO, HA-CHAN!
LET ME RE-TRACE...
"LEFT, RIGHT THERE!"
L
R
...
...OH.

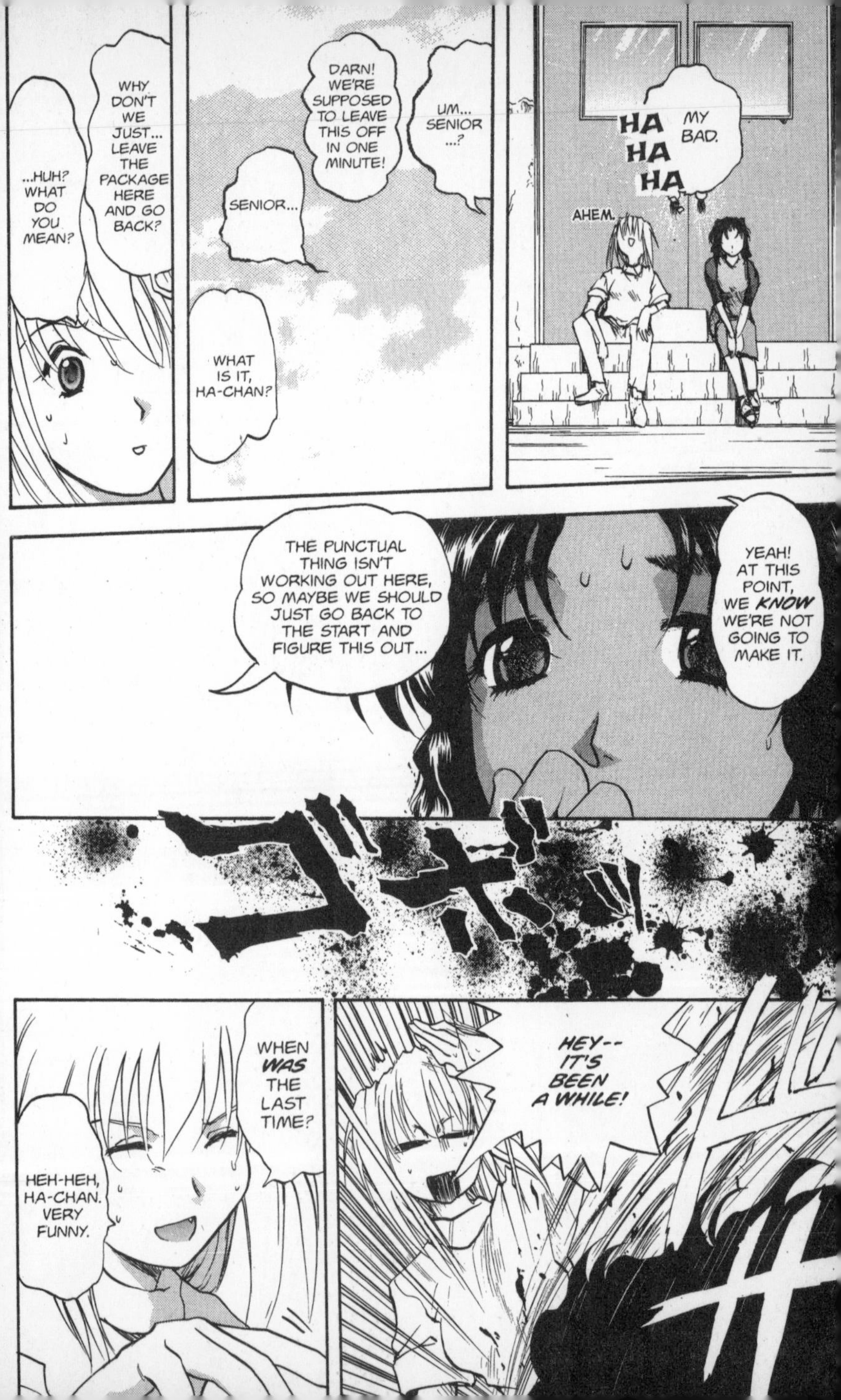
MY BAD.
HA HA HA
AHEM.
UM... SENIOR ...?
DARN! WE'RE SUPPOSED TO LEAVE THIS OFF IN ONE MINUTE!
SENIOR...
WHAT IS IT, HA-CHAN?
WHY DON'T WE JUST... LEAVE THE PACKAGE HERE AND GO BACK?
...HUH? WHAT DO YOU MEAN?
YEAH! AT THIS POINT, WE *KNOW* WE'RE NOT GOING TO MAKE IT.
THE PUNCTUAL THING ISN'T WORKING OUT HERE, SO MAYBE WE SHOULD JUST GO BACK TO THE START AND FIGURE THIS OUT...
ゴガッ!!
HEY-- IT'S BEEN A WHILE!
WHEN *WAS* THE LAST TIME?
HEH-HEH, HA-CHAN. VERY FUNNY.

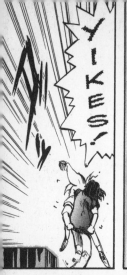

UM.
UH-OH.
YIKES!
WHAT'S GOING ON OVER THERE?
HUH? I'M GONNA TAKE A LOOK.
HEY-- IWATA!
TSK
MOB MENTALITY...

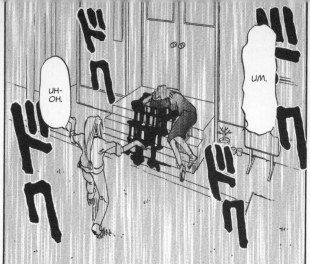

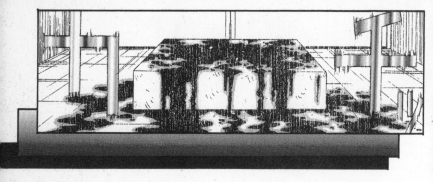

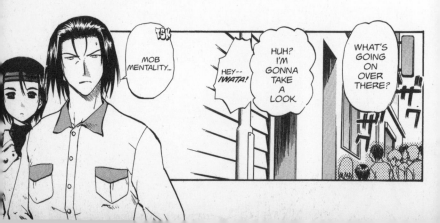

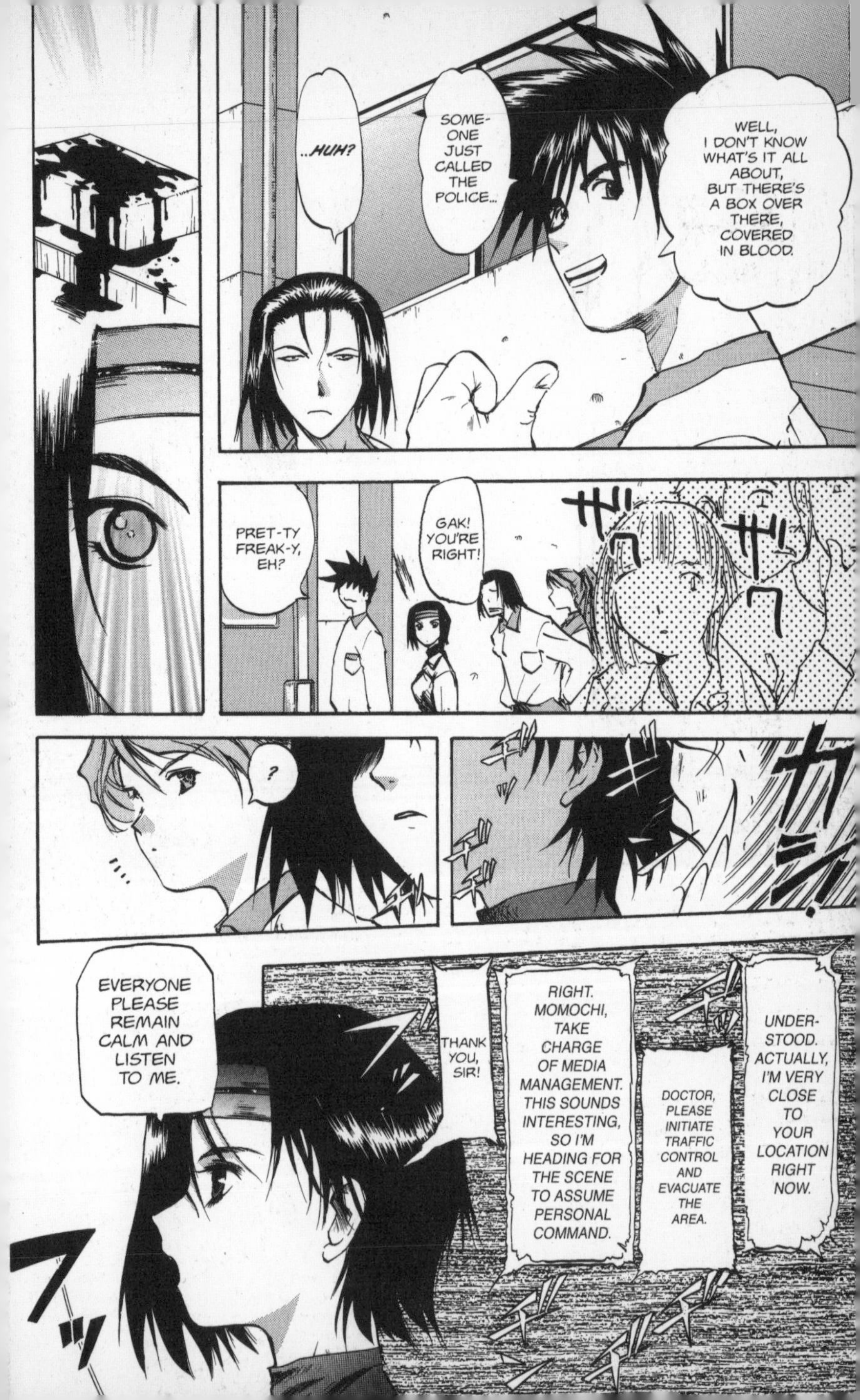
WELL, I DON'T KNOW WHAT'S IT ALL ABOUT, BUT THERE'S A BOX OVER THERE, COVERED IN BLOOD.
SOME-ONE JUST CALLED THE POLICE...
..HUH?
GAK! YOU'RE RIGHT!
PRET-TY FREAK-Y, EH?
?
UNDER-STOOD. ACTUALLY, I'M VERY CLOSE TO YOUR LOCATION RIGHT NOW.
DOCTOR, PLEASE INITIATE TRAFFIC CONTROL AND EVACUATE THE AREA.
RIGHT. MOMOCHI, TAKE CHARGE OF MEDIA MANAGEMENT. THIS SOUNDS INTERESTING, SO I'M HEADING FOR THE SCENE TO ASSUME PERSONAL COMMAND.
THANK YOU, SIR!
EVERYONE PLEASE REMAIN CALM AND LISTEN TO ME.

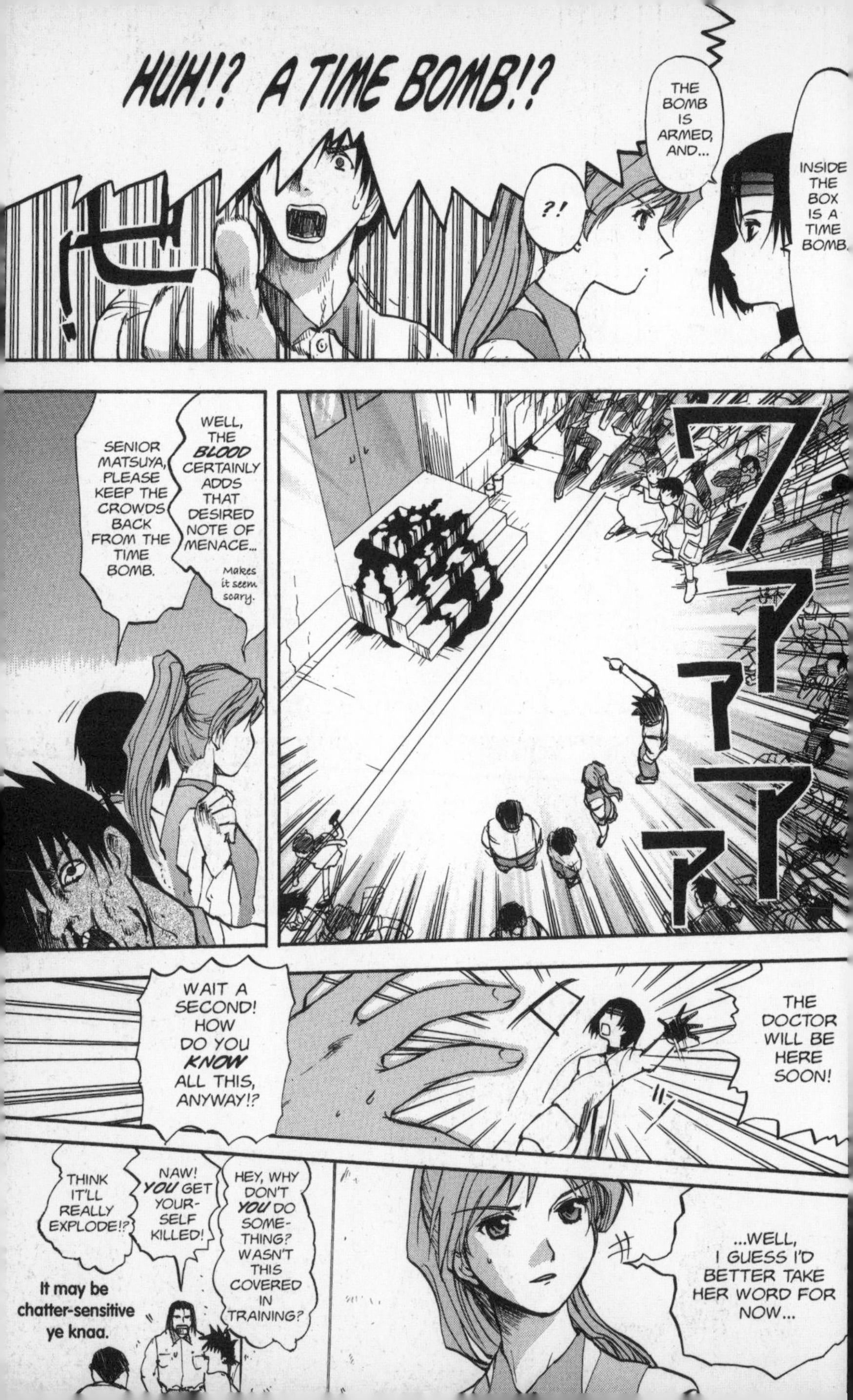
INSIDE THE BOX IS A TIME BOMB.
THE BOMB IS ARMED, AND...
?!
HUH!? A TIME BOMB!?
WELL, THE BLOOD CERTAINLY ADDS THAT DESIRED NOTE OF MENACE...
Makes it seem scary.
SENIOR MATSUYA, PLEASE KEEP THE CROWDS BACK FROM THE TIME BOMB.
THE DOCTOR WILL BE HERE SOON!
WAIT A SECOND! HOW DO YOU KNOW ALL THIS, ANYWAY!?
...WELL, I GUESS I'D BETTER TAKE HER WORD FOR NOW...
HEY, WHY DON'T YOU DO SOME-THING? WASN'T THIS COVERED IN TRAINING?
NAW! YOU GET YOUR-SELF KILLED!
THINK IT'LL REALLY EXPLODE!?
It may be chatter-sensitive ye knaa.

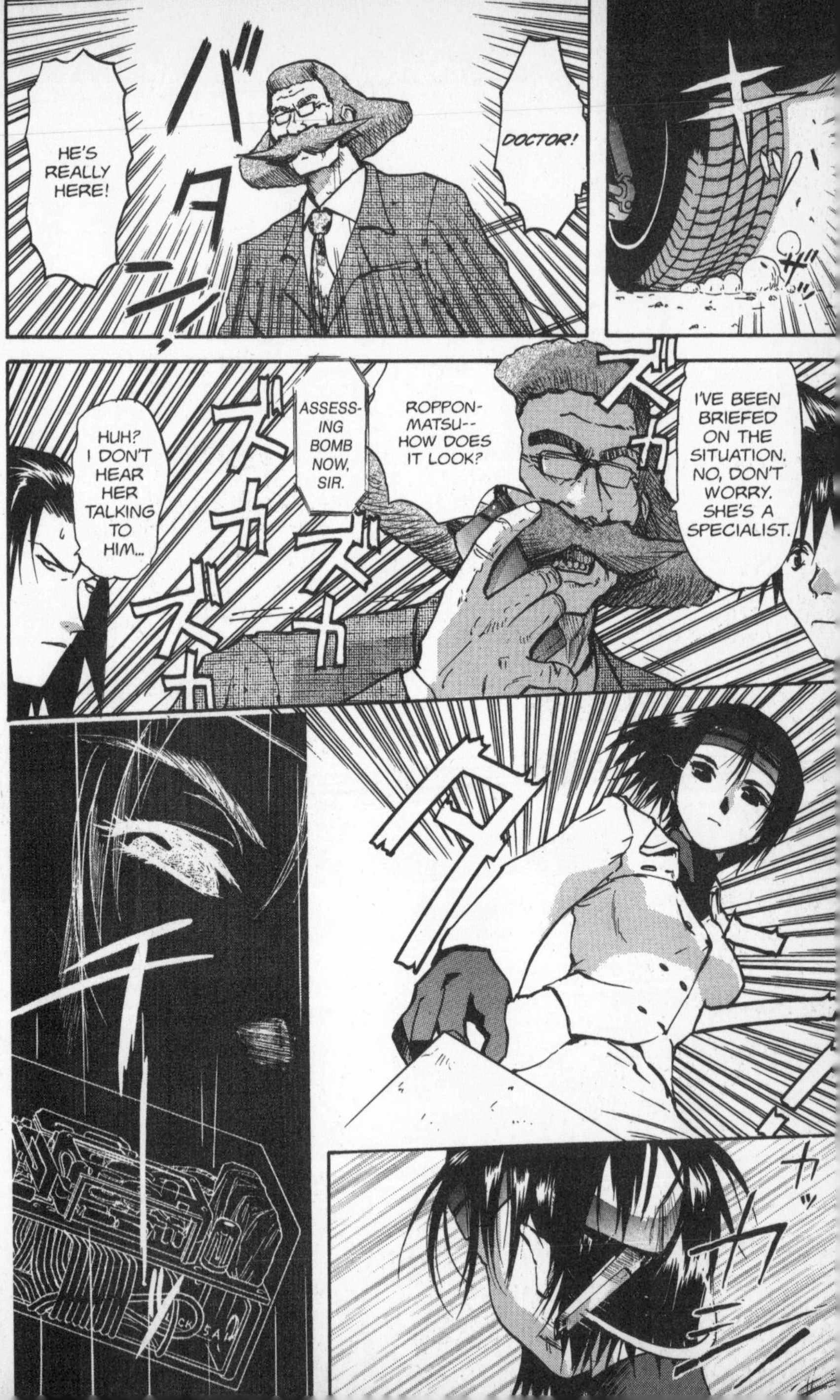
DOCTOR!
HE'S REALLY HERE!
I'VE BEEN BRIEFED ON THE SITUATION. NO, DON'T WORRY. SHE'S A SPECIALIST.
ROPPONMATSU-- HOW DOES IT LOOK?
ASSESSING BOMB NOW, SIR.
HUH? I DON'T HEAR HER TALKING TO HIM...

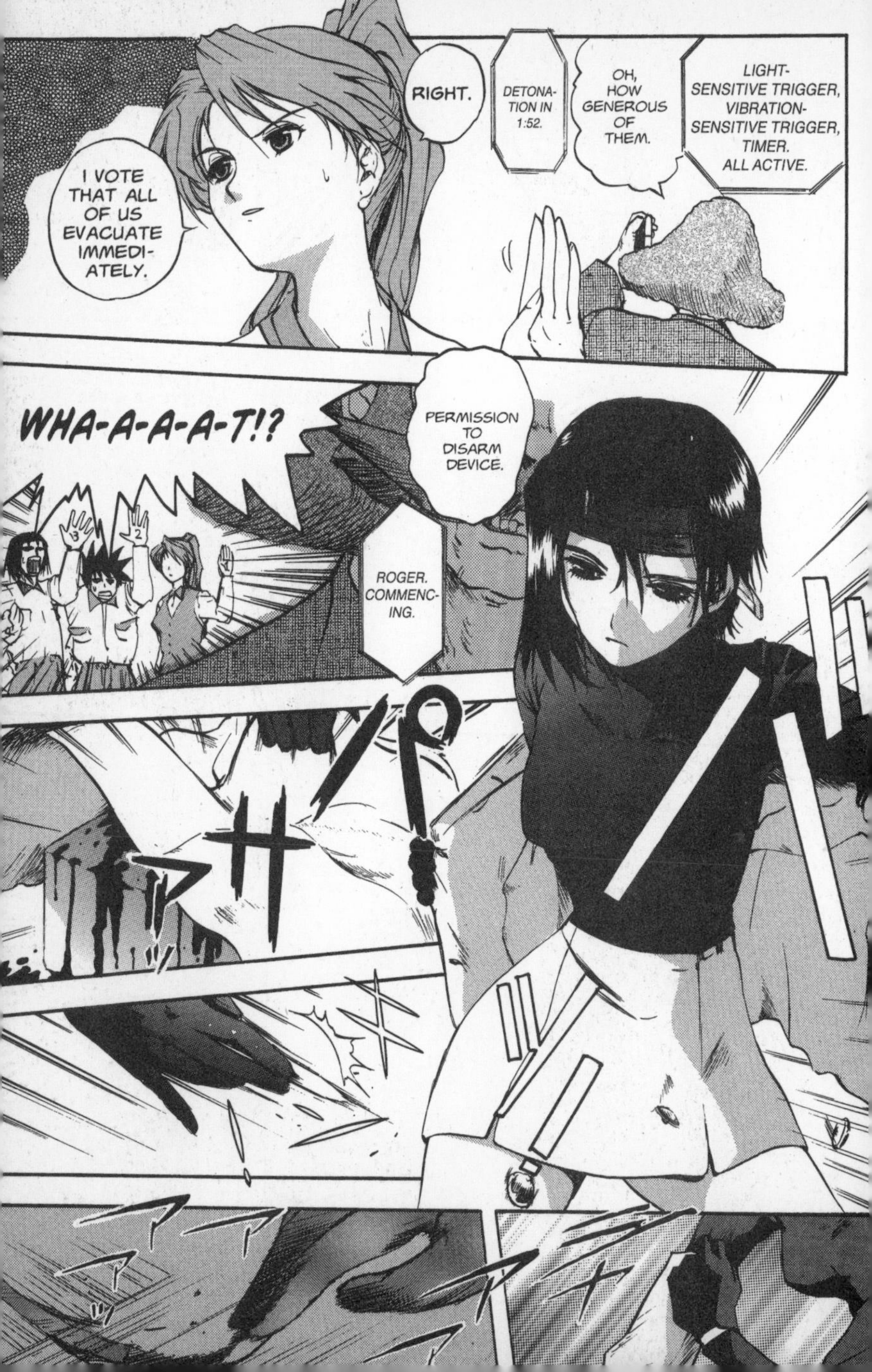
LIGHT-SENSITIVE TRIGGER, VIBRATION-SENSITIVE TRIGGER, TIMER. ALL ACTIVE.
OH, HOW GENEROUS OF THEM.
DETONATION IN 1:52.
RIGHT.
I VOTE THAT ALL OF US EVACUATE IMMEDIATELY.
PERMISSION TO DISARM DEVICE.
ROGER. COMMENCING.
WHA-A-A-A-T!?

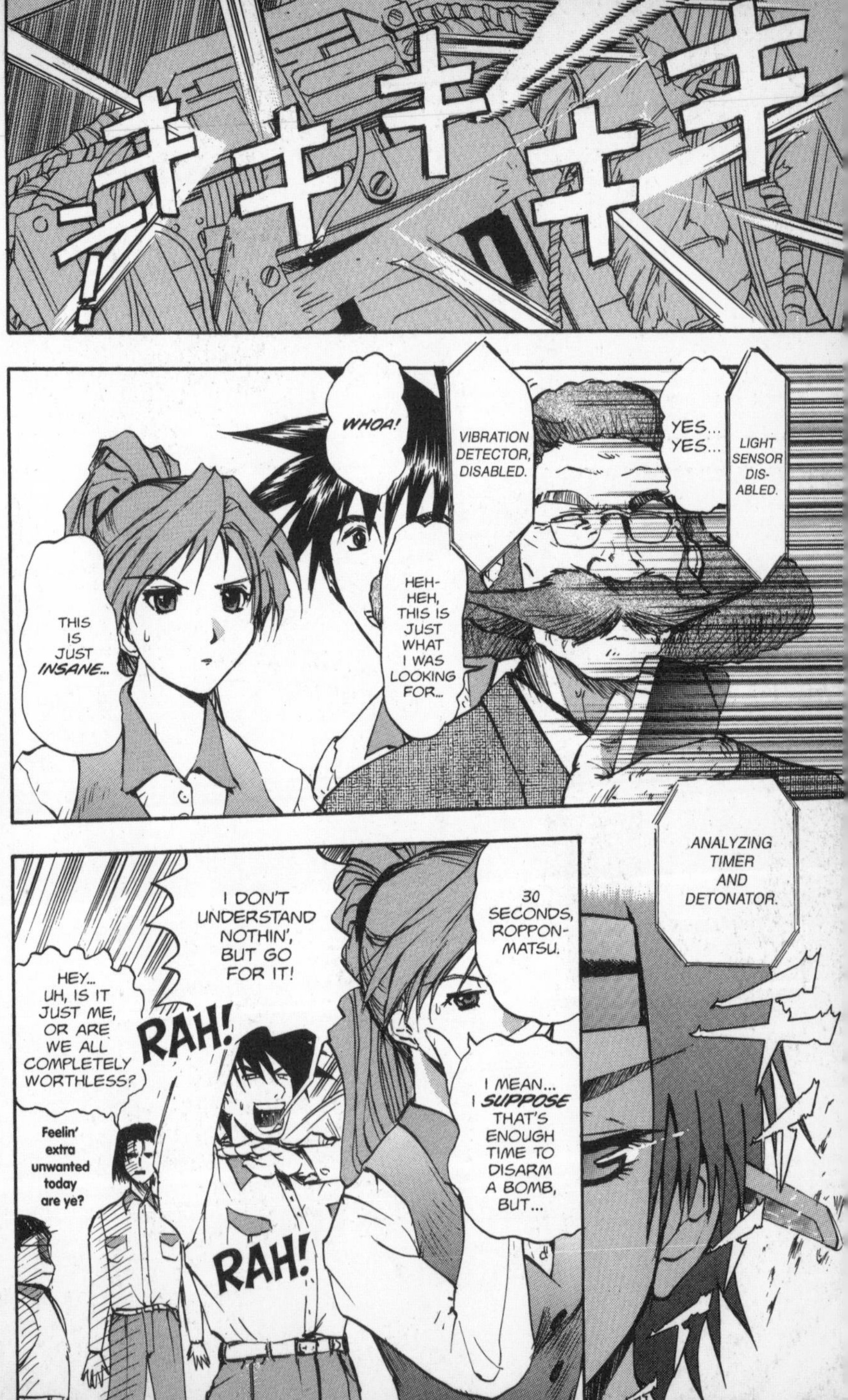
キキキキキ!
LIGHT SENSOR DIS-ABLED.
YES... YES...
VIBRATION DETECTOR, DISABLED.
WHOA!
HEH-HEH, THIS IS JUST WHAT I WAS LOOKING FOR...
THIS IS JUST INSANE...
ANALYZING TIMER AND DETONATOR.
30 SECONDS, ROPPON-MATSU.
I MEAN... I SUPPOSE THAT'S ENOUGH TIME TO DISARM A BOMB, BUT...
I DON'T UNDERSTAND NOTHIN', BUT GO FOR IT!
RAH!
RAH!
HEY... UH, IS IT JUST ME, OR ARE WE ALL COMPLETELY WORTHLESS?
Feelin' extra unwanted today are ye?

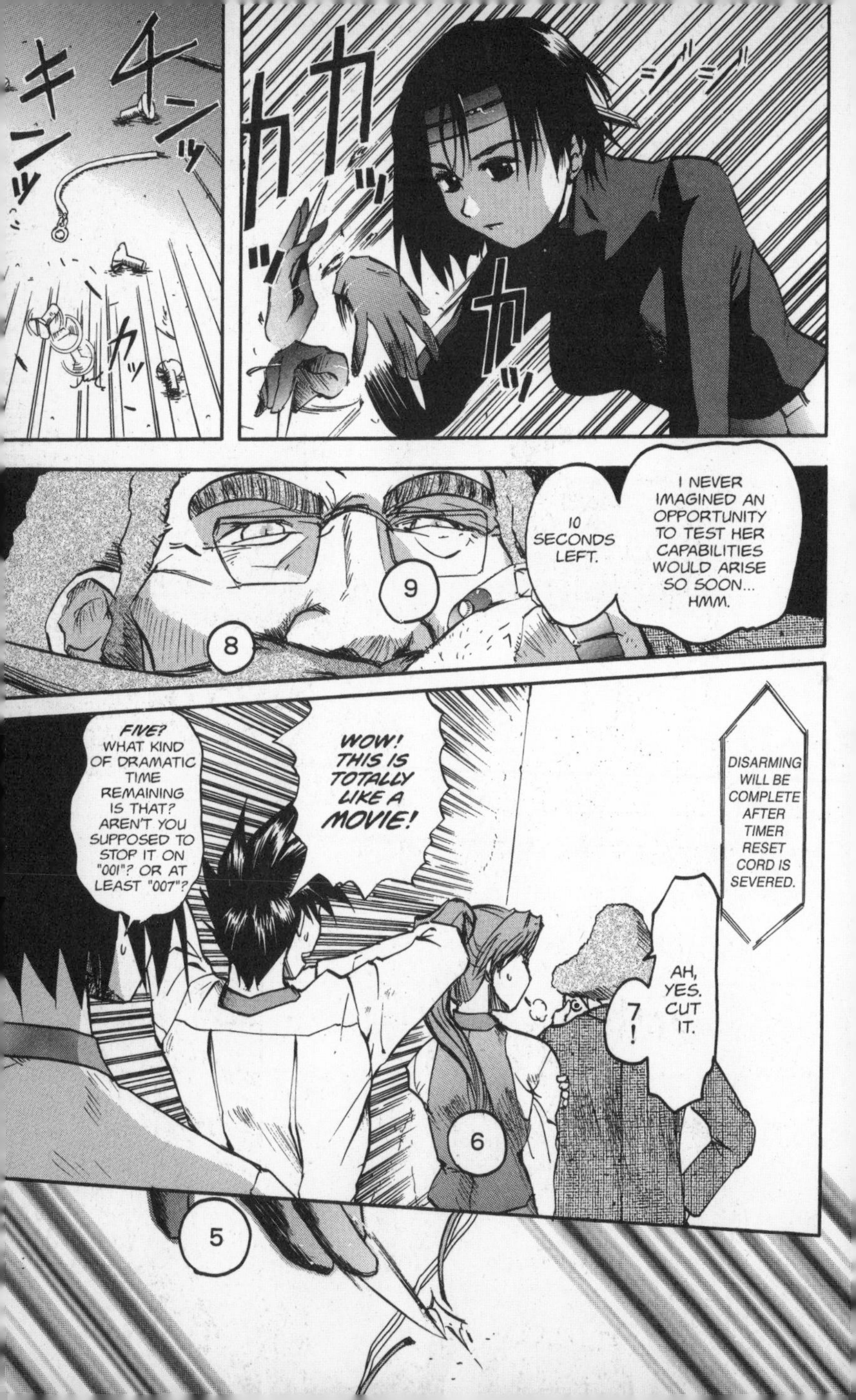

I NEVER IMAGINED AN OPPORTUNITY TO TEST HER CAPABILITIES WOULD ARISE SO SOON... HMM.
10 SECONDS LEFT.
9
8
DISARMING WILL BE COMPLETE AFTER TIMER RESET CORD IS SEVERED.
AH, YES. CUT IT.
7!
WOW! THIS IS TOTALLY LIKE A MOVIE!
FIVE? WHAT KIND OF DRAMATIC TIME REMAINING IS THAT? AREN'T YOU SUPPOSED TO STOP IT ON "001"? OR AT LEAST "007"?
6
5

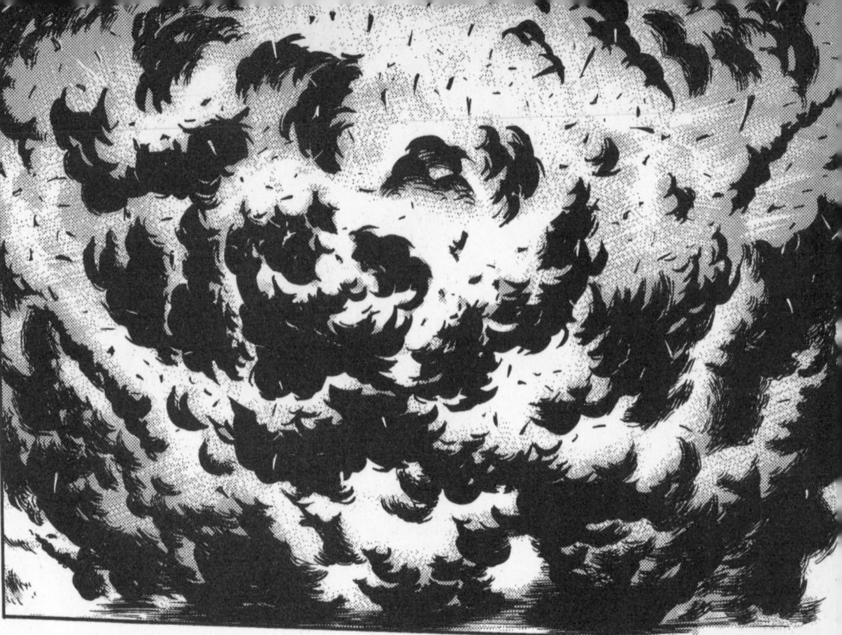

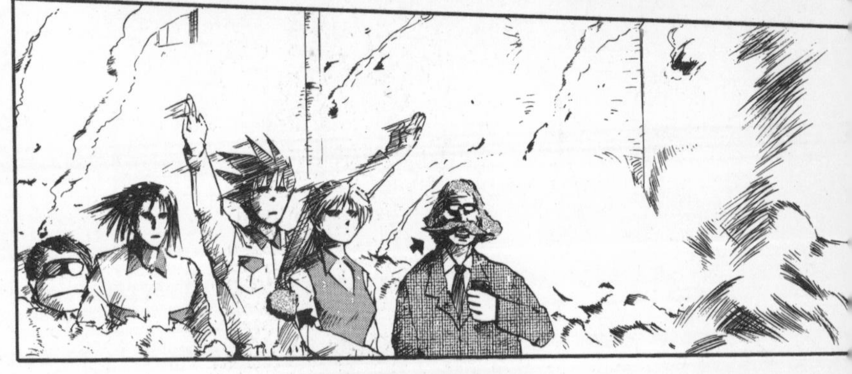

## END MISSION 5

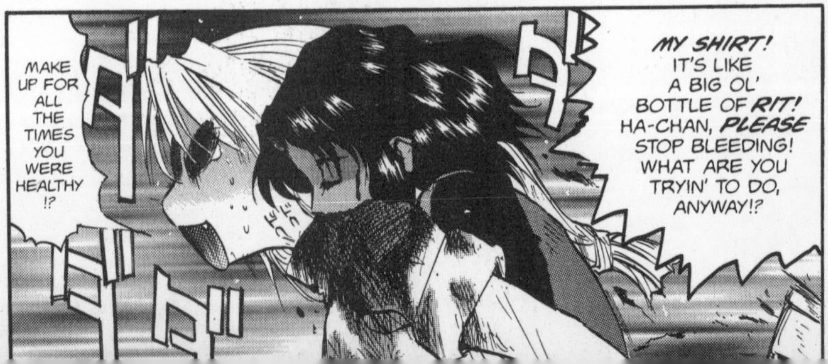
*MY SHIRT!* IT'S LIKE A BIG OL' BOTTLE OF *RIT!* HA-CHAN, *PLEASE* STOP BLEEDING! WHAT ARE YOU TRYIN' TO DO, ANYWAY!?
MAKE UP FOR ALL THE TIMES YOU WERE HEALTHY !?

Featured Character # (abbreviated because this was too much of a pain)

# GOJYOU SHIOUJI

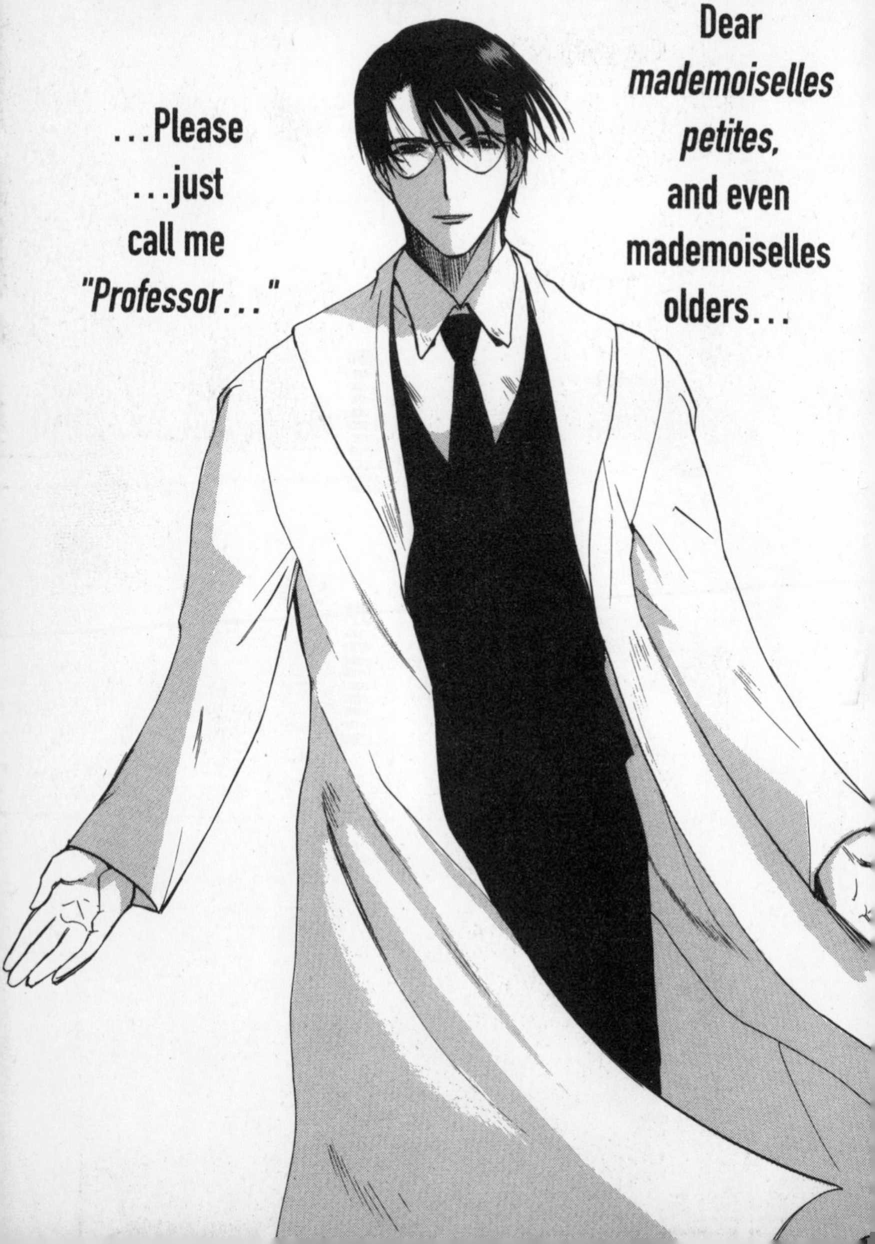
Dear *mademoiselles petites,* and even mademoiselles olders...
...Please ...just call me *"Professor..."*

Featured Character (?)

# ROPPONMATSU TYPE I

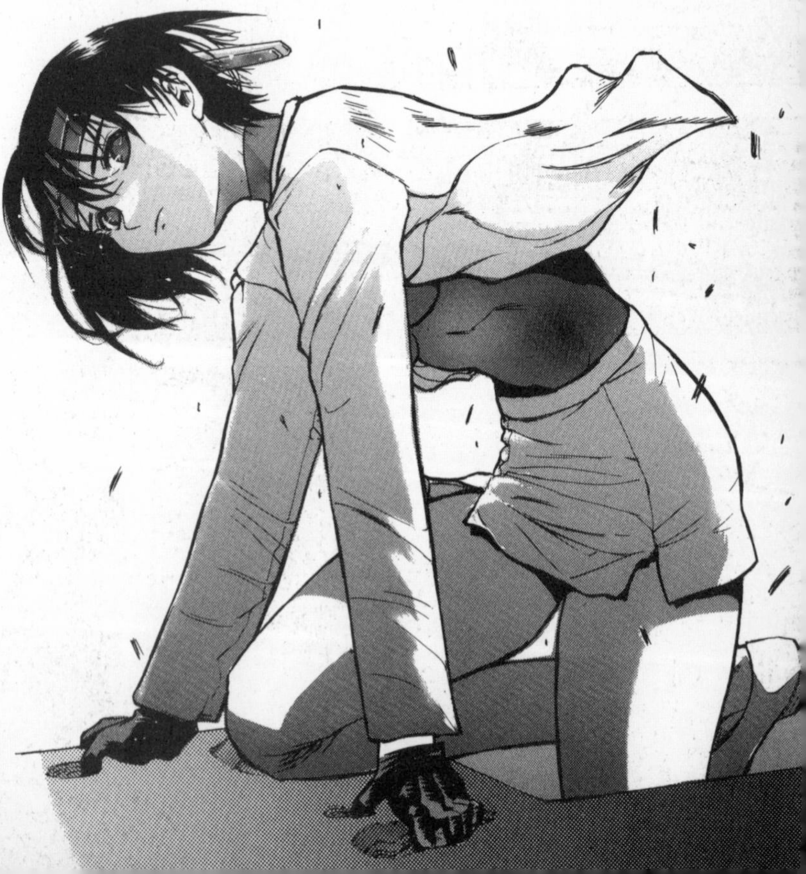

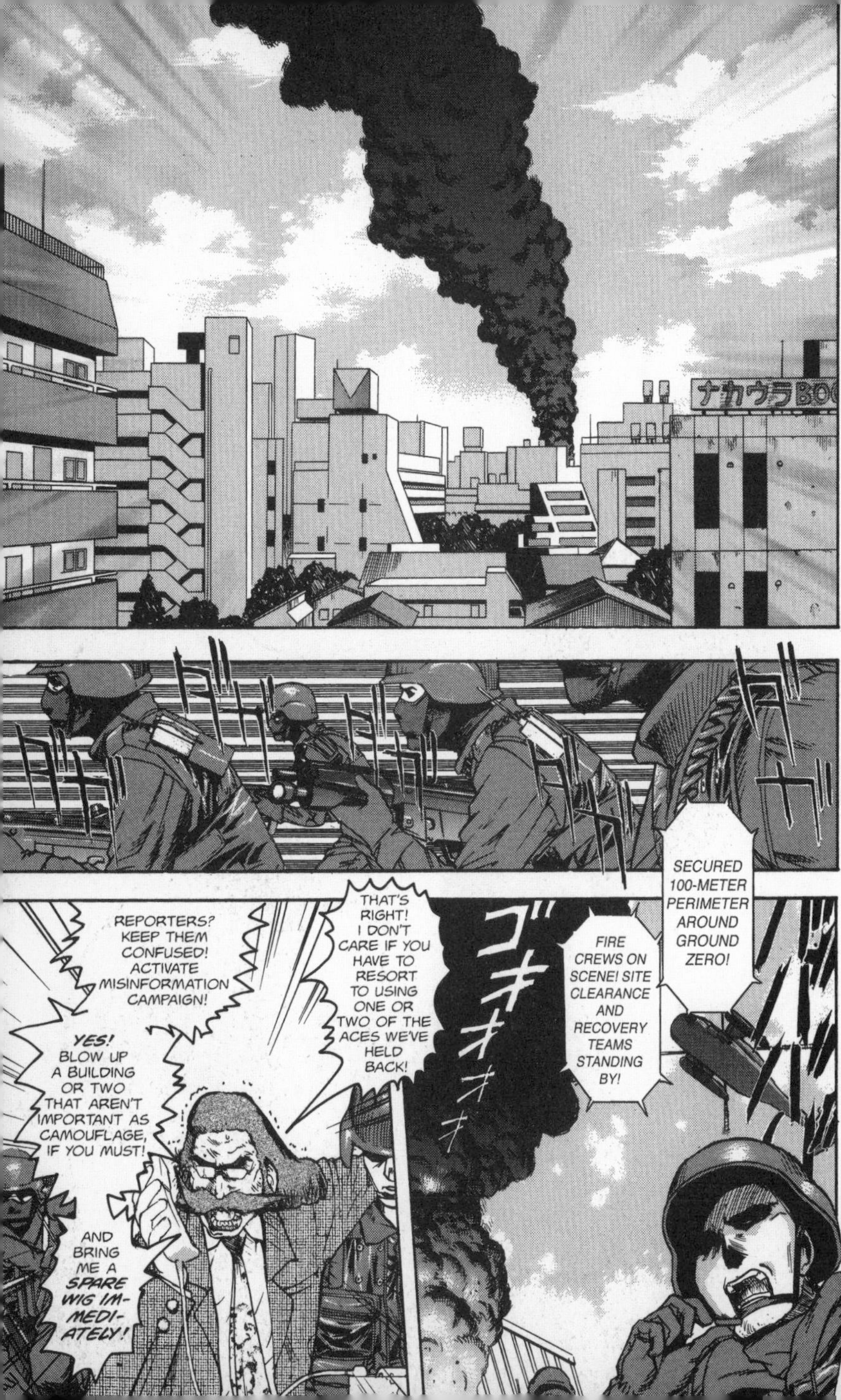
ナカウラBOO
SECURED 100-METER PERIMETER AROUND GROUND ZERO!
FIRE CREWS ON SCENE! SITE CLEARANCE AND RECOVERY TEAMS STANDING BY!
ゴオオオオオ
THAT'S RIGHT! I DON'T CARE IF YOU HAVE TO RESORT TO USING ONE OR TWO OF THE ACES WE'VE HELD BACK!
REPORTERS? KEEP THEM CONFUSED! ACTIVATE MISINFORMATION CAMPAIGN!
*YES!* BLOW UP A BUILDING OR TWO THAT AREN'T IMPORTANT AS CAMOUFLAGE, IF YOU MUST!
AND BRING ME A *SPARE WIG IMMEDIATELY!*

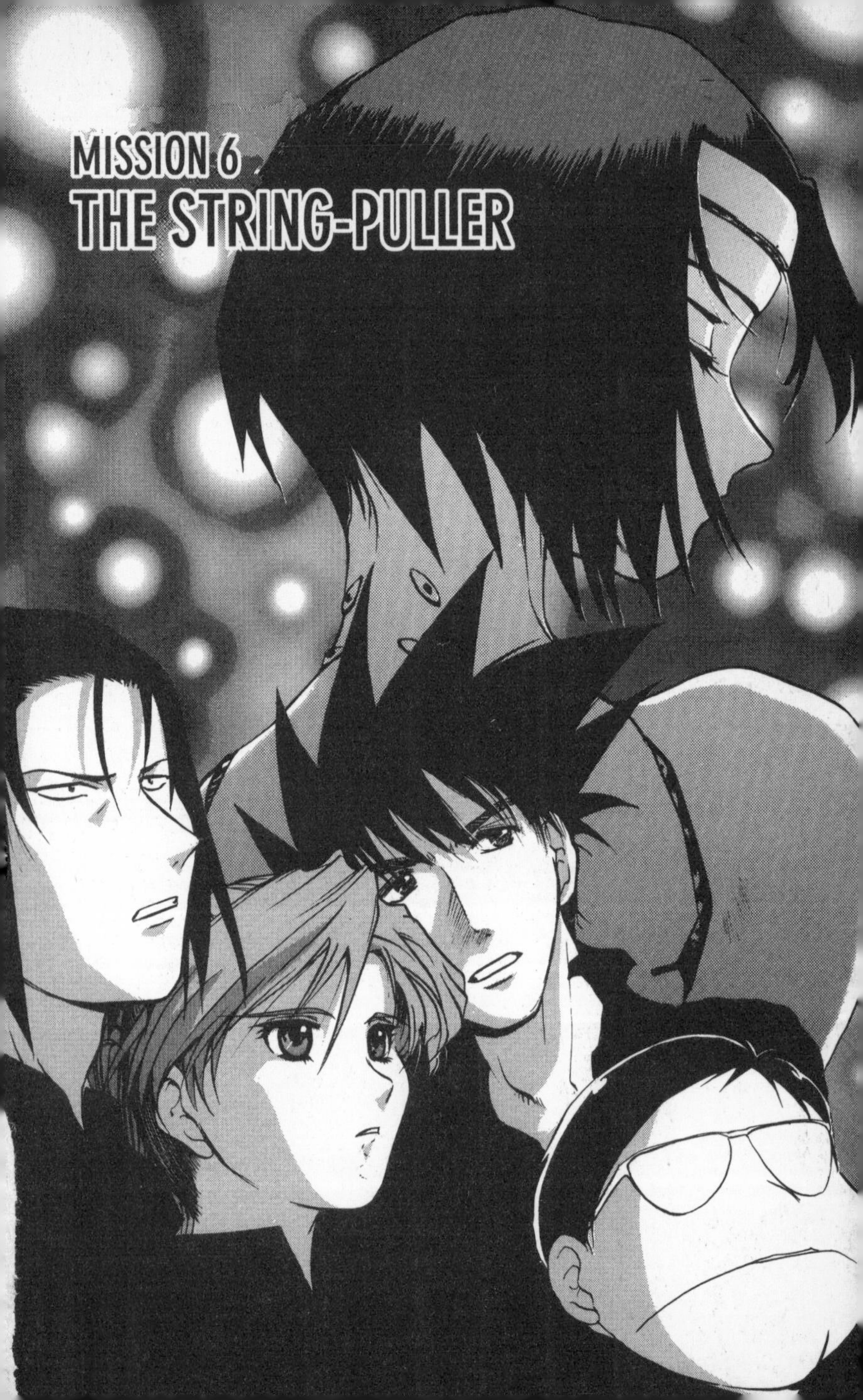
MISSION 6
THE STRING-PULLER

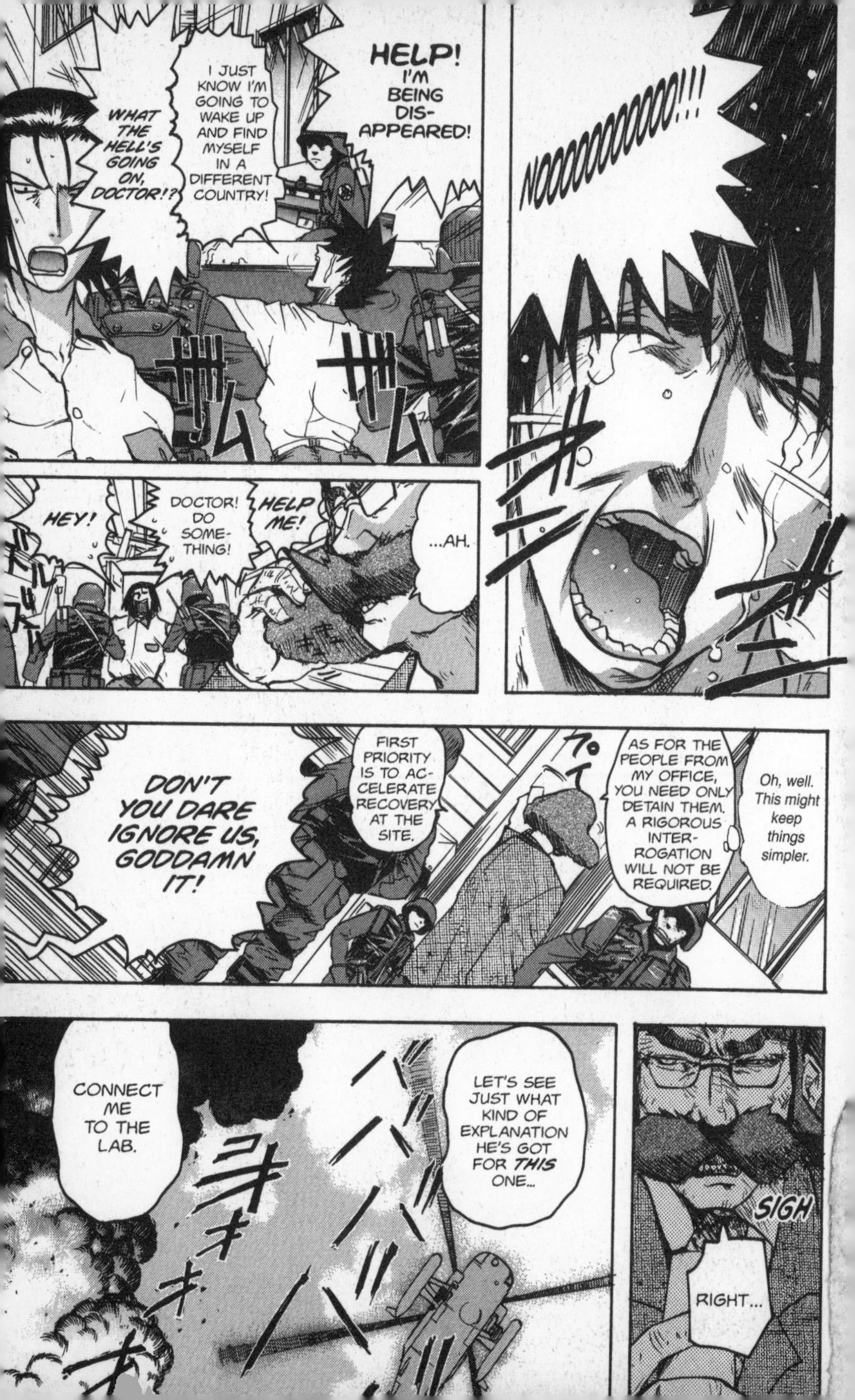

NOOOOOOOOOOO!!!
HELP! I'M BEING DIS-APPEARED!
I JUST KNOW I'M GOING TO WAKE UP AND FIND MYSELF IN A DIFFERENT COUNTRY!
WHAT THE HELL'S GOING ON, DOCTOR!?
...AH.
HELP ME!
DOCTOR! DO SOME-THING!
HEY!
Oh, well. This might keep things simpler.
AS FOR THE PEOPLE FROM MY OFFICE, YOU NEED ONLY DETAIN THEM. A RIGOROUS INTER-ROGATION WILL NOT BE REQUIRED.
FIRST PRIORITY IS TO AC-CELERATE RECOVERY AT THE SITE.
DON'T YOU DARE IGNORE US, GODDAMN IT!
SIGH
RIGHT...
LET'S SEE JUST WHAT KIND OF EXPLANATION HE'S GOT FOR THIS ONE...
CONNECT ME TO THE LAB.

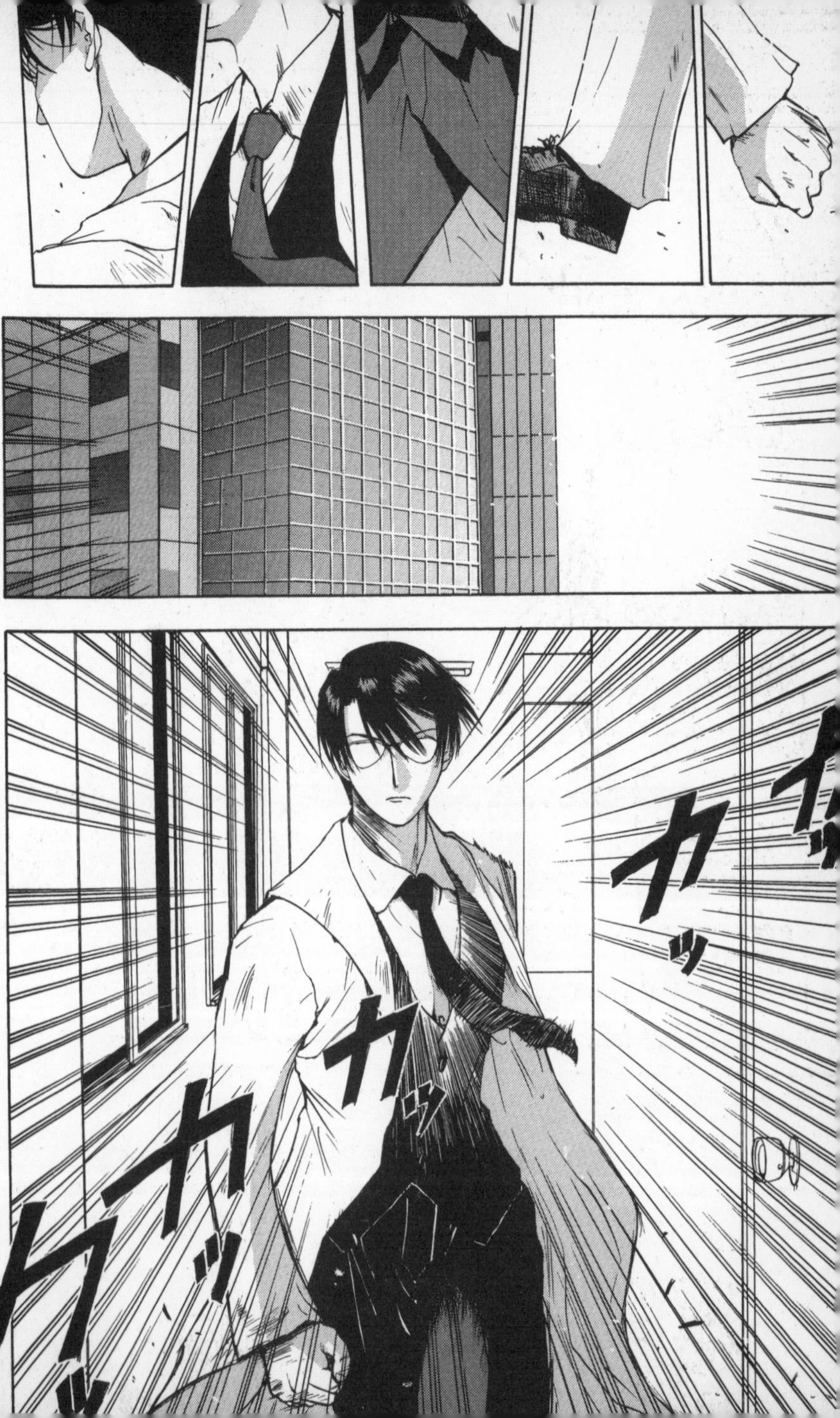

カッ
カッ

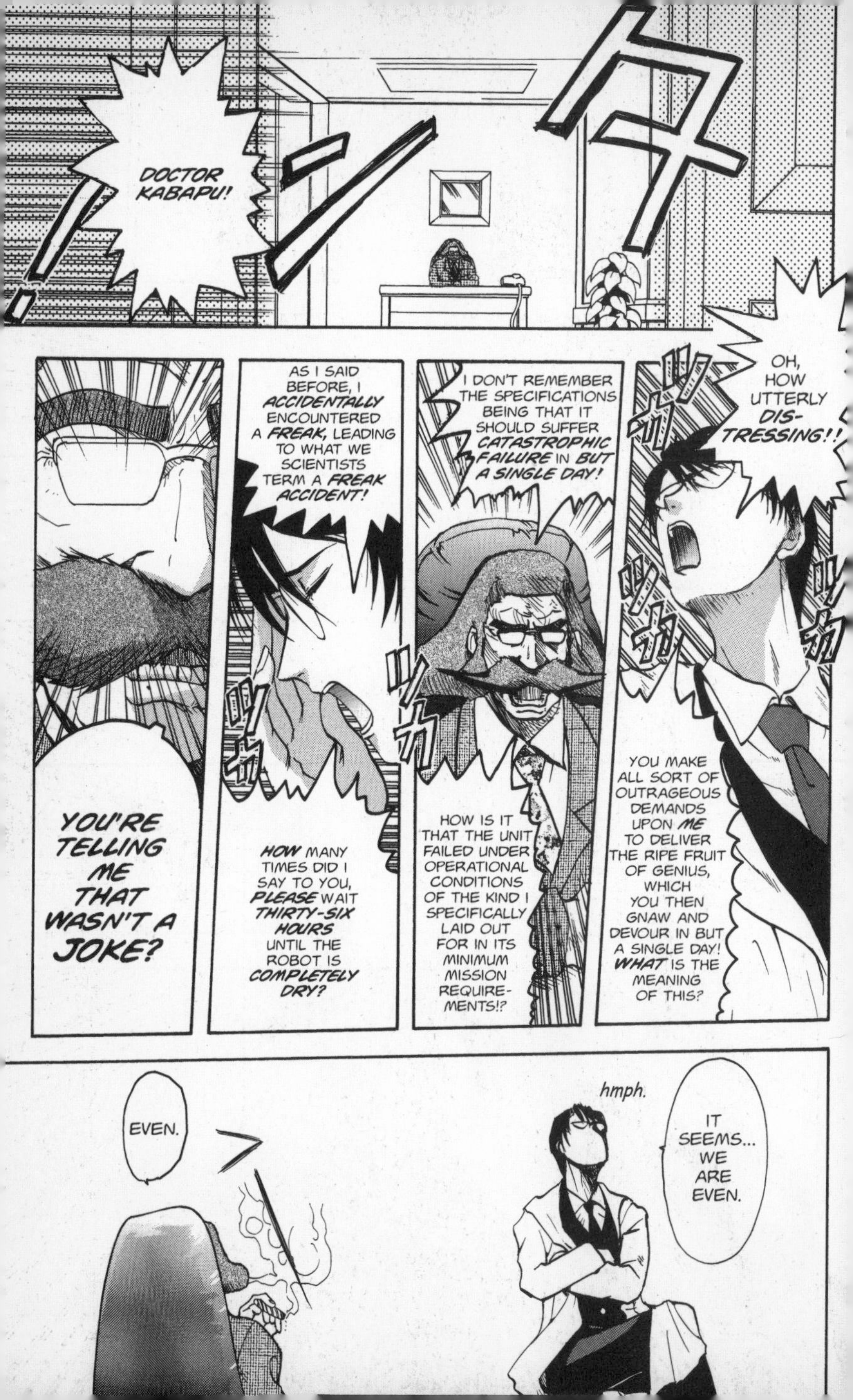
タン!
DOCTOR KABAPU!
OH, HOW UTTERLY DIS-TRESSING!!
YOU MAKE ALL SORT OF OUTRAGEOUS DEMANDS UPON ME TO DELIVER THE RIPE FRUIT OF GENIUS, WHICH YOU THEN GNAW AND DEVOUR IN BUT A SINGLE DAY! WHAT IS THE MEANING OF THIS?
I DON'T REMEMBER THE SPECIFICATIONS BEING THAT IT SHOULD SUFFER CATASTROPHIC FAILURE IN BUT A SINGLE DAY!
HOW IS IT THAT THE UNIT FAILED UNDER OPERATIONAL CONDITIONS OF THE KIND I SPECIFICALLY LAID OUT FOR IN ITS MINIMUM MISSION REQUIRE-MENTS!?
AS I SAID BEFORE, I ACCIDENTALLY ENCOUNTERED A FREAK, LEADING TO WHAT WE SCIENTISTS TERM A FREAK ACCIDENT!
HOW MANY TIMES DID I SAY TO YOU, PLEASE WAIT THIRTY-SIX HOURS UNTIL THE ROBOT IS COMPLETELY DRY?
YOU'RE TELLING ME THAT WASN'T A JOKE?
hmph.
IT SEEMS... WE ARE EVEN.
EVEN.

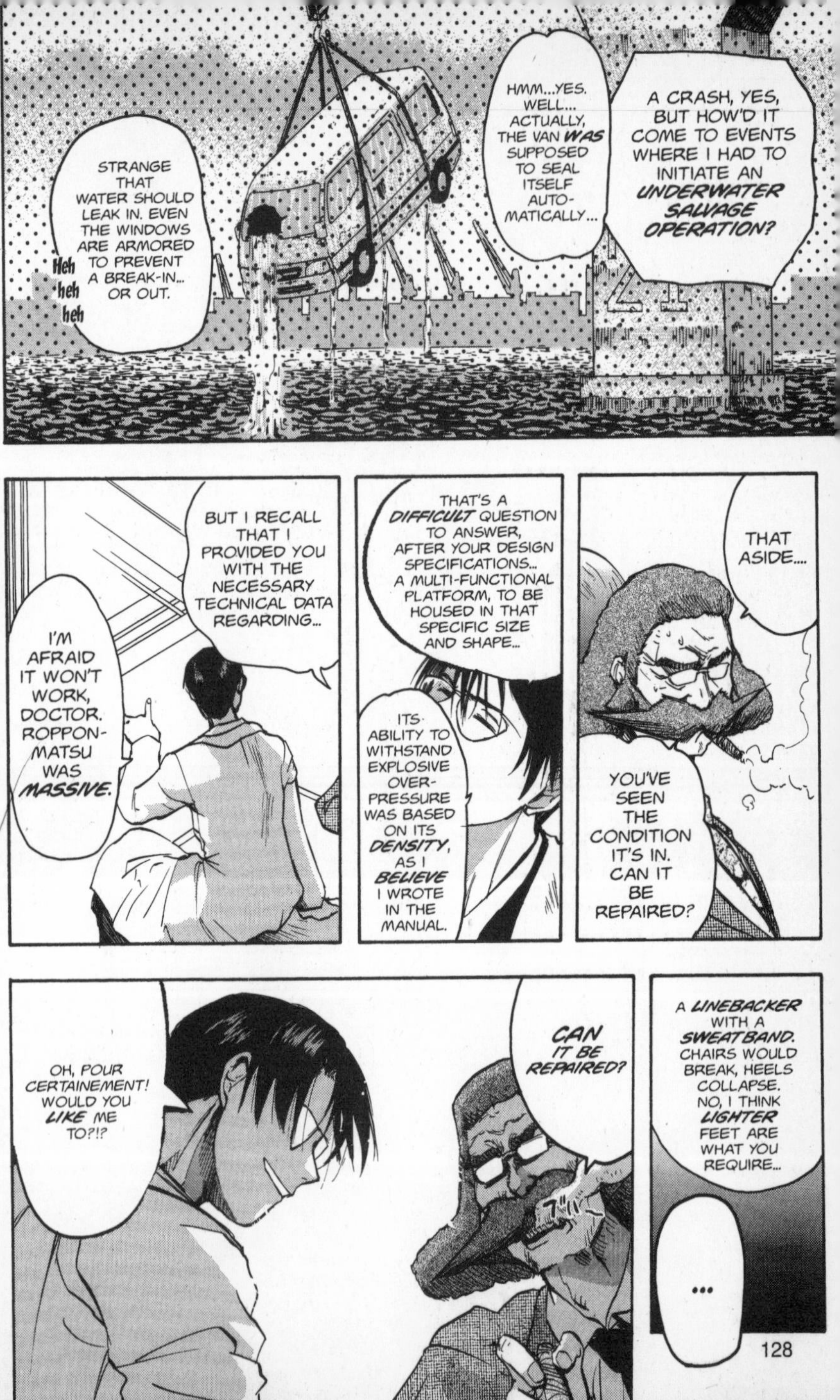
A CRASH, YES, BUT HOW'D IT COME TO EVENTS WHERE I HAD TO INITIATE AN UNDERWATER SALVAGE OPERATION?
HMM...YES. WELL... ACTUALLY, THE VAN WAS SUPPOSED TO SEAL ITSELF AUTO-MATICALLY...
STRANGE THAT WATER SHOULD LEAK IN. EVEN THE WINDOWS ARE ARMORED TO PREVENT A BREAK-IN... OR OUT.
Heh heh heh
THAT ASIDE....
YOU'VE SEEN THE CONDITION IT'S IN. CAN IT BE REPAIRED?
THAT'S A DIFFICULT QUESTION TO ANSWER, AFTER YOUR DESIGN SPECIFICATIONS... A MULTI-FUNCTIONAL PLATFORM, TO BE HOUSED IN THAT SPECIFIC SIZE AND SHAPE...
ITS ABILITY TO WITHSTAND EXPLOSIVE OVER-PRESSURE WAS BASED ON ITS DENSITY, AS I BELIEVE I WROTE IN THE MANUAL.
BUT I RECALL THAT I PROVIDED YOU WITH THE NECESSARY TECHNICAL DATA REGARDING...
I'M AFRAID IT WON'T WORK, DOCTOR. ROPPON-MATSU WAS MASSIVE.
A LINEBACKER WITH A SWEATBAND. CHAIRS WOULD BREAK, HEELS COLLAPSE. NO, I THINK LIGHTER FEET ARE WHAT YOU REQUIRE...
...
CAN IT BE REPAIRED?
OH, POUR CERTAINEMENT! WOULD YOU LIKE ME TO?!?

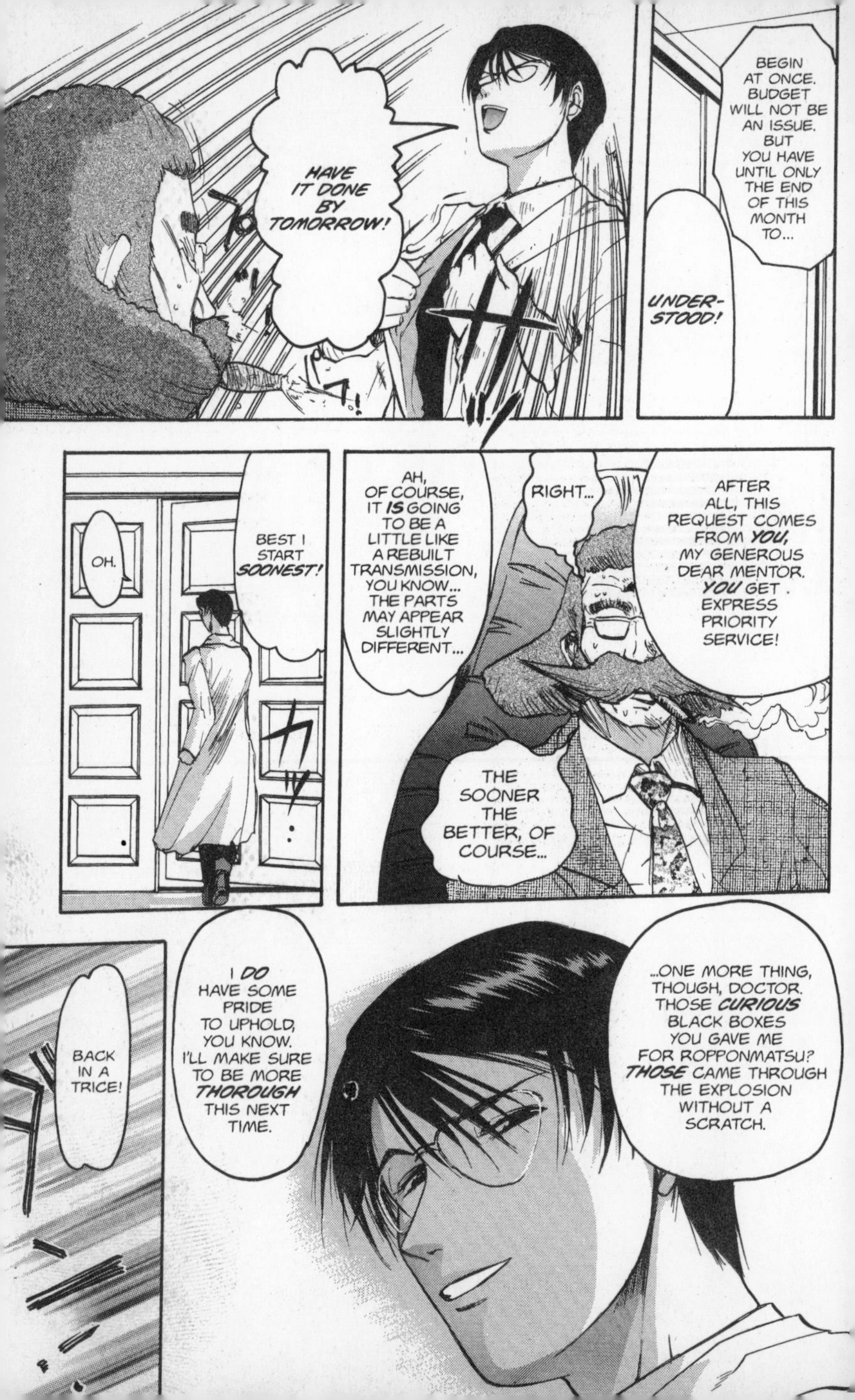
BEGIN AT ONCE. BUDGET WILL NOT BE AN ISSUE. BUT YOU HAVE UNTIL ONLY THE END OF THIS MONTH TO...
UNDER-STOOD!
HAVE IT DONE BY TOMORROW!
AFTER ALL, THIS REQUEST COMES FROM YOU, MY GENEROUS DEAR MENTOR. YOU GET EXPRESS PRIORITY SERVICE!
RIGHT...
AH, OF COURSE, IT IS GOING TO BE A LITTLE LIKE A REBUILT TRANSMISSION, YOU KNOW... THE PARTS MAY APPEAR SLIGHTLY DIFFERENT...
THE SOONER THE BETTER, OF COURSE...
BEST I START SOONEST!
OH.
...ONE MORE THING, THOUGH, DOCTOR. THOSE CURIOUS BLACK BOXES YOU GAVE ME FOR ROPPONMATSU? THOSE CAME THROUGH THE EXPLOSION WITHOUT A SCRATCH.
I DO HAVE SOME PRIDE TO UPHOLD, YOU KNOW. I'LL MAKE SURE TO BE MORE THOROUGH THIS NEXT TIME.
BACK IN A TRICE!

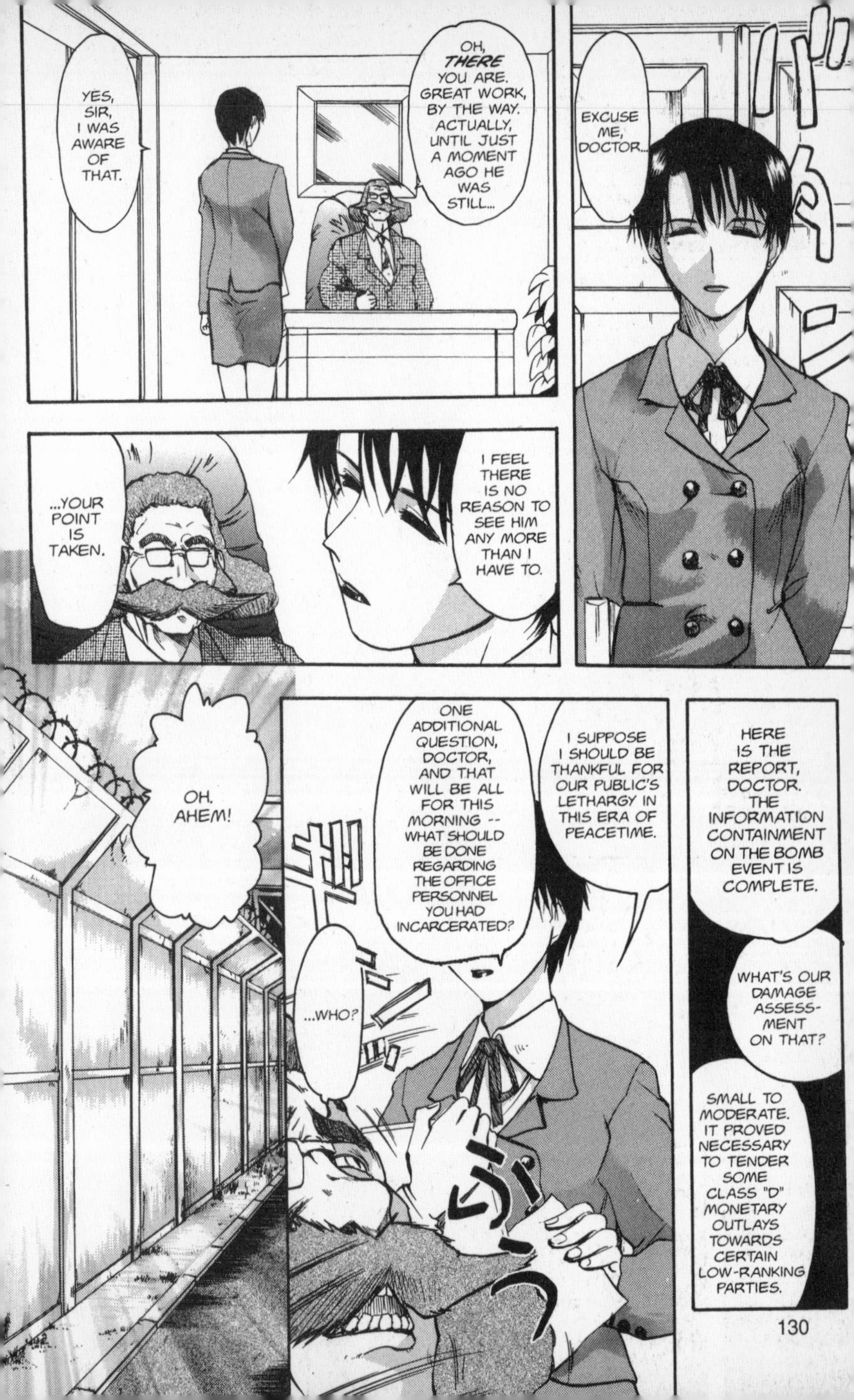
EXCUSE ME, DOCTOR...
OH, *THERE* YOU ARE. GREAT WORK, BY THE WAY. ACTUALLY, UNTIL JUST A MOMENT AGO HE WAS STILL...
YES, SIR, I WAS AWARE OF THAT.
I FEEL THERE IS NO REASON TO SEE HIM ANY MORE THAN I HAVE TO.
...YOUR POINT IS TAKEN.
HERE IS THE REPORT, DOCTOR. THE INFORMATION CONTAINMENT ON THE BOMB EVENT IS COMPLETE.
WHAT'S OUR DAMAGE ASSESS-MENT ON THAT?
SMALL TO MODERATE. IT PROVED NECESSARY TO TENDER SOME CLASS "D" MONETARY OUTLAYS TOWARDS CERTAIN LOW-RANKING PARTIES.
I SUPPOSE I SHOULD BE THANKFUL FOR OUR PUBLIC'S LETHARGY IN THIS ERA OF PEACETIME.
ONE ADDITIONAL QUESTION, DOCTOR, AND THAT WILL BE ALL FOR THIS MORNING -- WHAT SHOULD BE DONE REGARDING THE OFFICE PERSONNEL YOU HAD INCARCERATED?
...WHO?
OH. AHEM!

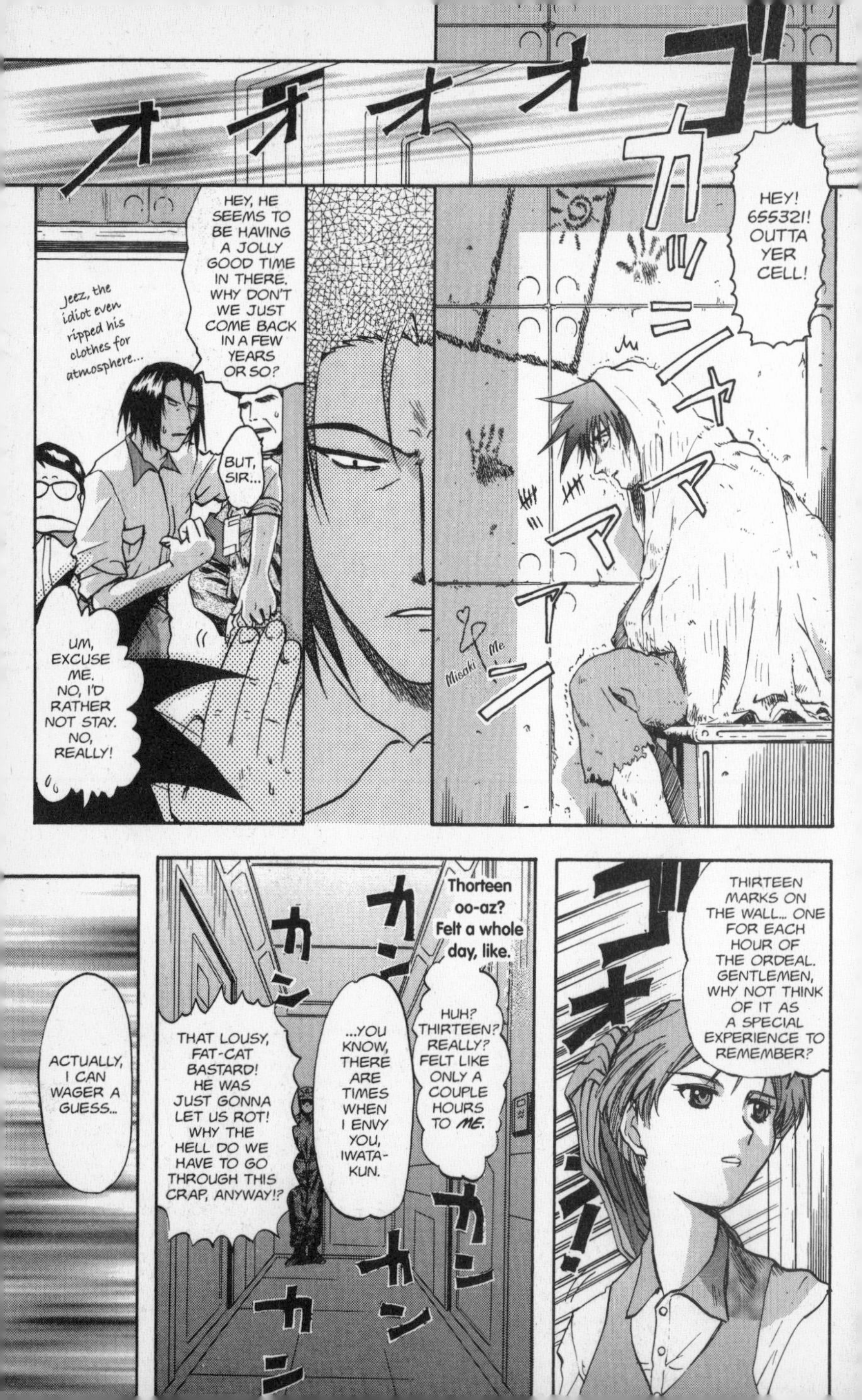
HEY! 655321! OUTTA YER CELL!
Misaki ♡ Me
HEY, HE SEEMS TO BE HAVING A JOLLY GOOD TIME IN THERE. WHY DON'T WE JUST COME BACK IN A FEW YEARS OR SO?
Jeez, the idiot even ripped his clothes for atmosphere...
BUT, SIR...
UM, EXCUSE ME. NO, I'D RATHER NOT STAY. NO, REALLY!
THIRTEEN MARKS ON THE WALL... ONE FOR EACH HOUR OF THE ORDEAL. GENTLEMEN, WHY NOT THINK OF IT AS A SPECIAL EXPERIENCE TO REMEMBER?
Thorteen oo-az? Felt a whole day, like.
HUH? THIRTEEN? REALLY? FELT LIKE ONLY A COUPLE HOURS TO ME.
...YOU KNOW, THERE ARE TIMES WHEN I ENVY YOU, IWATA-KUN.
THAT LOUSY, FAT-CAT BASTARD! HE WAS JUST GONNA LET US ROT! WHY THE HELL DO WE HAVE TO GO THROUGH THIS CRAP, ANYWAY!?
ACTUALLY, I CAN WAGER A GUESS...

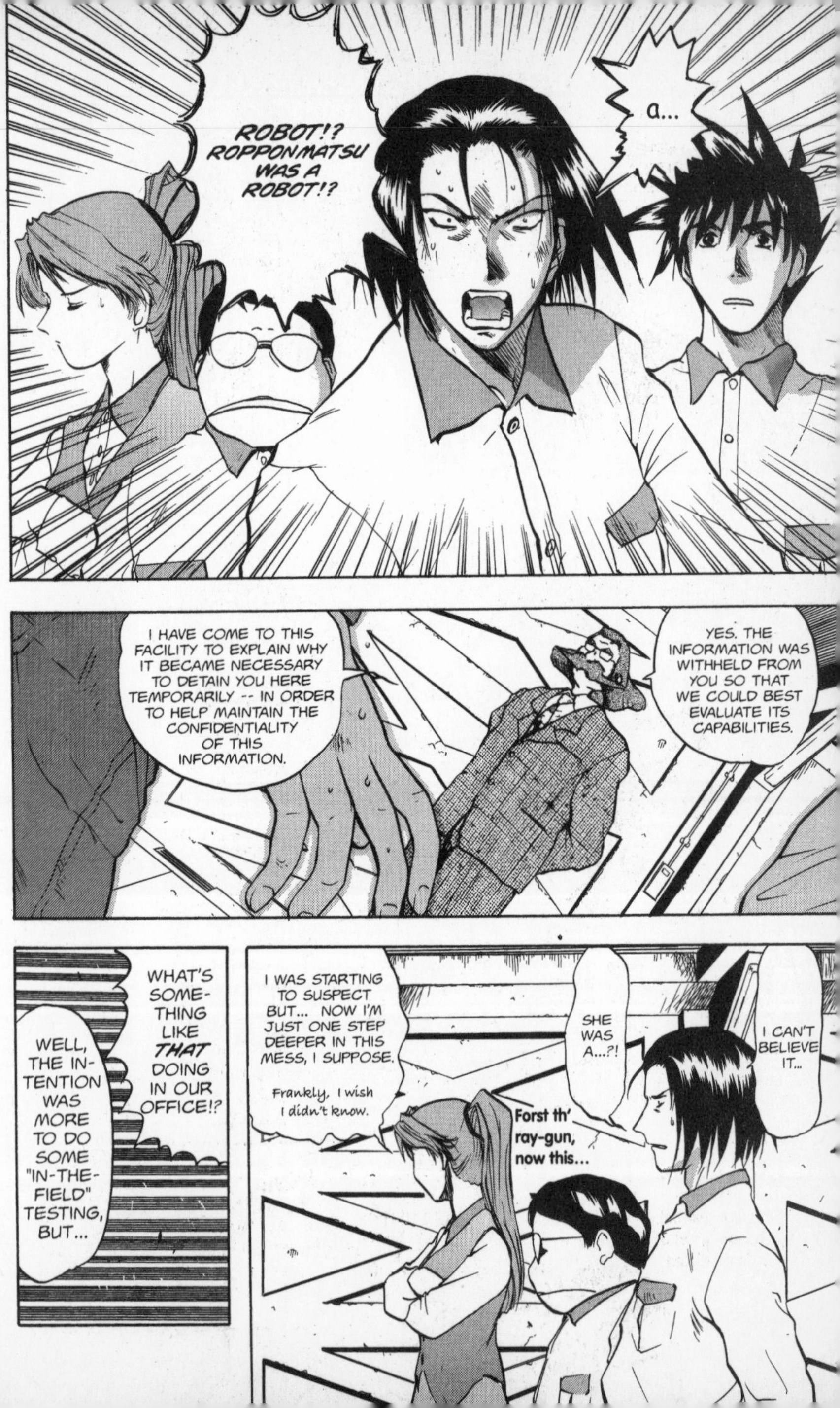
a...
ROBOT!? ROPPONMATSU WAS A ROBOT!?
YES. THE INFORMATION WAS WITHHELD FROM YOU SO THAT WE COULD BEST EVALUATE ITS CAPABILITIES.
I HAVE COME TO THIS FACILITY TO EXPLAIN WHY IT BECAME NECESSARY TO DETAIN YOU HERE TEMPORARILY -- IN ORDER TO HELP MAINTAIN THE CONFIDENTIALITY OF THIS INFORMATION.
I CAN'T BELIEVE IT...
SHE WAS A...?!
Forst th' ray-gun, now this...
I WAS STARTING TO SUSPECT BUT... NOW I'M JUST ONE STEP DEEPER IN THIS MESS, I SUPPOSE.
Frankly, I wish I didn't know.
WHAT'S SOME-THING LIKE THAT DOING IN OUR OFFICE!?
WELL, THE IN-TENTION WAS MORE TO DO SOME "IN-THE-FIELD" TESTING, BUT...

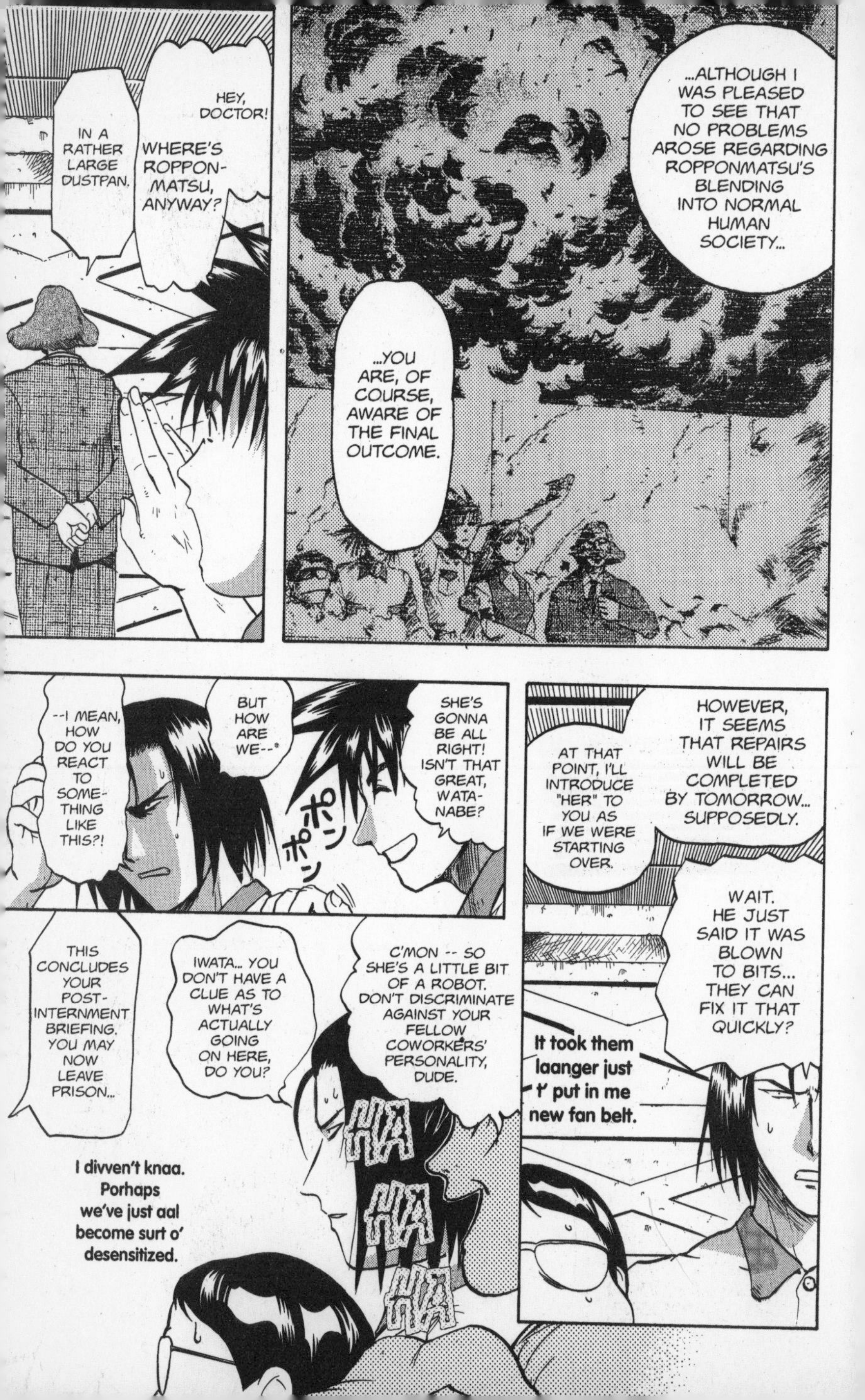
...ALTHOUGH I WAS PLEASED TO SEE THAT NO PROBLEMS AROSE REGARDING ROPPONMATSU'S BLENDING INTO NORMAL HUMAN SOCIETY...
...YOU ARE, OF COURSE, AWARE OF THE FINAL OUTCOME.
HEY, DOCTOR!
WHERE'S ROPPONMATSU, ANYWAY?
IN A RATHER LARGE DUSTPAN.
HOWEVER, IT SEEMS THAT REPAIRS WILL BE COMPLETED BY TOMORROW... SUPPOSEDLY.
AT THAT POINT, I'LL INTRODUCE "HER" TO YOU AS IF WE WERE STARTING OVER.
SHE'S GONNA BE ALL RIGHT! ISN'T THAT GREAT, WATANABE?
ポンポン
BUT HOW ARE WE--
--I MEAN, HOW DO YOU REACT TO SOMETHING LIKE THIS?!
WAIT. HE JUST SAID IT WAS BLOWN TO BITS... THEY CAN FIX IT THAT QUICKLY?
It took them laanger just t' put in me new fan belt.
C'MON -- SO SHE'S A LITTLE BIT OF A ROBOT. DON'T DISCRIMINATE AGAINST YOUR FELLOW COWORKERS' PERSONALITY, DUDE.
HA HA HA
IWATA... YOU DON'T HAVE A CLUE AS TO WHAT'S ACTUALLY GOING ON HERE, DO YOU?
THIS CONCLUDES YOUR POST-INTERNMENT BRIEFING. YOU MAY NOW LEAVE PRISON...
I divven't knaa. Porhaps we've just aal become surt o' desensitized.

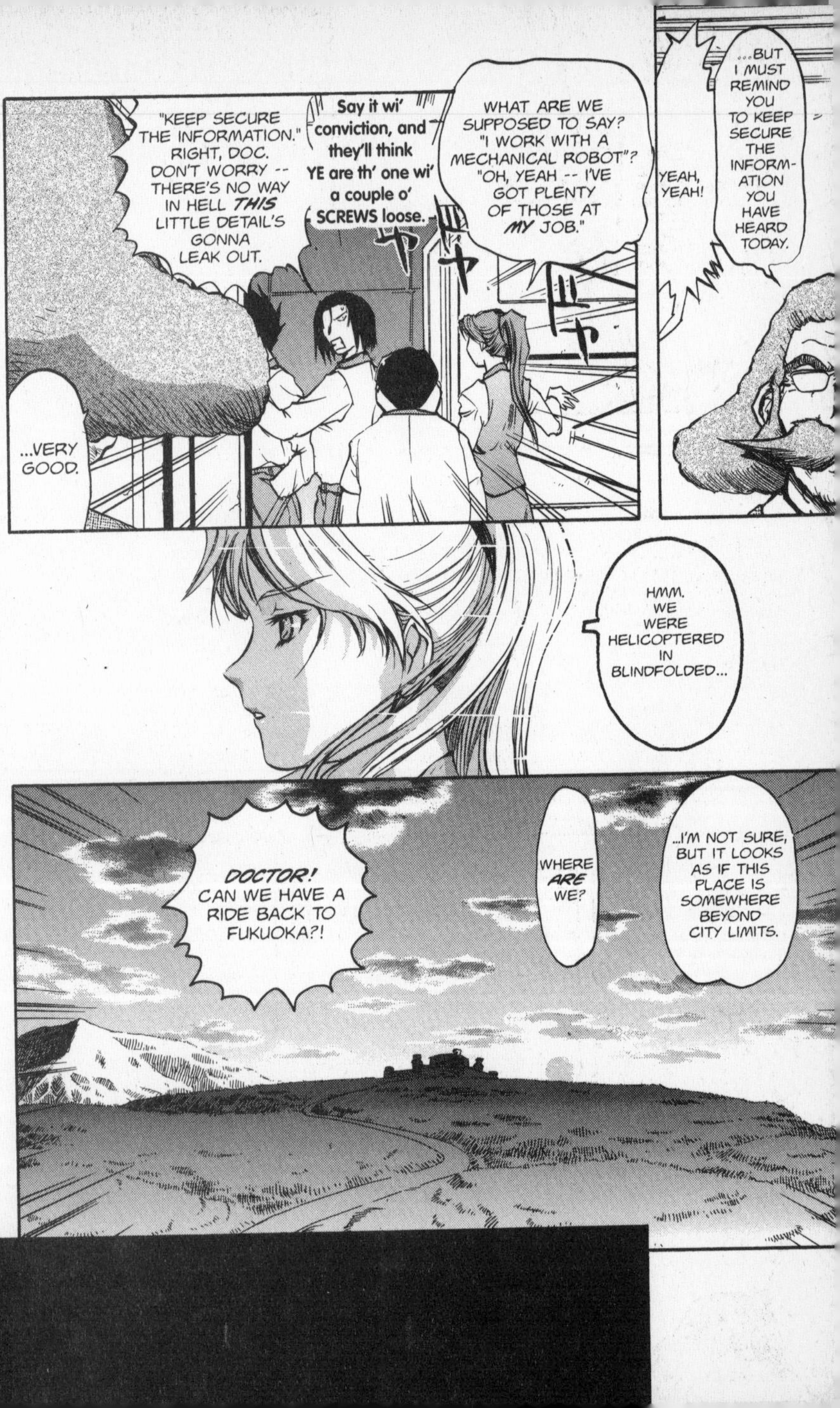
...BUT I MUST REMIND YOU TO KEEP SECURE THE INFORMATION YOU HAVE HEARD TODAY.
YEAH, YEAH!
WHAT ARE WE SUPPOSED TO SAY? "I WORK WITH A MECHANICAL ROBOT"? "OH, YEAH -- I'VE GOT PLENTY OF THOSE AT *MY* JOB."
Say it wi' conviction, and they'll think YE are th' one wi' a couple o' SCREWS loose.
"KEEP SECURE THE INFORMATION." RIGHT, DOC. DON'T WORRY -- THERE'S NO WAY IN HELL *THIS* LITTLE DETAIL'S GONNA LEAK OUT.
...VERY GOOD.
HMM. WE WERE HELICOPTERED IN BLINDFOLDED...
...I'M NOT SURE, BUT IT LOOKS AS IF THIS PLACE IS SOMEWHERE BEYOND CITY LIMITS.
WHERE *ARE* WE?
*DOCTOR!* CAN WE HAVE A RIDE BACK TO FUKUOKA?!

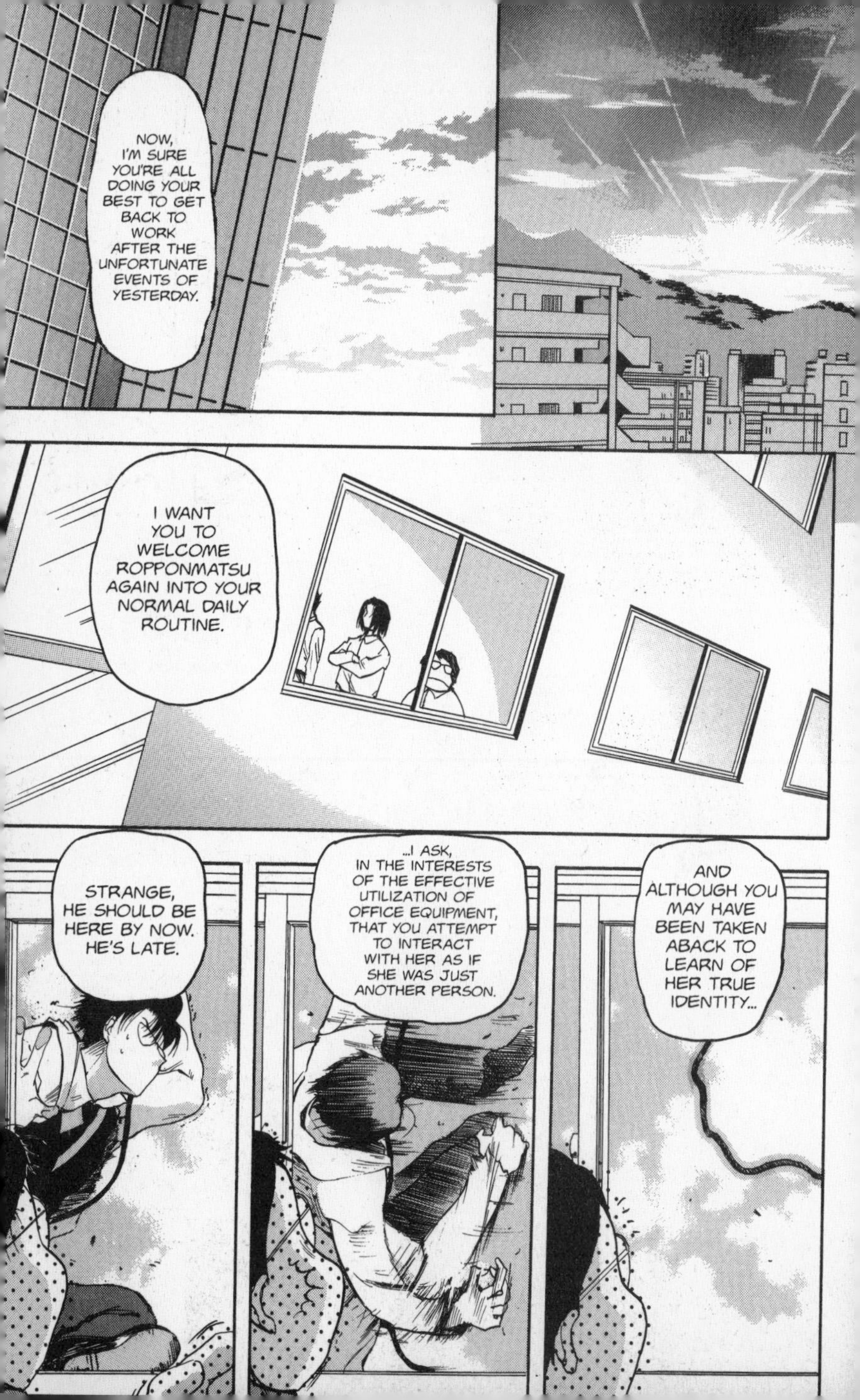
NOW, I'M SURE YOU'RE ALL DOING YOUR BEST TO GET BACK TO WORK AFTER THE UNFORTUNATE EVENTS OF YESTERDAY.
I WANT YOU TO WELCOME ROPPONMATSU AGAIN INTO YOUR NORMAL DAILY ROUTINE.
AND ALTHOUGH YOU MAY HAVE BEEN TAKEN ABACK TO LEARN OF HER TRUE IDENTITY...
...I ASK, IN THE INTERESTS OF THE EFFECTIVE UTILIZATION OF OFFICE EQUIPMENT, THAT YOU ATTEMPT TO INTERACT WITH HER AS IF SHE WAS JUST ANOTHER PERSON.
STRANGE, HE SHOULD BE HERE BY NOW. HE'S LATE.

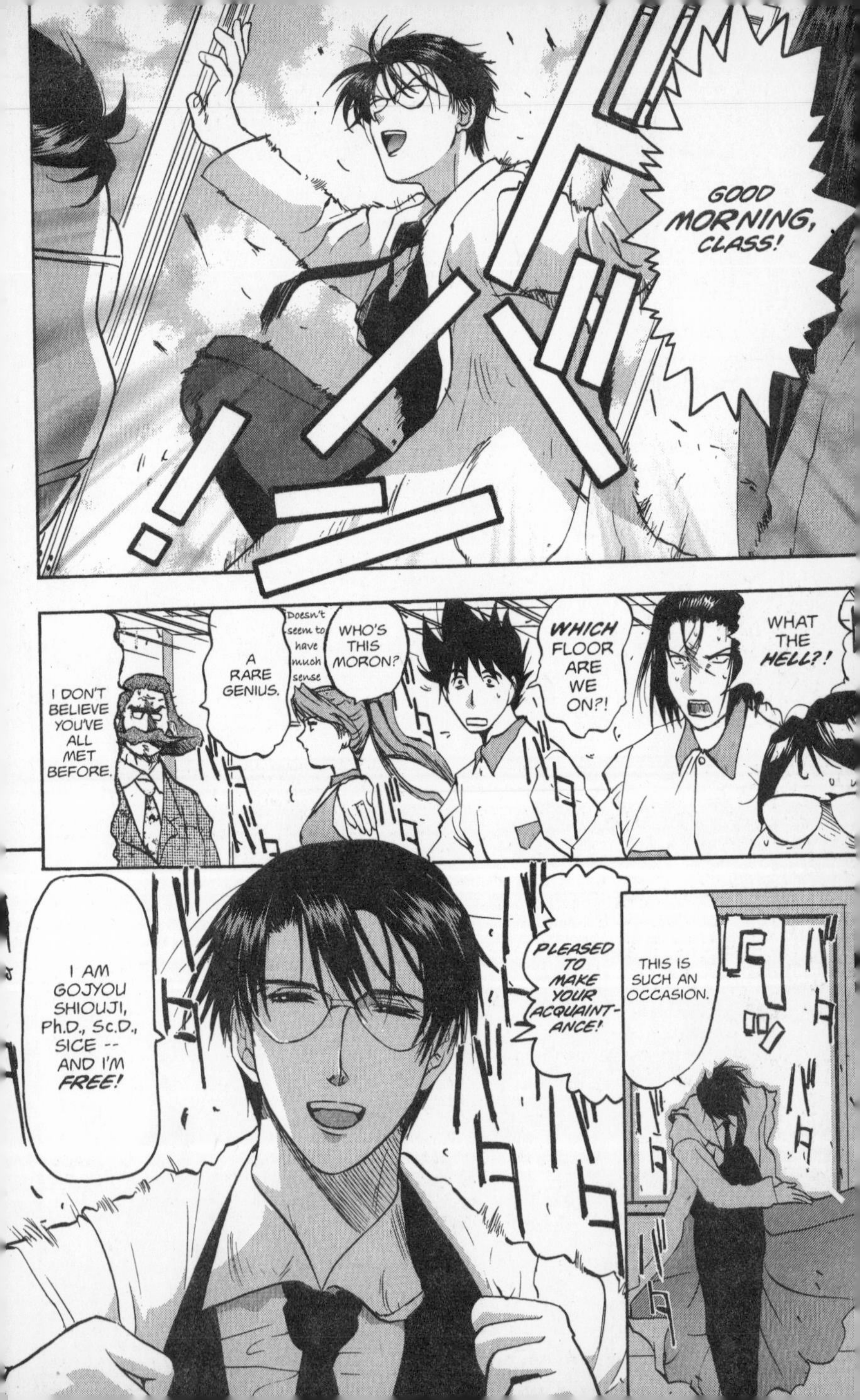
GOOD MORNING, CLASS!
WHAT THE HELL?!
WHICH FLOOR ARE WE ON?!
WHO'S THIS MORON?
Doesn't seem to have much sense
A RARE GENIUS.
I DON'T BELIEVE YOU'VE ALL MET BEFORE.
THIS IS SUCH AN OCCASION.
PLEASED TO MAKE YOUR ACQUAINTANCE!
I AM GOJYOU SHIOUJI, Ph.D., Sc.D., SICE -- AND I'M FREE!

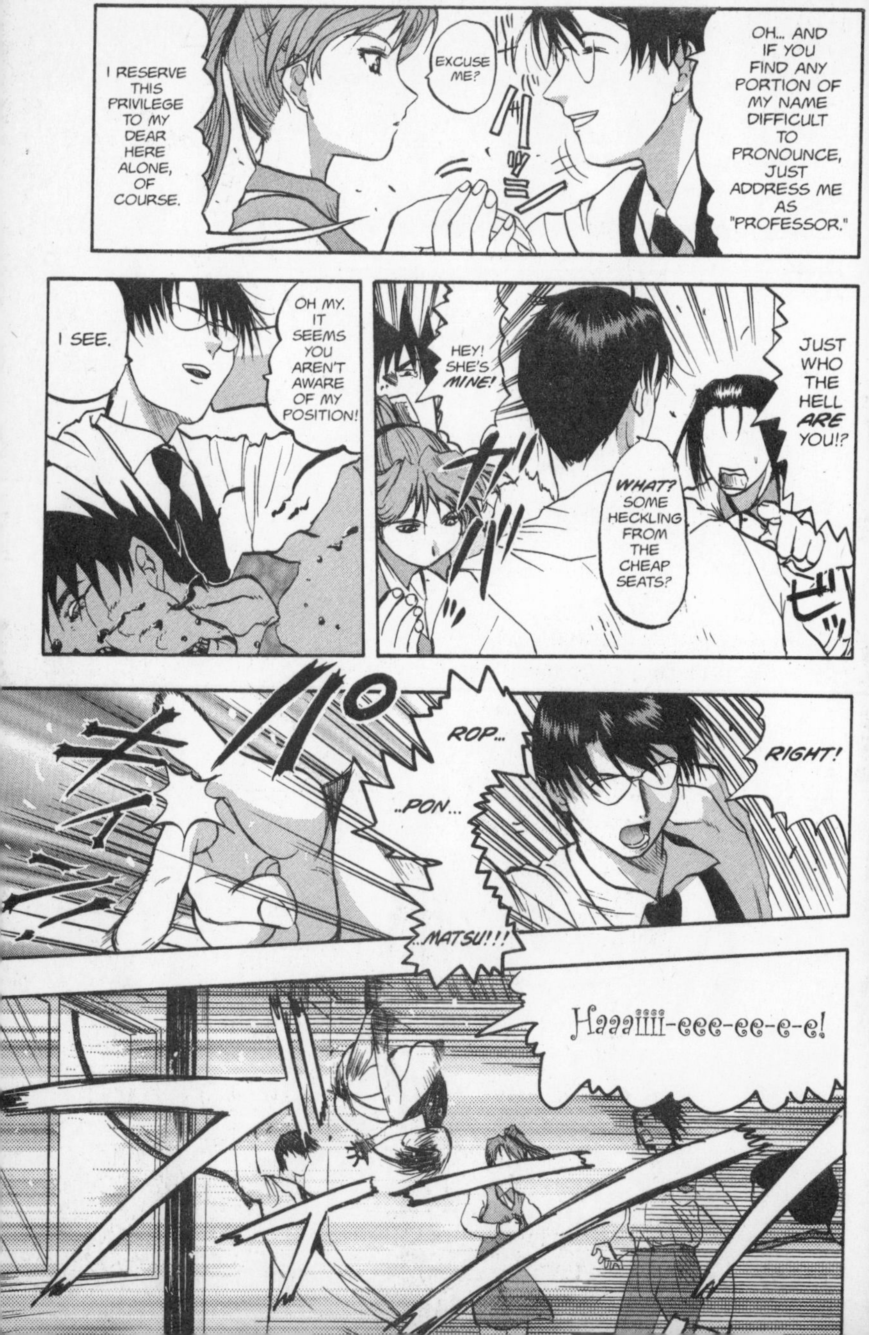
OH... AND IF YOU FIND ANY PORTION OF MY NAME DIFFICULT TO PRONOUNCE, JUST ADDRESS ME AS "PROFESSOR."
EXCUSE ME?
I RESERVE THIS PRIVILEGE TO MY DEAR HERE ALONE, OF COURSE.
JUST WHO THE HELL *ARE* YOU!?
HEY! SHE'S *MINE!*
*WHAT?* SOME HECKLING FROM THE CHEAP SEATS?
OH MY. IT SEEMS YOU AREN'T AWARE OF MY POSITION!
I SEE.
*RIGHT!*
*ROP...*
*..PON...*
*...MATSU!!!*
Haaaiiii-eee-ee-e-e!

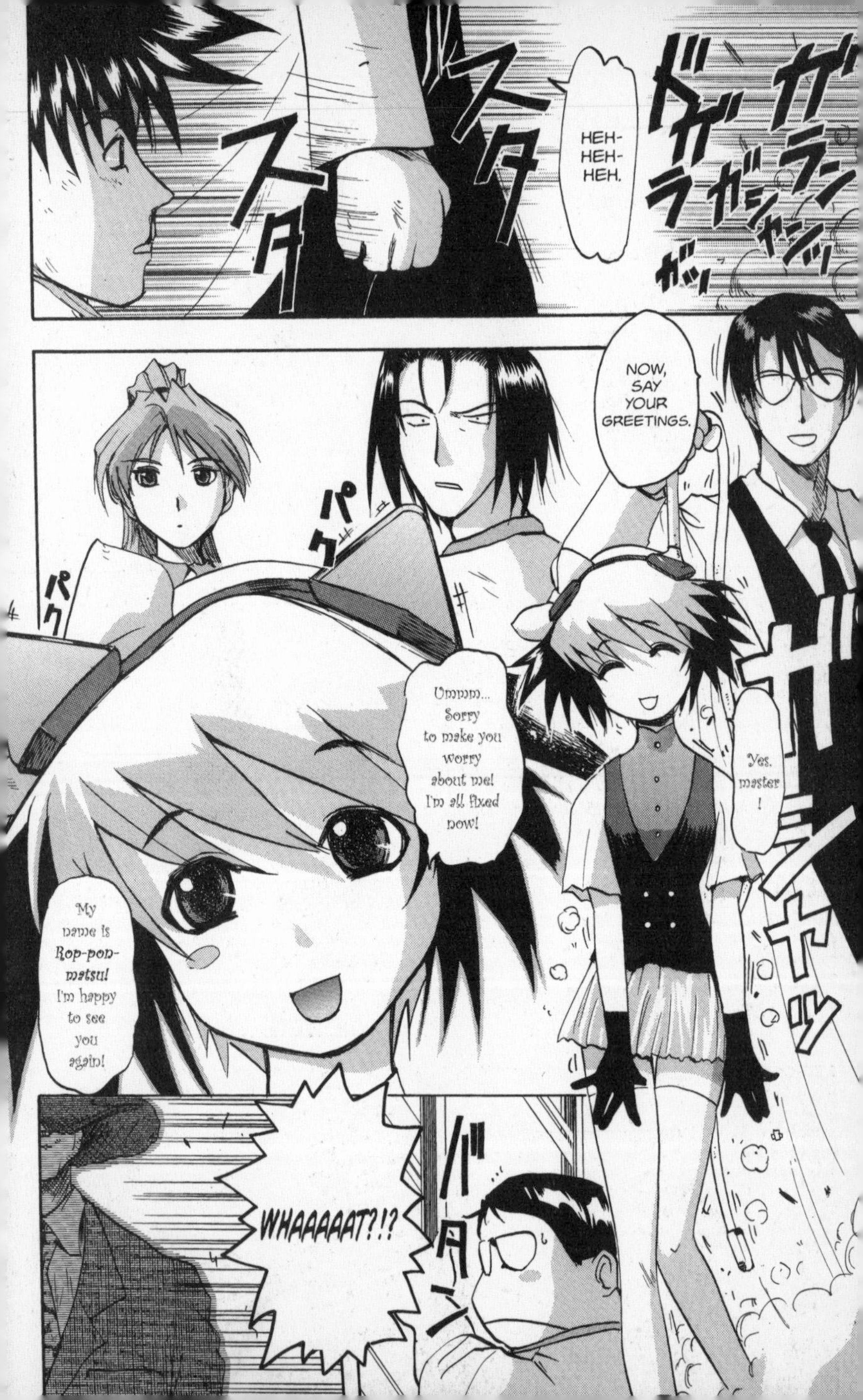
HEH-HEH-HEH.
NOW, SAY YOUR GREETINGS.
Yes, master!
Ummm... Sorry to make you worry about me! I'm all fixed now!
My name is Rop-pon-matsu! I'm happy to see you again!
WHAAAAAT?!?

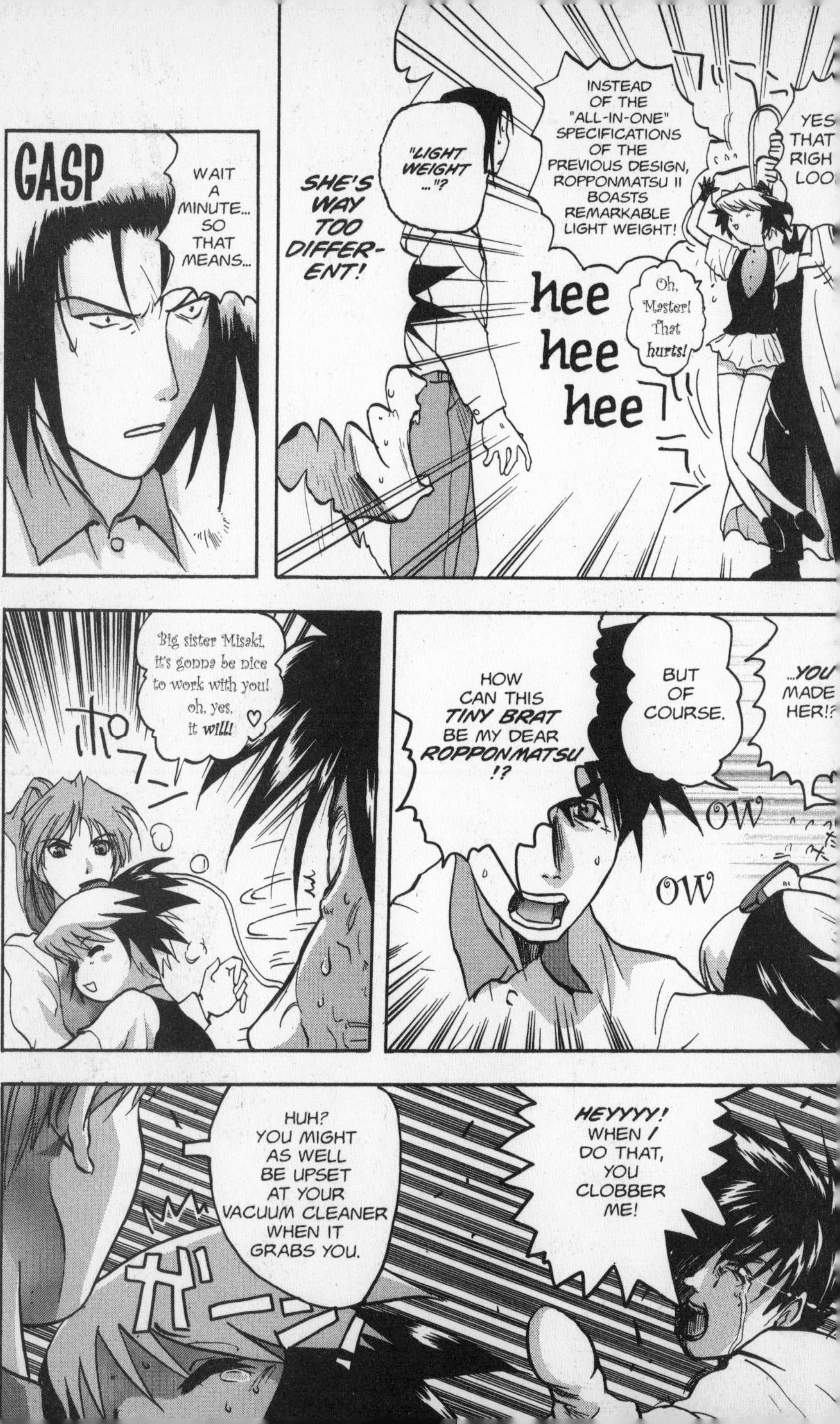
YES THAT RIGH LOO
INSTEAD OF THE "ALL-IN-ONE" SPECIFICATIONS OF THE PREVIOUS DESIGN, ROPPONMATSU II BOASTS REMARKABLE LIGHT WEIGHT!
Oh, Master! That hurts!
hee hee hee
"LIGHT WEIGHT ..."?
SHE'S WAY TOO DIFFER-ENT!
GASP
WAIT A MINUTE... SO THAT MEANS...
...YOU MADE HER!?
BUT OF COURSE.
HOW CAN THIS TINY BRAT BE MY DEAR ROPPONMATSU !?
OW
OW
Big sister Misaki, it's gonna be nice to work with you! oh, yes, it will! ♡
HEYYYY! WHEN I DO THAT, YOU CLOBBER ME!
HUH? YOU MIGHT AS WELL BE UPSET AT YOUR VACUUM CLEANER WHEN IT GRABS YOU.

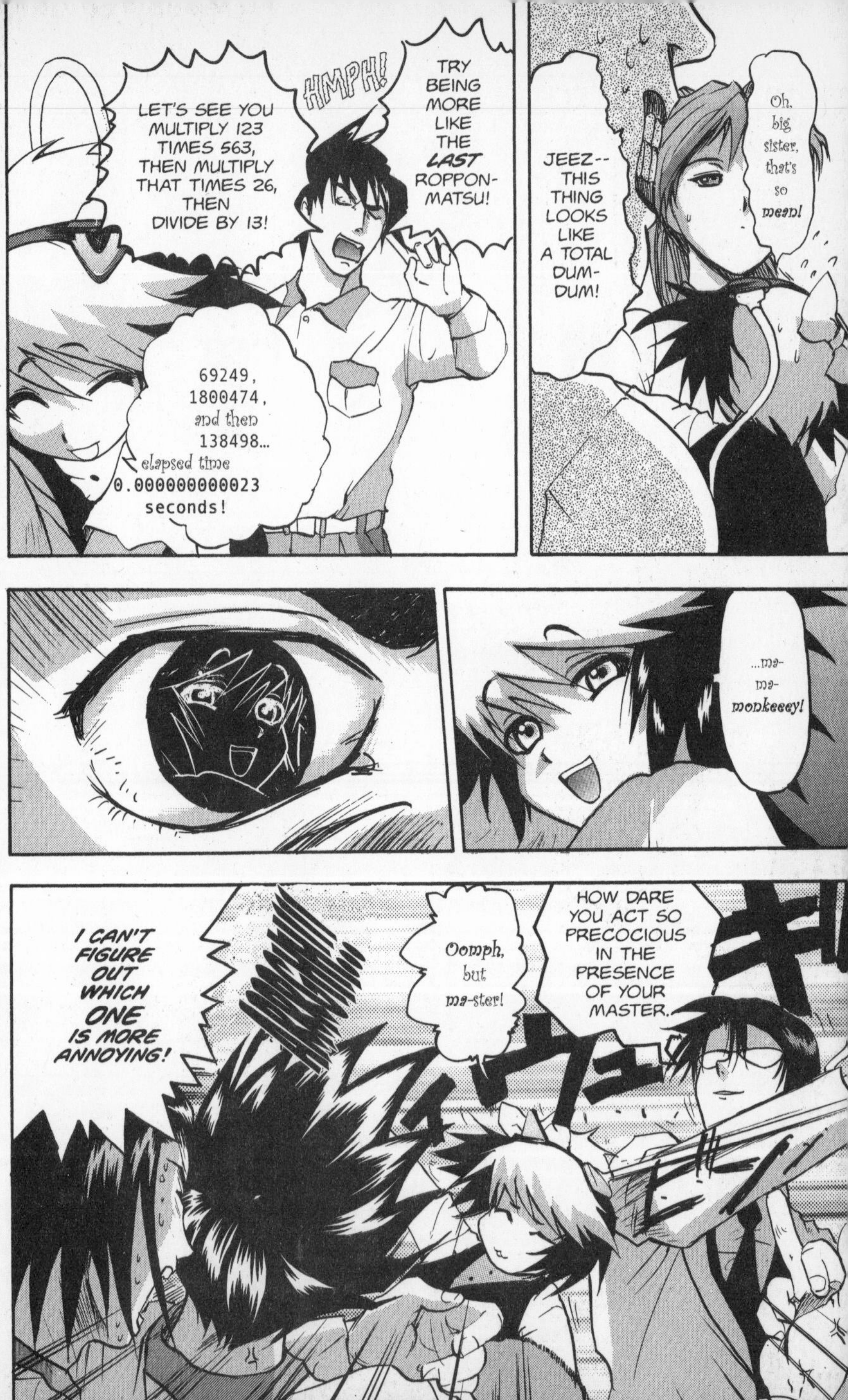
Oh, big sister, that's so mean!
JEEZ-- THIS THING LOOKS LIKE A TOTAL DUM-DUM!
TRY BEING MORE LIKE THE LAST ROPPON-MATSU!
HMPH!
LET'S SEE YOU MULTIPLY 123 TIMES 563, THEN MULTIPLY THAT TIMES 26, THEN DIVIDE BY 13!
69249, 1800474, and then 138498... elapsed time 0.000000000023 seconds!
...ma-ma-monkeeey!
HOW DARE YOU ACT SO PRECOCIOUS IN THE PRESENCE OF YOUR MASTER.
Oomph, but ma-ster!
I CAN'T FIGURE OUT WHICH ONE IS MORE ANNOYING!

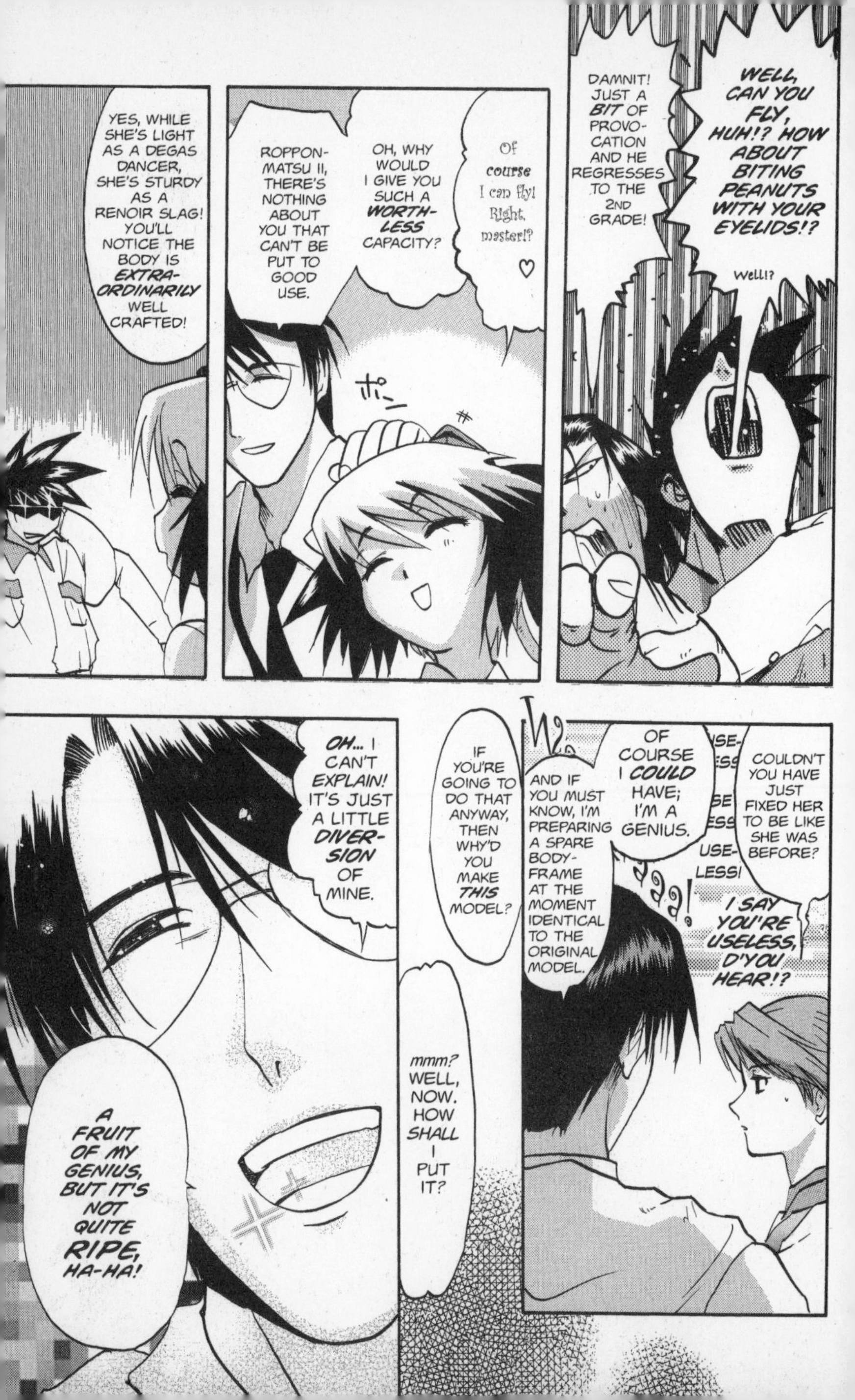
WELL, CAN YOU FLY, HUH!? HOW ABOUT BITING PEANUTS WITH YOUR EYELIDS!?
DAMNIT! JUST A BIT OF PROVOCATION AND HE REGRESSES TO THE 2ND GRADE!
Well!?
Of course I can fly! Right, master!? ♡
OH, WHY WOULD I GIVE YOU SUCH A WORTHLESS CAPACITY?
ROPPONMATSU II, THERE'S NOTHING ABOUT YOU THAT CAN'T BE PUT TO GOOD USE.
YES, WHILE SHE'S LIGHT AS A DEGAS DANCER, SHE'S STURDY AS A RENOIR SLAG! YOU'LL NOTICE THE BODY IS EXTRAORDINARILY WELL CRAFTED!
COULDN'T YOU HAVE JUST FIXED HER TO BE LIKE SHE WAS BEFORE?
USELESS!
I SAY YOU'RE USELESS, D'YOU HEAR!?
OF COURSE I COULD HAVE; I'M A GENIUS.
AND IF YOU MUST KNOW, I'M PREPARING A SPARE BODY-FRAME AT THE MOMENT IDENTICAL TO THE ORIGINAL MODEL.
IF YOU'RE GOING TO DO THAT ANYWAY, THEN WHY'D YOU MAKE THIS MODEL?
mmm? WELL, NOW. HOW SHALL I PUT IT?
OH... I CAN'T EXPLAIN! IT'S JUST A LITTLE DIVERSION OF MINE.
A FRUIT OF MY GENIUS, BUT IT'S NOT QUITE RIPE, HA-HA!

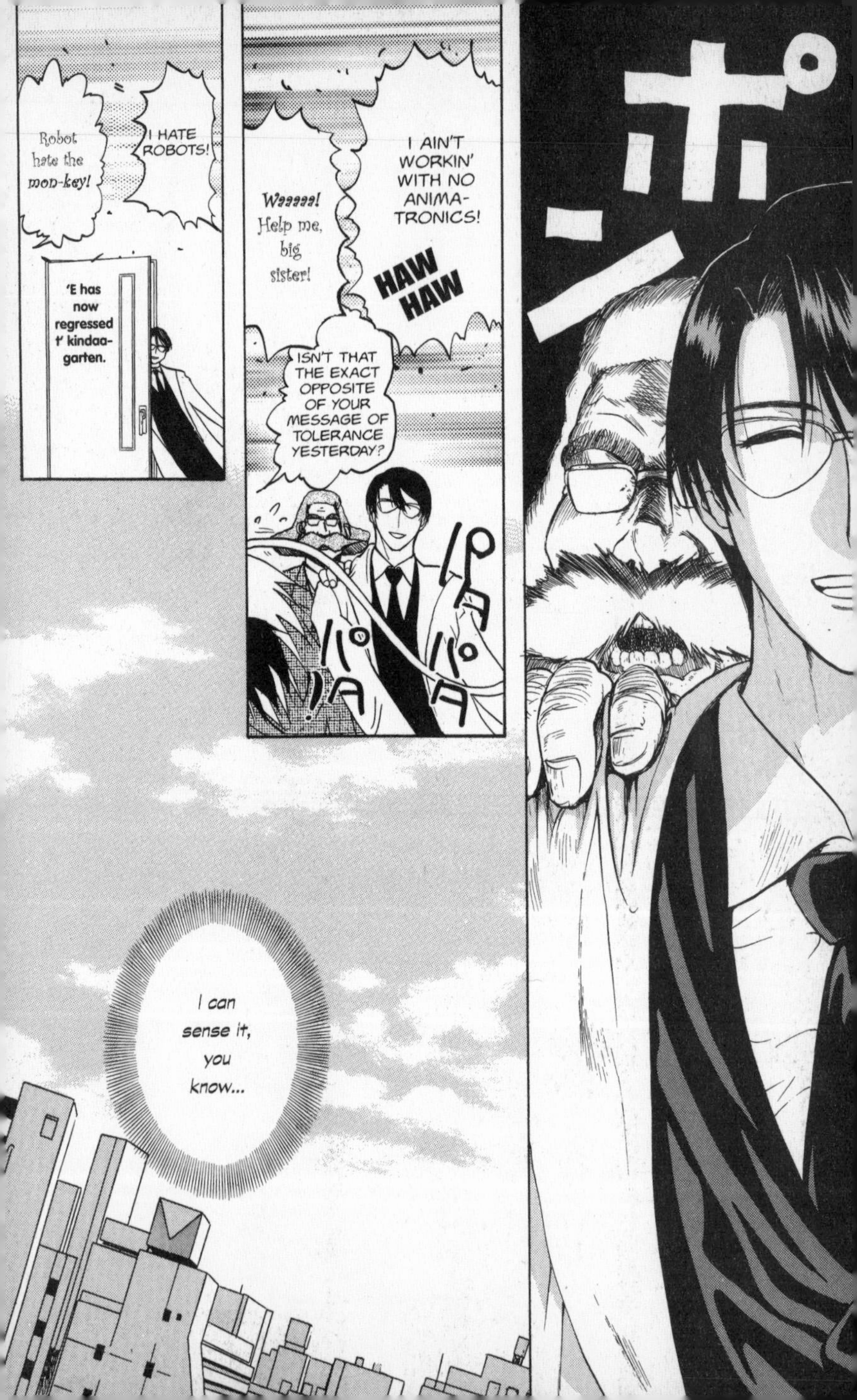
ポー
I AIN'T WORKIN' WITH NO ANIMA-TRONICS!
Waaaaa! Help me, big sister!
HAW HAW
ISN'T THAT THE EXACT OPPOSITE OF YOUR MESSAGE OF TOLERANCE YESTERDAY?
I HATE ROBOTS!
Robot hate the mon-key!
'E has now regressed t' kindaa-garten.
I can sense it, you know...

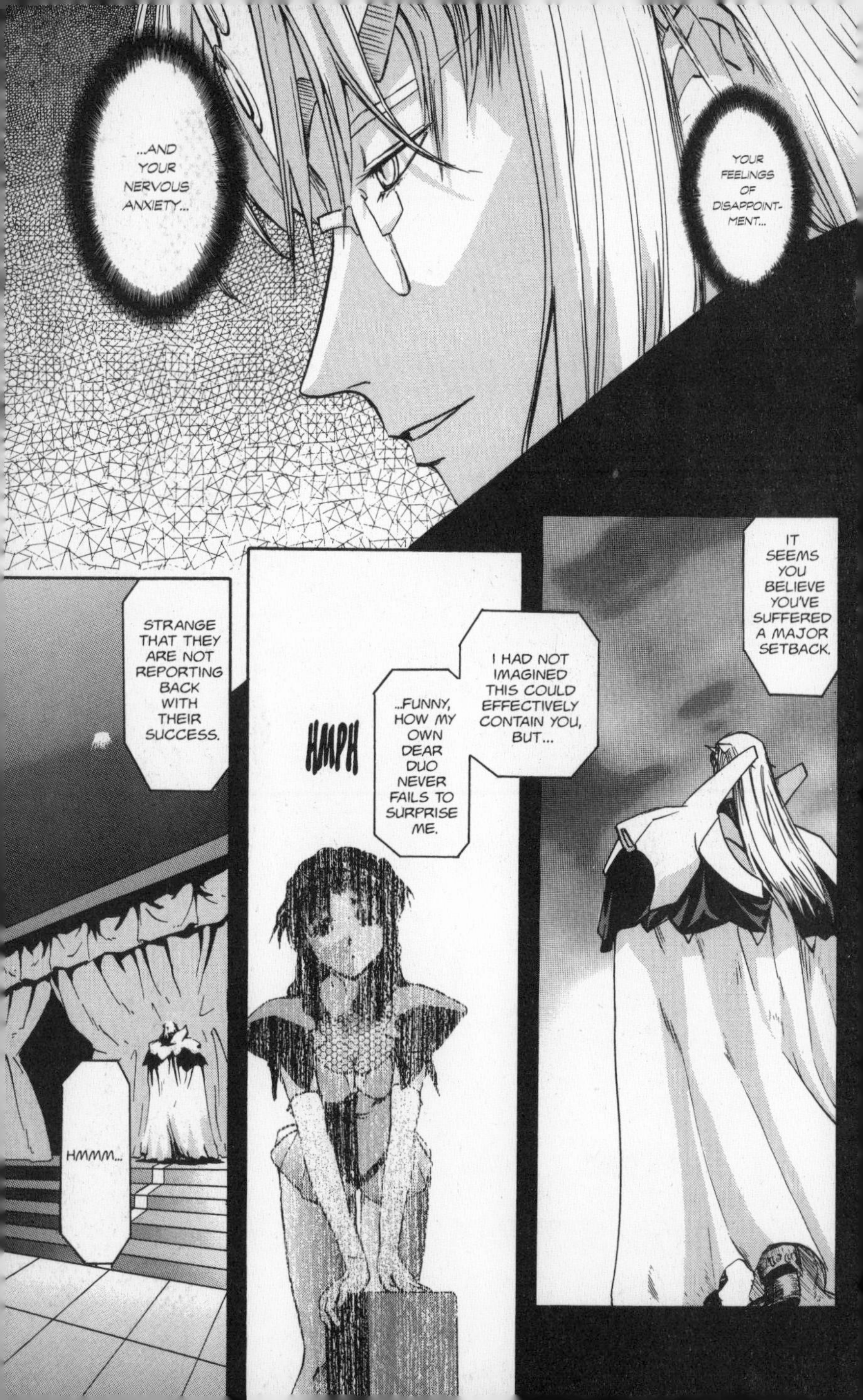
YOUR FEELINGS OF DISAPPOINT-MENT...
...AND YOUR NERVOUS ANXIETY...
IT SEEMS YOU BELIEVE YOU'VE SUFFERED A MAJOR SETBACK.
I HAD NOT IMAGINED THIS COULD EFFECTIVELY CONTAIN YOU, BUT...
...FUNNY, HOW MY OWN DEAR DUO NEVER FAILS TO SURPRISE ME.
HMPH
STRANGE THAT THEY ARE NOT REPORTING BACK WITH THEIR SUCCESS.
HMMM...

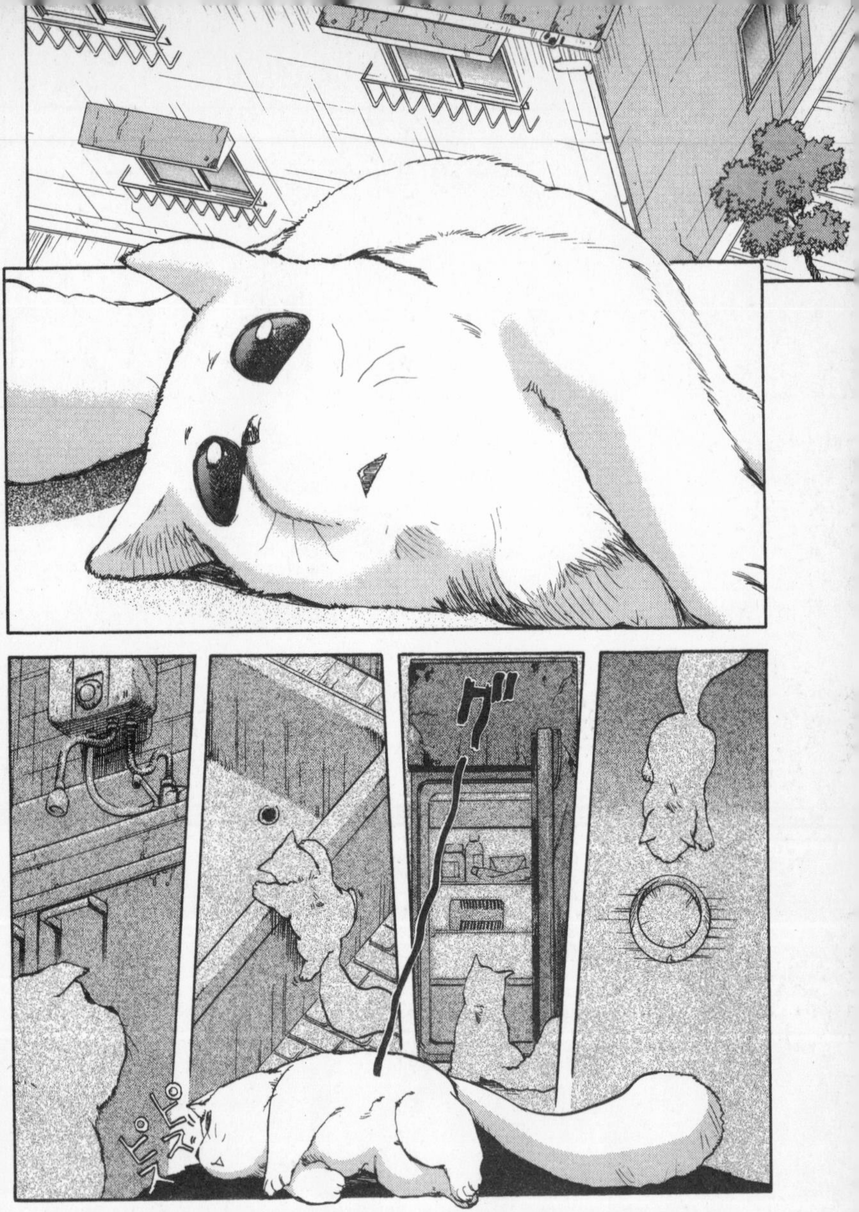
グ

**. . .AND NOW THE STORY MUST BACKTRACK ONE DAY!**

**END MISSION 6**

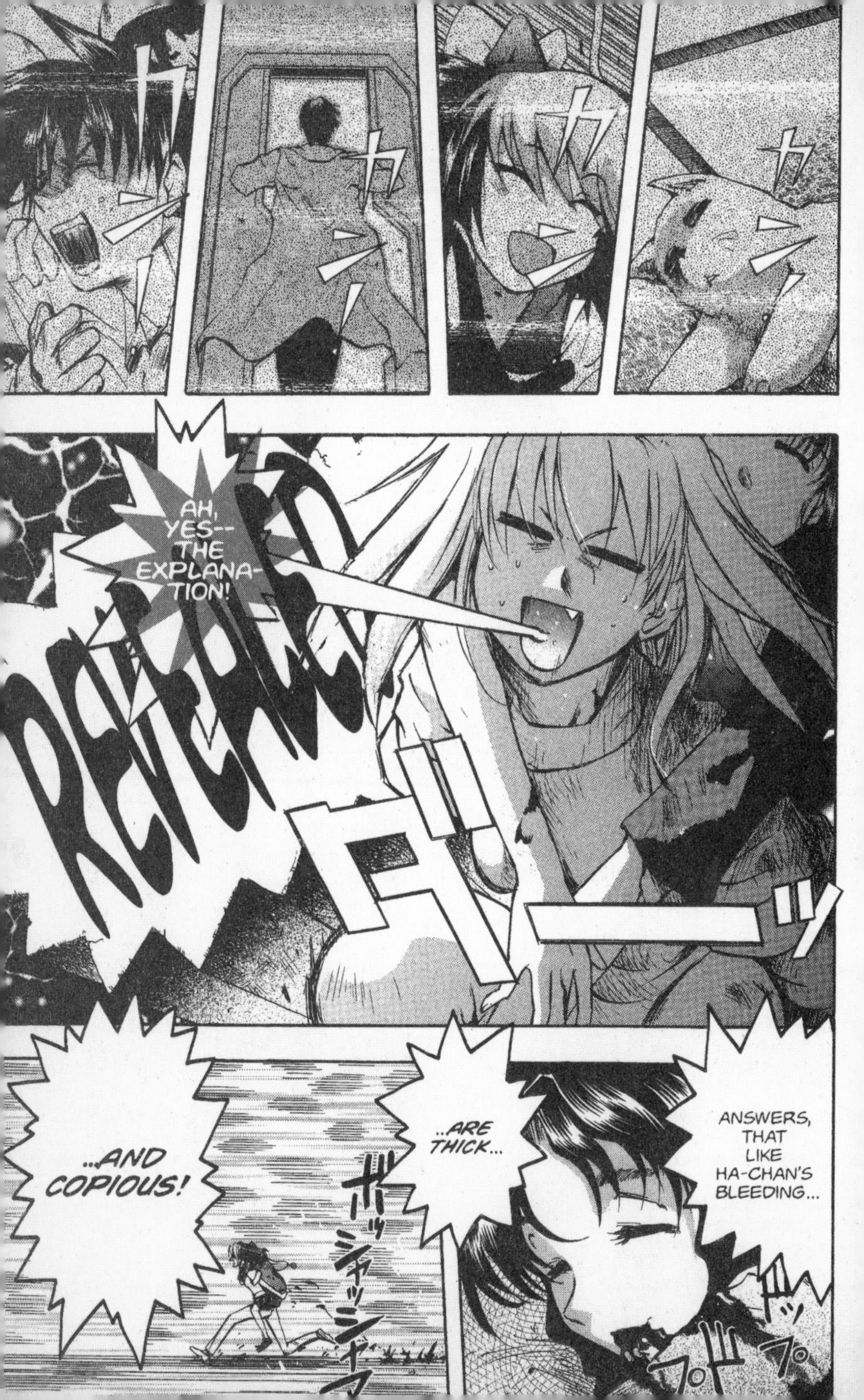
AH, YES-- THE EXPLANATION!
ANSWERS, THAT LIKE HA-CHAN'S BLEEDING...
...ARE THICK...
...AND COPIOUS!

## MISSION 7
# AND THE ONE THAT DANCES

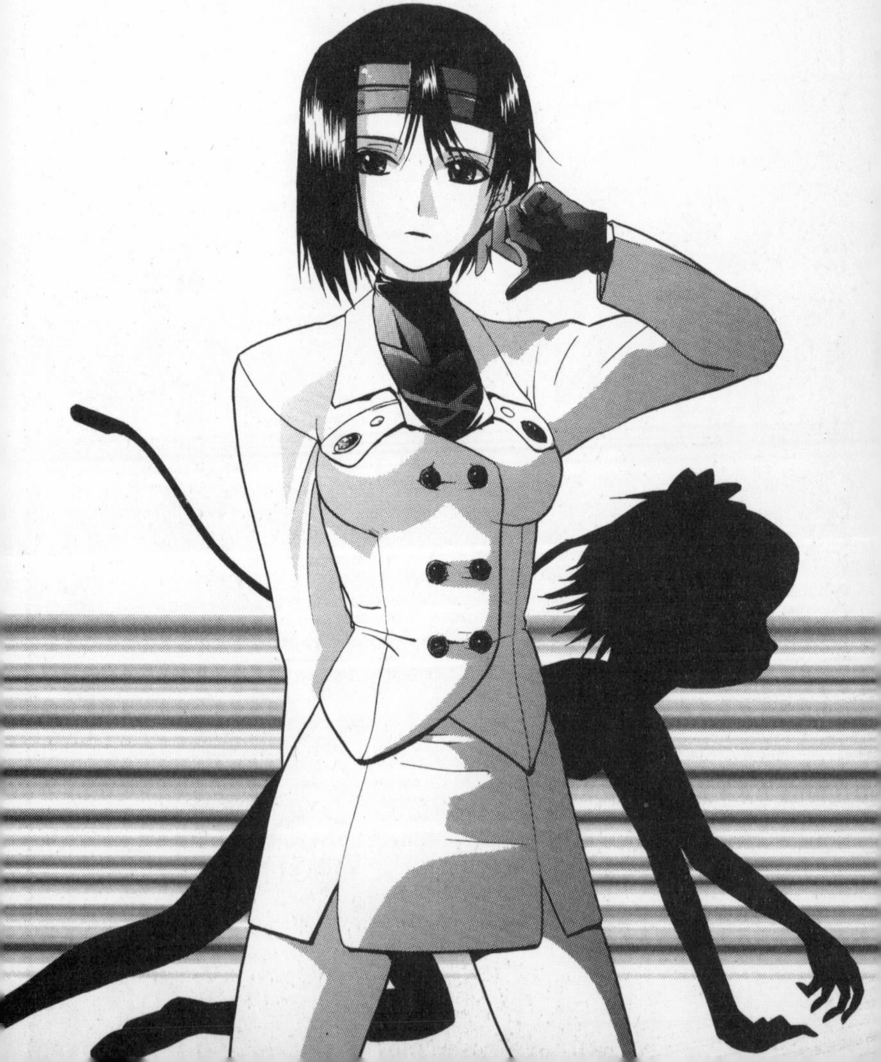

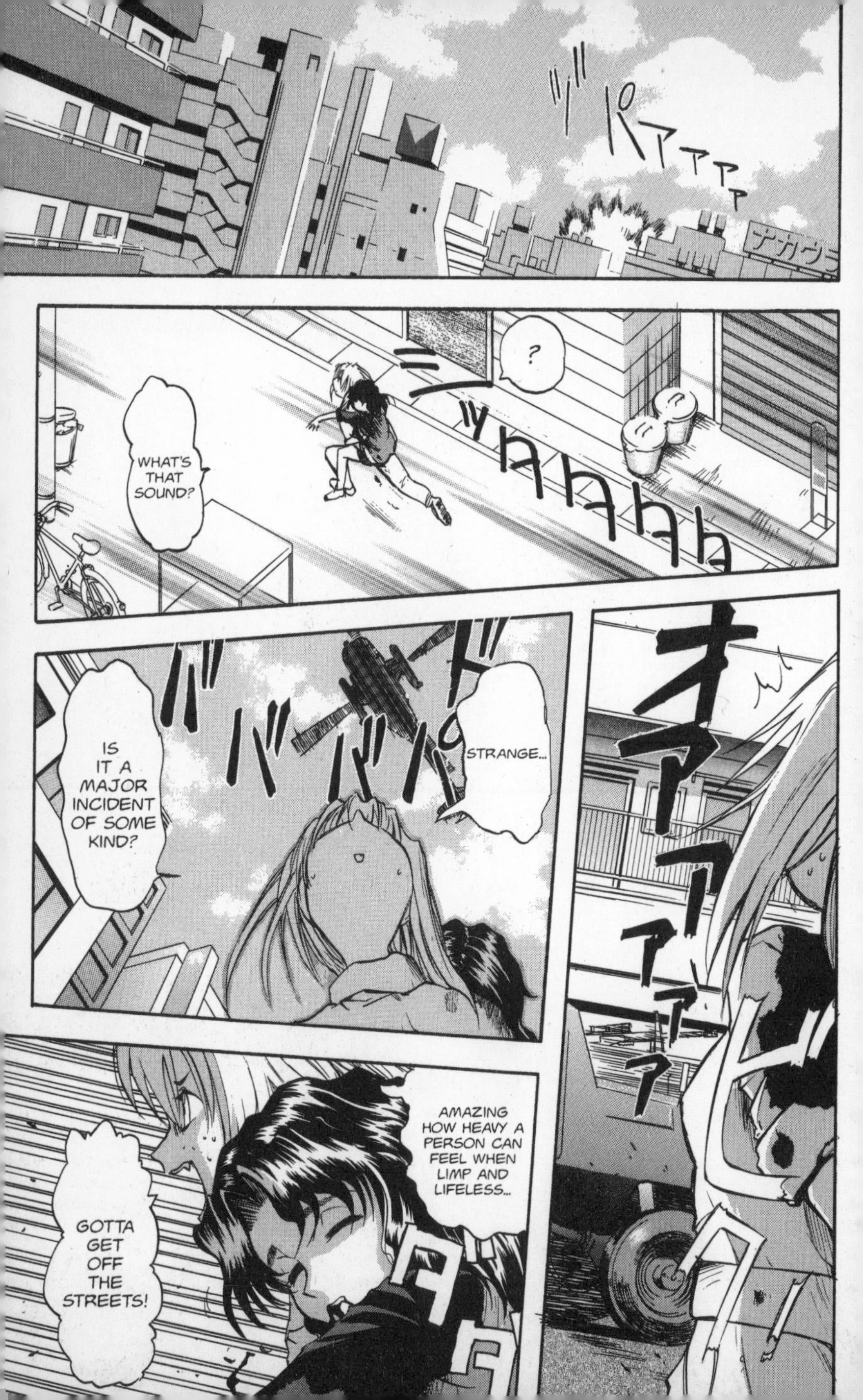
?
WHAT'S THAT SOUND?
STRANGE...
IS IT A MAJOR INCIDENT OF SOME KIND?
AMAZING HOW HEAVY A PERSON CAN FEEL WHEN LIMP AND LIFELESS...
GOTTA GET OFF THE STREETS!

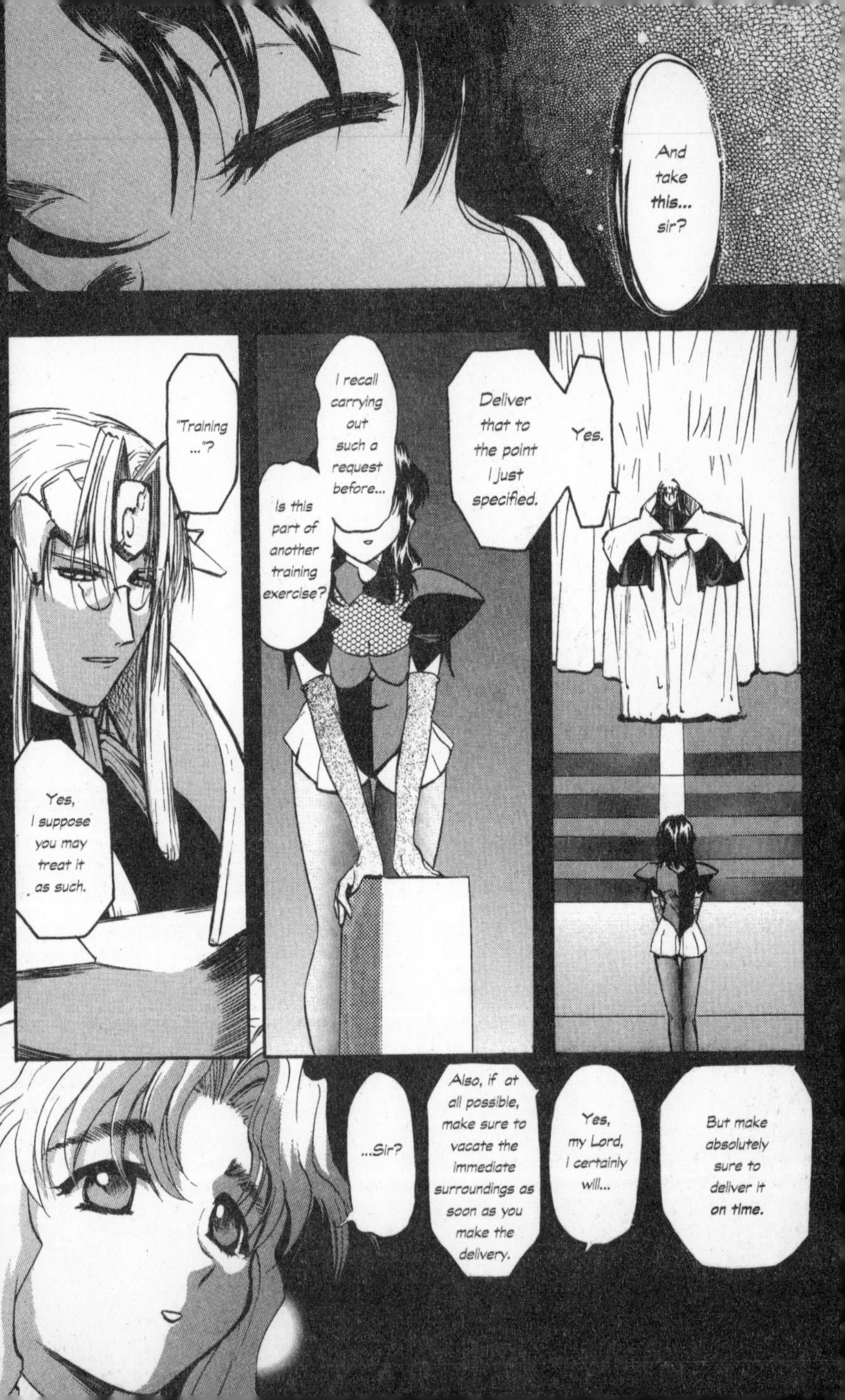

And take this... sir?
Deliver that to the point I just specified.
Yes.
I recall carrying out such a request before...
Is this part of another training exercise?
"Training ..."?
Yes, I suppose you may treat it as such.
But make absolutely sure to deliver it on time.
Yes, my Lord, I certainly will...
Also, if at all possible, make sure to vacate the immediate surroundings as soon as you make the delivery.
...Sir?

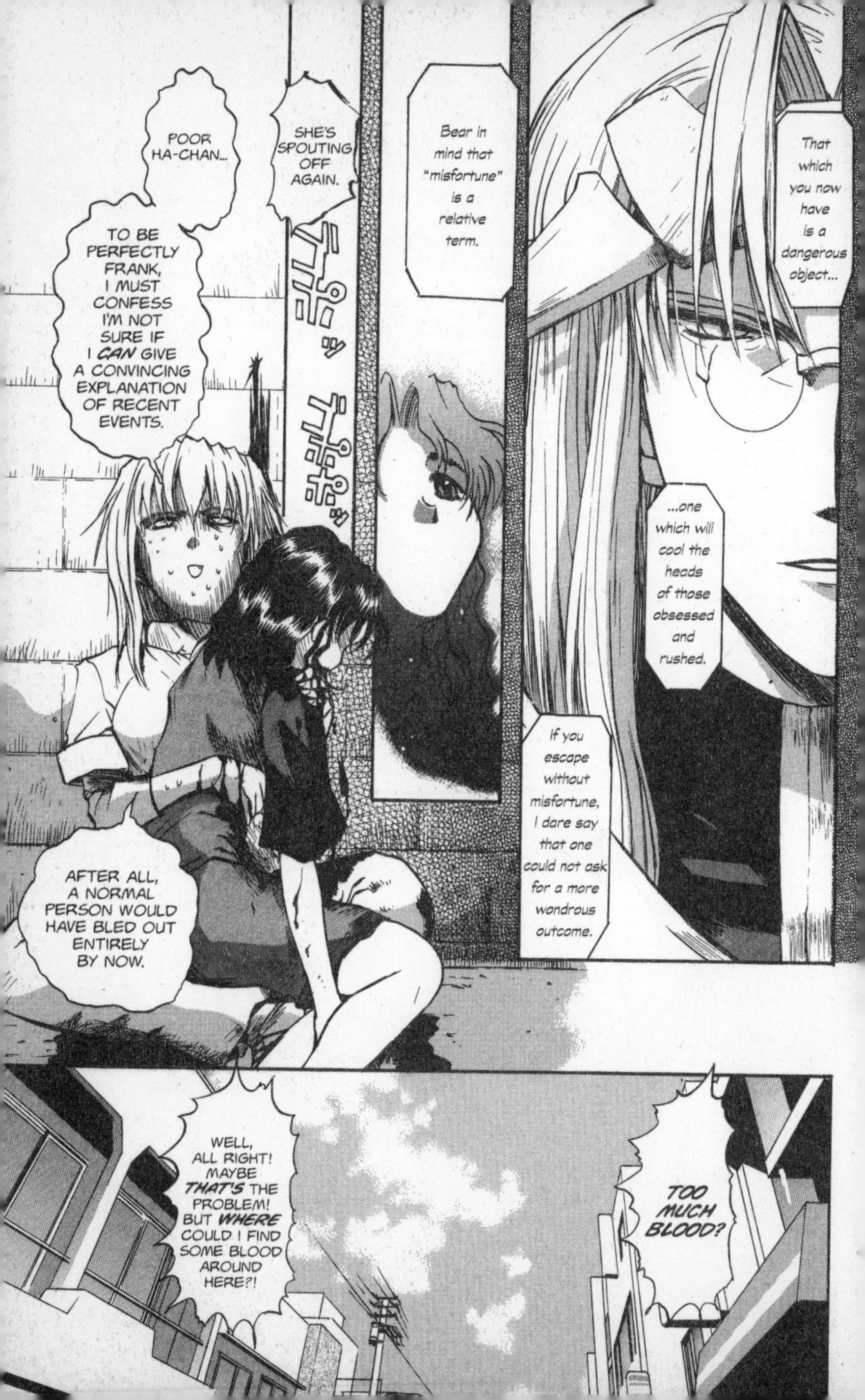
That which you now have is a dangerous object...
...one which will cool the heads of those obsessed and rushed.
If you escape without misfortune, I dare say that one could not ask for a more wondrous outcome.
Bear in mind that "misfortune" is a relative term.
SHE'S SPOUTING OFF AGAIN.
ゴポッ
ゴポポッ
POOR HA-CHAN...
TO BE PERFECTLY FRANK, I MUST CONFESS I'M NOT SURE IF I *CAN* GIVE A CONVINCING EXPLANATION OF RECENT EVENTS.
AFTER ALL, A NORMAL PERSON WOULD HAVE BLED OUT ENTIRELY BY NOW.
*TOO MUCH BLOOD?*
WELL, ALL RIGHT! MAYBE *THAT'S* THE PROBLEM! BUT *WHERE* COULD I FIND SOME BLOOD AROUND HERE?!

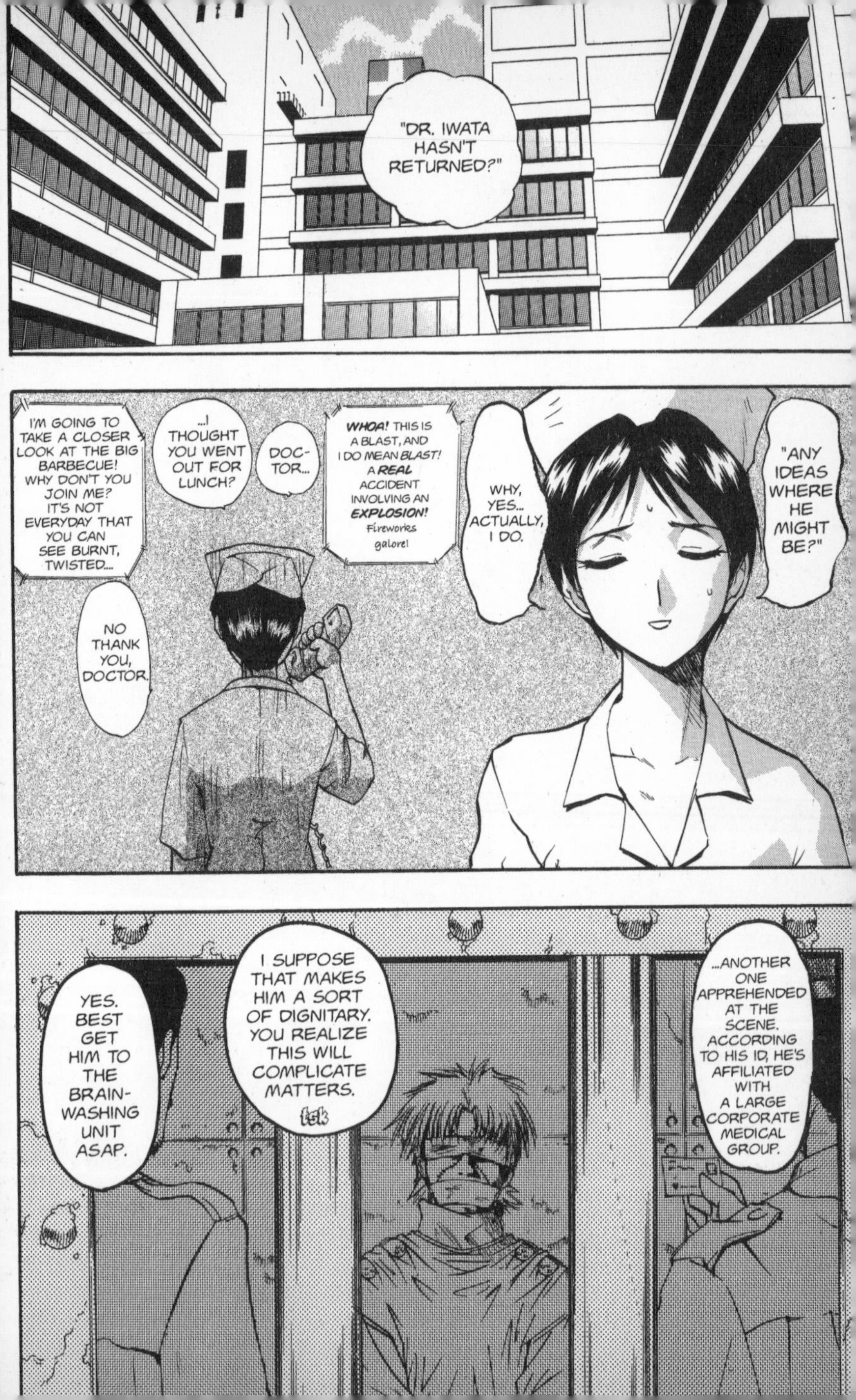
"DR. IWATA HASN'T RETURNED?"
"ANY IDEAS WHERE HE MIGHT BE?"
WHY, YES... ACTUALLY, I DO.
WHOA! THIS IS A BLAST, AND I DO MEAN BLAST! A REAL ACCIDENT INVOLVING AN EXPLOSION! Fireworks galore!
DOC-TOR...
...I THOUGHT YOU WENT OUT FOR LUNCH?
I'M GOING TO TAKE A CLOSER LOOK AT THE BIG BARBECUE! WHY DON'T YOU JOIN ME? IT'S NOT EVERYDAY THAT YOU CAN SEE BURNT, TWISTED...
NO THANK YOU, DOCTOR.
...ANOTHER ONE APPREHENDED AT THE SCENE. ACCORDING TO HIS ID, HE'S AFFILIATED WITH A LARGE CORPORATE MEDICAL GROUP.
I SUPPOSE THAT MAKES HIM A SORT OF DIGNITARY. YOU REALIZE THIS WILL COMPLICATE MATTERS.
tsk
YES. BEST GET HIM TO THE BRAIN-WASHING UNIT ASAP.

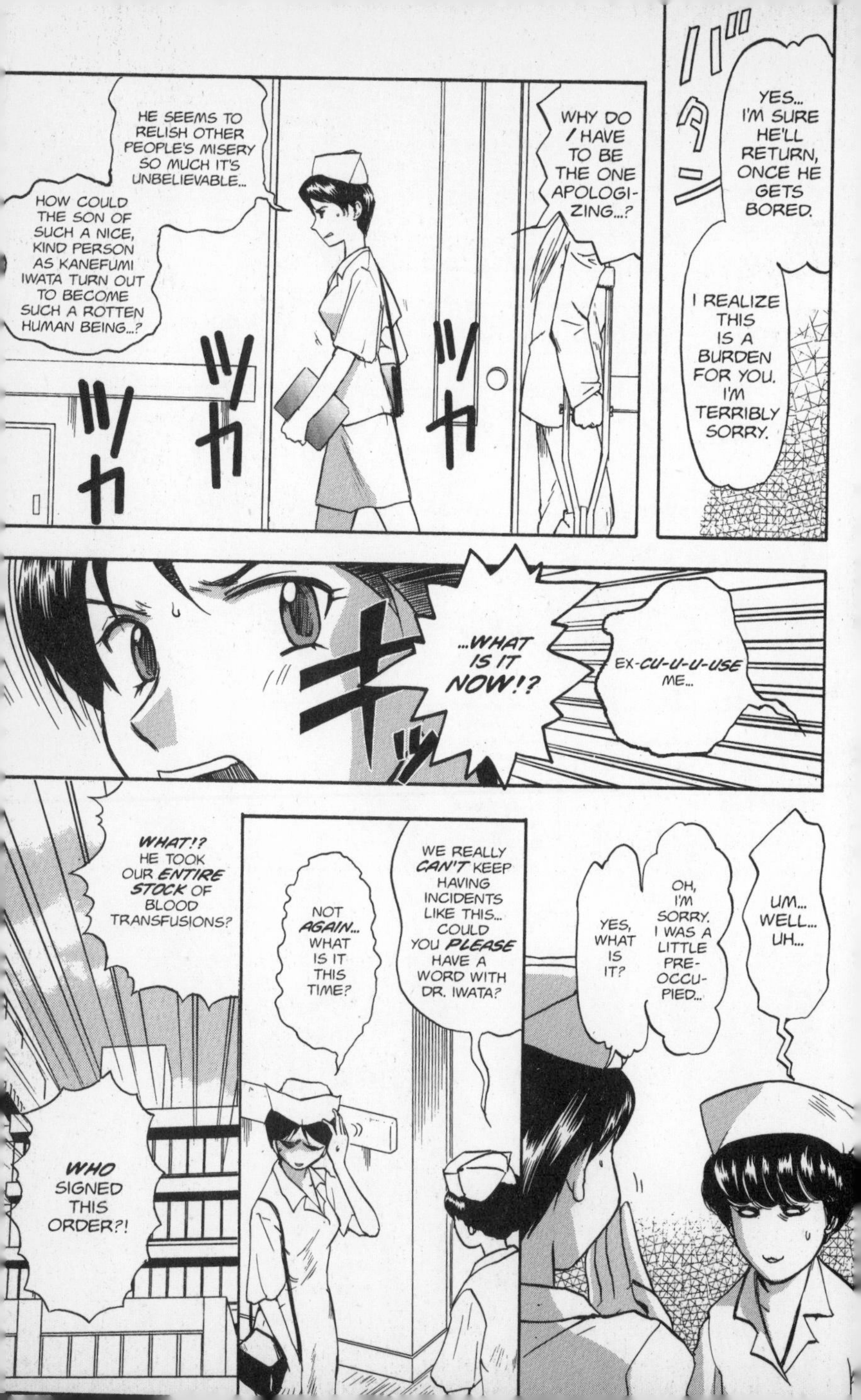
YES... I'M SURE HE'LL RETURN, ONCE HE GETS BORED.
I REALIZE THIS IS A BURDEN FOR YOU. I'M TERRIBLY SORRY.
WHY DO I HAVE TO BE THE ONE APOLOGIZING...?
HE SEEMS TO RELISH OTHER PEOPLE'S MISERY SO MUCH IT'S UNBELIEVABLE...
HOW COULD THE SON OF SUCH A NICE, KIND PERSON AS KANEFUMI IWATA TURN OUT TO BECOME SUCH A ROTTEN HUMAN BEING...?
EX-CU-U-U-USE ME...
...WHAT IS IT NOW!?
UM... WELL... UH...
OH, I'M SORRY. I WAS A LITTLE PRE-OCCUPIED...
YES, WHAT IS IT?
WE REALLY CAN'T KEEP HAVING INCIDENTS LIKE THIS... COULD YOU PLEASE HAVE A WORD WITH DR. IWATA?
NOT AGAIN... WHAT IS IT THIS TIME?
WHAT!? HE TOOK OUR ENTIRE STOCK OF BLOOD TRANSFUSIONS?
WHO SIGNED THIS ORDER?!

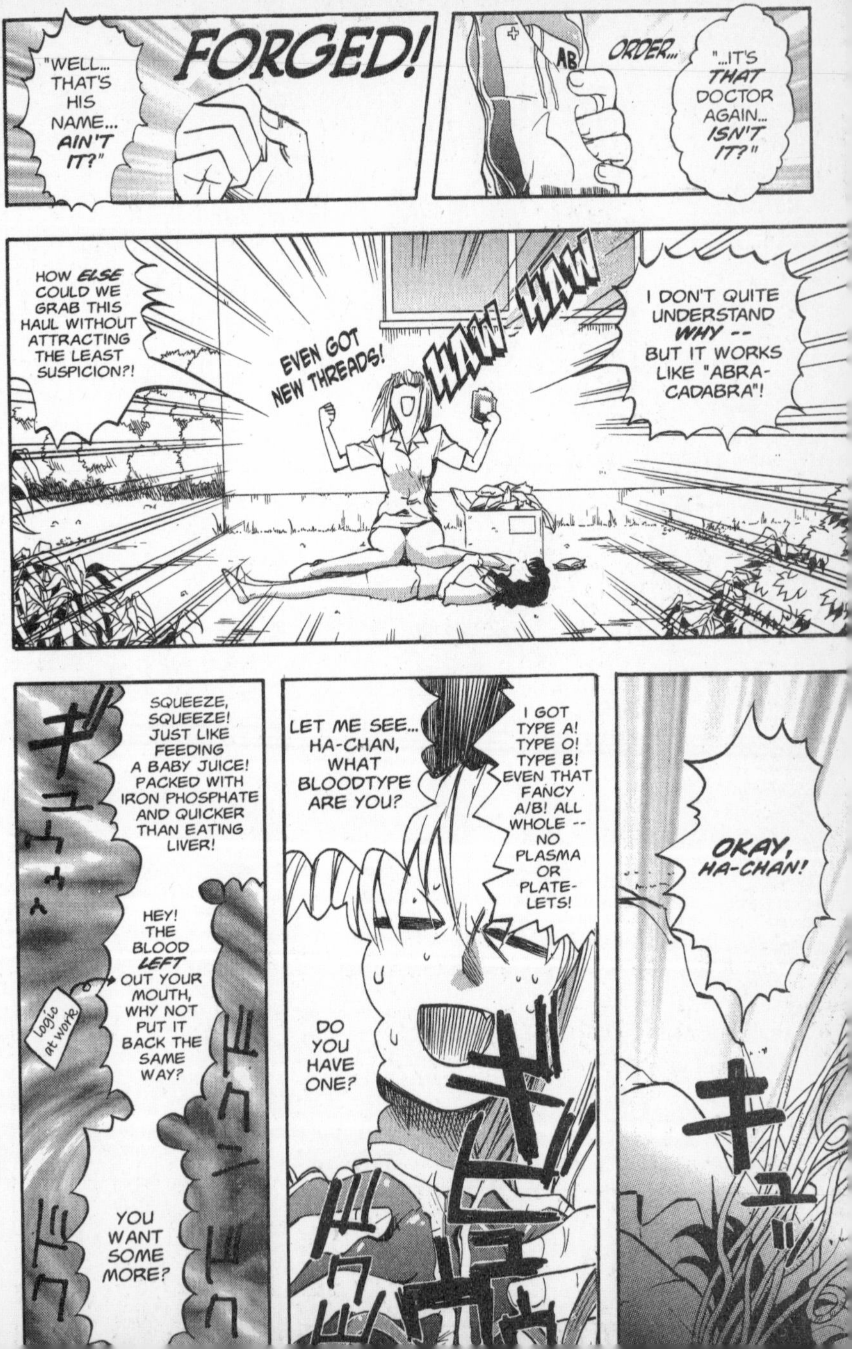
"...IT'S THAT DOCTOR AGAIN... ISN'T IT?"
ORDER...
AB
FORGED!
"WELL... THAT'S HIS NAME... AIN'T IT?"
I DON'T QUITE UNDERSTAND WHY -- BUT IT WORKS LIKE "ABRA-CADABRA"!
HAW HAW
EVEN GOT NEW THREADS!
HOW ELSE COULD WE GRAB THIS HAUL WITHOUT ATTRACTING THE LEAST SUSPICION?!
OKAY, HA-CHAN!
I GOT TYPE A! TYPE O! TYPE B! EVEN THAT FANCY A/B! ALL WHOLE -- NO PLASMA OR PLATE-LETS!
LET ME SEE... HA-CHAN, WHAT BLOODTYPE ARE YOU?
DO YOU HAVE ONE?
SQUEEZE, SQUEEZE! JUST LIKE FEEDING A BABY JUICE! PACKED WITH IRON PHOSPHATE AND QUICKER THAN EATING LIVER!
HEY! THE BLOOD LEFT OUT YOUR MOUTH, WHY NOT PUT IT BACK THE SAME WAY?
Logic at work
YOU WANT SOME MORE?

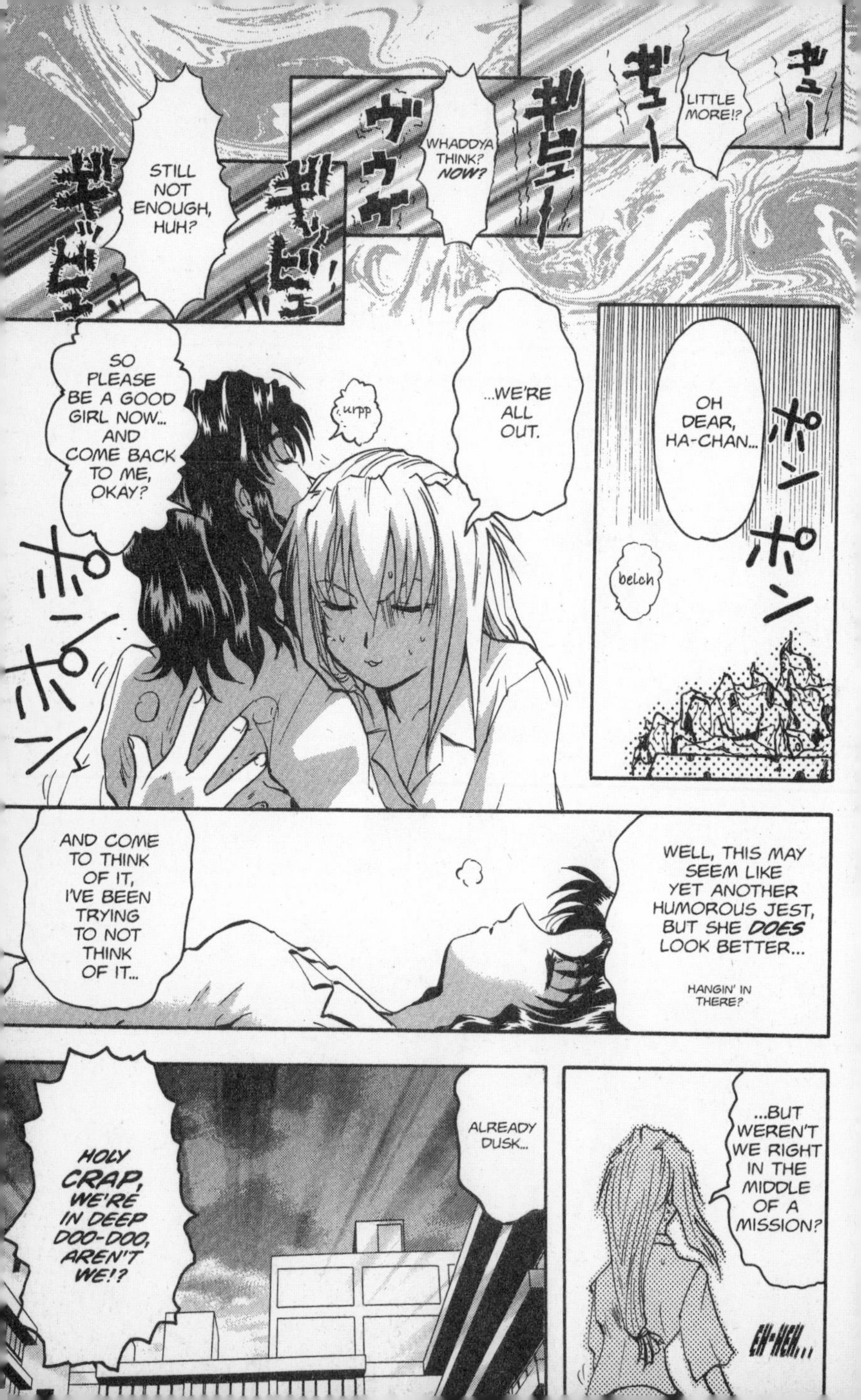
LITTLE MORE!?
WHADDYA THINK? *NOW?*
STILL NOT ENOUGH, HUH?
OH DEAR, HA-CHAN...
belch
...WE'RE ALL OUT.
urpp
SO PLEASE BE A GOOD GIRL NOW... AND COME BACK TO ME, OKAY?
WELL, THIS MAY SEEM LIKE YET ANOTHER HUMOROUS JEST, BUT SHE *DOES* LOOK BETTER...
HANGIN' IN THERE?
AND COME TO THINK OF IT, I'VE BEEN TRYING TO NOT THINK OF IT...
...BUT WEREN'T WE RIGHT IN THE MIDDLE OF A MISSION?
EH-HEH...
ALREADY DUSK...
*HOLY CRAP, WE'RE IN DEEP DOO-DOO, AREN'T WE!?*

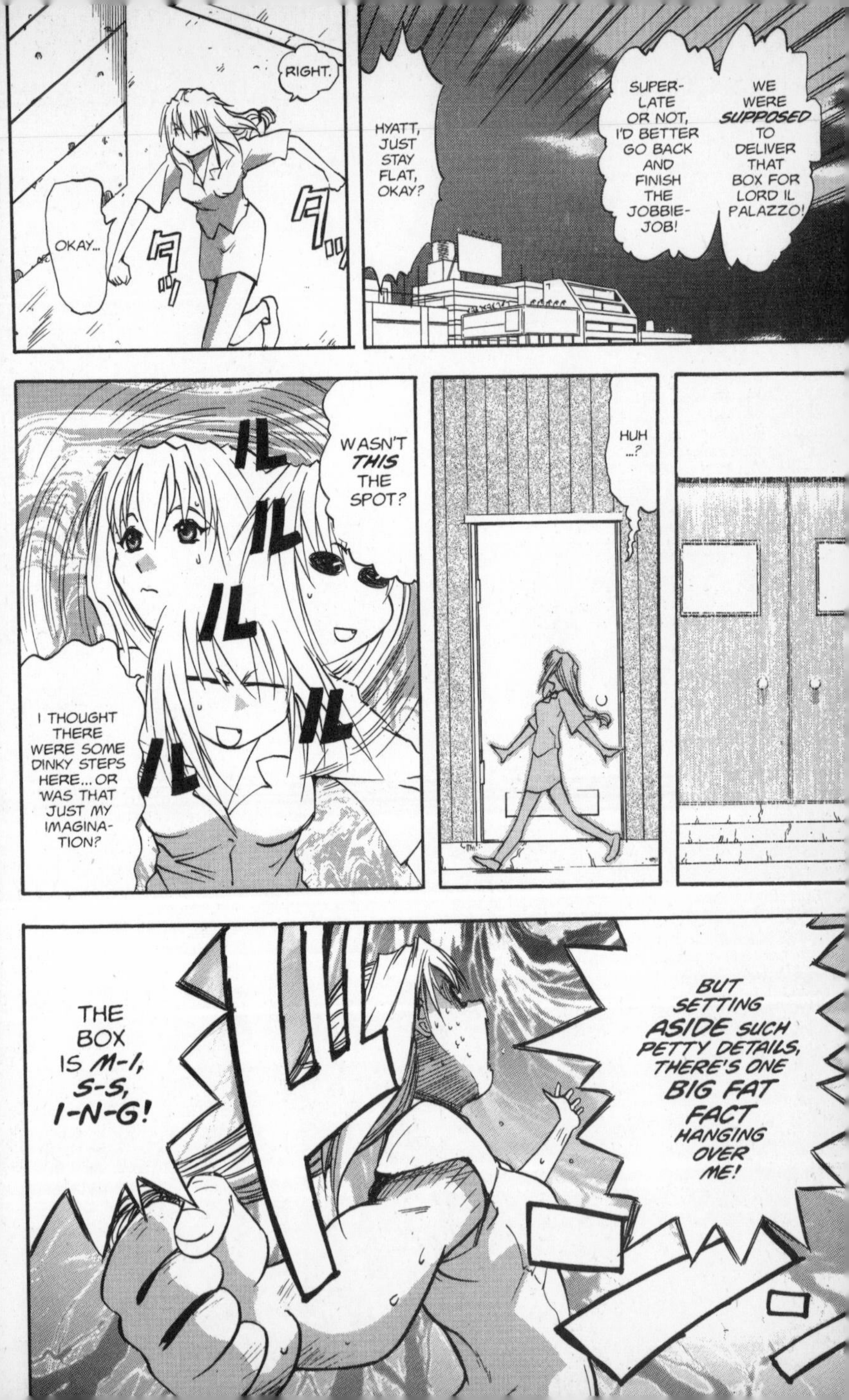
WE WERE SUPPOSED TO DELIVER THAT BOX FOR LORD IL PALAZZO!
SUPER-LATE OR NOT, I'D BETTER GO BACK AND FINISH THE JOBBIE-JOB!
HYATT, JUST STAY FLAT, OKAY?
RIGHT.
OKAY...
タッ
タッ
HUH ...?
WASN'T THIS THE SPOT?
IL IL IL IL IL
I THOUGHT THERE WERE SOME DINKY STEPS HERE... OR WAS THAT JUST MY IMAGINATION?
BUT SETTING ASIDE SUCH PETTY DETAILS, THERE'S ONE BIG FAT FACT HANGING OVER ME!
THE BOX IS M-I, S-S, I-N-G!

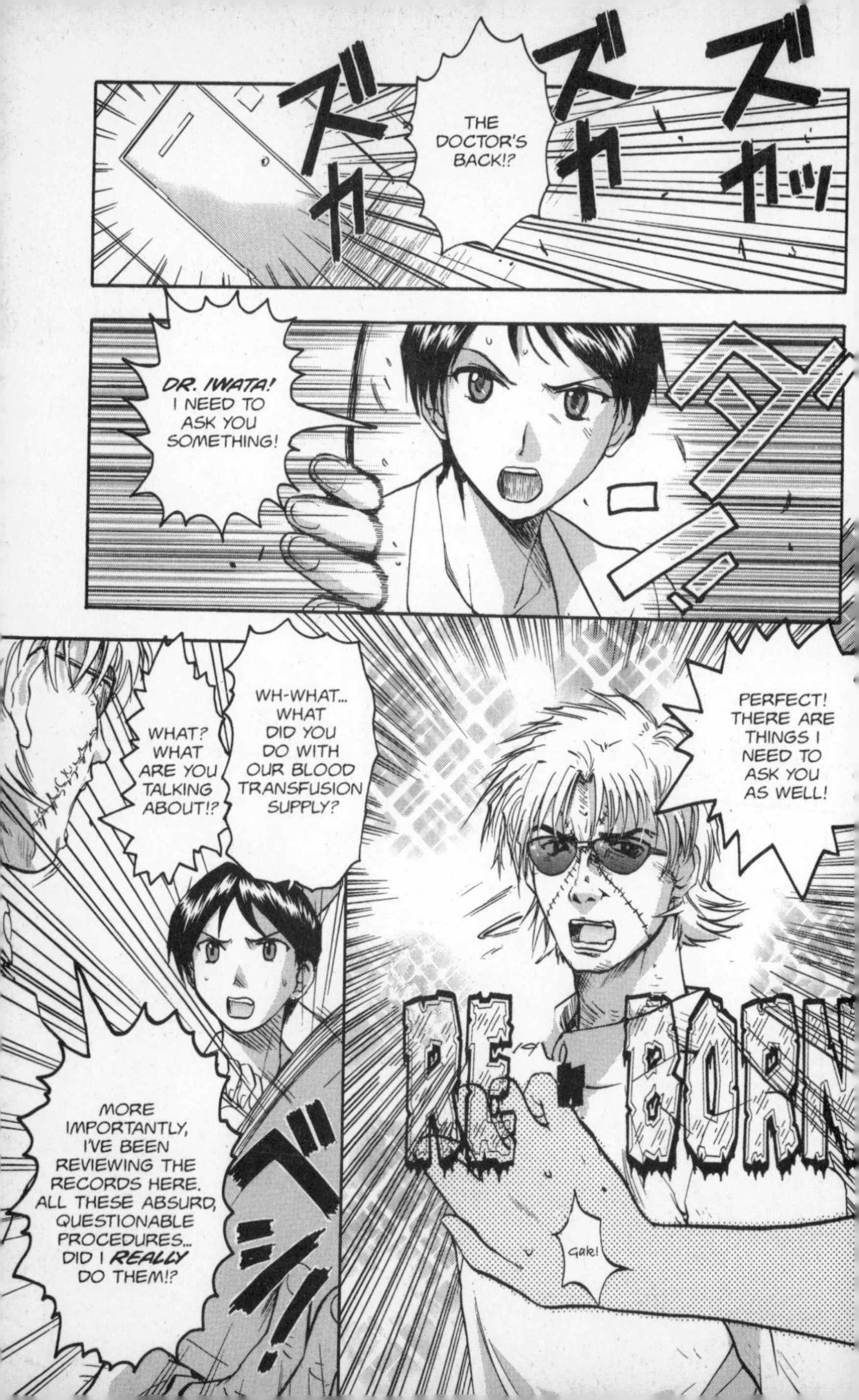
ズカッ
ズカ
THE DOCTOR'S BACK!?
ズカ
DR. IWATA! I NEED TO ASK YOU SOMETHING!
PERFECT! THERE ARE THINGS I NEED TO ASK YOU AS WELL!
RE-BORN
Gak!
WH-WHAT... WHAT DID YOU DO WITH OUR BLOOD TRANSFUSION SUPPLY?
WHAT? WHAT ARE YOU TALKING ABOUT!?
MORE IMPORTANTLY, I'VE BEEN REVIEWING THE RECORDS HERE. ALL THESE ABSURD, QUESTIONABLE PROCEDURES... DID I *REALLY* DO THEM!?

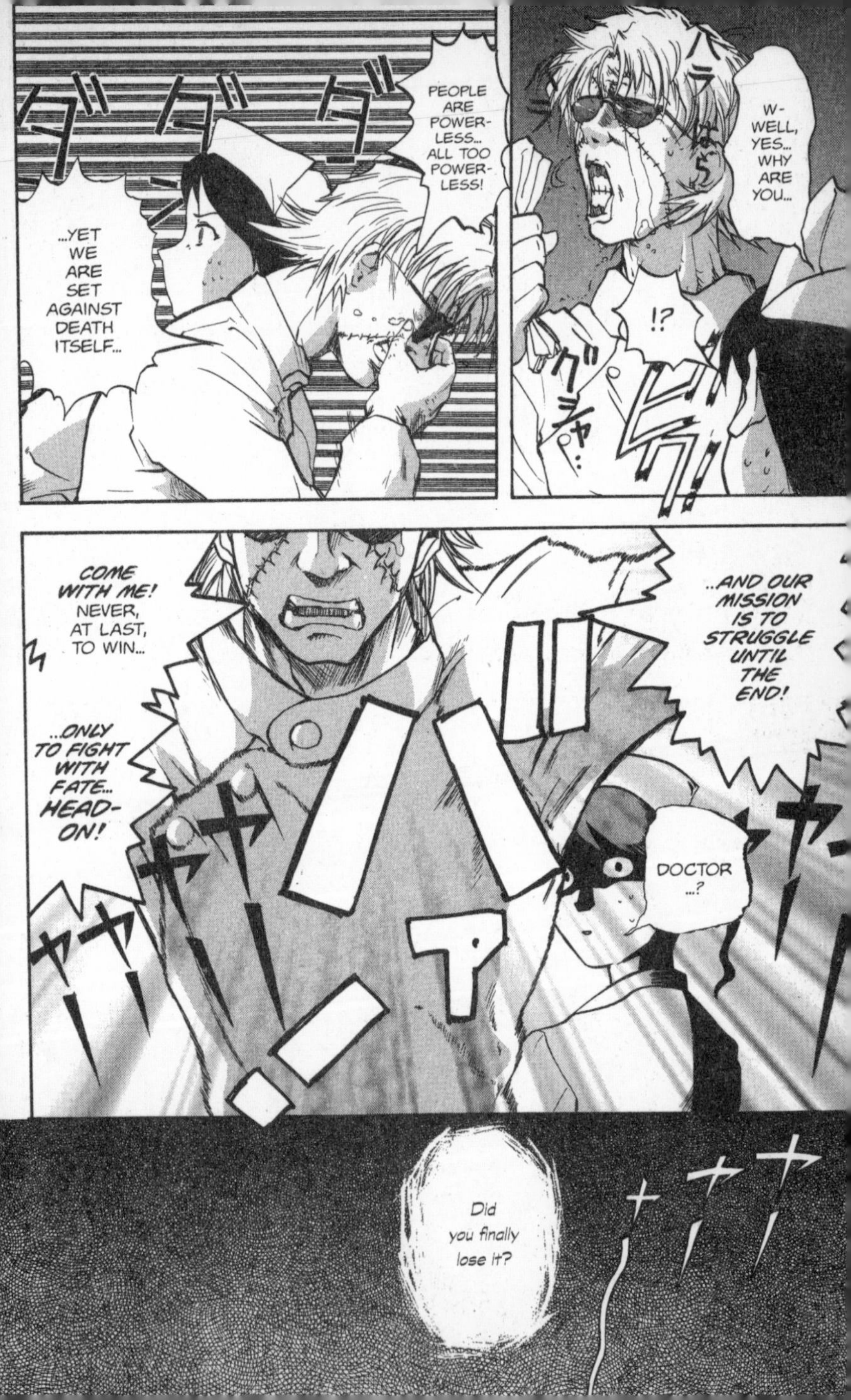
W-WELL, YES... WHY ARE YOU...
!?
PEOPLE ARE POWER-LESS... ALL TOO POWER-LESS!
...YET WE ARE SET AGAINST DEATH ITSELF...
...AND OUR MISSION IS TO STRUGGLE UNTIL THE END!
COME WITH ME! NEVER, AT LAST, TO WIN...
...ONLY TO FIGHT WITH FATE... HEAD-ON!
DOCTOR ...?
Did you finally lose it?

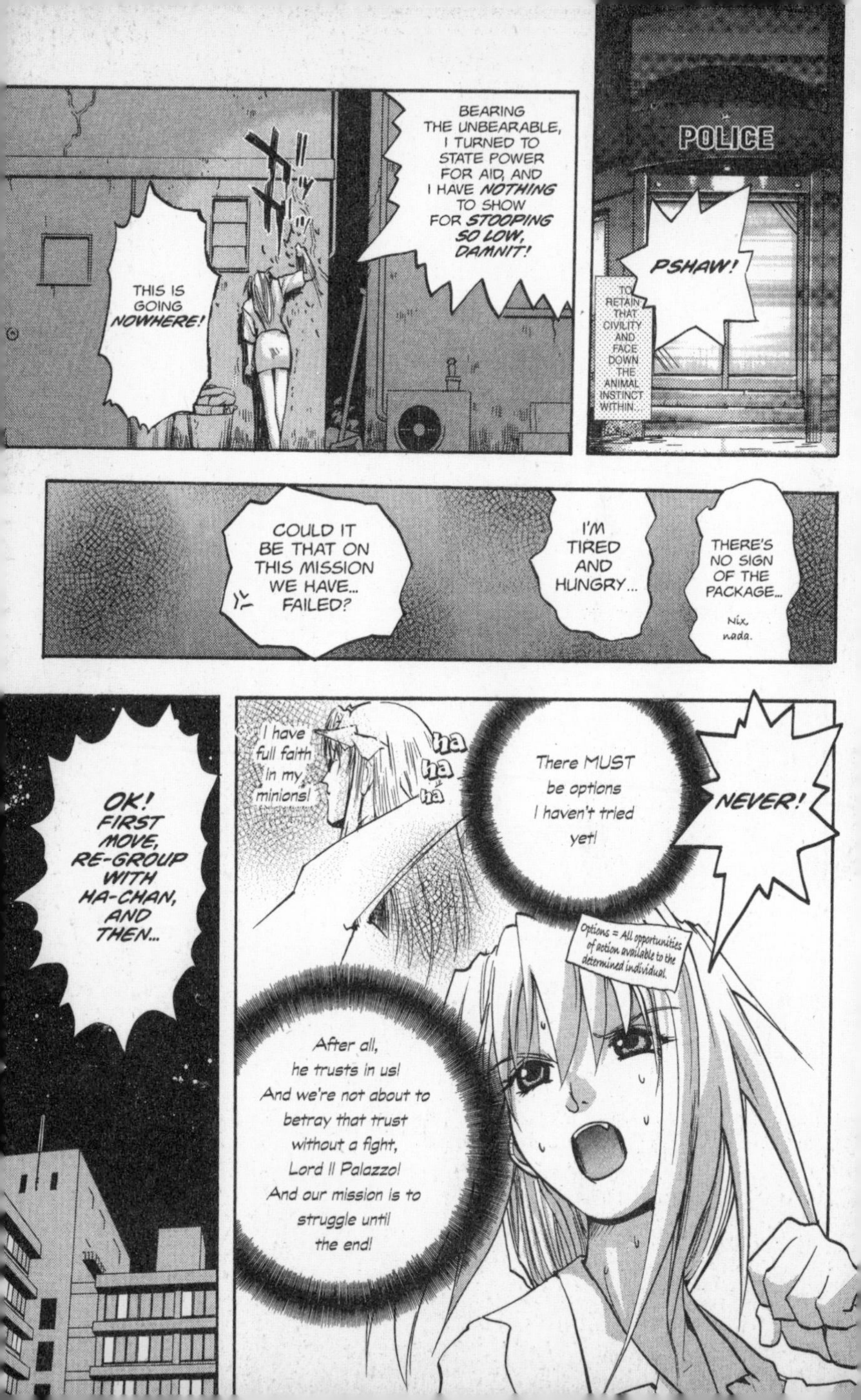
POLICE
PSHAW!
TO RETAIN THAT CIVILITY AND FACE DOWN THE ANIMAL INSTINCT WITHIN.
BEARING THE UNBEARABLE, I TURNED TO STATE POWER FOR AID, AND I HAVE NOTHING TO SHOW FOR STOOPING SO LOW, DAMNIT!
THIS IS GOING NOWHERE!
THERE'S NO SIGN OF THE PACKAGE...
Nix, nada.
I'M TIRED AND HUNGRY...
COULD IT BE THAT ON THIS MISSION WE HAVE... FAILED?
NEVER!
There MUST be options I haven't tried yet!
I have full faith in my minions!
ha ha ha
Options = All opportunities of action available to the determined individual.
After all, he trusts in us! And we're not about to betray that trust without a fight, Lord Il Palazzo! And our mission is to struggle until the end!
OK! FIRST MOVE, RE-GROUP WITH HA-CHAN, AND THEN...

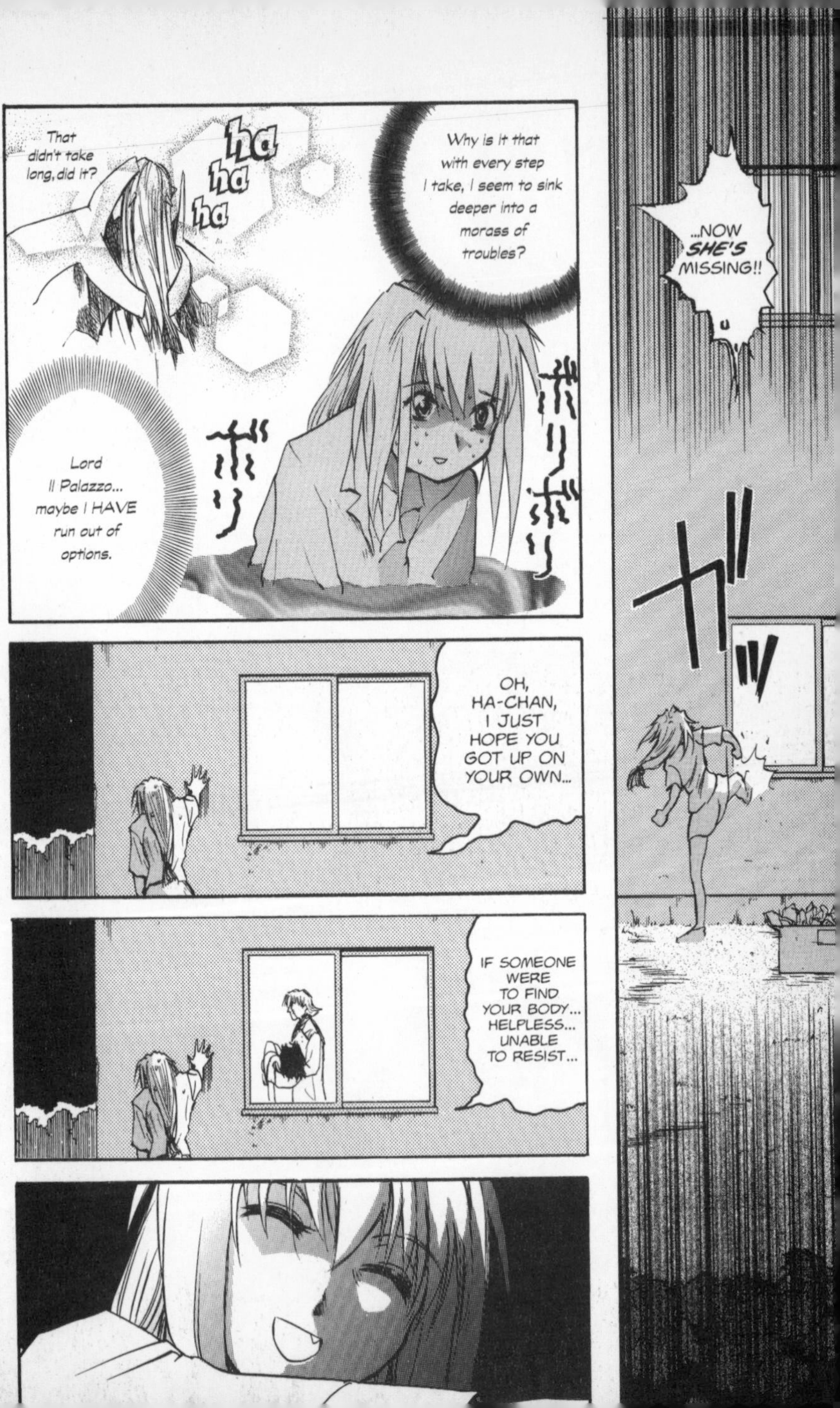
...NOW SHE'S MISSING!!
Why is it that with every step I take, I seem to sink deeper into a morass of troubles?
ha ha ha
That didn't take long, did it?
Lord Il Palazzo... maybe I HAVE run out of options.
OH, HA-CHAN, I JUST HOPE YOU GOT UP ON YOUR OWN...
IF SOMEONE WERE TO FIND YOUR BODY... HELPLESS... UNABLE TO RESIST...

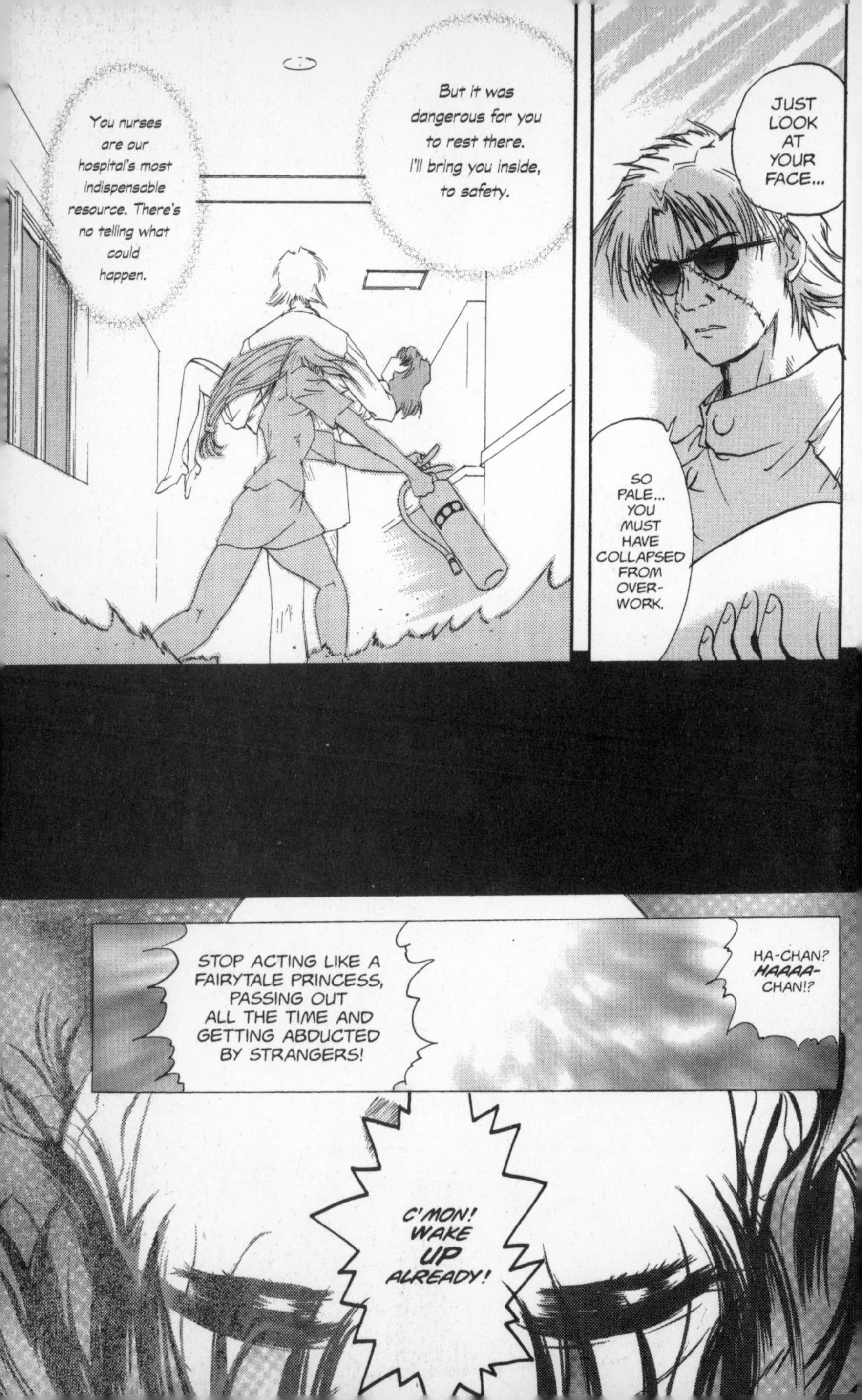
JUST LOOK AT YOUR FACE...
SO PALE... YOU MUST HAVE COLLAPSED FROM OVER-WORK.
But it was dangerous for you to rest there. I'll bring you inside, to safety.
You nurses are our hospital's most indispensable resource. There's no telling what could happen.
HA-CHAN? HAAAA-CHAN!?
STOP ACTING LIKE A FAIRYTALE PRINCESS, PASSING OUT ALL THE TIME AND GETTING ABDUCTED BY STRANGERS!
C'MON! WAKE UP ALREADY!

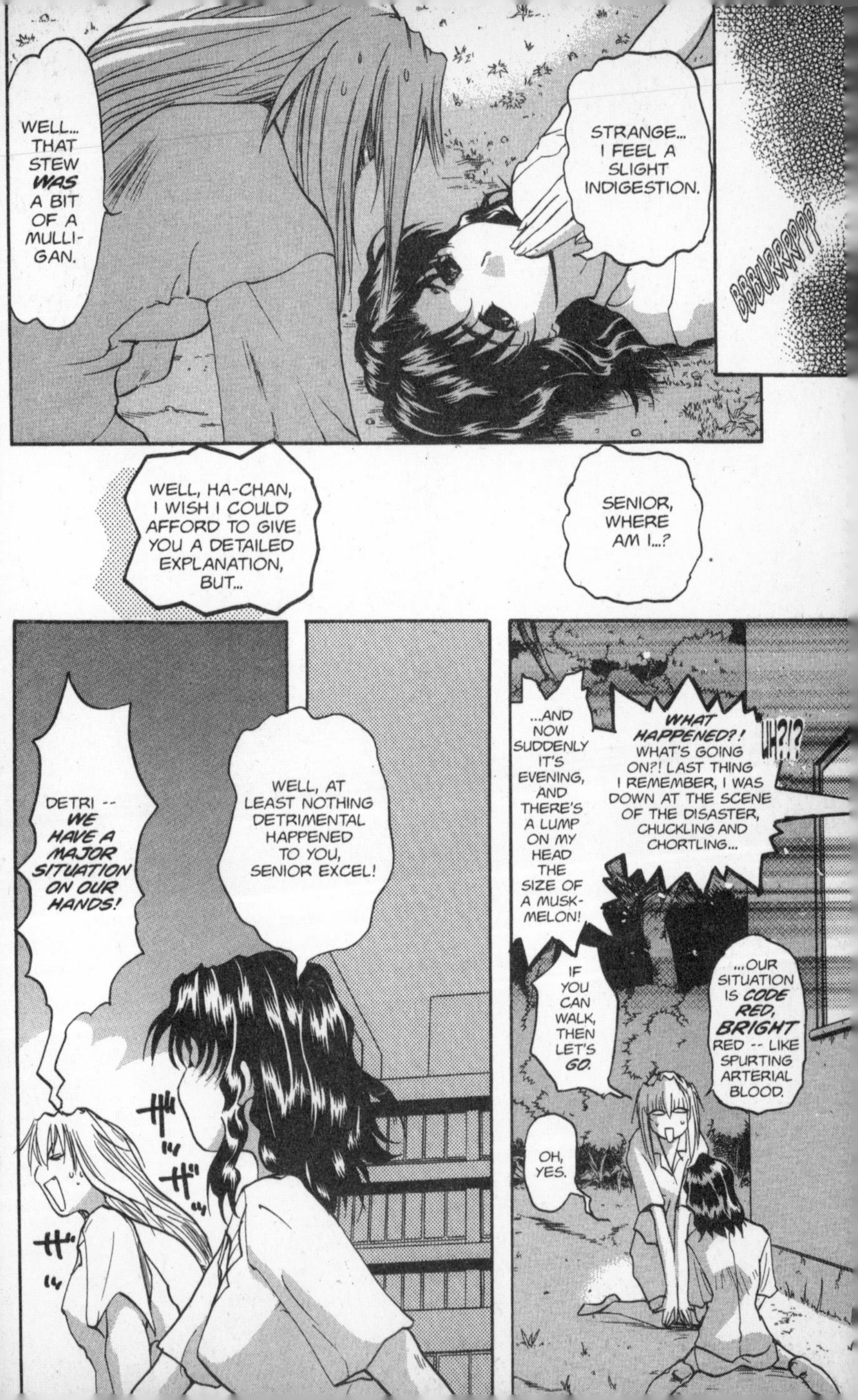
STRANGE... I FEEL A SLIGHT INDIGESTION.
BBBURRRRPPP
WELL... THAT STEW *WAS* A BIT OF A MULLI-GAN.
SENIOR, WHERE AM I...?
WELL, HA-CHAN, I WISH I COULD AFFORD TO GIVE YOU A DETAILED EXPLANATION, BUT...
UH?!?
*WHAT HAPPENED?!* WHAT'S GOING ON?! LAST THING I REMEMBER, I WAS DOWN AT THE SCENE OF THE DISASTER, CHUCKLING AND CHORTLING...
...AND NOW SUDDENLY IT'S EVENING, AND THERE'S A LUMP ON MY HEAD THE SIZE OF A MUSK-MELON!
...OUR SITUATION IS *CODE RED, BRIGHT* RED -- LIKE SPURTING ARTERIAL BLOOD.
IF YOU CAN WALK, THEN LET'S *GO.*
OH, YES.
WELL, AT LEAST NOTHING DETRIMENTAL HAPPENED TO YOU, SENIOR EXCEL!
DETRI -- *WE HAVE A MAJOR SITUATION ON OUR HANDS!*

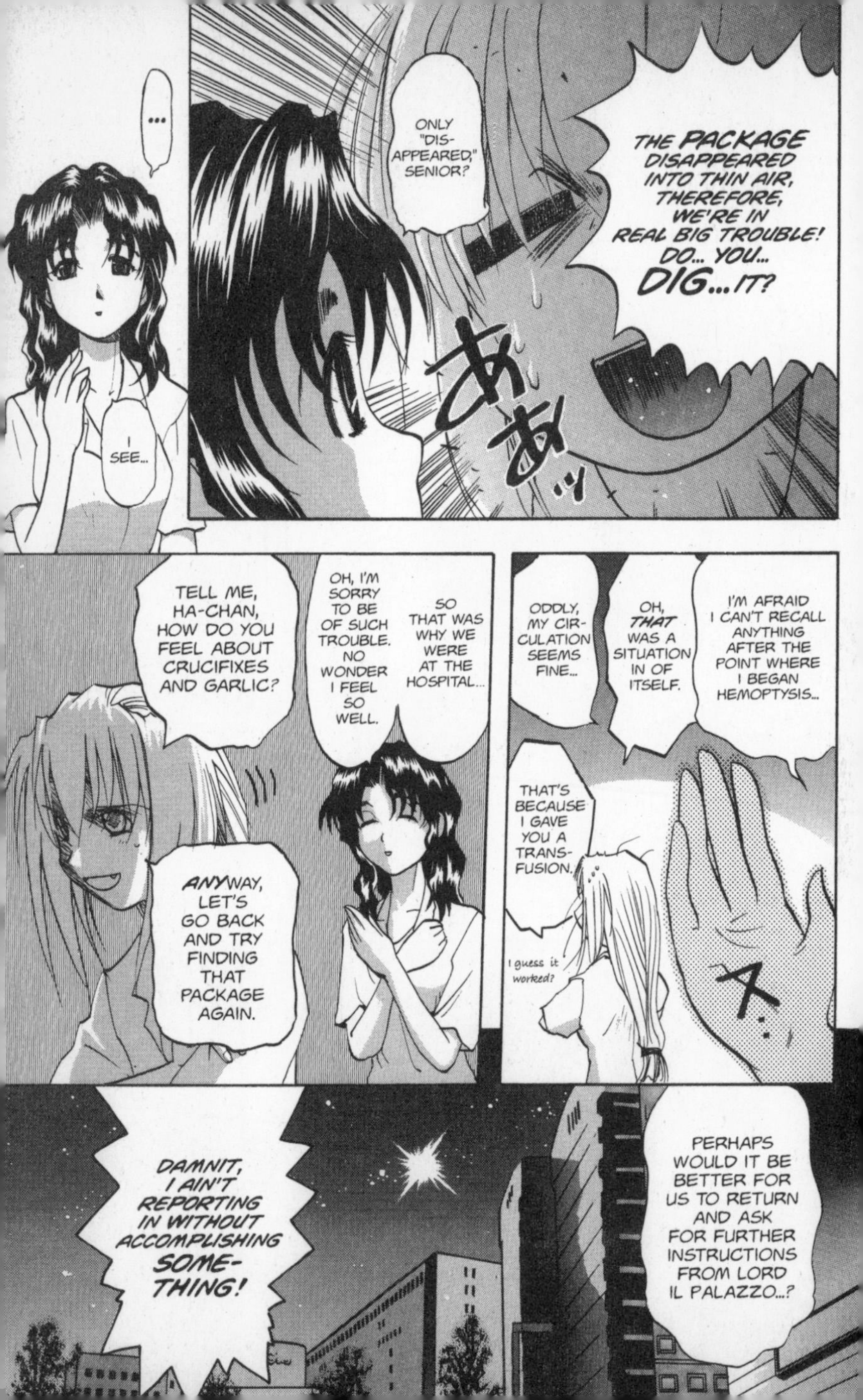
THE PACKAGE DISAPPEARED INTO THIN AIR, THEREFORE, WE'RE IN REAL BIG TROUBLE! DO... YOU... DIG...IT?
ONLY "DIS-APPEARED," SENIOR?
ああッ
...
I SEE...
I'M AFRAID I CAN'T RECALL ANYTHING AFTER THE POINT WHERE I BEGAN HEMOPTYSIS...
OH, THAT WAS A SITUATION IN OF ITSELF.
ODDLY, MY CIR-CULATION SEEMS FINE...
THAT'S BECAUSE I GAVE YOU A TRANS-FUSION.
I guess it worked?
SO THAT WAS WHY WE WERE AT THE HOSPITAL...
OH, I'M SORRY TO BE OF SUCH TROUBLE. NO WONDER I FEEL SO WELL.
TELL ME, HA-CHAN, HOW DO YOU FEEL ABOUT CRUCIFIXES AND GARLIC?
ANYWAY, LET'S GO BACK AND TRY FINDING THAT PACKAGE AGAIN.
PERHAPS WOULD IT BE BETTER FOR US TO RETURN AND ASK FOR FURTHER INSTRUCTIONS FROM LORD IL PALAZZO...?
DAMNIT, I AIN'T REPORTING IN WITHOUT ACCOMPLISHING SOME-THING!

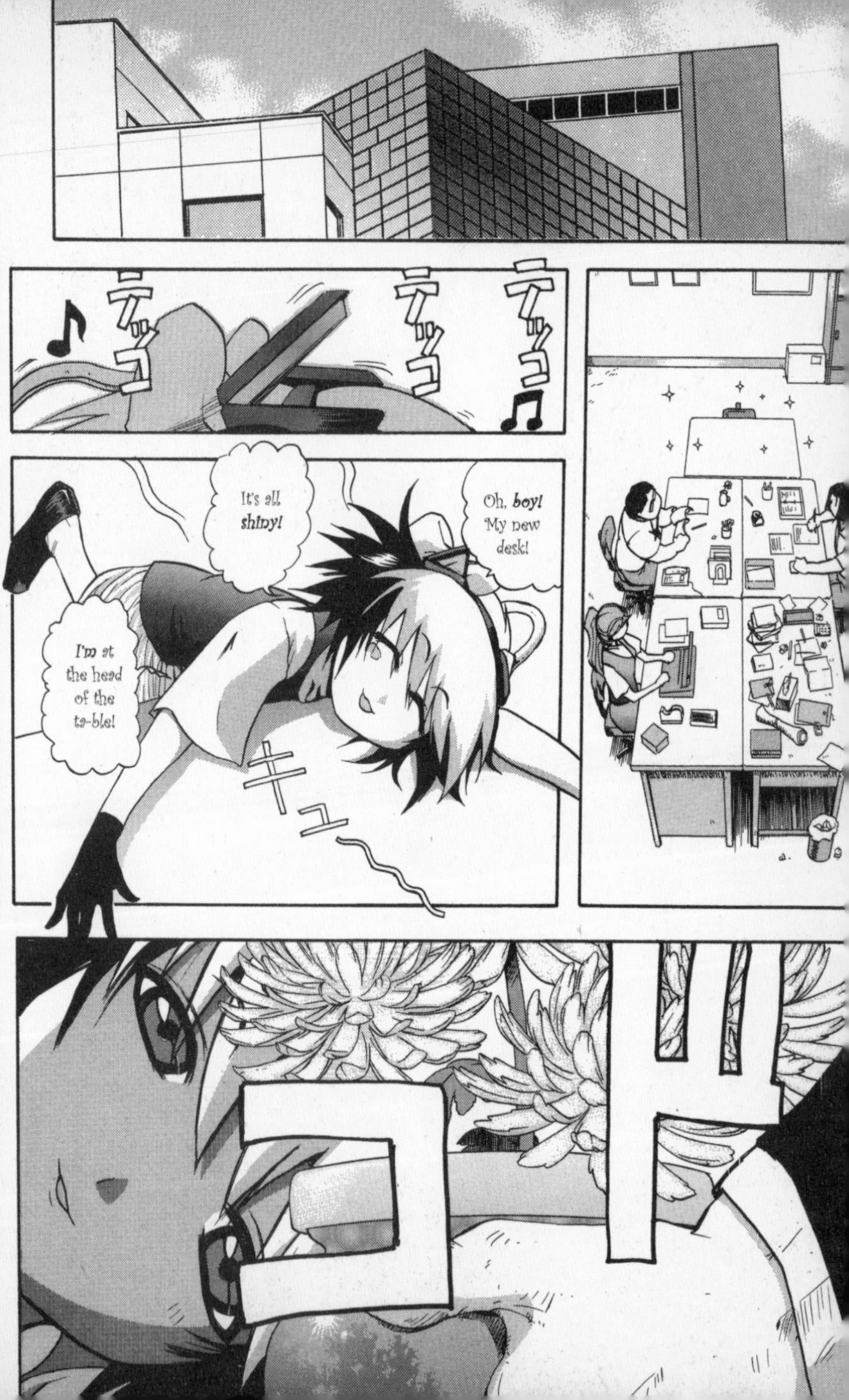
テッコ
テッコ
テッコ
Oh, boy! My new desk!
It's all shiny!
I'm at the head of the ta-ble!
キュ〜

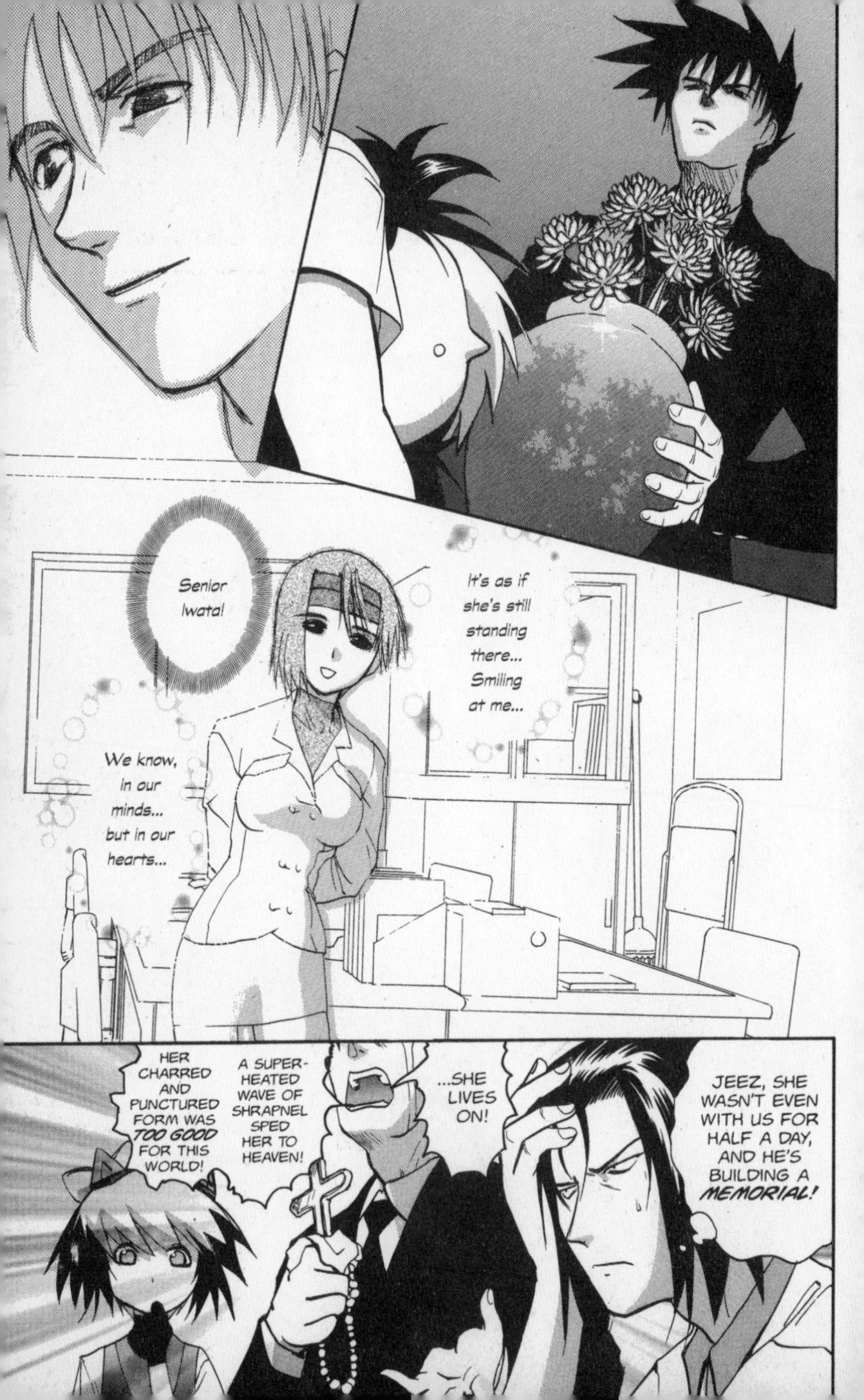
It's as if she's still standing there... Smiling at me...
Senior Iwata!
We know, in our minds... but in our hearts...
JEEZ, SHE WASN'T EVEN WITH US FOR HALF A DAY, AND HE'S BUILDING A ***MEMORIAL!***
...SHE LIVES ON!
A SUPER-HEATED WAVE OF SHRAPNEL SPED HER TO HEAVEN!
HER CHARRED AND PUNCTURED FORM WAS ***TOO GOOD*** FOR THIS WORLD!

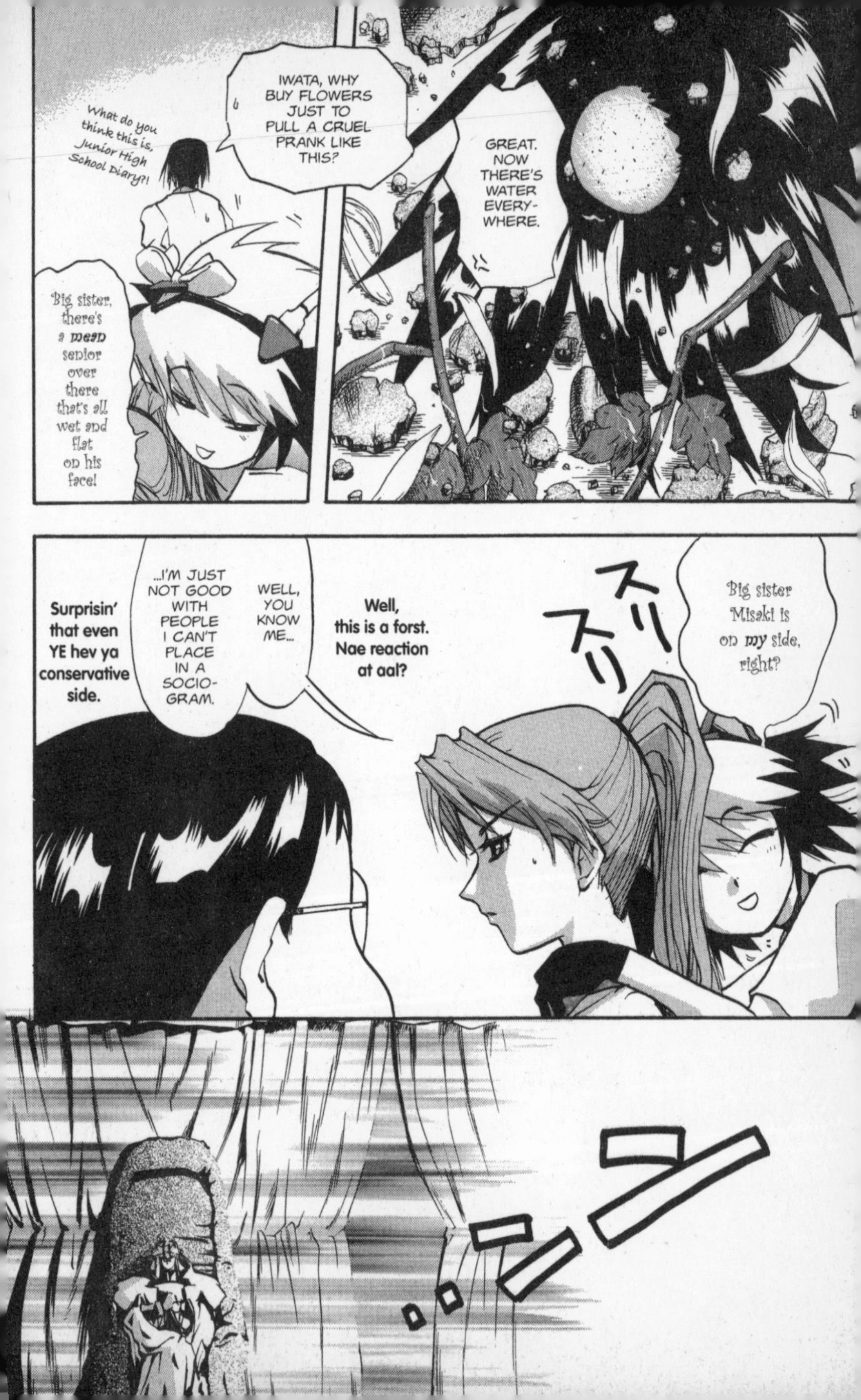
GREAT. NOW THERE'S WATER EVERY-WHERE.
IWATA, WHY BUY FLOWERS JUST TO PULL A CRUEL PRANK LIKE THIS?
What do you think this is, Junior High School Diary?!
Big sister, there's a *mean* senior over there that's all wet and flat on his face!
Big sister Misaki is on *my* side, right?
スリ
スリ
Well, this is a forst. Nae reaction at aal?
WELL, YOU KNOW ME...
...I'M JUST NOT GOOD WITH PEOPLE I CAN'T PLACE IN A SOCIO-GRAM.
Surprisin' that even YE hev ya conservative side.

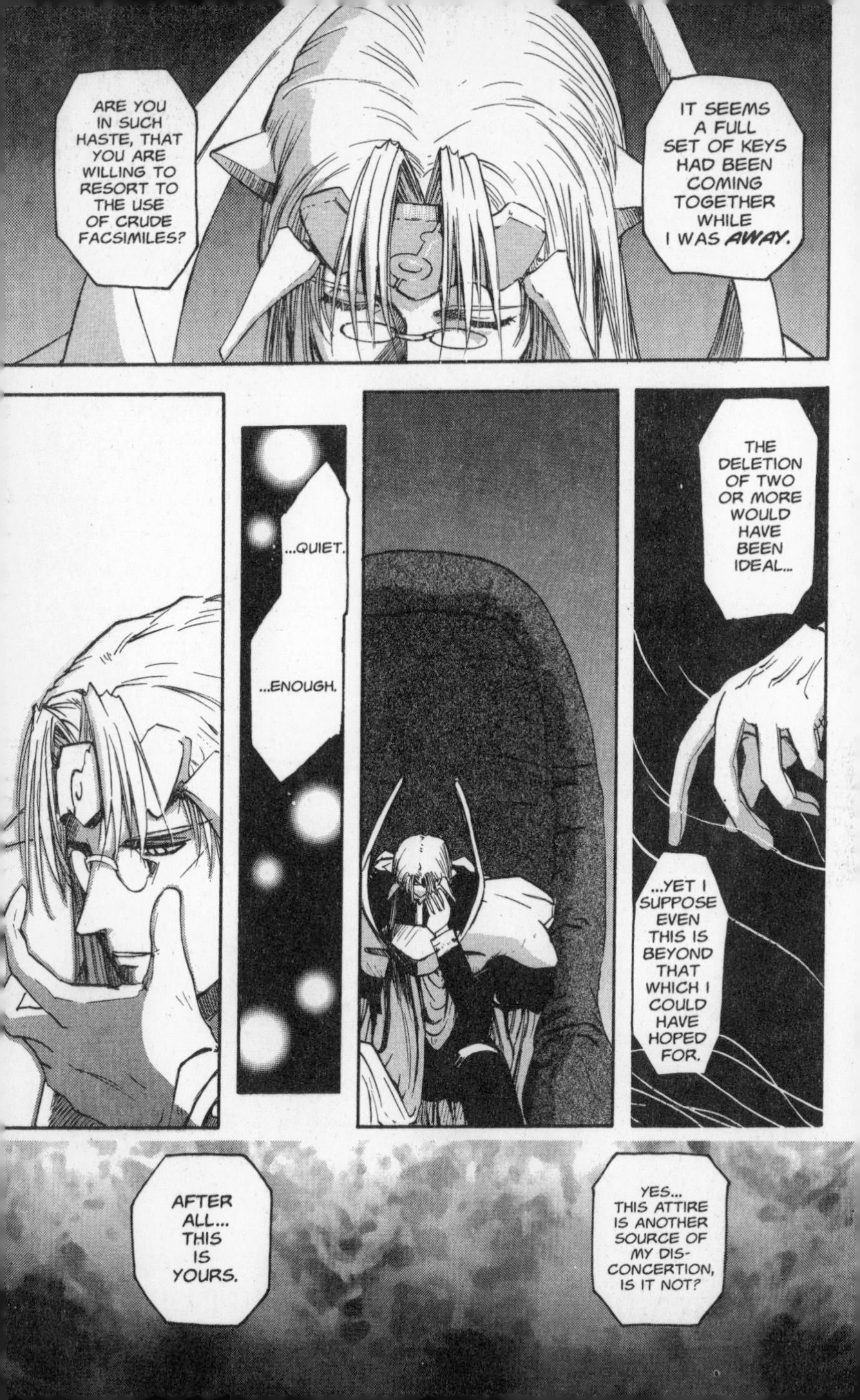
IT SEEMS A FULL SET OF KEYS HAD BEEN COMING TOGETHER WHILE I WAS *AWAY.*
ARE YOU IN SUCH HASTE, THAT YOU ARE WILLING TO RESORT TO THE USE OF CRUDE FACSIMILES?
THE DELETION OF TWO OR MORE WOULD HAVE BEEN IDEAL...
...YET I SUPPOSE EVEN THIS IS BEYOND THAT WHICH I COULD HAVE HOPED FOR.
...QUIET.
...ENOUGH.
YES... THIS ATTIRE IS ANOTHER SOURCE OF MY DIS-CONCERTION, IS IT NOT?
AFTER ALL... THIS IS YOURS.

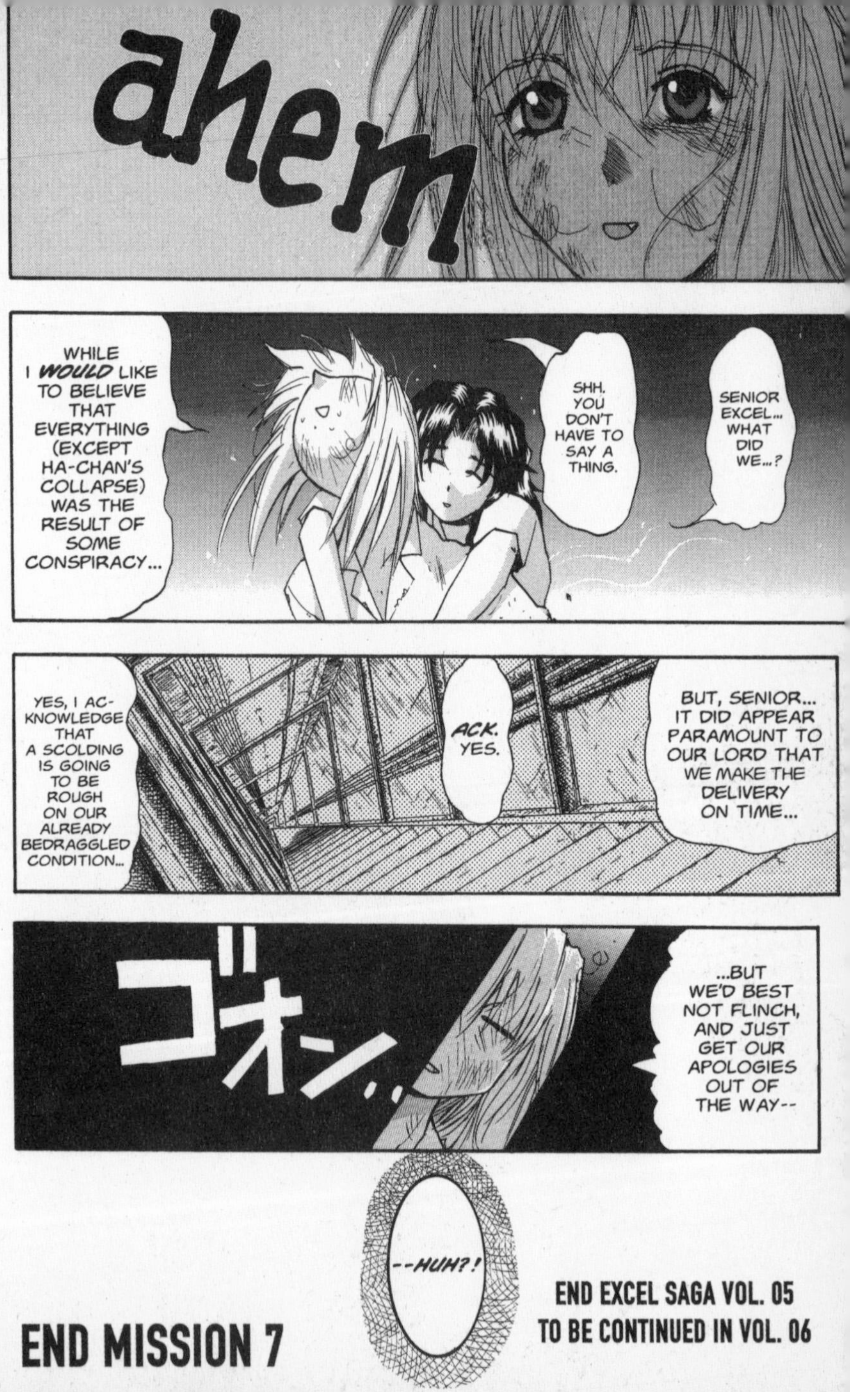
ahem
SENIOR EXCEL... WHAT DID WE...?
SHH. YOU DON'T HAVE TO SAY A THING.
WHILE I *WOULD* LIKE TO BELIEVE THAT EVERYTHING (EXCEPT HA-CHAN'S COLLAPSE) WAS THE RESULT OF SOME CONSPIRACY...
BUT, SENIOR... IT DID APPEAR PARAMOUNT TO OUR LORD THAT WE MAKE THE DELIVERY ON TIME...
*ACK.* YES.
YES, I AC-KNOWLEDGE THAT A SCOLDING IS GOING TO BE ROUGH ON OUR ALREADY BEDRAGGLED CONDITION...
...BUT WE'D BEST NOT FLINCH, AND JUST GET OUR APOLOGIES OUT OF THE WAY--
ゴォン..
--HUH?!
END MISSION 7
END EXCEL SAGA VOL. 05
TO BE CONTINUED IN VOL. 06

# Special Edition

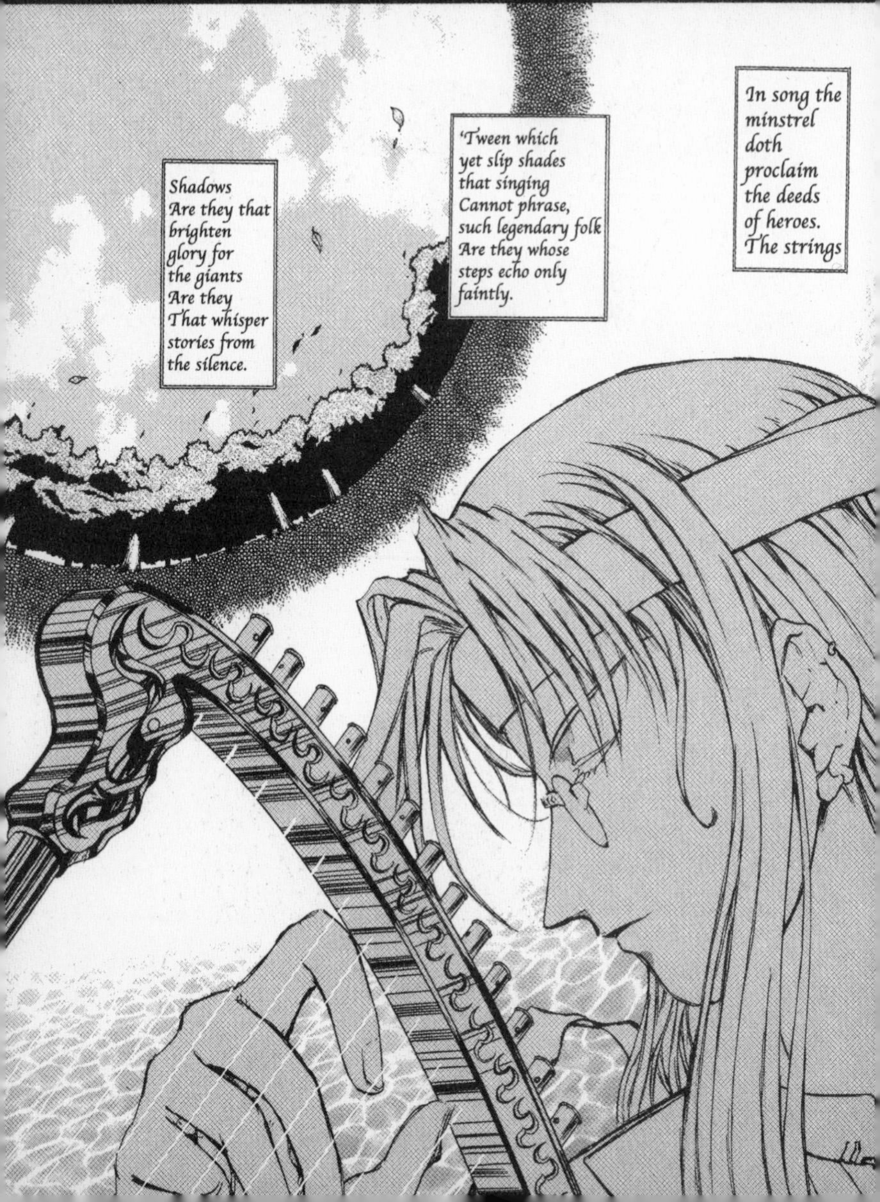
In song the minstrel doth proclaim the deeds of heroes. The strings
'Tween which yet slip shades that singing Cannot phrase, such legendary folk Are they whose steps echo only faintly.
Shadows Are they that brighten glory for the giants Are they That whisper stories from the silence.

## BONUS MISSION

# THE SPRING PROGRAMMING SPECIAL

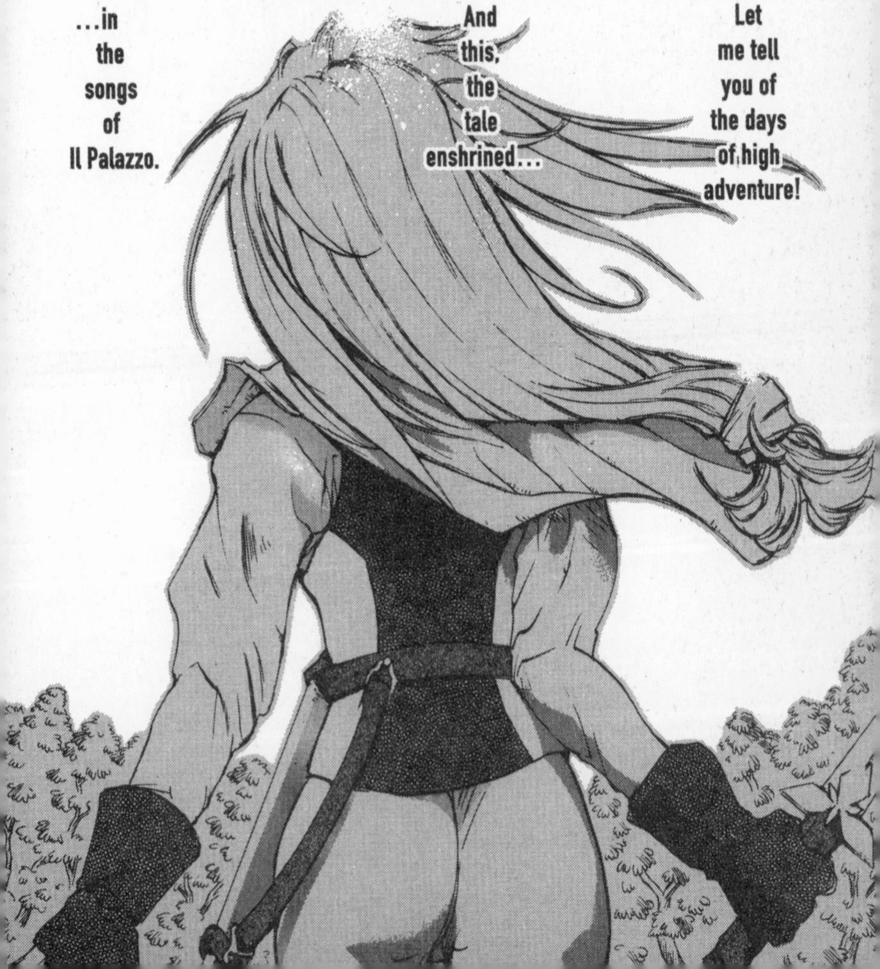
Let me tell you of the days of high adventure!
And this, the tale enshrined...
...in the songs of Il Palazzo.

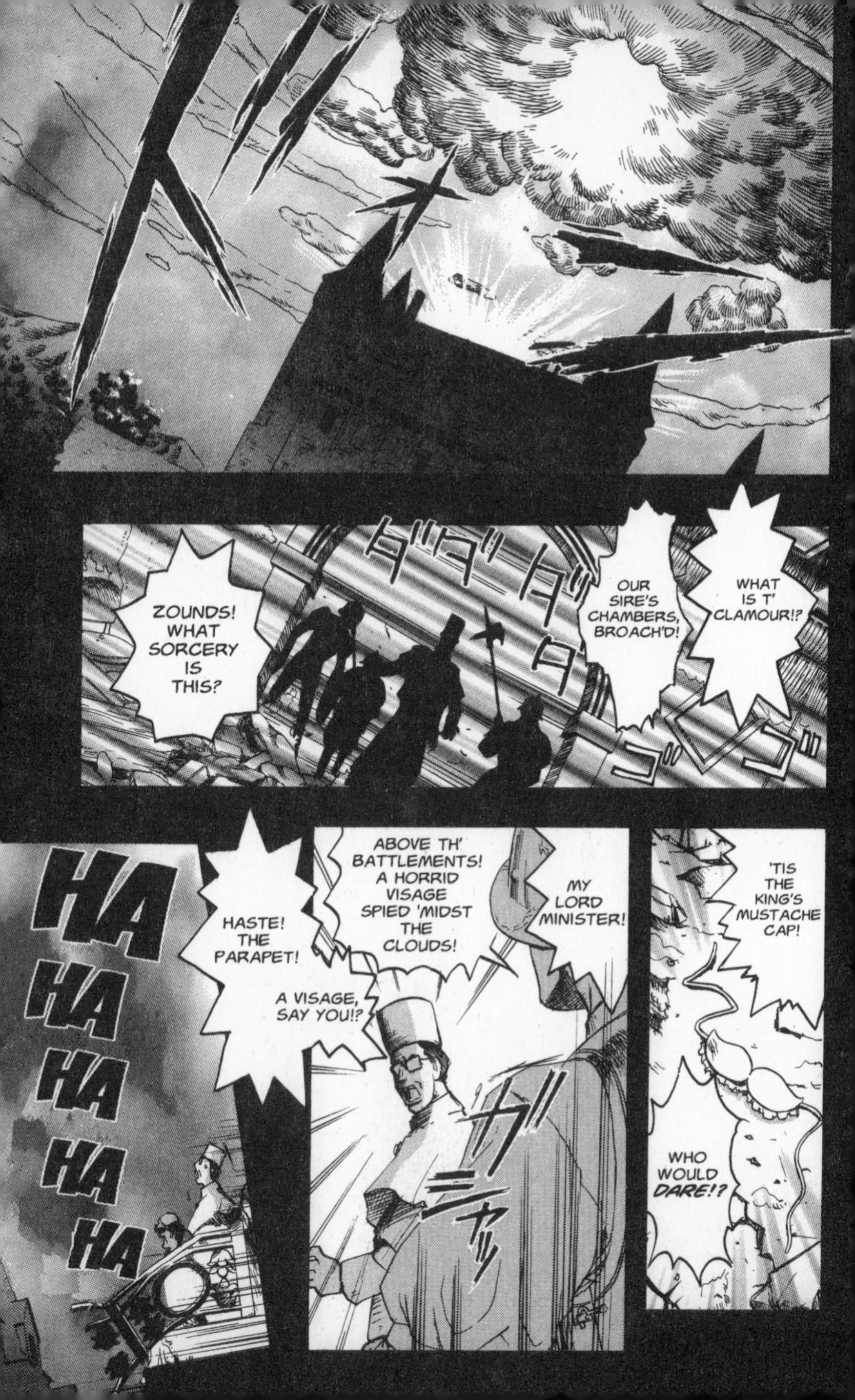
WHAT IS T' CLAMOUR!?
OUR SIRE'S CHAMBERS, BROACH'D!
ZOUNDS! WHAT SORCERY IS THIS?
'TIS THE KING'S MUSTACHE CAP!
WHO WOULD *DARE!?*
MY LORD MINISTER!
ABOVE TH' BATTLEMENTS! A HORRID VISAGE SPIED 'MIDST THE CLOUDS!
A VISAGE, SAY YOU!?
HASTE! THE PARAPET!
HA HA HA HA HA HA

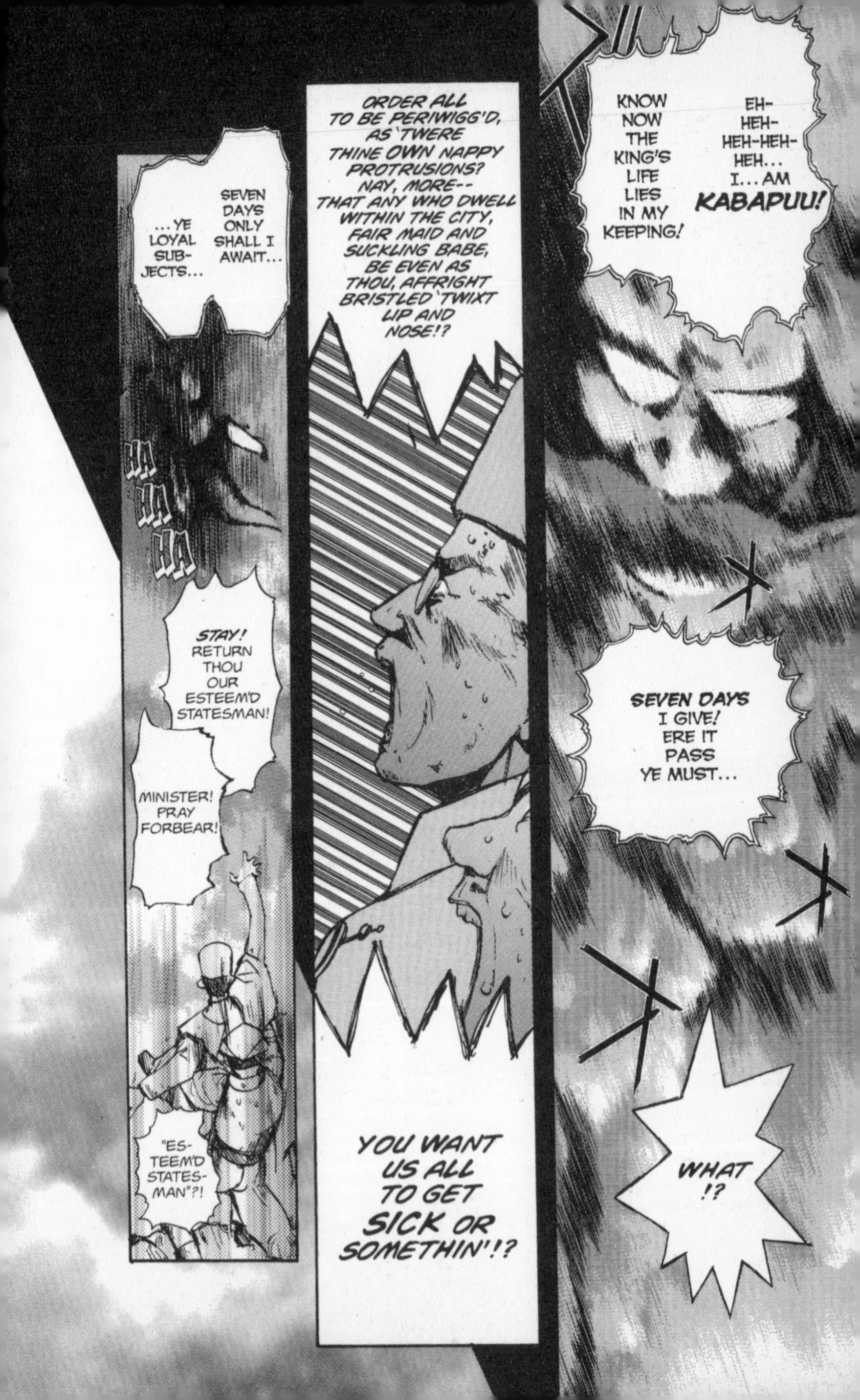

EH-HEH-HEH-HEH-HEH... I... AM KABAPUU!
KNOW NOW THE KING'S LIFE LIES IN MY KEEPING!
SEVEN DAYS I GIVE! ERE IT PASS YE MUST...
WHAT!?
ORDER ALL TO BE PERIWIGG'D, AS 'TWERE THINE OWN NAPPY PROTRUSIONS? NAY, MORE-- THAT ANY WHO DWELL WITHIN THE CITY, FAIR MAID AND SUCKLING BABE, BE EVEN AS THOU, AFFRIGHT BRISTLED 'TWIXT LIP AND NOSE!?
YOU WANT US ALL TO GET SICK OR SOMETHIN'!?
SEVEN DAYS ONLY SHALL I AWAIT...
...YE LOYAL SUBJECTS...
HA HA HA
STAY! RETURN THOU OUR ESTEEM'D STATESMAN!
MINISTER! PRAY FORBEAR!
"ES-TEEM'D STATES-MAN"?!

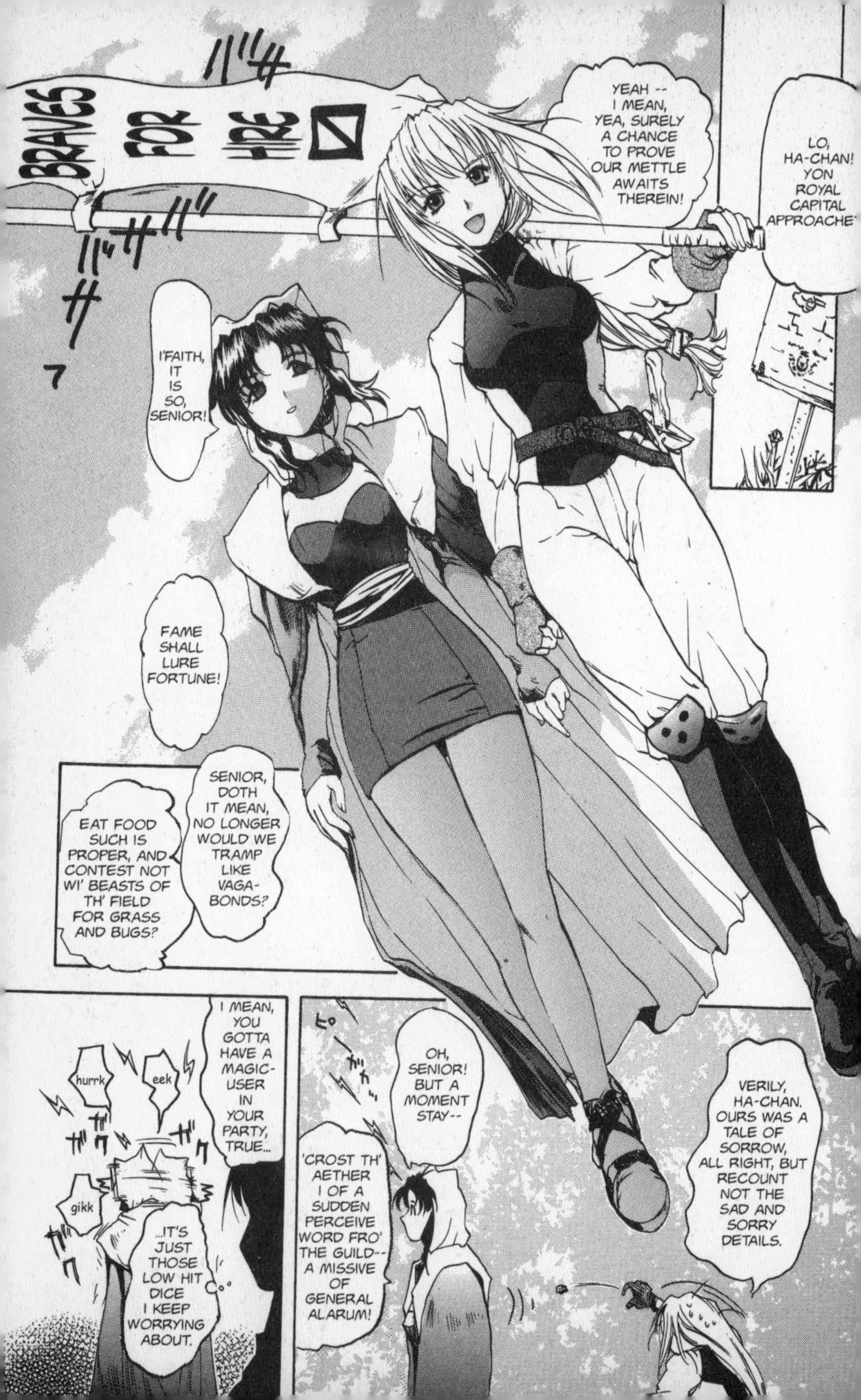
LO, HA-CHAN! YON ROYAL CAPITAL APPROACHE
YEAH -- I MEAN, YEA, SURELY A CHANCE TO PROVE OUR METTLE AWAITS THEREIN!
BRAVES FOR HIRE
7
I'FAITH, IT IS SO, SENIOR!
FAME SHALL LURE FORTUNE!
SENIOR, DOTH IT MEAN, NO LONGER WOULD WE TRAMP LIKE VAGA-BONDS?
EAT FOOD SUCH IS PROPER, AND CONTEST NOT WI' BEASTS OF TH' FIELD FOR GRASS AND BUGS?
VERILY, HA-CHAN. OURS WAS A TALE OF SORROW, ALL RIGHT, BUT RECOUNT NOT THE SAD AND SORRY DETAILS.
OH, SENIOR! BUT A MOMENT STAY--
'CROST TH' AETHER I OF A SUDDEN PERCEIVE WORD FRO' THE GUILD-- A MISSIVE OF GENERAL ALARUM!
I MEAN, YOU GOTTA HAVE A MAGIC-USER IN YOUR PARTY, TRUE...
eek
hurrk
gikk
...IT'S JUST THOSE LOW HIT DICE I KEEP WORRYING ABOUT.

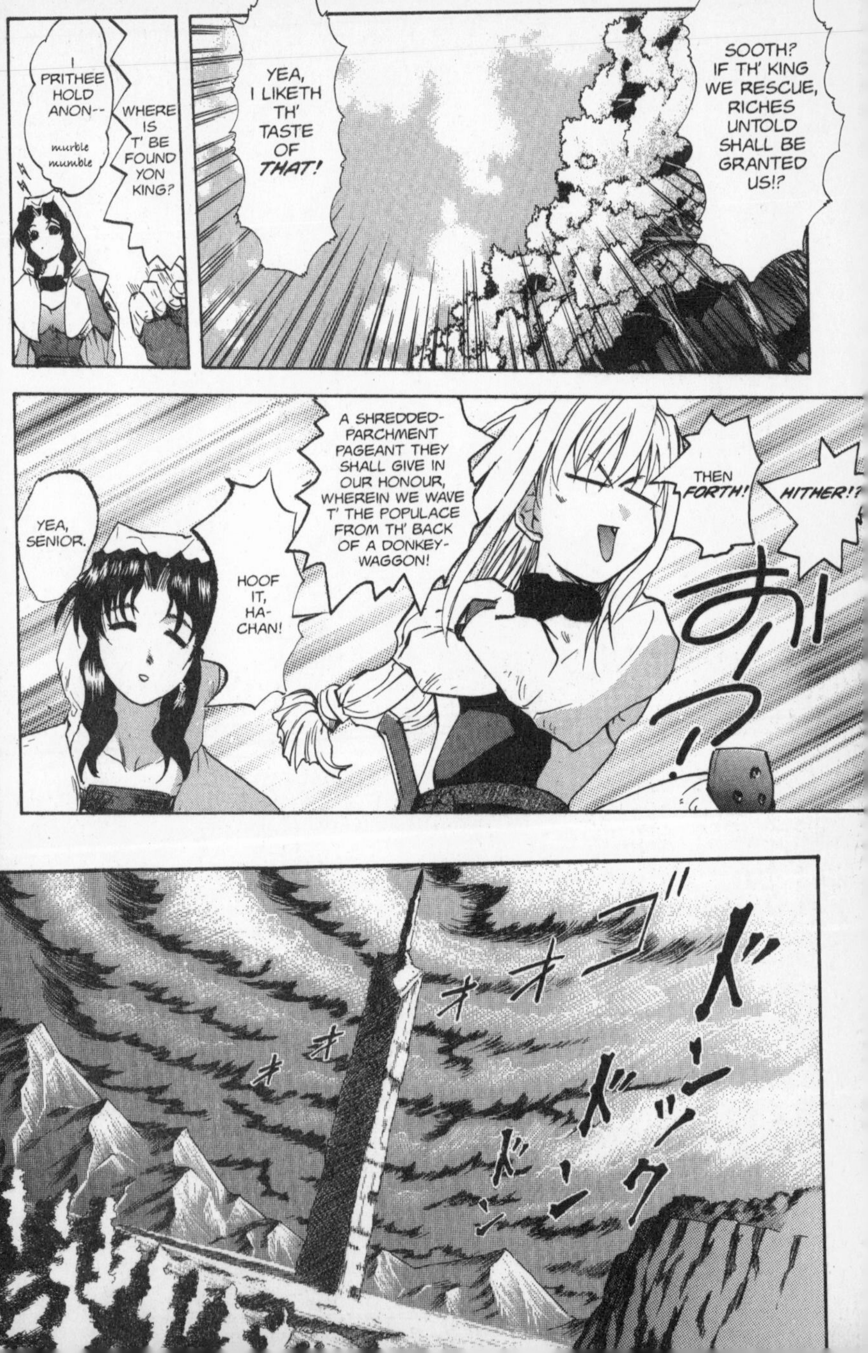
SOOTH? IF TH' KING WE RESCUE, RICHES UNTOLD SHALL BE GRANTED US!?
YEA, I LIKETH TH' TASTE OF *THAT!*
WHERE IS T' BE FOUND YON KING?
I PRITHEE HOLD ANON-- murble mumble
*HITHER!?*
THEN *FORTH!*
A SHREDDED-PARCHMENT PAGEANT THEY SHALL GIVE IN OUR HONOUR, WHEREIN WE WAVE T' THE POPULACE FROM TH' BACK OF A DONKEY-WAGGON!
おーっ!?
HOOF IT, HA-CHAN!
YEA, SENIOR.
ゴオオオオ

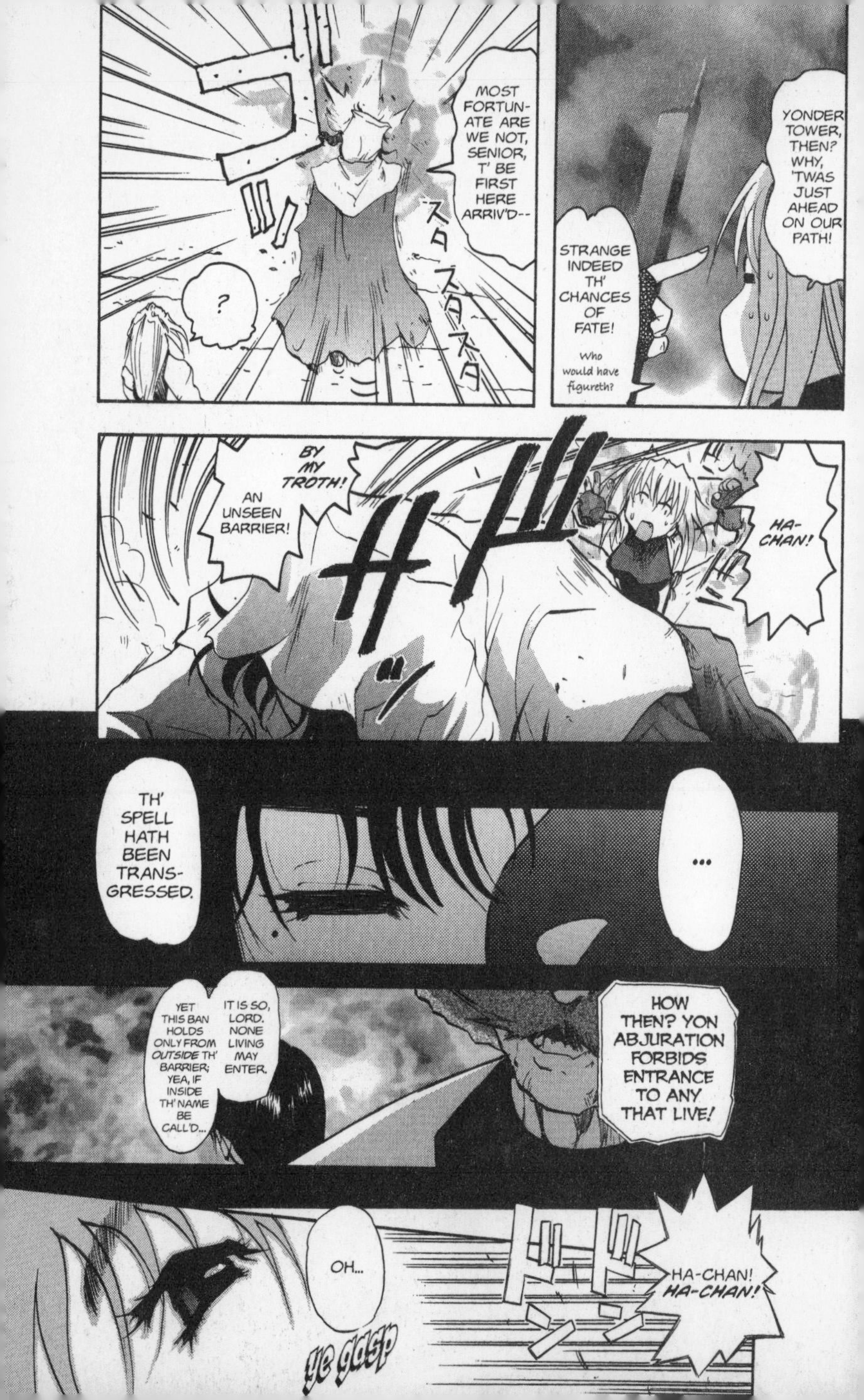

YONDER TOWER, THEN? WHY, 'TWAS JUST AHEAD ON OUR PATH!
STRANGE INDEED TH' CHANCES OF FATE!
Who would have figureth?
MOST FORTUN-ATE ARE WE NOT, SENIOR, T' BE FIRST HERE ARRIV'D--
?
HA-CHAN!
BY MY TROTH!
AN UNSEEN BARRIER!
...
TH' SPELL HATH BEEN TRANS-GRESSED.
HOW THEN? YON ABJURATION FORBIDS ENTRANCE TO ANY THAT LIVE!
IT IS SO, LORD. NONE LIVING MAY ENTER.
YET THIS BAN HOLDS ONLY FROM *OUTSIDE* TH' BARRIER; YEA, IF INSIDE TH' NAME BE CALL'D...
HA-CHAN! *HA-CHAN!*
OH...
ye gasp

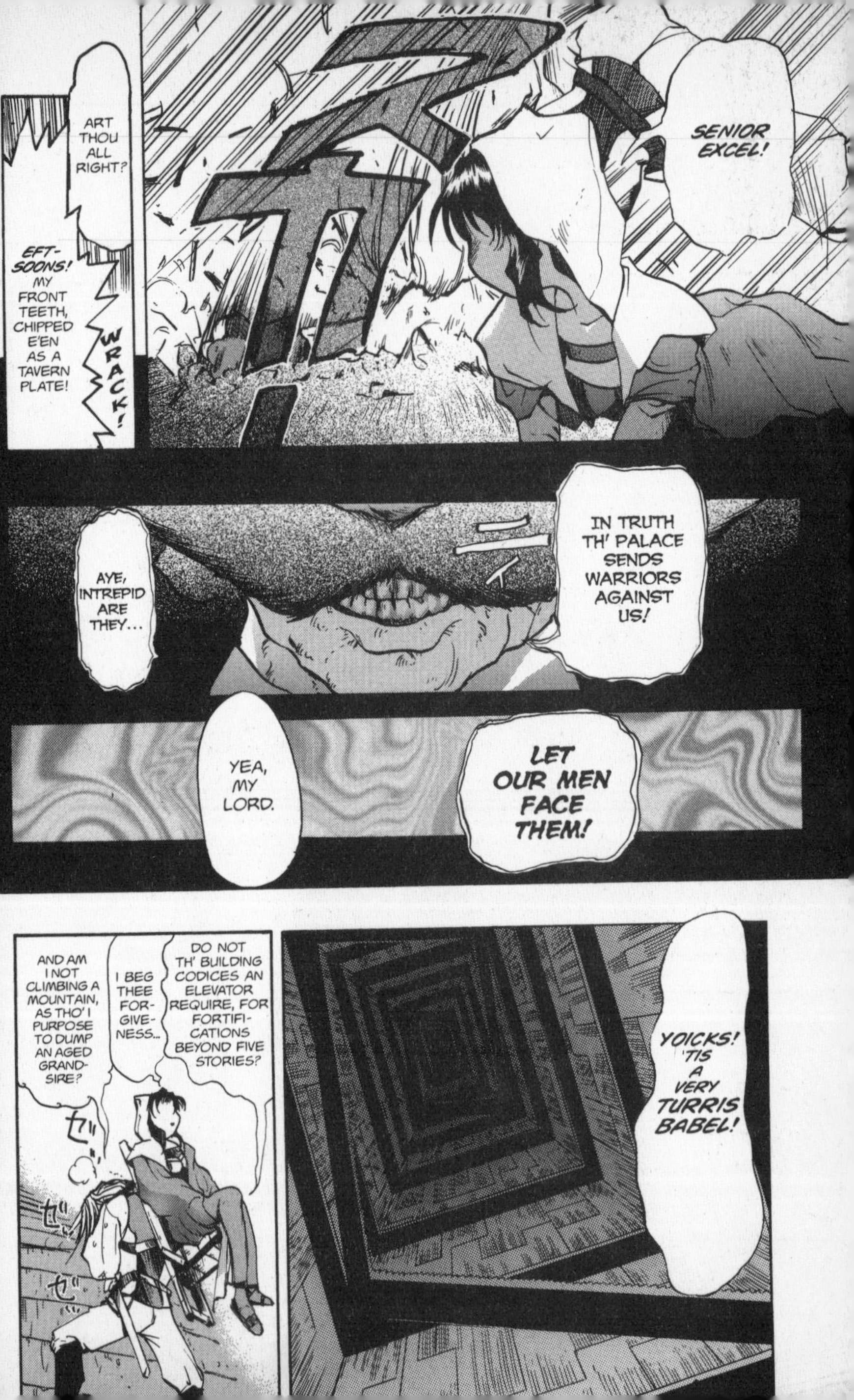
SENIOR EXCEL!
ART THOU ALL RIGHT?
EFT-SOONS! MY FRONT TEETH, CHIPPED E'EN AS A TAVERN PLATE!
WRACK!
IN TRUTH TH' PALACE SENDS WARRIORS AGAINST US!
AYE, INTREPID ARE THEY...
LET OUR MEN FACE THEM!
YEA, MY LORD.
YOICKS! 'TIS A VERY TURRIS BABEL!
DO NOT TH' BUILDING CODICES AN ELEVATOR REQUIRE, FOR FORTIFICATIONS BEYOND FIVE STORIES?
I BEG THEE FORGIVENESS...
AND AM I NOT CLIMBING A MOUNTAIN, AS THO' I PURPOSE TO DUMP AN AGED GRANDSIRE?

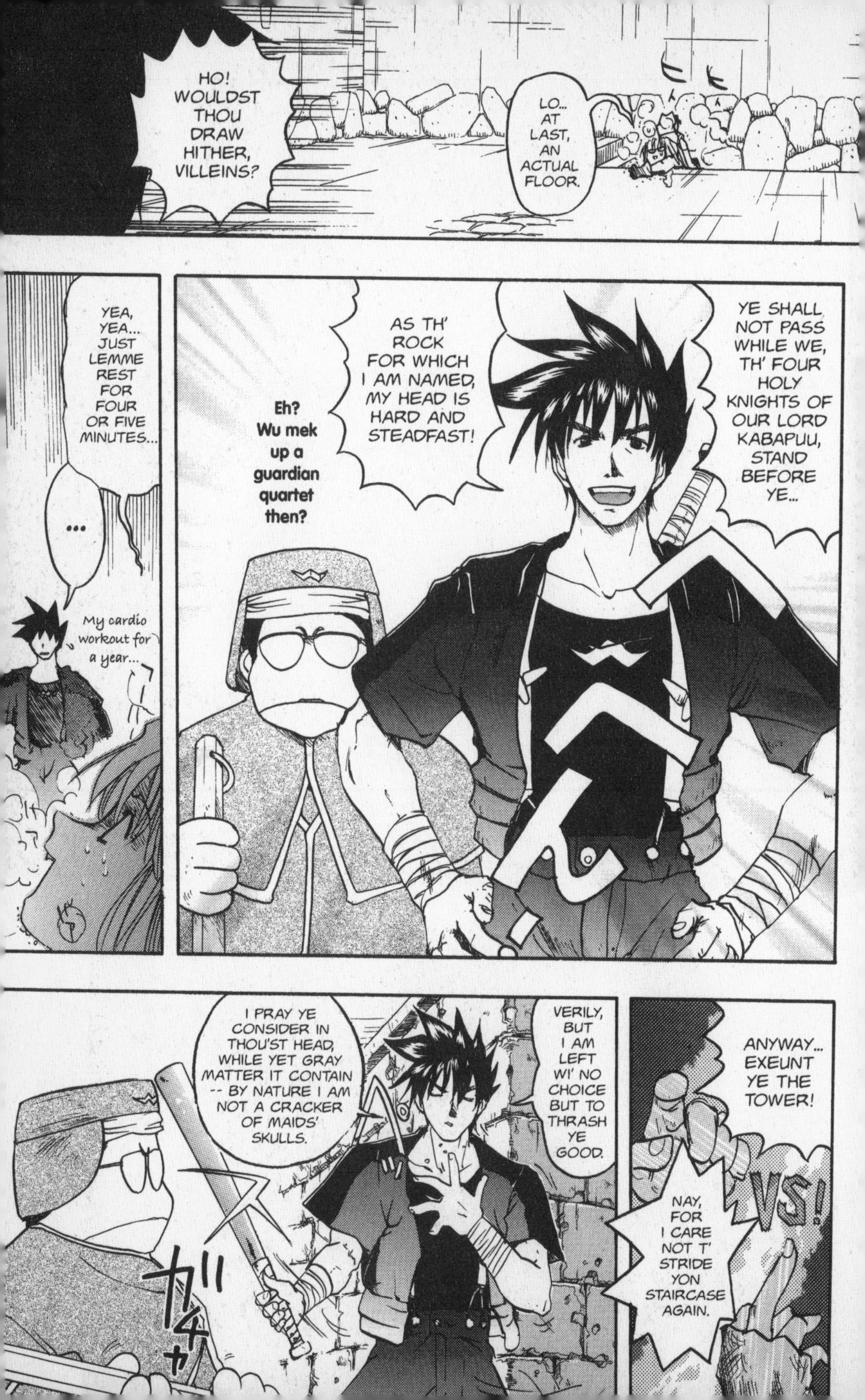
LO... AT LAST, AN ACTUAL FLOOR.
HO! WOULDST THOU DRAW HITHER, VILLEINS?
YE SHALL NOT PASS WHILE WE, TH' FOUR HOLY KNIGHTS OF OUR LORD KABAPUU, STAND BEFORE YE...
AS TH' ROCK FOR WHICH I AM NAMED, MY HEAD IS HARD AND STEADFAST!
Eh? Wu mek up a guardian quartet then?
YEA, YEA... JUST LEMME REST FOR FOUR OR FIVE MINUTES...
...
My cardio workout for a year...
ANYWAY... EXEUNT YE THE TOWER!
VS!
NAY, FOR I CARE NOT T' STRIDE YON STAIRCASE AGAIN.
VERILY, BUT I AM LEFT WI' NO CHOICE BUT TO THRASH YE GOOD.
I PRAY YE CONSIDER IN THOU'ST HEAD, WHILE YET GRAY MATTER IT CONTAIN -- BY NATURE I AM NOT A CRACKER OF MAIDS' SKULLS.

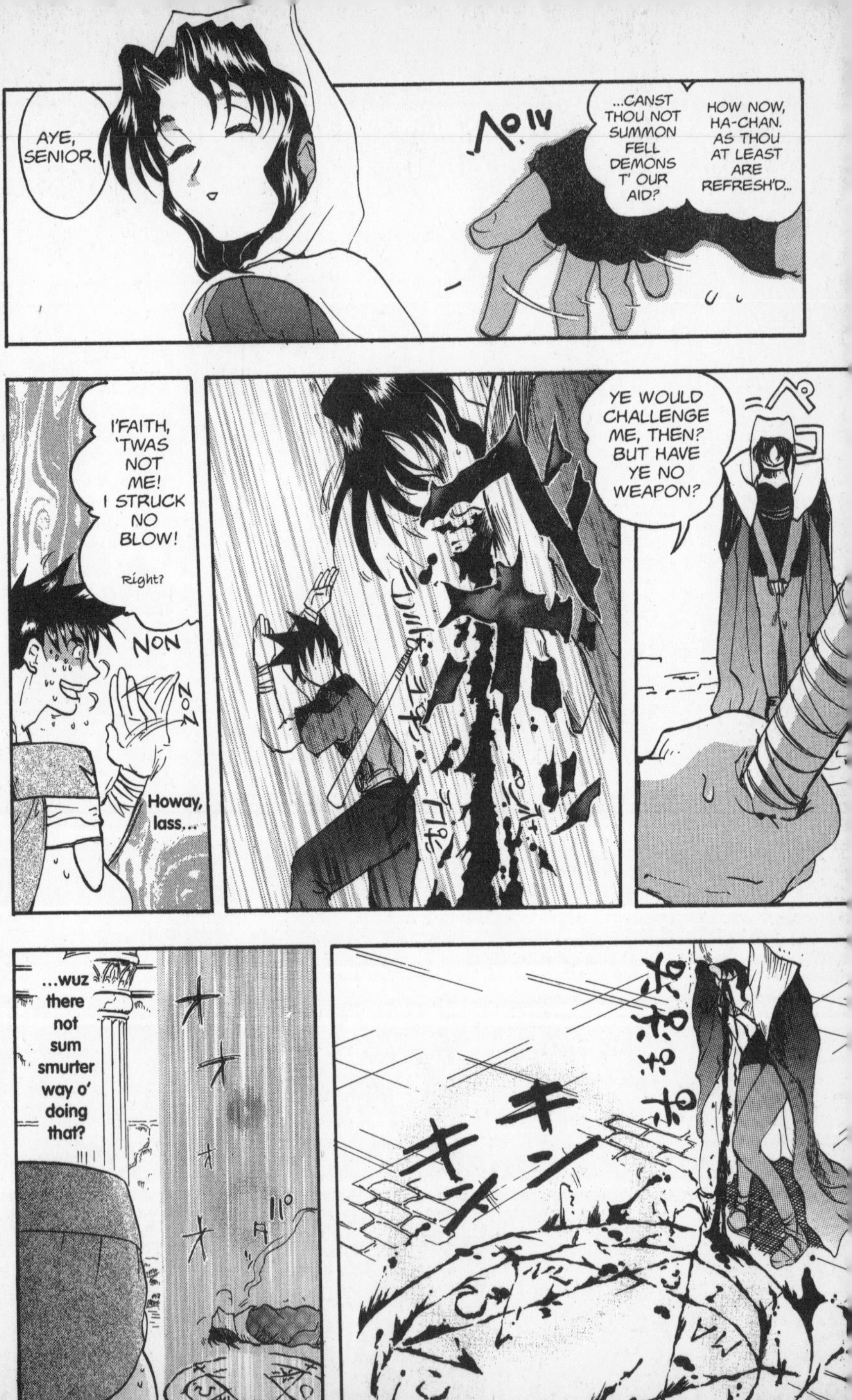
HOW NOW, HA-CHAN. AS THOU AT LEAST ARE REFRESH'D...
...CANST THOU NOT SUMMON FELL DEMONS T' OUR AID?
AYE, SENIOR.
YE WOULD CHALLENGE ME, THEN? BUT HAVE YE NO WEAPON?
I'FAITH, 'TWAS NOT ME! I STRUCK NO BLOW!
Right?
NON
NON
Howay, lass...
...wuz there not sum smurter way o' doing that?

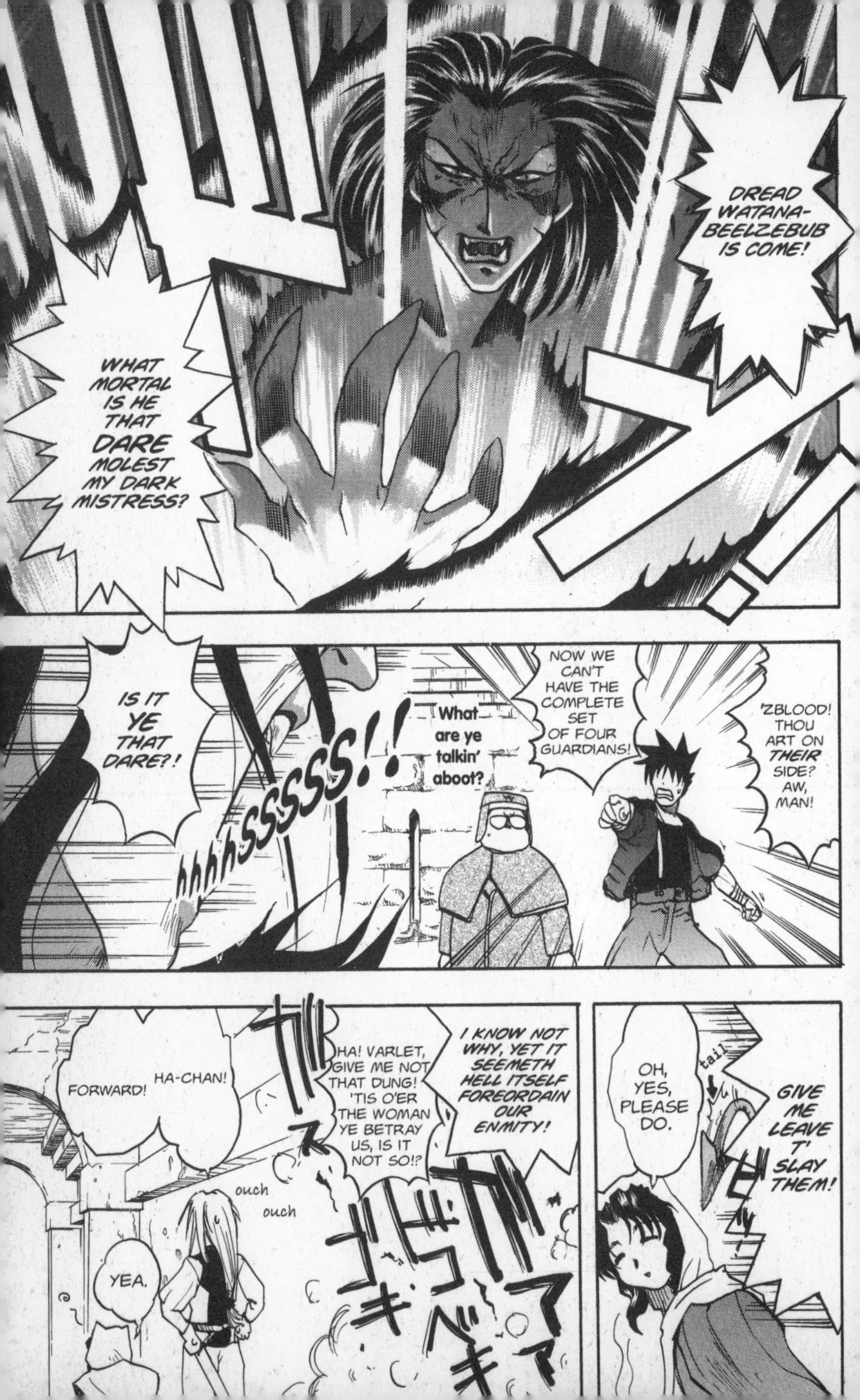
DREAD WATANA-BEELZEBUB IS COME!
WHAT MORTAL IS HE THAT DARE MOLEST MY DARK MISTRESS?
'ZBLOOD! THOU ART ON THEIR SIDE? AW, MAN!
NOW WE CAN'T HAVE THE COMPLETE SET OF FOUR GUARDIANS!
What are ye talkin' aboot?
hhhhSSSSSS!!
IS IT YE THAT DARE?!
GIVE ME LEAVE T' SLAY THEM!
tail
OH, YES, PLEASE DO.
I KNOW NOT WHY, YET IT SEEMETH HELL ITSELF FOREORDAIN OUR ENMITY!
HA! VARLET, GIVE ME NOT THAT DUNG! 'TIS O'ER THE WOMAN YE BETRAY US, IS IT NOT SO!?
HA-CHAN!
FORWARD!
ouch
ouch
YEA.

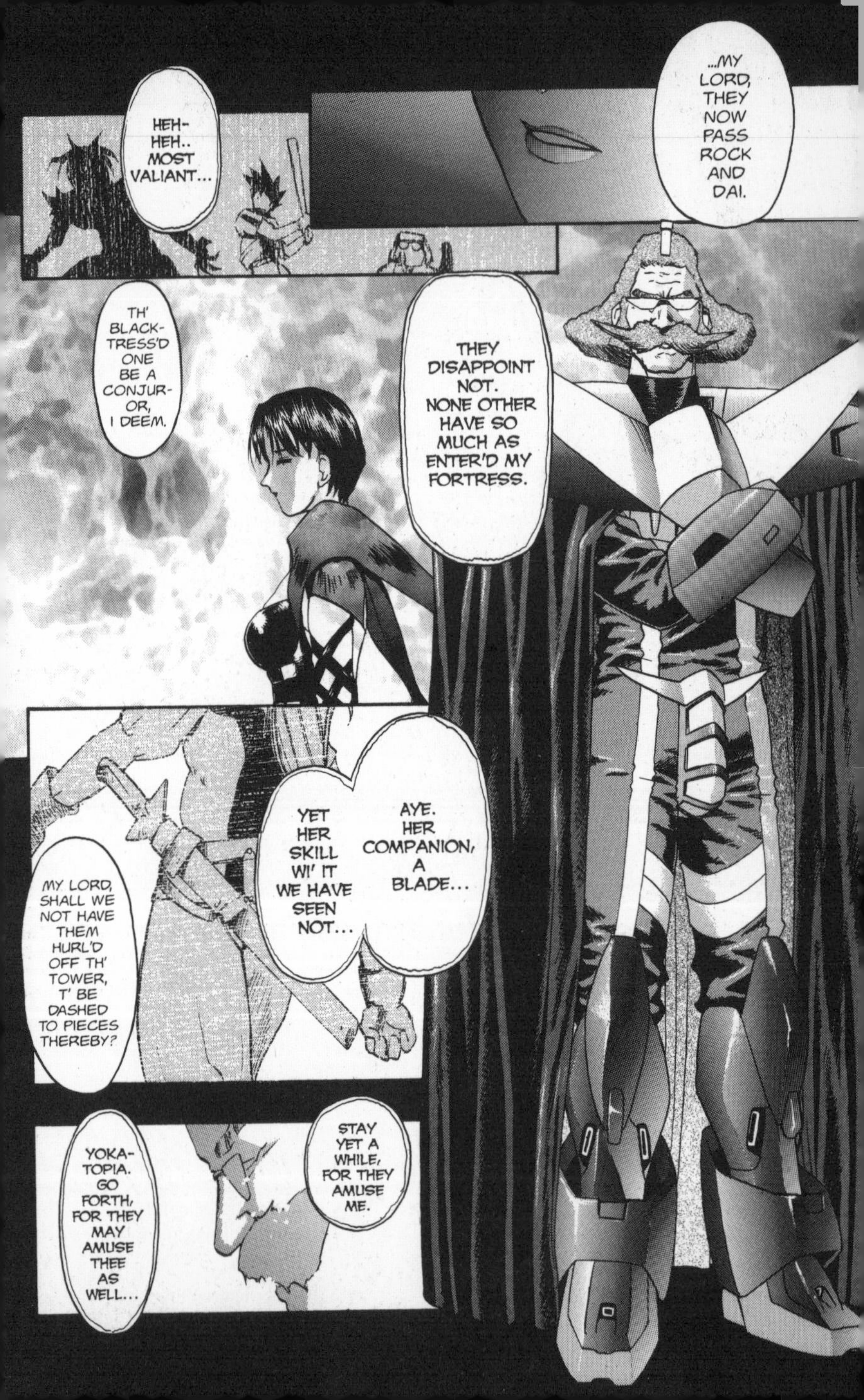
...MY LORD, THEY NOW PASS ROCK AND DAI.
HEH-HEH.. MOST VALIANT...
THEY DISAPPOINT NOT. NONE OTHER HAVE SO MUCH AS ENTER'D MY FORTRESS.
TH' BLACK-TRESS'D ONE BE A CONJUR-OR, I DEEM.
AYE. HER COMPANION, A BLADE...
YET HER SKILL WI' IT WE HAVE SEEN NOT...
MY LORD, SHALL WE NOT HAVE THEM HURL'D OFF TH' TOWER, T' BE DASHED TO PIECES THEREBY?
STAY YET A WHILE, FOR THEY AMUSE ME.
YOKA-TOPIA. GO FORTH, FOR THEY MAY AMUSE THEE AS WELL...

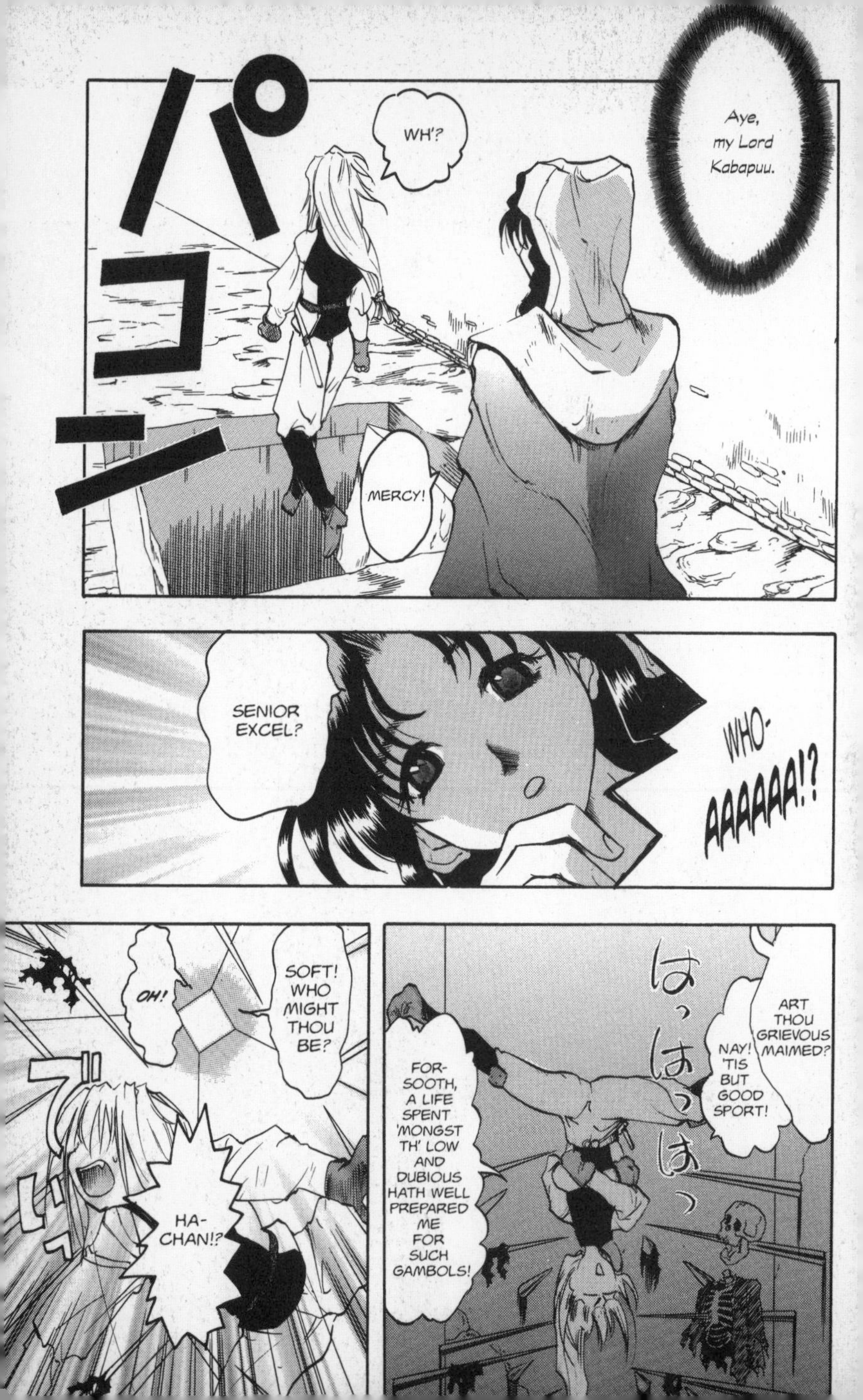

Aye, my Lord Kabapuu.
WH'?
パコーン
MERCY!
WHO-AAAAAA!?
SENIOR EXCEL?
はっはっはっ
ART THOU GRIEVOUS MAIMED?
NAY! 'TIS BUT GOOD SPORT!
FOR-SOOTH, A LIFE SPENT 'MONGST TH' LOW AND DUBIOUS HATH WELL PREPARED ME FOR SUCH GAMBOLS!
SOFT! WHO MIGHT THOU BE?
OH!
HA-CHAN!?

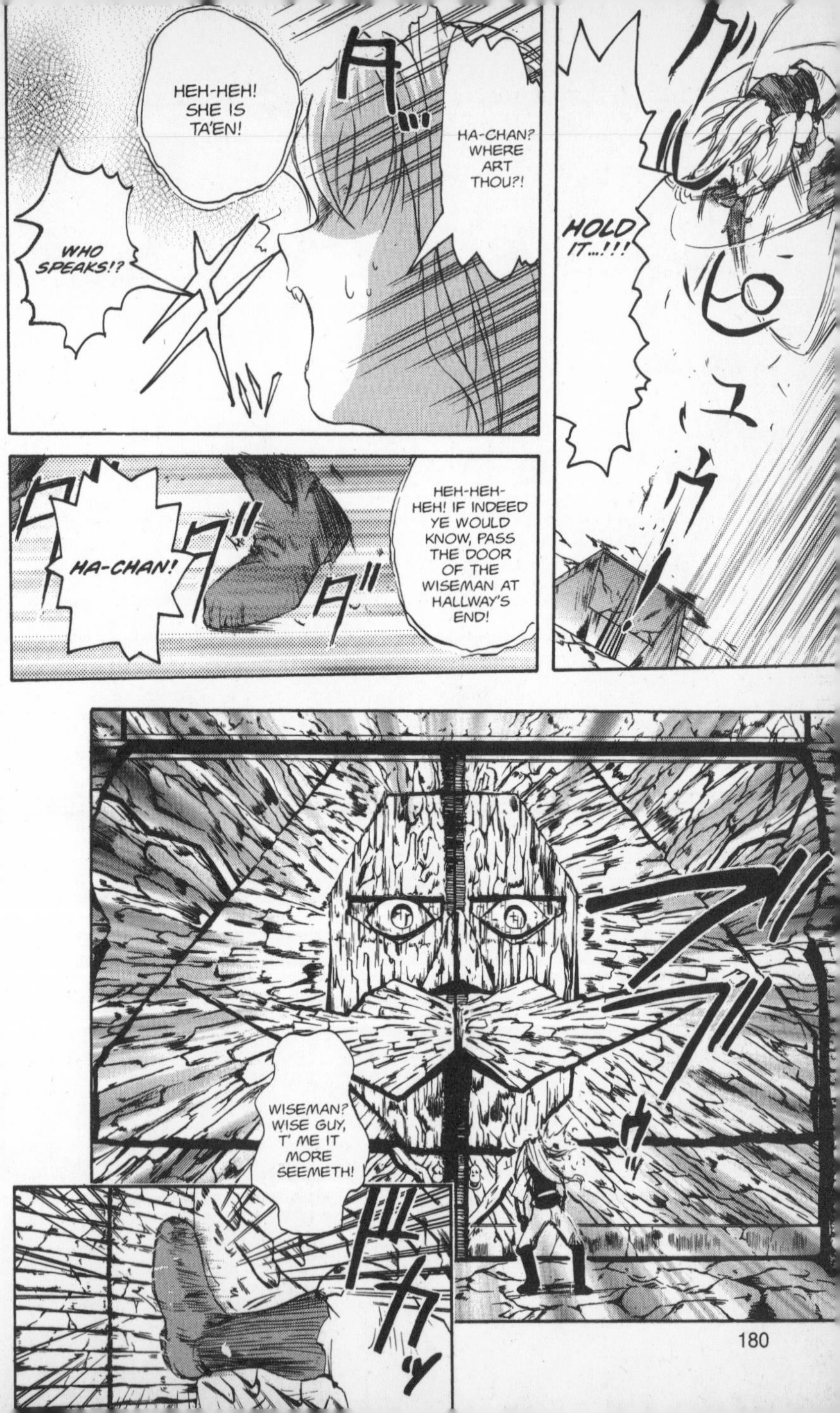
HOLD IT...!!!
HA-CHAN? WHERE ART THOU?!
HEH-HEH! SHE IS TA'EN!
WHO SPEAKS!?
HEH-HEH-HEH! IF INDEED YE WOULD KNOW, PASS THE DOOR OF THE WISEMAN AT HALLWAY'S END!
HA-CHAN!
WISEMAN? WISE GUY, T' ME IT MORE SEEMETH!

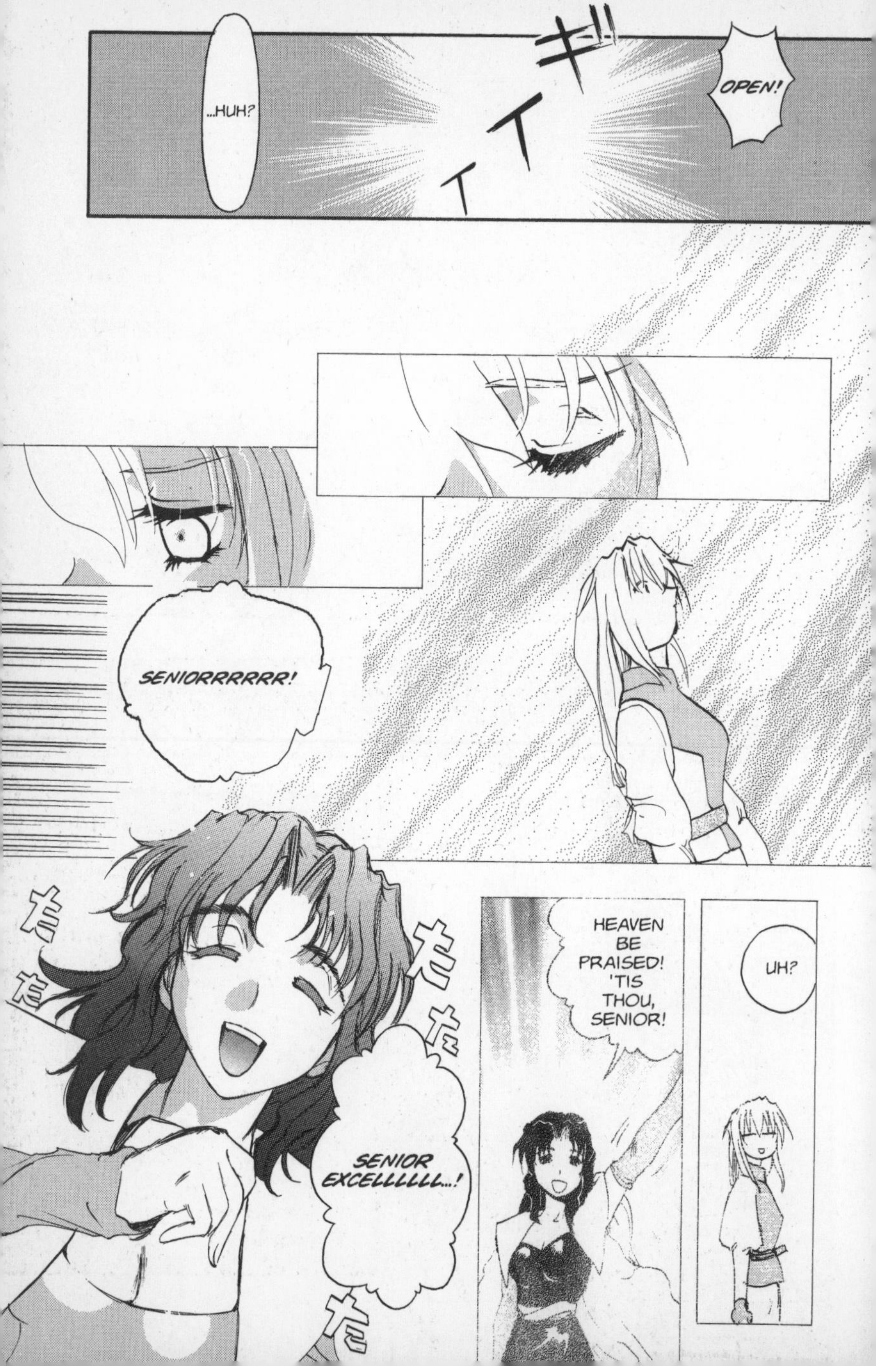

OPEN!
ギイイ
...HUH?
SENIORRRRRR!
UH?
HEAVEN BE PRAISED! 'TIS THOU, SENIOR!
たたた
SENIOR EXCELLLLLLL...!
たた

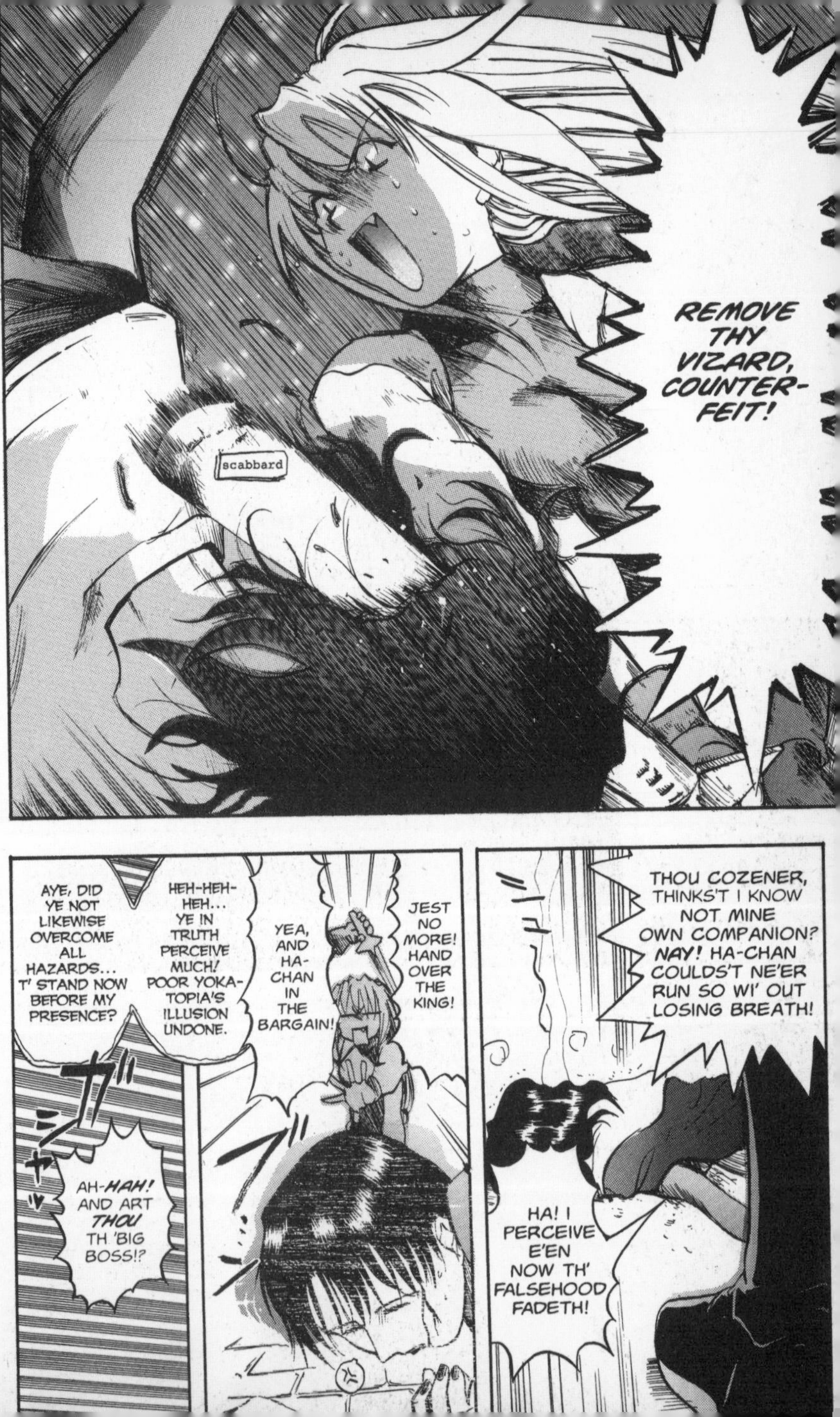
REMOVE THY VIZARD, COUNTER-FEIT!
scabbard
THOU COZENER, THINKS'T I KNOW NOT MINE OWN COMPANION? NAY! HA-CHAN COULDS'T NE'ER RUN SO WI' OUT LOSING BREATH!
HA! I PERCEIVE E'EN NOW TH' FALSEHOOD FADETH!
JEST NO MORE! HAND OVER THE KING!
YEA, AND HA-CHAN IN THE BARGAIN!
HEH-HEH-HEH... YE IN TRUTH PERCEIVE MUCH! POOR YOKA-TOPIA'S ILLUSION UNDONE.
AYE, DID YE NOT LIKEWISE OVERCOME ALL HAZARDS... T' STAND NOW BEFORE MY PRESENCE?
AH-HAH! AND ART THOU TH 'BIG BOSS!?

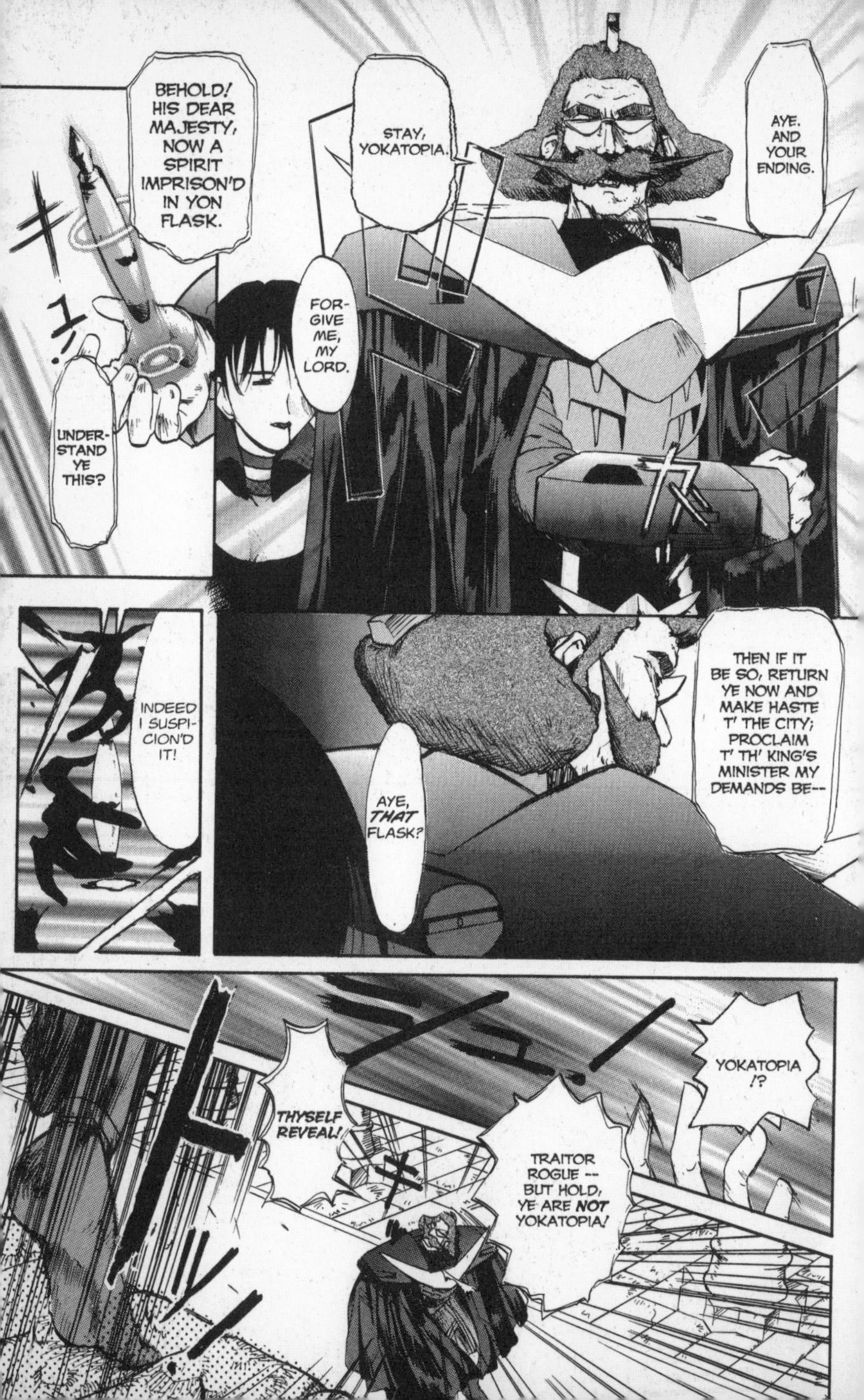
AYE. AND YOUR ENDING.
STAY, YOKATOPIA.
FOR-GIVE ME, MY LORD.
BEHOLD! HIS DEAR MAJESTY, NOW A SPIRIT IMPRISON'D IN YON FLASK.
UNDER-STAND YE THIS?
THEN IF IT BE SO, RETURN YE NOW AND MAKE HASTE T' THE CITY; PROCLAIM T' TH' KING'S MINISTER MY DEMANDS BE--
AYE, *THAT* FLASK?
INDEED I SUSPICION'D IT!
YOKATOPIA !?
TRAITOR ROGUE -- BUT HOLD, YE ARE *NOT* YOKATOPIA!
*THYSELF REVEAL!*

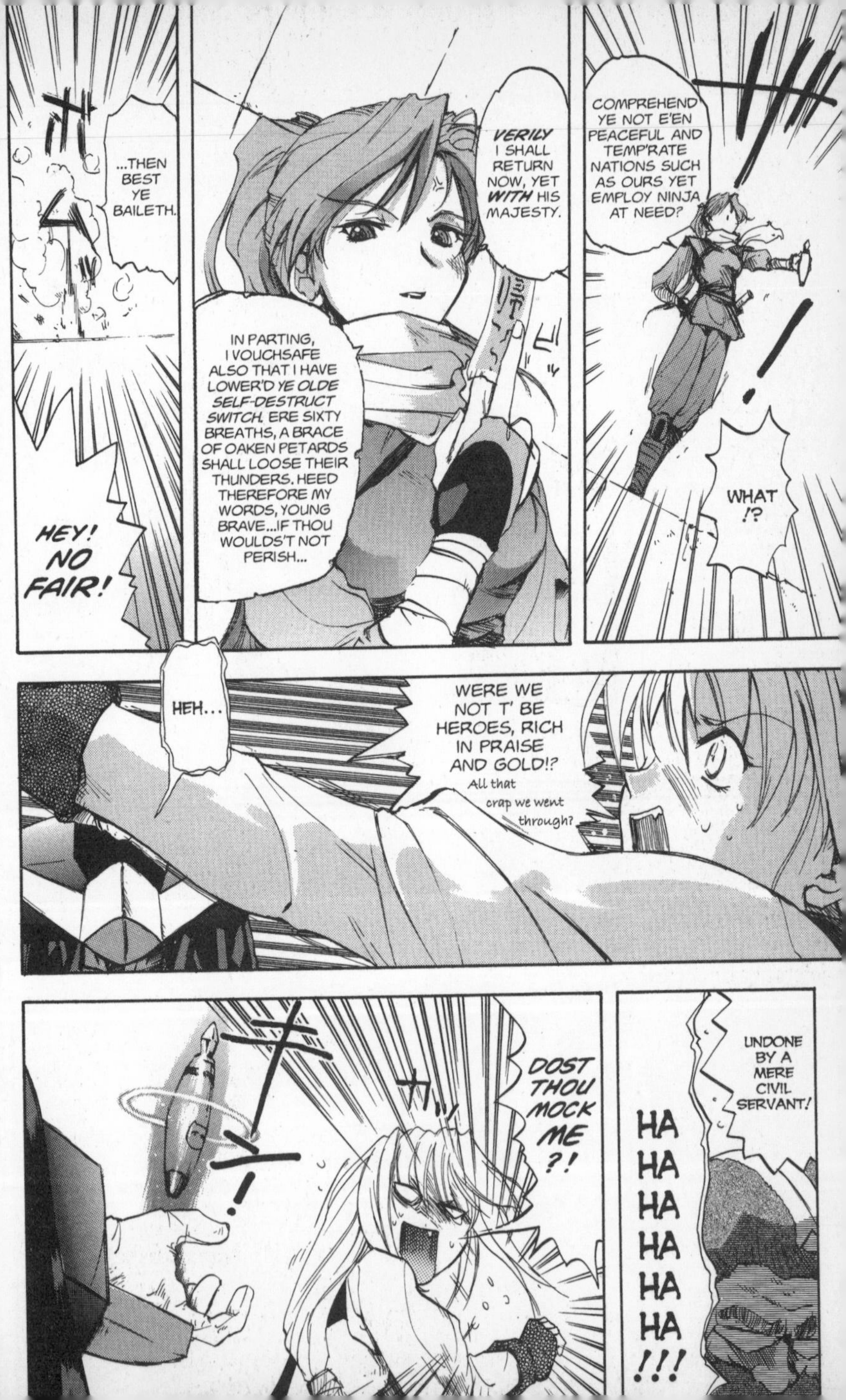
COMPREHEND YE NOT E'EN PEACEFUL AND TEMP'RATE NATIONS SUCH AS OURS YET EMPLOY NINJA AT NEED?
WHAT !?
VERILY I SHALL RETURN NOW, YET WITH HIS MAJESTY.
IN PARTING, I VOUCHSAFE ALSO THAT I HAVE LOWER'D YE OLDE SELF-DESTRUCT SWITCH. ERE SIXTY BREATHS, A BRACE OF OAKEN PETARDS SHALL LOOSE THEIR THUNDERS. HEED THEREFORE MY WORDS, YOUNG BRAVE...IF THOU WOULDS'T NOT PERISH...
...THEN BEST YE BAILETH.
HEY! NO FAIR!
WERE WE NOT T' BE HEROES, RICH IN PRAISE AND GOLD!?
All that crap we went through?
HEH...
UNDONE BY A MERE CIVIL SERVANT!
HA HA HA HA HA HA HA !!!
DOST THOU MOCK ME ?!

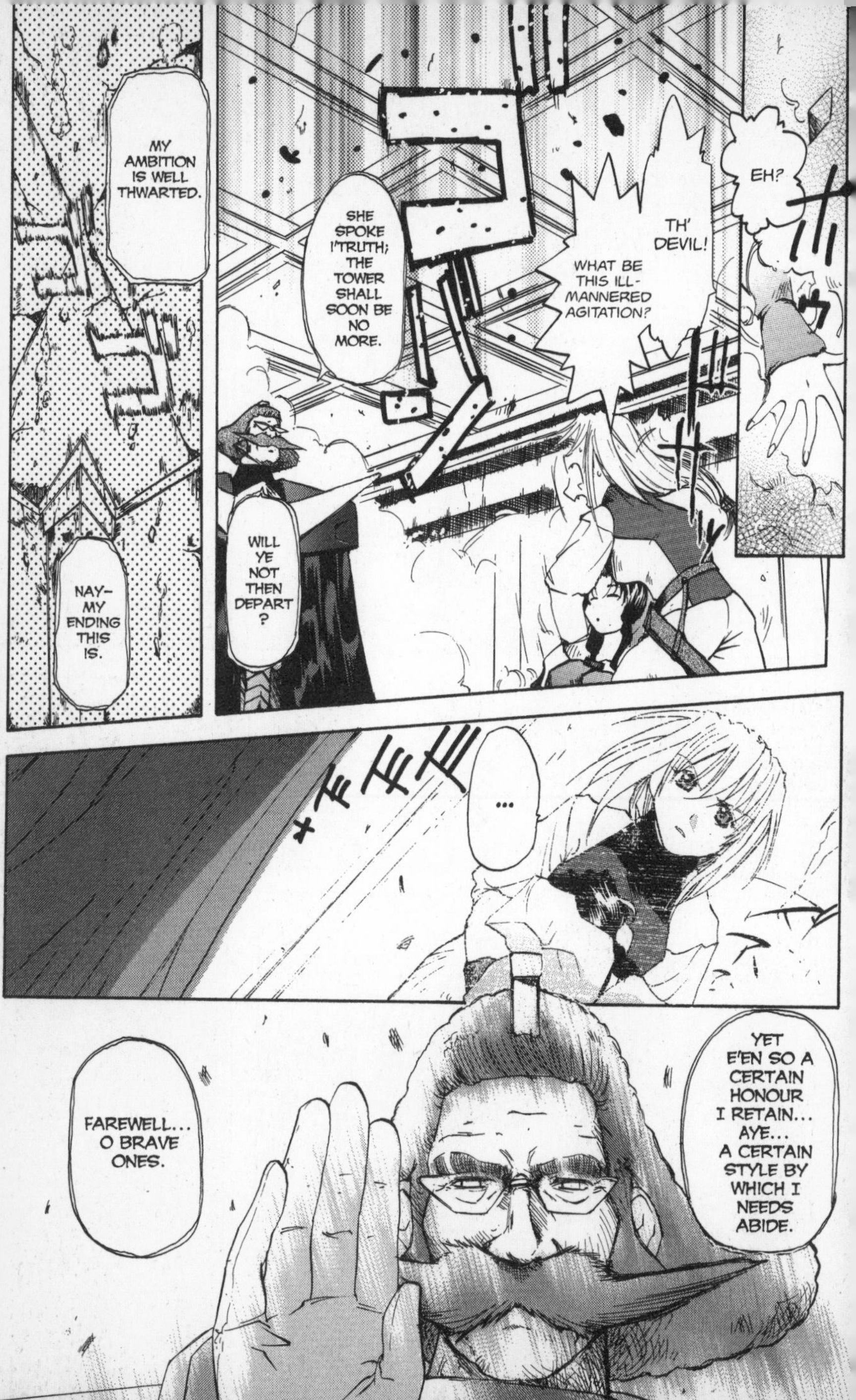
EH?
TH' DEVIL!
WHAT BE THIS ILL-MANNERED AGITATION?
SHE SPOKE I'TRUTH; THE TOWER SHALL SOON BE NO MORE.
WILL YE NOT THEN DEPART?
MY AMBITION IS WELL THWARTED.
NAY-MY ENDING THIS IS.
...
YET E'EN SO A CERTAIN HONOUR I RETAIN... AYE... A CERTAIN STYLE BY WHICH I NEEDS ABIDE.
FAREWELL... O BRAVE ONES.

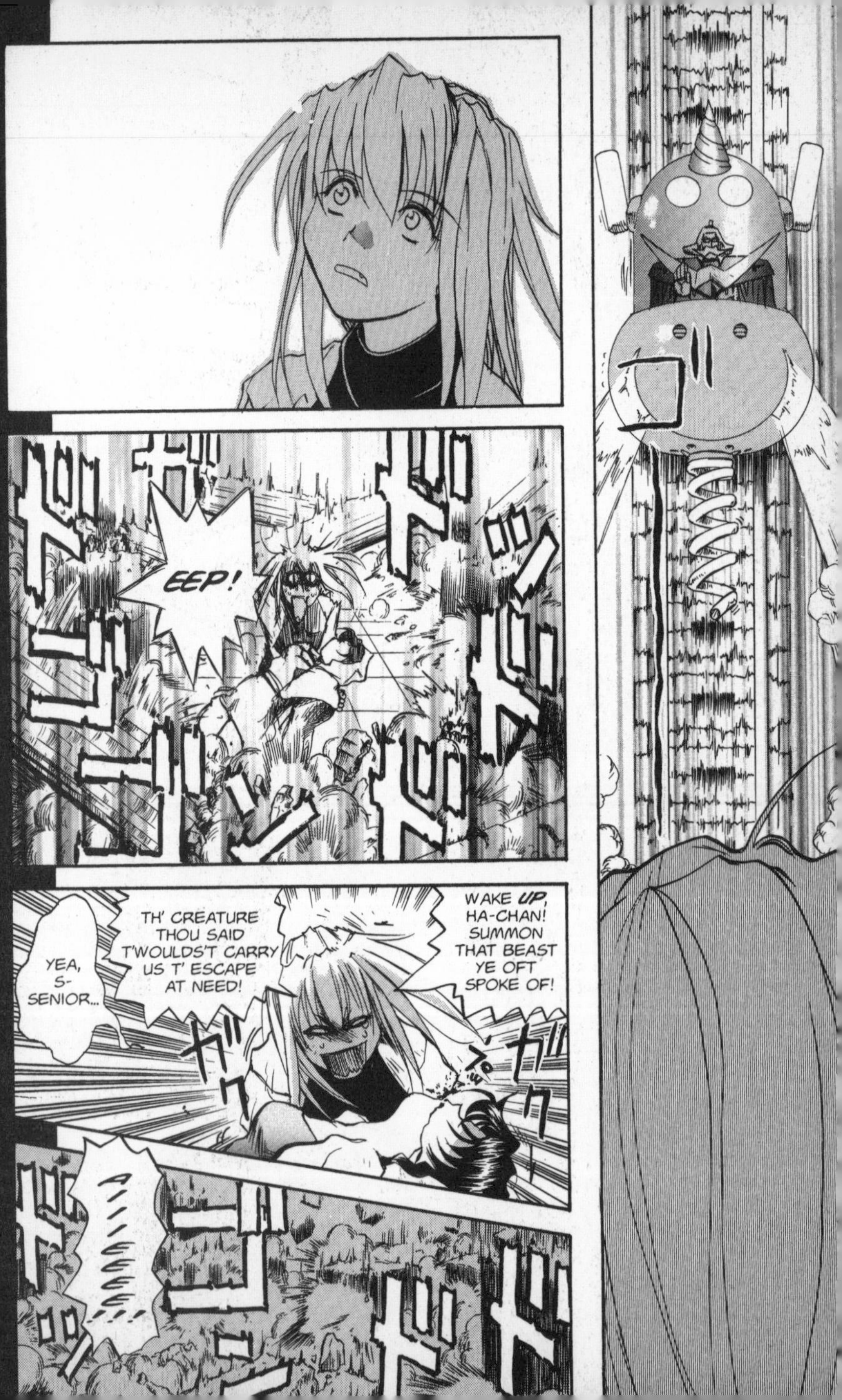
EEP!
WAKE *UP*, HA-CHAN! SUMMON THAT BEAST YE OFT SPOKE OF!
TH' CREATURE THOU SAID T'WOULDS'T CARRY US T' ESCAPE AT NEED!
YEA, S-SENIOR...
AIIEEEE-!!!

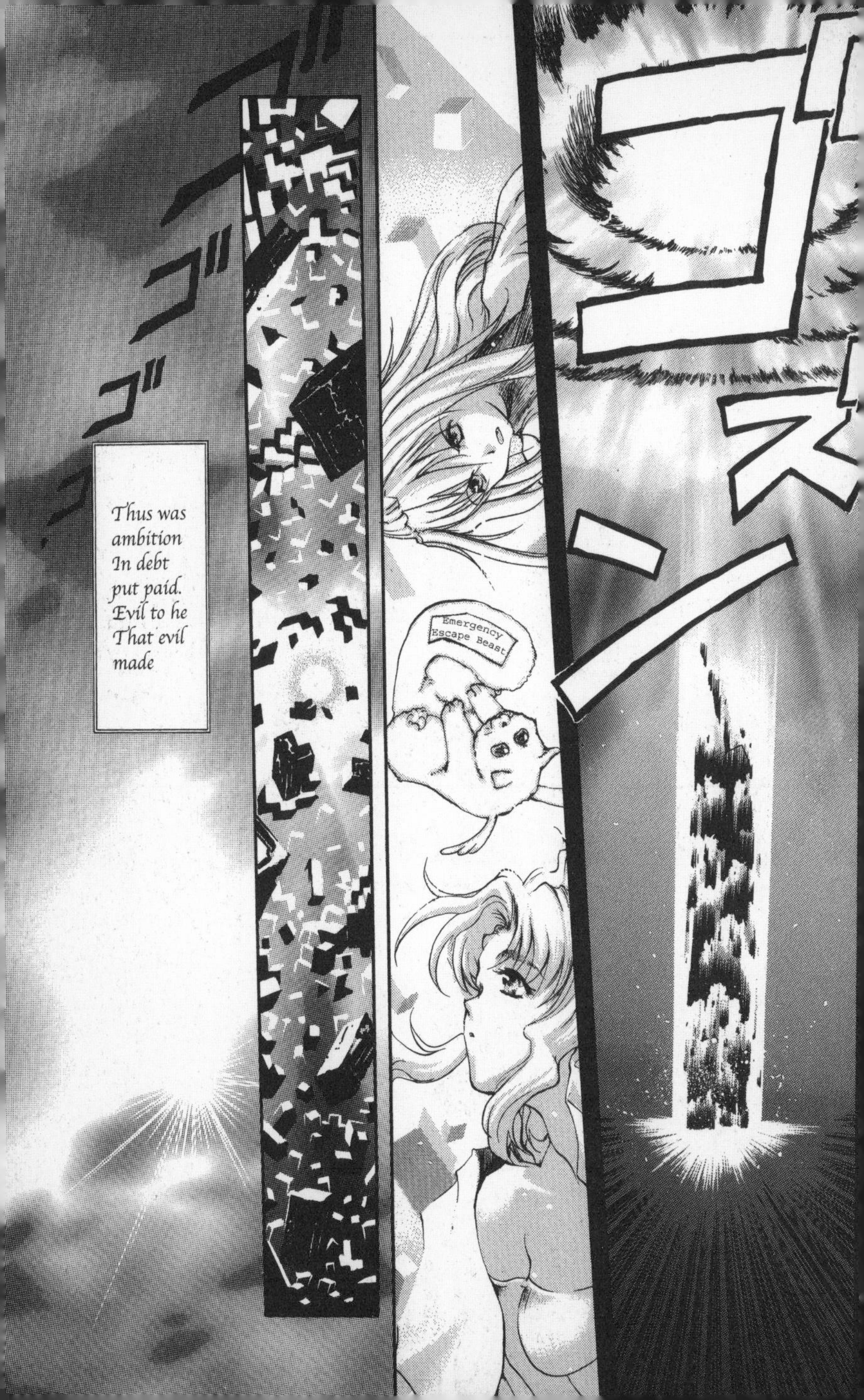
Emergency Escape Beast
Thus was ambition In debt put paid. Evil to he That evil made

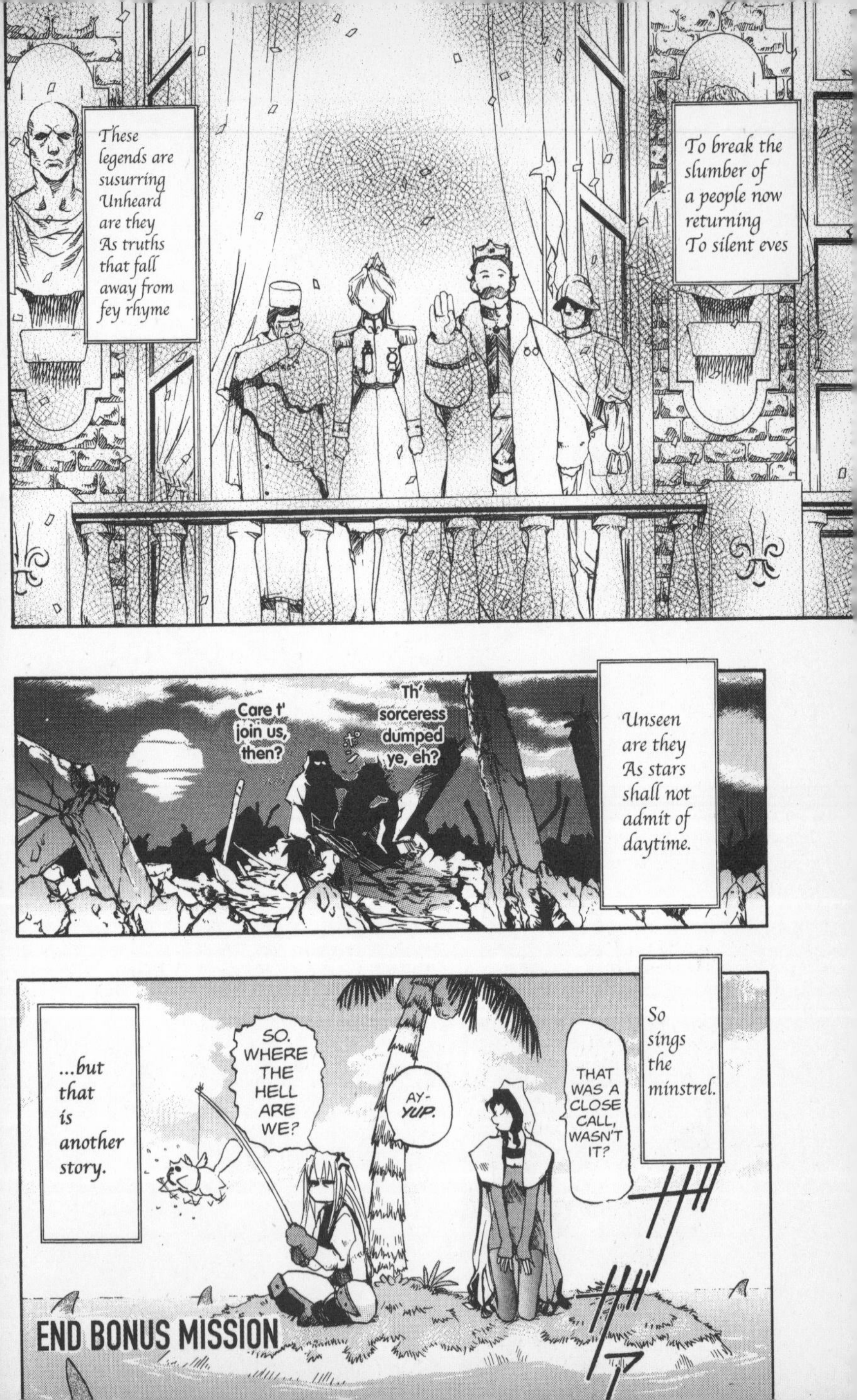

To break the slumber of a people now returning To silent eves
These legends are susurring Unheard are they As truths that fall away from fey rhyme
Unseen are they As stars shall not admit of daytime.
Th' sorceress dumped ye, eh?
Care t' join us, then?
So sings the minstrel.
THAT WAS A CLOSE CALL, WASN'T IT?
AY-YUP.
SO. WHERE THE HELL ARE WE?
...but that is another story.
END BONUS MISSION

Do my intro in the next volume, okay?

Scenes from the Personal Life of Rikdo Koshi Vol.⑦

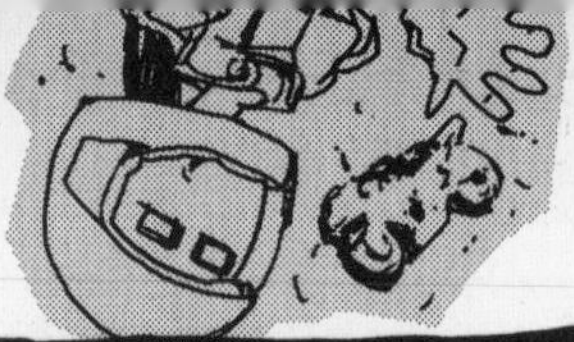

## We Who Are Unsure What to Say

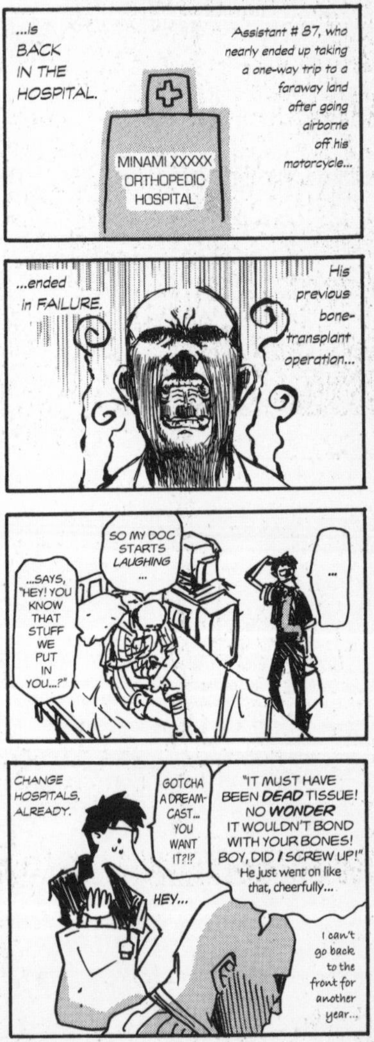

Assistant # 87, who nearly ended up taking a one-way trip to a faraway land after going airborne off his motorcycle...
...is BACK IN THE HOSPITAL.
MINAMI XXXXX ORTHOPEDIC HOSPITAL
His previous bone-transplant operation...
...ended in FAILURE.
...
SO MY DOC STARTS LAUGHING ...
...SAYS, "HEY! YOU KNOW THAT STUFF WE PUT IN YOU...?"
"IT MUST HAVE BEEN DEAD TISSUE! NO WONDER IT WOULDN'T BOND WITH YOUR BONES! BOY, DID I SCREW UP!" He just went on like that, cheerfully...
GOTCHA A DREAMCAST... YOU WANT IT?!?
CHANGE HOSPITALS, ALREADY.
I can't go back to the front for another year...
HEY...


## We, The Media Elite: Part 2

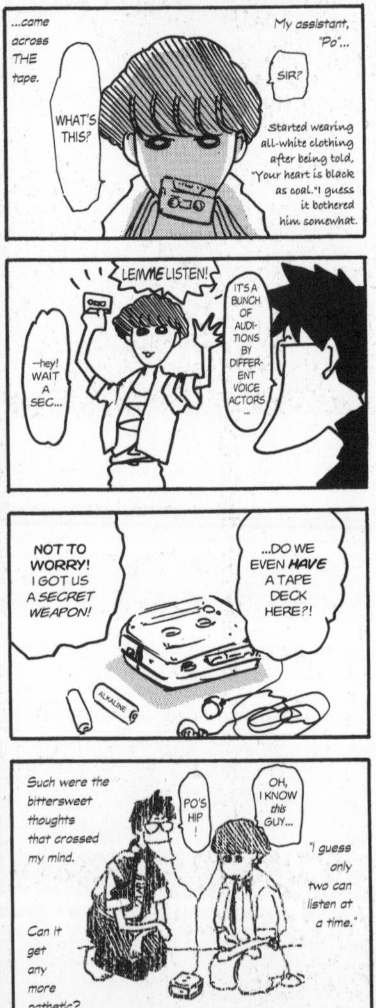

My assistant, "Po"...
SIR?
Started wearing all-white clothing after being told, "Your heart is black as coal." I guess it bothered him somewhat.
WHAT'S THIS?
...came across THE tape.
IT'S A BUNCH OF AUDITIONS BY DIFFERENT VOICE ACTORS...
LEMME LISTEN!
--hey! WAIT A SEC...
...DO WE EVEN HAVE A TAPE DECK HERE?!
NOT TO WORRY! I GOT US A SECRET WEAPON!
ALKALINE
OH, I KNOW this GUY...
"I guess only two can listen at a time."
PO'S HIP!
Such were the bittersweet thoughts that crossed my mind.
Can it get any more pathetic?

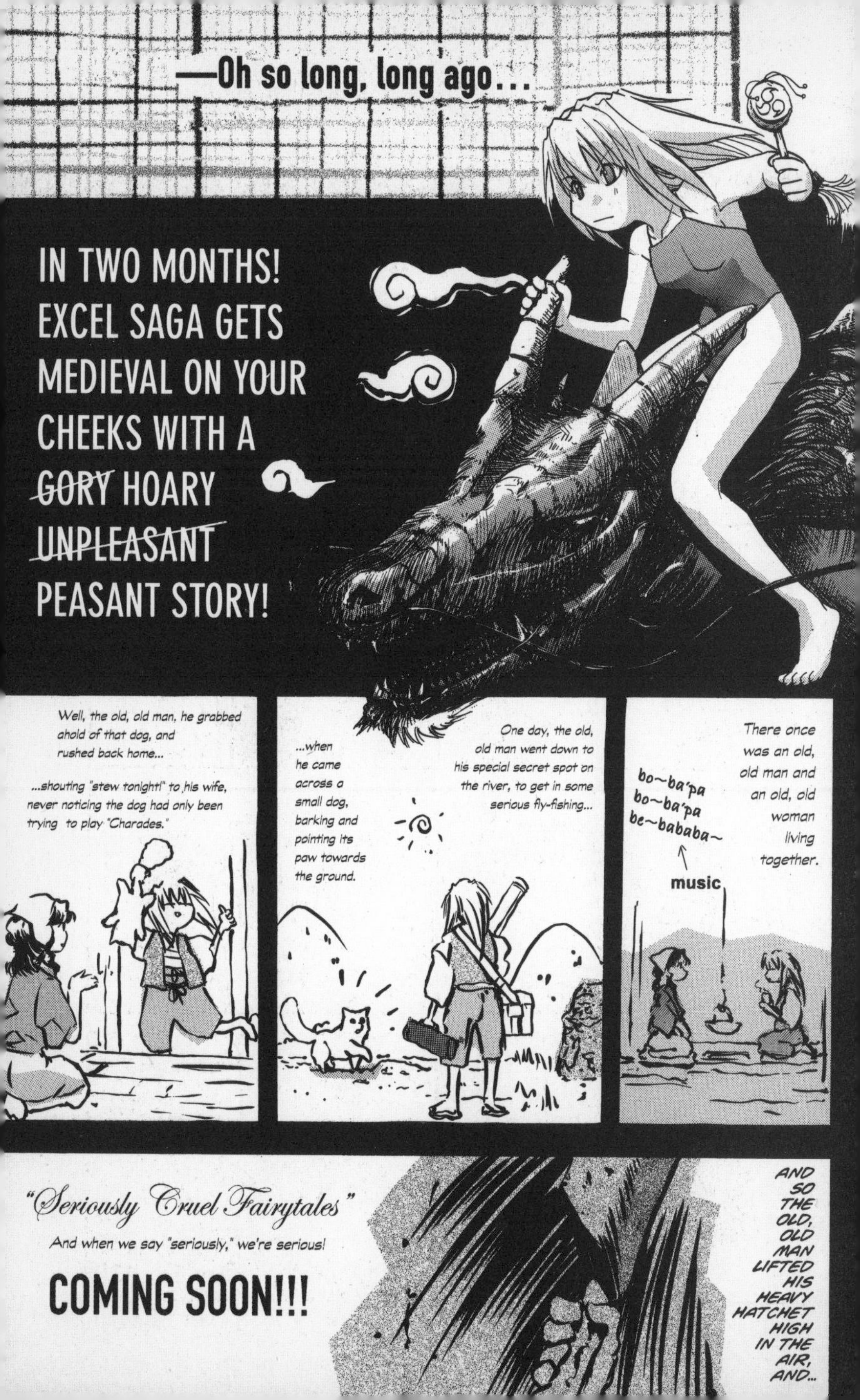
—Oh so long, long ago...
IN TWO MONTHS! EXCEL SAGA GETS MEDIEVAL ON YOUR CHEEKS WITH A ~~GORY~~ HOARY ~~UNPLEASANT~~ PEASANT STORY!
There once was an old, old man and an old, old woman living together.
bo~ba'pa bo~ba'pa be~bababa~
music
One day, the old, old man went down to his special secret spot on the river, to get in some serious fly-fishing...
...when he came across a small dog, barking and pointing its paw towards the ground.
Well, the old, old man, he grabbed ahold of that dog, and rushed back home...
...shouting "stew tonight!" to his wife, never noticing the dog had only been trying to play "Charades."
AND SO THE OLD, OLD MAN LIFTED HIS HEAVY HATCHET HIGH IN THE AIR, AND...
"Seriously Cruel Fairytales"
And when we say "seriously," we're serious!
COMING SOON!!!

# Guide to *Excel Saga* 05's Sound Effects!

5-2————FX    k'GrunCH k'GrunCH k'GrunCH k'GruN'CH (gori gofun', sound, snow packing below)

5-3————FX    k'Thud! (goton, sound)

5-4————FX    k'GroaR gG'ROAR GG'RROAROOAR (gofu gobu goon, sound, engine roaring while in low gear)

5-5-1————FX    Klunk K'Thunk (goto, sound)

7-1————FX    kk'KRAC'KK (kaoon, sound)

7-3————FX    H'FFF (hou, sound, breathing out)

8-5————FX    cl'chak (gacha', sound)

9-2/3————FX    K'ThuK (goton, sound)

9-4————FX    P'fft! (pan!, sound, gentle sound)

9-5————FX    G'Thok (gotsun, sound)

10-1————FX    K'ThuKk (goto', sound)

12-1————FX    K'chank (katan, sound)

12-2-1————FX    Sssk Sssk (shi¨, sound, dental sound created with use of toothpick)

12-2-2————FX    KI'chak (kacha, sound)

12-5————FX    Z'lurrrp (zu¨, sound, slurping)

13-1————FX    T'ing a lingG T'ing a lingG (chirin, sound, bell)

14-4————FX    B'thump! (batan, sound)

15-2————FX    K'ReeReeReeRee K'ReeReeReeReeRee Gk'ReeReeRee... (kashushushu goriri, sound, ignition turning)

15-4————FX    thud (do, sound)

16-1-1————FX    (upper left): G'thak (ga, sound)

16-1-2————FX    (mid right): b'thudd(doko, sound)

16-1-3————FX    (mid left): k'thud (koga, sound)

16-1-4————FX    (lower right): k'Grak (gu', sound)

16-1-5————FX    (lower left): v'woosh (bun, sound, going through the air)

16-4————FX    K'lachk... (cha..., sound)

17-1————FX    g'Runch (gyu, sound, crunching snow)

17-2————FX    Zz'runch Zz'runch (zamu, sound, walking through snow)

17-3————FX    Th'chakk (gasa, sound)

17-4-1————FX    V'thunch wh'thunchunch (za' botebote, sound, snow piling on)

17-4-2————FX    th'chakk (gasa, sound)

17-4-3————FX    V'thunch vvh'thunchunch (za' botebote, sound, snow piling on)

Most of Rikdo Koshi's original sound FX are left in their original Japanese in the Viz edition of Excel Saga; exceptions being handwritten dialogue and "drawn" notes that have the character of captions. Although these sounds are all listed as "FX," they are of two types: onomatopoeia (in Japanese, *giseigo*) where the writing is used in an attempt to imitate the actual sound of something happening, and mimesis (in Japanese, *gitaigo*) where the writing is used to attempt to convey rhetorically a state, mood, or condition.

Whereas the first type of FX will invariably be portrayed with kana, the second may use kana and/or kanji. One should note that there is often overlap between these two types. Onomatopoeia notes: *Sound* refers to audible sounds being generated somehow. *Movement* refers to the physical movement, or lack of movement, of something; not audible or mostly not audible. *Depiction* refers to the psychological state of something or someone. Now, you've made it this far through the book backwards, so I'm guessing I don't have to tell you what I am, in fact, about to tell you. All numbers are given in the original Japanese reading order: right-to-left.

A special thanks, by the way, to all the readers who have both made *Excel Saga* a success, and who are also strong enough, man enough, and fan enough to endure *Oubliette* each and every time. Just for a bit of a laugh and a carry on, write *Oubliette* c/o Excel Saga, VIZ, LLC, P.O. Box 77064, San Francisco, CA, 94107.

26-5——FX plllr pllr pllr k'chak (pururururu chi, sound)

26-6-1——FX V'WoooWooo (ooo, sound)

26-6-2——FX VW'WOOFOOO (byuooo, sound)

29-2——FX klak klak klak (ka', sound)

29-5-1——FX k'lakk k'lakk (kotsu, sound)

29-5-2——FX k'ruch k'runsh (gusha, sound)

29-6——FX K'thunk (katan, sound)

29-7——FX G'THUNK (gata, sound)

29-8——FX Gg'reekk (gishi, sound)

31-1——FX Munch munch (ga', depiction)

31-2——FX Zz'lurpp (zuzu, sound)

31-3-1——FX Kunch Munch (bari bori, depiction and sound)

31-3-2——FX g'Munchk mnchunk mg'lunch (gatsu kucha mogu, depiction and sound)

32-2——FX Munch munch (mori mori, depiction)

32-3——FX G'ulp (gokkun, sound and depiction)

32-4——FX Sh'SHINNG (aaa, depiction, dramatic build up)

33-4——FX Ggrip (ga', depiction)

33-5——Iwa (out of wb): Get it?

34-1-1——FX p'ting (piku, depiction)

34-1-2——FX sh'shing! (bi', depiction, pointing Watanabe)

34-2——FX gglarre! (kishi, depiction, dead serious)

34-4——FX Kk'thud! (gatan, sound)

34-5——FX Klang klang klang (kan, sound, metallic, running down the stairs of the apartment)

35-2——FX Shsh'arath (shuruu, sound, smooth clothing sound)

35-6——FX k'chakk (koto, sound)

36-4——FX Dribblb (deroro, motion, melting)

37-1——FX k'lak (ka', sound)

37-2——FX k'lak k'lak (ka', sound)

37-3——FX ph'chak (za', depiction, presenting something)

38-4——FX K'lak (ka', sound)

40-2——FX ha'HYA! (hea', dialog and depiction, posing, comic)

40-4——FX Gasp (ha', depiction)

41-1——FX Th-thump! (gokii, depiction)

17-5——FX Chak (cha', sound)

17-6——FX Z'CHAKK! (zaka', sound)

18-1——FX zZ'thunch! (zafu', sound, something walking midst underbrush and snow)

18-1/3——FX K'CHAKK!... (gaki, sound, hard metallic sound)

18-6-1——FX klakklakklak (katakata, depiction and movement, shivering)

18-6-2——FX klakklakklak (katakata, depiction and movement, shivering)

18-6-3——FX th'chakk (zari, sound, the grainy feel of a chemical reaction agent type heat pack)

19-1-1——FX v'WHROooAR (byuooo, sound, strong winds)

19-1-2——FX v'WHROooAR (byuooo, sound, strong winds)

19-4-1——FX Wh'THUD! (doka', sound)

19-4-2——FX K'THUNK! (gan', sound)

19-4-3——FX rattle rattle (do' boko', sound)

20-1——FX Ph'tungg (puchin, depiction, unbuttoning)

20-4——FX Skk'RCH Skk'RCH (keki, sound, scratching, comic)

21-6——FX Fssk (su', motion)

21-7——FX K'lonk K'lonk (kotsu, sound)

22-1——FX slurp slurp (peta, depiction)

22-3-1——FX Sniff sniff (fun, sound)

22-3-2——FX ph'tap (ton, sound, light tapping)

22-7——FX Bb'LAMmmm (dooonnn, sound, heavy gunshot)

23-2——FX K'thunk (koto, sound)

23-3-1——FX Kla'chak (gacha, sound)

23-3-2——FX K'lonk K'lonk k'lonk (kotsu, sound)

23-7——FX flap flap (pata, motion)

23-8——FX flap flap flap (pata, motion)

24-1——FX wh'BAAAANGgg (zugaa, sound)

24-2——FX B'THUMPT! (ban, sound)

24-3——FX VGRGGGROARRR (gooooo, sound, fire)

24-6——FX RrROARRR (ooo, sound, fire)

25-2——FX Wobble (fura, motion and depiction)

25-5——FX VGRGGGROARRR (gooooo, sound, fire)

25-6——FX VGRGGGROARRR (gooooo, sound, fire)

25-8——FX kl'chak kl'chak (kasha, sound)

26-4——FX Pip pip pip pip ppip (pi, sound, electronic)

# OUBLIETTE
## Your *Excel Saga* bonus section!

55-1-2——FX (bottom right): rustle rustle (zawa, sound, crowds)

55-1-3——FX h'OO~~~Nk (pu'puaaa)

55-1-4——FX (bottom left): rustle rustle (zawa, sound, crowds)

55-2-1——FX rustle rustle (zawa, sound, crowds)

55-2-2——FX k'thunkk (katan, sound)

55-2-3——FX sh'shin! (bi', motion)

55-4——FX Flap flap (pata pata, motion)

55-5——FX b'thump! (batan, sound)

56-1——FX zz'rak zz'rak zz'rak (zaka, sound, forceful walking)

56-2——FX zz'rak (jari, sound, abrasive)

56-6——FX smak smak (pan pan, hands)

56-7——FX Fap fap (pan, sound)

57-1——FX Zz'thak! (gasa', sound)

57-2——FX th'chakk z'thachk th'chakk (gasa goso gasa, sound and depiction, shuffling about)

57-5——FX Zz'chak! (zya', sound)

57-5/6——FX gg'naPp (guki, depiction, bending a joint the wrong way)

57-8——FX Z'chak Ch'chak (chyaka, sound)

58-3——FX Zz'shing! (bishi!, depiction)

58-4-1——FX (upper): Whoosh whoosh (bun, motion, fast)

58-4-2——FX (lower): glare glare (ka', depiction)

58-4-3——FX (next to Mince): krrk krrk (kuri, motion, cute turning)

59-2-1——FX Th'chakkchakkchakk (zarazara, sound)

59-2-2——FX Glugluglugl ug (go' go', sound and depiction)

59-4——FX th'THUD! (do', sound)

60-5——FX Glare! (ki', depiction and motion, turning head and glaring)

61-4-1——FX v'WHROooAR (byuooo, sound, strong winds)

61-4-2——FX Zz'shingg! (zazann, sound and depiction)

62-1——FX bRAKaRAKaRAKaRAK (bararara, sound, SMG fire)

62-2——FX k'BOOm (doon, sound, explosion)

62-3——FX o'ROOOARRR (ooo, sound, engine roar)

62-4-1——FX vPvPvPvPvP (babababa, sound, helicopter sounds)

62-4-2——FX zz'ak zz'ak (za', sound)

41-2——FX P'thap! (pu', sound, blowing out the nose plugs)

41-4——FX Zz'shing (za', depiction, posing)

42-1——FX Da-daaamp! (ban, depiction, dramatic presentation)

42-3——FX Zz'shing! (za', depiction)

43-4——FX RRROARRR (ooo, depiction, surprised crowd)

43-6——FX KK'REEK (kyu, depiction, squeaking sound generated from pushing something in)

44-1——FX Sh'shing!! (pishi, depiction, posing)

44-4-1——FX Ch'chak (chi', sound)

44-4-2——FX A'RATH (basa, sound, clothing)

44-4-3——FX Th'THUMP! (biku, depiction, reaction)

45-5——FX P'ting! (biku, depiction)

46-3——FX v'VREEE (puaaa, sound, high pitch engine sound)

46-4——FX BB'AMP'P (ban', sound)

47-2——FX Kla'chak (gacha, sound)

47-3——FX klak klak klak (katsu, sound)

47-5——FX klak... (katsu, sound)

48-2——FX k'runch (kaki, sound)

48-3——FX Klak (katsu, sound)

48-4——FX klak klak klak (katsu,' sound)

49-1——FX v'REEEEM (pyuuun, sound, electronic-think robots and such)

49-2——FX Ggrip (gu', depiction)

49-3——FX Huffff (dialog)

50-1——FX b'thump (batan, sound)

50-3——FX z'thrsh z'thrsh z'thrsh z'thrshsh (zaza, sound, water)

50-4——FX V'woooo~~~ (hyuu, sound, lonely wind)

53-1——FX zz'sSHING (zan, depiction, posing)

53-2——FX Fsfssk (baba', motion)

53-3——FX Fssk (hyu', motion)

53-4——FX k'fssk (kukiki, motion, minimal)

53-6——FX TaDa taDa taDa taDAAA Ta~~~, tat tat DAAA~ (chara', sound, music, jazz like)

53-7——FX z'chak! (zya', sound)

53-9——FX wB'BAAAMM!! (zudon!, sound, loud)

55-1-1——FX ba-Boom ba-boomboom (dontsuku, depiction, festive atmosphere)

9-2——FX V'TINGG V'TINGG V'TINGG (bikun', motion, spasm)

9-3——FX DAAASH! (da~, depiction, running)

9-4——FX zz'RASH! (za'ha, motion, quick movement)

9-6-1——FX Wheez' wheez' wheez' wheez' (zei', sound)

9-6-2——FX fssk (su', motion)

0-1-1——FX thBPLth (bu', sound, plosive bilabial)

0-1-2——FX zz'CHAK (zyaki, sound)

0-2——FX Zz'rackk (zya', sound, abrasive)

0-3——FX VV'REEEN' (chuiin, sound, electronic acceleration, à la The Bionic Woman)

1-1——FX K'BAAAAM! (agyun!, sound, gunshot)

1-3-1——FX Zz'rakk (za', sound, abrasive)

1-3-2——FX Humph (ke', dialog)

1-3-3——FX Zz'rakk (zaku', sound, abrasive)

1-5-1——FX Zz'rakk z'raakk (za', sound, abrasive)

1-5-2——FX DASH (da', depiction)

2-1-1——FX h'HOOONK (bu~, sound)

2-1-2——FX g'THUDD (ga', motion)

2-4——FX v'WhoooSH (ooo, sound, fast movement)

2-7-1——FX k'lang (kan, sound)

2-7-2——FX g'thud (gan, sound)

2-7-3——FX vV'Plash (posha~n, sound, liquid splash down)

3-1——FX zz'rakkazz (ga'kakaka, sound, metal, abrasive)

3-3-1——FX ha'Haoonk (paaan, sound)

3-3-2——FX k'chak (zya', sound)

3-7——FX K'BLAAAM! (baan, sound)

3-8——FX P'ff't (fu', sound, blowing exhale)

4-1-1——FX K'KRK (kuru, motion, turning)

4-1-2——FX crumble (boro, depiction)

4-3-1——FX Wobble wobble (yota, motion)

4-3-2——FX Yikes! Aieee (kyaaa' kyaaa', dialog)

4-6——FX V'TINGG V'TINGG V'TINGG (bikun', motion, spasm)

5-1-1——FX k'reek k'reek k'reek k'reek k'reek (kara, sound)

1-2——FX Th-thump!! (biku, depiction)

62-5——FX b'BAAAM KI'BANGg (boon bon, sound, gas explosions)

62-6——FX A'Rath (ba', sound and depiction, clothing)

63-1-1——FX B'BAMBAMBAM (ban, sound)

63-1-2——FX th-thump! (biku', depiction)

63-2-1——FX Flap flap (hira hira, motion, flaping about hand)

63-2-2——FX th-thump th-thump (dokidoki, depiction, rapid heartbeat)

64-1——FX v'BANGg (ban, sound)

64-2——FX Teeter (yura, motion)

64-3——FX ph'pht (poi, movement, lightly tossing things in)

65-2——FX th'THUt th'THUt th'THUt th'THUt th'THUt th'THUt th'THUt th'THUt (dada, movement, fast running)

65-3-1——FX bB'THUMD! (ban, sound)

65-3-2——FX wheez wheez (ze', sound)

66-2-1——FX AIEEE (dialog)

66-2-2——FX bB'THUMD! (ban, sound)

66-3——FX Zz'rrk (zuzu, motion, slowly sliding down)

66-4——FX Pipeeep pipeeep (pi~ pipipi~, sound, electronic)

66-5——FX p'ting! (pi~n, depiction, reaction to something)

67-3——FX zZ'chunk (zu..., depiction, weighed down by something)

67-4——FX Shuffle shuffle (jita, motion, playing about)

67-5——FX BAAANG (baan, sound)

67-6——FX sprinkle sprinkle (para, motion, something loose falling apart)

67-7——FX G'chak (ga!, motion)

68-1——FX V'TINGG V'TINGG V'TINGG (bikun', motion, spasm)

68-2-1——FX (large): V'TINGG V'TINGG V'TINGG (bikun', motion, spasm)

68-2-2——FX (small, upper): k'thunk (kaku, motion, going limp)

68-2-3——FX (small, mid): p'ting (hiku, depiction, reaction)

68-2-4——FX (small, bottom right): chomp (gabu', motion, biting)

68-3——FX V'TINGG V'TINGG V'TINGG (bikun', motion, spasm)

68-5——FX Th'CRASSH (bakan, sound)

68-6——FX th'chingching th'ching (zyara, sound, loose change)

69-1-1——FX A'RUTH (ba', sound, clothes, getting up suddenly)

82-5——FX  b'thump (batan, sound)

83-2——FX  vmvmvmvm (tokakaka, sound, slow movement)

83-3——FX  z'KRErerere... KRECH! (dokyakyakya, sound, tires squealing)

83-4-1——FX  Rattle rattle (biribiri, sound, vibration)

83-4-2——FX  Rattle (biri, sound, vibration)

83-5——FX  vV'GRDOOAR (gyuooo, sound, engine going full bore)

84-1——FX  DASH (da', motion)

84-2——FX  Waddle waddle (nota nota, depiction, slow movement)

84-3——FX  sh shing! (bi', depiction, posing)

84-4——FX  T'thutt (ta', sound)

85-1-1——FX  V'ROAAMMMM (buooo, sound)

85-1-2——FX  vG'THUD! (baan, sound)

85-2——FX  th'CRASSSH (gashaaan, sound)

85-3-1——FX  v'THUDD (dan, sound, landing on both feet)

85-3-2——FX  twirl! (uryun!, motion)

85-4——FX  phew (ho', dialog)

85-5-1——FX  ph'SSSH (shu', sound)

85-5-2——FX  ch chinkchinkchink (kan, sound)

86-1——FX  kla'ThumKK! (gapan!, sound, opening door)

86-4-1——FX  g'thuk (gon, sound)

86-4-2——FX  Zz'rak (ga', sound)

86-5——FX  k-thunk k-thunk (gaku, motion, shaking)

86-6-1——FX  P'TING (piku, depiction, reaction)

86-6-2——FX  whiRRR... (hyooo, sound, computer equipment booting up)

87-3-1——FX  B'thump (batan, sound)

87-3-2——FX  zzhhrr zzhhrr (ja ja, tires spinning against ground)

87-3-3——FX  vroom (buon, engine firing up)

87-4——FX  sk'REECHREECHREEEECH (gyagyagya, sound, tires spinning)

87-6——FX  v'ROARRR (gaooo, sound, engine revving up)

88-3——FX  V'ROOAARRRR (gooo, sound, driving fast)

88-4——FX  Ggrip (ga', depiction)

88-5——FX  Rattle rattle (kata, sound, vibration)

89-1——FX  Ph'thapp! (ben, sound)

77-3——FX  G'CHUNKK (gooun, sound)

77-3/4——FX  K'lak (katsu, sound)

77-5——FX (far left and right): Whisper whisper (boso, depiction)

77-6——FX  G'CHUNKK (gooun, sound)

77-7——FX  K'thud (go', sound)

78-1——FX  p'pfft (poro, depiction, something falling off)

78-3-1——FX  Ph'VOOSH! (kun, motion)

78-3-2——FX  Twirl twirl (kirikiri, motion, comic)

78-3-3——FX  K'THUD (doga, sound)

78-3-4——FX  Falter wobble (furakurin, depiction)

78-3-5——FX  Ch thumpp (gusha, sound)

79-1——FX  k'lak k'lak k'lak (katsu, sound)

79-2-1——FX  sk'RAT'chch shuffle sk'RAT'chch shuffle sk'RAT'chch shuffle (kari jita, sound and depiction)

79-2-2——FX  fssk (su', motion)

79-3——FX  p'fumpp (pito', depiction, reattaching something)

79-4——FX  sh ZINGg' (bi', depiction)

79-5——FX  kk'off kau'ff kOAff kauuf koaff (geeho gee booeho geho eho, sound, coughing)

79-6——FX  k'lak k'lak (katsu, sound)

80-1——FX  k'lak (katsu, sound)

80-3-1——FX  klak (katsu, sound)

80-3-2——FX  KI'chak (gacha, sound)

80-4——FX  B'thump (batan, sound)

80-5——FX  Kre'roarrrr (kooo, sound, airplane engine, residual)

81-1——FX  VV'REEEEuuuEE'n (gyuoon, sound, aircraft engine sound)

81-5——FX  zz'chak! (nza', sound, abrasive)

82-1——FX  zz'ark zz'ark zz'ark zz'ark zz'ark (za', sound)

82-3-1——FX  A'RUTH (suku, motion, getting up)

82-3-2——FX  vW'RUTH (basa, sound, clothing)

82-4-1——FX  SH'SHIN___G! (kipi___n, depiction, scary glare)

82-4-2——FX  k'chak (paka, sound and depiction, opening, wrist watch)

82-4-3——FX  VW'WOMP! (pan!, sound and motion)

82-4-4——FX  vv'v'ROMMm (burun', sound, engine starting)

98-2——FX Fssk (su, motion)

98-4——FX 'OOORMmm (oon, sound, dramatic)

98-5——FX Wheez wheez (zei zei, sound)

100——FX 'EY, SIR!! (oi'su, dialog)

101-1——FX B'thap (dan, sound)

102-2/4—FX vGrmvGrmvGrmvGrm (gogogogo, depiction, dramatic buildup)

102-5——FX v'VuMPP! (ban, depiction, dramatic)

103-5——FX K'THUNK (gata', sound)

104-1——FX p'ting (pita', depiction, sudden freeze)

104-4——FX Ggrip (gu', depiction)

105-4——FX B'thump (batan, sound)

105-5——FX klak (ka'..., sound)

105-6——FX klak klak klak (ka', sound)

106-2——FX Flaplaplaplaplap (bararara, sound, flipping through many pages)

106-5——FX Phew (huu, dialog)

107-4——FX K'THUNKK (gatan', sound)

108-1——FX k'tak k'tak k'tak (kata, sound, typing)

108-2——FX P'thmpt (pon, sound, light tap)

108-4——FX k'tak (kata, sound, typing)

108-5——FX D'~ing (chi~n, sound)

109-1——FX Kla'chunk Kla'chunk (gako, sound, elevator doors opening)

109-2——FX ph'thungg (gon, sound, increasing weight)

109-3/4—FX b'buzzzzzzzzzz (bu~, sound, buzzer)

109-4-1—FX Kreek (kiri, depiction, mechnical creaking sounds adapted to depict increasing tension and anger)

109-4-2—FX Kreek (kiri, depiction, mechnical creaking sounds adapted to depict increasing tension and anger)

109-4-3—FX S'SHO~CK (ga~n, depiction)

109-5——FX D'~ing (chi~n, sound)

109-6——FX Wh'RRRR (wuiii, sound, mechanical)

110-2——FX Ph'fft (pou, depiction, tossing into air)

110-3——FX Fssk (kui, motion, turning objection around)

112-5——FX h'KOaUGHh (gofu', sound, coughing up something)

112-6——FX WH'THUD! (dosa, motion, collapse)

113-1——FX blub blub blub blub (doku doku, depiction, blood pouring out)

89-2——FX K'thud (do', sound, leaning back on chair)

90-1-1——FX CHOP! (chopu'! Yes—you got it.)

90-1-2——FX K'THUNK (meki, sound)

90-3——FX rattle rattle rattle rattle rattle rattle (ka ka ka, sound, extreme vibration)

90-4——FX sk'REECH (gya, sound)

90-5——FX A'ARATH!! (ba', motion)

91-1-1——FX kG'CHUNK (dogin, sound)

91-1-2——FX fssk! (kun', motion)

91-2-1——FX zz'zrakzrakzrak (gagaga, sound, abrasive)

91-2-2——FX wobble wobble (tsuuu~~, motion)

91-3——FX Ggrip! (gu', motion)

91-4——FX kreek (kori, sound)

91-5——FX v'VROAMM! (gao', sound)

92-2——FX Kl'chakchakchakchakchakchakchakc hakchakchakchakchak (ga, sound and depiction)

92-5——FX nonchalantly (shire, depiction)

92-6——FX 'OARRR (aaan, sound)

93-1——FX H'OOONK (paaa, sound)

93-2——FX Glare (ka', depiction)

93-3——FX SK'REECH K'REECH KREEK SK'REECH (gyaakaka karii gun!, sound)

93-4-1——FX v'WHOOSH! (hyu'!, motion)

93-4-2——FX ph'VREEE!! (supa~n, motion, cut clear across.)

94-1-1——FX v'ROARRR (gooo, sound)

94-1-2——FX Clap clap (pachi pachi, sound)

94-2——FX Fssk (su', motion)

94-3——FX VV'KREEECH (dogya, sound)

94-5——FX 'OARRR (aan, sound)

94-6——FX V'ROAAARRR (ooooo, sound)

95-3——FX K'THUD WHUD WHUD (dogagaga, sound)

95-4/5——FX V'VHOOOSH (bashu', sound)

95-6——FX Flap flap flap (bata, motion)

96-1——FX V'GROARRRR (gooo, sound)

96-4——FX whp'VPLAAASH (zaboaaa, sound)

96-5——FX Zz'rakk (zyari, sound)

97-3——FX z'thrsh z'thrsh z'thrsh z'thrshsh (zaaa, sound, water)

120-3-1 —— FX    t'thuthuthuthut (dadada, sound, running)

120-3-2 —— FX    (small, next to Excel's neck): blupblupblup (doku-doku, depiction, steady flow)

123-2 —— FX    g'duthduthduthduth (daga dagam, sound, running with heavy equipment)

123-3-1 —— FX    vWPvWPvWPvWPvWPvWP (bababba, sound, helicopter sounds, reinforced)

123-3-2 —— FX    VGRGGGGROARRR (gooooo, sound, fire)

125-1 —— FX    Shake shake (bun bun, motion, shaking head)

125-2 —— FX    Z'chak z'chak (zamu, sound, heavy and deliberate)

125-3-1 —— FX    (next to hair add on): K'reek k'reek (kyu kyu, sound, tightening or fastening something)

125-3-2 —— FX    Zz'rak zz'rak (zuruzuru, depiction, being dragged in)

125-4 —— FX    fssk (pui, motion, looking away, slightly comic -> quick motion)

125-6-1 —— FX    vWPvWPvWPvWPvWP (bababba, sound, helicopter sounds, reinforced)

125-6-2 —— FX    vV'VGRGGGGROARRR (kooooo, sound, fire)

126-7 —— FX    k'lak'lak'lak'lak'lak (ka', sound)

127-1 —— FX    th'THUD! (tan!, sound, opening door)

127-2 —— FX    zk'lak zk'lak zk'lak   (ga tsuka, sound, reinforced, walking, incoming)

127-3/4 —— FX    zk'lak zk'lak (tsuka, sound, reinforced, walking, incoming)

127-6 —— FX    PH'fff (fu¯, depiction, smoke exhale)

127-7 —— FX    VV'phfffff (buha¯, sound, exhaling)

129-2-1 —— FX    Fssk (sa', motion)

129-2-2 —— FX    ph'POP (pofu, sound, popping sound from blowing into cigar)

129-2-3 —— FX    p'PLth!! (pu'l, sound, plosive bilabial)

129-4 —— FX    KK'lak (katsu, sound)

129-6 —— FX    B'thud! (dan!, sound)

130-1 —— FX    B'thmp... (batan..., sound)

130-5-1 —— FX    K'REEK (gishi', sound)

130-5-2 —— FX    WHOOSH (fuu, sound)

131-1/2-1 —— FX    g'GrGrGrGrGr (gooo, sound, heavy mechanical)

131-1/2-2 —— FX    Kk'LAAANnnk! (ka'shaaan, sound, mechanical, light)

131-5 —— FX    g'Grrrrn! (gooon!, sound, heavy mechanical, opening door)

131-6 —— FX    Klank klank klank klank klank (kan, sound)

133-4 —— FX    Phap phap (pon, sound and motion, light tapping)

113-2 —— FX    Dash! (da', motion)

113-6 —— FX    Rustle rustle (zawa zawa, depiction)

114-2 —— FX    rustle rustle (zawa, depiction)

114-4-1 —— FX    ka'shnnk! (kashi, sound, light mechanical sound)

114-4-2 —— FX    K'KREEK (gin, sound, activation of equipment sound)

114-4/5 —— FX    Bzzt bzzzzt bzt bzzt (zi, sounds, mechanical operation sounds)

114-6-1 —— FX    Bzzt bzzzzt bzt bzzt (zi, sounds, mechanical operation sounds)

114-6-2 —— FX    B'chnkk (bu, sound, termination of line)

114-6-3 —— FX    Fssk (fu, motion)

115-1 —— FX    sh'ZINGg' (bi', depiction and movement, fast movement followed by sudden stop)

115-2 —— FX    GASP! (waaa, depiction and sound, crowd gasping)

115-4 —— FX    T'thut (ta', motion, running)

116-1-1 —— FX    sc'reech (ki', sound)

116-1-2 —— FX    zz'rk (za', sound, abrasive)

116-2 —— FX    B'thump! (batan!, sound)

116-3-1 —— FX    zk'lak (zuka, sound, reinforced)

116-3-2 —— FX    zk'lak zk'lak (zuka, sound, reinforced)

116-4 —— FX    t'thup! (tan, depiction, dramatic reinforcement)

116-5-1 —— FX    k'chak (ka', sound)

116-5-2 —— FX    ka'shnnk! (kashi, sound, light mechanical sound)

116-6 —— FX    vr¯¯¯¯ (chi¯¯¯¯, sound, scanning)

117-3 —— FX    a'RUTH! (ba!, sound, removing clothing in a rush)

117-4 —— FX    ph'thap! (pasa', sound, light)

117-5 —— FX    k'CHING! (kin!, sound)

117-6 —— FX    sh'SHI¯¯¯ng (shaaa, depiction and motion, severing something)

117-7 —— FX    sh'I¯¯¯ng (shaaa, depiction and motion, severing something)

118-1 —— FX    k'fssk k'fssk k'fsskfssk! (kikikikin!, sound and depiction, quickly cutting here and there)

118-3 —— FX    K'rrrrrm (chiiin, sound, high pitched mechanical activation sound)

119-1-1 —— FX    Bzzt bzzt (zi, sounds, mechanical operation sounds)

119-1-2 —— FX    chak k'chak chak (ka, sound, mechanical cutting sounds)

119-2 —— FX    ch'ching kk'inkk k'thakk (chin kin' ka', sounds, various metallic impact sounds)

134-2——FX Bustle bustle (doya doya, depiction)

136-1——FX TA'DMMT'!! (doban!, depiction, dramatic)

136-2——FX (throughout background): vWumPvWumP vWumPvWumPvWumP (batabata, sound, helicopter sounds, slower rotation)

136-3-1——FX th'ap! (ta', sound, touching ground)

136-3-2——FX (through out background): vWumPvWumPvWumP vWumPvWumP (batabata, sound, helicopter sounds, slower rotation)

136-4——FX (through out background): vWumPvWumPvWumPvWumPvWumP (batabata, sound, helicopter sounds, slower rotation)

137-1-1——FX A'ruth a'rrUth (basa, motion and sound, hair flapping about)

137-1-2——FX gg'rasp (ha'shi, motion, grasping her hands, comic)

137-2-1——FX sh'shing! (bi', depiction, pointing)

137-2-2——FX AA'RUTH! (gaba', motion)

137-4——FX K'SSNAPP! (pakkiin!, sound)

137-5——FX V'WHOOOSH! (buiin!, motion, swift)

138-1-1——FX k'Kthak th'KRASH wh'THUDD k'thatch (garan gashan' dogara ga', sound, crashing and thrashing)

138-1-2——FX t'thut t'thut (suta suta, motion, fast walking)

138-2——FX gk'KCHunk (gasha', sound)

138-3——FX Flap flap (paku paku, motion, of ear like sensors on head)

138-5——FX V'Thump (batan, sound, closing window)

139-1——FX (above and below): S'way s'way (buran, motion, being suspended and swaying about)

139-3——FX tt'thut tt'thu (teke teke, motion, walking)

139-4——FX GLOMP (pofun, sound)

139-5——FX SHO~~~~CK!! (ga~n!, depiction)

140-5-1——FX gK'REEKk (gyuu, motion, pulling -> sound)

140-5-2——FX yank (bin, depiction, a line becoming taut -> motion)

141-2——FX P'thmpt (pon, sound, light tap)

142-1——FX P'thmpt (pon, sound, heavy tap)

142-2——FX T'thut t'thut t'thut (pata pata, motion, walking and rushing about, hurriedly)

143-3——FX P'ff't (fu', sound, blowing exhale)

144-7-1——FX gG'rmblermblrm~~~~ (gu~, sound, hunger)

144-7-2——FX (white): s'niff s'niff (pisu pisu, sound, short bursts of sniffing)

145-1——FX k'lank (kan, sound, mechanical)

145-2——FX k'lank (kan, sound, mechanical)

145-3——FX k'lank (kan, sound, mechanical)

145-4——FX k'lank (kan, sound, mechanical)

145-5——FX DAAAAAAA (daaaaa', sound trumpet)

145-6——FX b'lup b'lup (do'pu dopu, depiction, blood flow)

145-7——FX v'WHISSOOSHPHOOSH (ho'sha'shaa, sound, running, excessive comic exaggeration)

147-1——FX v'BLAAAAMmm (zupaaa, sound)

147-2——FX ph'thuthuthuthut (shi'tatatata, motion, fast running, comic)

147-3-1——FX v'VRROARrr (oaaa, sound, vehicle driving by)

147-3-2——FX th'THUMP! (biku, motion, reation -> sudden heartbeat)

147-4——FX v'WhoPvPvPvPvP (dopabababa, sound, helicopter sounds)

147-5——FX v'Thuthut (dada, sound, running)

149-3——FX B'lupp bV'lupp (gopo' gopopo', depiction, blood flow)

150-1——FX B'thmp (bata, sound)

150-2——FX Kl'thak Kl'thak Kl'thak (tsuka, sound)

151-3——FX Glare (ki', depiction)

152-4——FX s'Squeeze! (kyu', depiction, squeezing)

152-5-1——FX ZG'GUEEEZE~~~~ (gibyuuu, depiction, massive injection)

152-5-2——FX b'lup'lup (doku doku, depiction, blood pumping in)

152-6-1——FX ss'queeeze~ (gyuuu, depiction)

152-6-2——FX (background, lower): b'lup b'lup b'lup (dokun dokun, blood flow)

153-1-1——FX s'QUEEEZE~~~~ (gyuuu, depiction, massive injection)

153-1-2——FX s'QUEEEZE~~~~ (gyuuu, depiction, massive injection)

153-2-1——FX zZ'GUEEEZE~~~~ (gyubyuu, depiction, massive injection)

153-2-2——FX ~~~QUEEEZ~~~~ (gyuuu, depiction, massive injection)

153-3-1——FX zZ'GUE'EEEZ! (gi'byuu, depiction, massive injection)

153-3-2——FX zZ'GUE'EEEZ! (gi'byuu, depiction, massive injection)

153-4——FX p'fft p'fft (pon pon, sound, tossing light objects away)

153-5——FX Phap phap (pon, sound and motion, light tapping)

154-2——FX T'thut t'thut (ta', sound, running)

154-5——FX V'whrwhrwhrwhr (rururu, depiction, looking about, new and comic, working off of FX of turning about [kuru] and of mechanics [kyururu])

154-6——FX Ta'DMPPP!! (donn, depiction, dramatic reinforcement)

155-1——FX zk'lak zk'lak zk'lak (zuka, sound, reinforced)

# OUBLIETTE
## Your *Excel Saga* bonus section!

172-3——FX Oh YEAH! (ootsu! dialog)

172-4-1——FX (far right): T'dum t'dum tattat'dumdum T'dum t'dum tattat'dumdum (dontsuku dontsuku, sound, drums [film score like])

172-4-2——FX V'WHOOROARRR (gooo, sound, wind, dramatic)

173-2-1——FX t'thut t'thut t'thut t'thut (suta suta, motion, walking)

173-2-2——FX G'THUD! (go', sound)

173-3-1——FX b'ang b'ang (don don, sound)

173-3-2——FX wh'thmp (dosa', sound, collapsing)

173-6——FX b'ang b'ang (don don, sound)

174-1——FX F'SSHINK! (suka!, motion and depiction, [suddenly] getting through effortlessly)

174-3——FX Grin (nii, depiction)

174-6——FX Wheez wheez wheez (ze', sound)

175-1——FX wheeeez wheeeez (hii hii, depiction and sound)

175-2——FX Ha-HAH! (he hen! dialog)

175-3——FX Phew~~~ hu'eeez Huff huff (fu~ ha~ haa haa, sounds)

175-5-1——FX P'ffput (pe', sound, spitting)

175-5-2——FX fssk (su, motion)

175-5-3——FX th'chak (gacha, sound)

176-1——FX Phap (pe', motion, crude hand movement)

176-2——FX bow (peko, motion)

176-3-1——FX (large): gG'HOUGHH! (bebo, sound, coughing up a lot of blood in one burst)

176-3-2——FX thr'plash k'plash phap'lash blup'lash (besho dopo gopo pazya, sound, splashing sounds)

176-5-1——FX b'lupplupplupp (popopo, sound)

176-5-2——FX krek'shing! thk'shing! (kin kin, sound and depiction, something coming together to form a large whole)

176-6-1——FX v'VRRRRM (ooo, sound and depiction, something materializing)

176-6-2——FX ph'thmp (pata, sound and depiction, collapsing, comic)

177-1——FX Da'DMMP!! (don!, depiction, dramatic appearance)

177-3——FX Zz'SHING! (bi, depiction, dramatic, putting somebody on the spot)

177-4-1——FX vH'ROAARRGH (goaaa, sound, beast like roaring)

177-4-2——FX k'THUD wh'thak kk'KRACK G'THUD (doko beki geki gako, sounds)

179-1——FX k'KLNK! (pakon, sound, sudden opening)

179-3——FX Hahaha (ha' ha' ha', dialog)

155-2——FX vW'THMP! (tan!, sound)

155-4——FX Ph'THAP!! (beshi, sound)

156-1-1——FX TEARS STREAMING TEARS STREAMING (hara hara, depiction, crying in a state of emotional distress)

156-1-2——FX (black): th'KRsh... (gusha, sound, crumpling paper)

156-1-3——FX (white): th-THUMP! (biku, depiction, reaction -> heart jumping)

156-2——FX D'THUP D'THUP D'THUP (dan dan, sound, walking loud, stamping down feet)

156-3-1——FX Aa-AH~~ Aa-A'AAH~~~ Aa-AH~~ Aaa~AH^~~A~ (ya~, sound, dramatic film score where they preciousness of life is being celebrated, James Horner and Randy Newman like music)

156-3-2——FX vh'RUTH! (baa!, sound and motion, spreading out arms)

156-3-3——FX AaAH~ AaA'AAH~~AaAH Aaa~AH^~~A~ (as 156-3-1)

156-4——FX Aaa~AH^~~A~Aaa~AH^~~A~AA^~~~~ (as 156-3-1)

157-2——FX K'THUD K'THUD (ga', sound)

158-1——FX K'THUD (ga', sound)

158-2——FX B'LUP B'LUP B'LUP (bori bori, sound, sinking)

160-6——FX zz'chak zz'chak zz'ckak (za', sound)

161-1——FX OH GOD! (aa', dialog)

161-3——FX Fssk... (su.., motion, slight)

162-3——FX giddy giddy giddy (te'ko, depiction and motion, being happy and giddy)

162-4——FX Whee~~~ (kyu~~, depiction, emotionally uplifted, happiness -> dialog)

162-5——FX K'THUK (doko, sound, heavy)

164-3——FX Snuggle snuggle (suri suri, motion)

164-4——FX 'nnNNN... (nnn..., depiction and sound, vastness of ACROSS Base)

166-4——FX v'GGGrrn... (goon, sound, heavy door opening)

169-1——FX k'BLAAAM (doon, sound)

169-2-1——FX (white): V'Groarr (gogo, sound)

169-2-2——FX (black): th'THUt th'THUt th'THUt th'THUt th'THUt th'THUt th'THUt th'THUt (dada, movement, fast running)

169-4——FX Kla'CHAK! (gasha', sound)

170-1——FX (in bg): ZZ'ROARRR (zuooo, depiction, dramatic)

171-2——FX flap flap f'flap (basa basa basa', motion)

171-4——FX K'REE~, ggrakvraakRAKkreekya~ (pi~ gaka', sound, modem session start sound)

171-5——FX K'THNKT KK'thnKT k'THUNK K'ththNK (gaku gaku ga gaku, depiction and motion, seizure like movements)

179-4——FX Hup!! (dei', dialog)

180-1-1——FX twirl twirl (guru, motion)

180-1-2——FX v'WHOOOSH! (pyuuu, motion)

180-2-1——FX T'thut! (ta', sound)

180-2-2——FX Glare! (ki', depiction)

180-3——FX T'thud T'thud T'thud T'thud (dadada, sound)

180-4——FX thBPLth (bu', sound, plosive bilabial)

180-5——FX Whd'THUD! (doka, sound)

181-1——FX K'REEEEEk (giii, sound)

181-7——FX (in bg): t'thut t'thut t'thut t'thut (tatata, sound)

182-2——FX K'hSH~~~~ (shu~, depiction, giving off steam)

182-3——FX v'VRMMM (Bu...n, depiction, image changing)

182-4——FX Th'chakk! (gasha', sound)

183-1-1——FX Ta'DMPPP!! (donn, depiction, dramatic reinforcement)

183-1-2——FX thnk! (ga', swinging gesture)

183-2——FX krek'shing! (kin kin, depiction, sudden appearance)

183-4——FX zz'fssk! (zon, motion, fast and taking something)

183-5——FX Fssk! (shu!, motion)

183-6-1——FX Glare! (ki', depiction)

183-6-2——FX T'thutt! (to'!, sound)

184-1——FX zz'chak! (za!, sound and depiction, going into pose)

184-2——FX zZ'shing! (bi', motion and depiction)

184-3——FX K'BLOOM! (bomu', sound)

184-6-1——FX Glare! (ka', depiction)

184-6-2——FX krek'shing! (kin!, depiction, sudden appearance)

185-1——FX K'BLOOM! (bou, sound)

185-2-1——FX wh'thmp (dosa', sound, collapsing)

185-2-2——FX kK'BANNGGH (goban, sound)

185-3——FX G'GROARRR (gogo, sound)

185-4-1——FX v'GrGrGrGr... (zuzuzu, sound)

185-4-2——FX kl'THUD V'THUD G'THUD... (dododoo, sound)

186-1——FX g'VWHOOOSH (go~, sound)

186-3——FX g'THUD g'THUD g'THUD g'THUD (do' dodo gadogogon, sound

186-4-1——FX K'thunk k'thunk (gaku gaku, motion, shaking)

186-4-2——FX splirt! (pu', depiction, blood spriting out)

186-5-1——FX KG'WHUDD'THUDD'THUDD (dogogogon, sound)

186-5-2——FX th'THUD! Th'THUD! (do', sound)

186-5-3——FX kl'THUD gG'THUD... (gon do', sound)

187-1——FX vWH'VOOOMm (gosun, sound, major explosion)

187-4——FX g'THUTHUDDTHUDDD (gogogo, sound)

188-2——FX P'thmpt (pon, sound, light tap)

188-3——FX zz'plashzz (zazaa, sound)

5-4 In Japan, the legal drinking age is 20--this is the age at which you are legally considered to be a full adult, including the right to smoke, drink, vote, and pay taxes, although not necessarily in that order. Just as in America, however, certain rights are granted earlier, at 18—including the ability to drive (when the editor was 16 with a just-issued license, he had the privilege of briefly serving as the chauffeur of Hideo Ogata, editor of *Animage*, who remarked the experience was a thrill he could not have enjoyed in Japan), as well as the authority to play pachinko, buy porno, and join the army--by which I mean of course, the Self-Defense Force. Maybe you're wondering what the hell this note has to do with anything in Page 5, panel 4. Please examine closely the beer ad on the back of the ski resort guide that Iwata's reading. The liquor industry adopted this public service message in a polite bid to curtail underage drinking, as beer, whisky and saké are available from public vending machines in Japan. When the editor was 16 with a just-used airplane ticket to Tokyo, he had the privilege of repeatedly availing himself of these devices, remarking the experience was a thrill he could not have enjoyed in America.

9-2 The word "pension" is the common title attached to the names of (remote) recreational retreats and/or villas in Japan. It's a loanword taken not from English but French; in continental Europe the term is often used to refer to boardinghouses and small hotels, both urban and rural.

14-3-1 The bit about "self-defense" would not be in the original. While it is legal but difficult in Japan to own a rifle or shotgun for hunting and target practice (and therefore Rumiko Takahashi was able to put a "shotgun wedding" joke in her manga *Maison Ikkoku*, where Godai imagines Kozue's dad will help him resolve his indecisive nature with a brief brandish of the 12-gauge) and legal but almost impossible to own a pistol there, Japanese people would not be inclined to think of firearms in a personal self-defense role. Even cops in Japan are expected to be able to handle themselves with martial arts or non-lethal weapons in a confrontation; Sumiyoshi's quote of *Ninja Force Moonlight* (see Vol. 03, note for 157-3), "Your pistol is the weapon of last resort," actually reflects real Japanese police attitudes.

Attorney and author Dave Kopel (an active member of both the NRA and ACLU) has a thought-provoking law review article on Japanese gun law history, which you can locate at the URL http://www.davekopel.org/2A/LawRev/Japanese_Gun_Control.htm. Although one statement within the article—that "the military barely exists" in Japan risks misleading the reader (their military, that is, readers right up to this point, simply because the Japanese also celebrate Valentine's Day on February 14th. The twist is that only girls give to boys in Japan on the 14th, whereas the Japanese (or, to be more accurate, the Japanese chocolate companies) developed their own reciprocal holiday a month later on March 14th, when only boys give to girls. Susan Yee's story on Valentine's Day for sushiandtofu.com (located at the URL http://www.sushiandtofu.com/sushi_and_tofu/features_sheLovesMe.htm) will not only fill in details, but suggest the rather surprising thing Misaki was trying to do in 50.3.

53 I never thought I'd see the day when the 1977-80 *Lupin III* TV series (the second of the three Lupin anime TV series to date) was on nationwide American television. I literally dreamed of this when I was in high school in the mid-80s—I remember a dream where, in the dream, I woke up in the middle of the night and went downstairs to the living room, turning on the TV to find *Lupin III* was playing. As Calvin said, "My dreams are becoming way too literal"; aren't otaku supposed to fantasize *about* the anime, not merely *about watching* the anime? So even for fans new to Japanese animation and comics, there's a good chance you might recognize whose style Excel is trying to emulate here.

However, as DJ Quik said, "I don't compare my rhyme style to no gat/'Cause to me that bullshit is super wack," as are many things about the dubbed version of *Lupin III* shown on Adult Swim. You have to understand that this is one of the all-time classics in Japan, a show fondly remembered there by both hardcore anime fans and the general public. The dub's attempt to add contemporary references to the script to make you think it was made recently is not only bizarre to the point of suggesting genuine mental disorder (as no attempt is made to change the show's 70s fashion, disco music, or of course, its dated style of animation), it's simply wrong—what would people think if you re-ran *Kojak*, but with newly inserted jokes about *American Idol* and Paris Hilton?

And also, I don't know who the American voice actor who plays Jigen is, but he is no Kiyoshi Kobayashi, the man who established the character in Japan. Again, this is no mere nit-pick—in their time, the original cast of *Lupin III* were the best-regarded and highest-paid voice actors in Japan. Jigen Daisuke was the epitome of cool—although Jet Black from *Cowboy Bebop* is often thought of as that show's "Jigen" character, in actuality Spike, too—sardonic and collected as well as lanky and deadly—is probably more "Jigen" than "Lupin." If only the late James Coburn (who did a star voice acting turn as Henry J. Waternoose in *Monsters, Inc.*) could have been the one to give us an American Jigen; for Coburn himself was said to have been *Lupin III* creator Monkey Punch's original inspiration for the character. I can believe it—check out Coburn's 1966 film *Our Man Flint*; he really *was* that lanky.

58-4-2 The original terms were *chaka* and *hajiki*. Chaka is the slang employed by the Yakuza for a gun. As you might guess, it's based on the sound of cocking a hammer. *Hajiki*, on the other hand, is the slang employed by police referring to a gun; *Viz* Visual Entertainment producer Toshi Yoshida vouchsafed to the editor the term is from the verb *hajiku*, to bounce or ricochet—also occurring in the sardonic phrase for one who has taken in more lead than was good for him: *hajikareta*, "(he was) bounced." Just as in America, however, Japanese cops will in fact often use criminals' slang, and vice-versa.

as Kopel intends to suggest, barely exists in Japan as an instrument of *policy*—however, not only does the SDF certainly exist, but it is a modern and well-funded military by world standards) Kopel's piece otherwise strikes the editor as researched and convincing. Differing in its assertion of some details of the Japanese law is an article by Masaaki Ishida at http://yarchive.net/gun/politics/japan_gun.html. Mr. Ishida, a member of the National Rifle Association of Japan (just a *little* different from the American NRA) gives many interesting specifics on what the Japanese law requires of gun owners.

25-8 Saga Prefecture (the nation of Japan is divided into 47 prefectures, but as Japan is about the size of California, one should perhaps think in terms of county-sized areas rather than states) is just to the southwest of Fukuoka Prefecture—itself, of course, named for the storied "City of F." Note that likewise the original manga here spoke of the ski resort being located on "Mt. T" in "S Prefecture." This was another example of the odd self-censorship one can often find in manga, where entire major cities are referred to only by initial, out of fear local civic organizations might take offense.

This is also (in part) why a disproportionate number of stories seem to take place in Tokyo, in whose greater metropolitan area only one out of seven Japanese actually live. People will believe anything about Tokyo. Of course, the manga industry (including Shonen Gahosha, the original publisher of Excel Saga) is centered there, and it is Japan's greatest city; it's not so different from DC Comics' avatars of NYC, Metropolis and Gotham City—or for that matter—the Marvel Universe, which has always been openly centered around Manhattan Island. By the way, if you yourself would ever like to go ski Tenzan and avenge the guys' night of horror, Snowjapan.com offers the lowdown at: http://www.snowjapan.com/e/resorts/resortdetail.php?resid=344

28-3 The portable Sony MiniDisc player was always much more popular in Japan than the U.S., despite the fact that (unlike most portable CD players), you can record on it, too. Like Sony's Betamax, MD was never much supported by U.S. releases in the format; unlike Beta vs. VHS however, MiniDiscs were understood to be somewhat inferior in recording quality to the CD. In April, though, Sony will try again in the U.S. with the new Hi-MD, whose improved sound quality and 1GB capacity offers 45 hours of music capacity versus 80 min. on the original MD format. It's seen in part as a way to compete with products such as the iPod.

36-4-1 Dr. Kabapu originally made reference to two times of the year in Japan, *chugen* (near the summer solstice) and *seibo* (more commonly called *o-seibo*—this season is six months later, near the end of the year) in which both individuals and companies will send gifts to those whom they feel they have consideration or respect, or to those whom they at least wish to give the appearance of feeling consideration or respect. On these occasions, VIZ, LLC receives such things as tins of rice crackers, cookie assortments, boxes of chocolates, etc., much of the largesse being distributed to the office as a whole. I recall one year a great glass carboy of pistachios, epic in size, whose unshelling was a tale but slowly told.

52-2-2 This whole storyline works pretty well for American

not add the suffix "-kun" when addressing Matsuya (Iwata simply says "Misaki" most of the time) but is using it when talking to Ropponmatsu Type I. For this reason, we need to impress upon the readers that Iwata is being selective in addressing Ropponmatsu Type I.

106-6 Japanese phrase is *gyakufuu*, meaning an unfavorable shift in wind.

125-2-1 The term *rachi*, or abduction, carries no specific cultural baggage, but *rachirareru*, which is what Iwata shouts out in the original, is a slang form of the same verb that is now associated more specifically with two kinds of notorious kidnappings: that of Japanese by the domestic cult Aum Shinrikyo, and by North Korean intelligence. The editor thought of the modish English transitive use of "he was disappeared" versus the familiar, intransitive "he disappeared." The former, pending certain 2004 Supreme Court rulings, has been used in America mostly to refer to hi-jinks abroad; inspired by the Spanish *desaparecidos*, the people "disappeared" by authoritarian Latin American regimes in the 70s and 80s. The North Korean abductions, by the way, were supposedly to teach their spies about contemporary Japan, but the editor cannot but regard the practice as more than cruel, but bizarre—not only can many Koreans speak, and physically pass for, Japanese anyway, but why didn't they just watch some goddamn trendy dramas? Speaking as a resident of the world's #1 spy target, I can categorically state that the KGB never had to resort to such shenanigans.

141-1-1 Common schoolyard taunt regarding the extreme but useless capabilities of a person (or robot), although perhaps carrying less sting in the era of *Fear Factor*. Original reference goes back to the much-beloved (except in the U.S. of A.) manga and anime series *Doraemon*, where Nobita must perform this de-shelling feat to impress his friends. It henceforth entered the Japanese language as a phrase to be invoked in such situations.

142-2-1 Iwata originally makes reference not to "animatronics" but "electric dolls," cheap pseudo-robot toys sold in Japan.

150-2-3 Dr. Iwata's heartless cheers at the situation are a creative adaptation of an old Japanese custom. Long ago in the Tokugawa Era (see 184-1-1 below), audiences would always yell out in praise the names of the fireworks makers whenever they went to see them being shot off at a display. The two most famous fireworks firms were called "Tamaya" and "Kagiya." Some might be tempted to translated the two names as "Balls Retailer" (shades of Inspector Clouseau) and "Keys Retailer," but this would be incorrect; rather, they are proper names. Since it would be useless to try to relay all this culture-specific information in one line, the translator chose to represent the spirit behind the line spoke—"Yeah, those fireworks kick ass!" Note this footnote was first written, in a modified form, to accompany the official translation of *Sakura Wars: The Movie* from Geneon (formally Pioneer).

151-2-2 The original text has Fukuya refer to Dr. Sekifumi Iwata's father, Kanefumi, as *ojisan*, which can have two meanings. It can either mean Fukuya and Kanefumi are uncle and niece, or that Fukuya respects Kanefumi as an older person and is using the title *ojisan* as a sign of respect. The word "uncle" in English can have a similar meaning, but usually only young children refer to non-related older men as "uncle."

61-1 What an excellent opportunity to make more fun of the SDF. But why use several paragraphs to do so here, when no less sober an authority than *The Christian Science Monitor* can do better, merely by reporting the news? Look, maybe the Japanese military really is full of otaku. Well if so—otaku, please. What the hell is this, *Mao-Chan*? I'm not saying this approach wouldn't have actually worked back in the 1980s, but did you expect a response from all those kids who grew up in 90s Japan seeing Shinji ask Gendo "No, *Dad*—what about *you?*" http://www.csmonitor.com/2003/0825/p07s01-woap.html

61-5~64-1: Here, however, Excel is trying to emulate the style of Maki Umezaki, one of the stars of Akihiro Ito's *Geobreeders*, a next-door neighbor to *Excel Saga*, as they both run in the same Japanese monthly magazine, *Young King Ours*.

63-3-2 Excel's original reference is to *naniwa bushi*, traditional narrative ballads recited by a solo chanter, accompanied by the playing of the shamisen. *Naniwa* is an old-fashioned term for the Osaka area, and it was there the style originated in the mid-Tokugawa period. *Naniwa bushi* tend to stress sentimental themes of sacrifice, especially on a matter of the heart or soul, and hence it has come to convey a tear-jerker ending.

91-5-1: Owing to such factors as a greater distribution and use of public transportation, a larger percentage of Japanese than Americans lack drivers' licenses, and many Japanese high schools do not offer driver's ed. (a salutary chill is evoked by the fact the editor spent his own drivers' ed. class drawing manga in his notebook). Whereas buying a cheap used car is a common entry into driving for many young Americans, the registration system is rigged against it in Japan—after a car gets a few years old, it starts becoming really expensive to renew its tags. This is why so many Japanese used cars get exported to poorer nations (particularly Russia, where there is a huge demand for them) instead of bought by Japanese. The system is, of course, designed for the benefit of the Japanese auto industry, not the consumer, "encouraging" the public to buy a new car more often. An additional irony comes from the notorious practice of the Japanese government subsidizing highway building to benefit construction firms (major political contributors); highways which remain underutilized in part because of other policies that discourage wider auto ownership. . . ("Return to START and roll dice again").

92-5-2 The same word, "law," would be used in English were we to refer either to laws in the scientific sense, or laws in the legal sense, but in Japanese different words are used——*housoku* meaning law when applied to science, and *houritsu* meaning law when applied to the legal system.

92-6-1 Excel's epithet here is lifted directly from the world's greatest comics magazine, Newcastle-on-Tyne's very own *Viz*—specifically, the story "Charlie Heston's Cold, Dead Hands" (Issue #127, Aug 2003, p. 30) where a young British schoolboy has as his constant magical companion the disembodied, assault gun-clutching hands of Charlton Heston.

106-2 Japanese phrase is *senpai kaze*, literally "senior wind" ("senpai" is what Hyatt calls Excel in the original Japanese).

106-5-3 Why preserve the -kun here? Well notice that Iwata does

# OUBLIETTE

## Your *Excel Saga* bonus section!

municipally-subsidized to do so—freely roaming around. Fukuoka Tower of song and legend (173-1) was built for the 1989 Expo as well.

174-6-3 Excel refers to ye olde Japanese custom (though by no means limited to Japan) of peasant families abandoning their old relatives—especially unwanted old women—in times of famine and dearth. Perhaps unsurprisingly, little actual information concerning the details of the practice survives, but the story of this heartbreak and sorrow (presumably these aged family members were never annoying and cranky) is told often enough in Japan to schoolchildren that most people there have at least heard of it.

175-2-1 The translator and many readers already know this, but the editor never plays video games himself (although he does like to watch—huh-huh-huh). In many console or computer games, before you can battle the big boss, you must fight the middle management of darkness. Often this will consist of a set of four top-ranked henchmen of varying powers and abilities, referred to as the boss's *shitennou* (the term here given as "guardian quartet" or "four guardians"). The term originally came from the set of four guardian Deva Kings in Buddhism (for an excellent online resource, please consult http://www.onmarkproductions.com/html/)shitenno.shtml). Note that in contemporary Japanese usage *shitennou* need not refer to figures in the realm of fantasy or myth; indeed people will speak of individuals who are a company's *shitennou*, for instance. An academic might even describe Lacan, Foucault, Barthes, and Derrida as the "*shitennou* of structuralism/post-structuralism." This last detail, by the way, is perhaps the clearest example *Oubliette* will ever feature of the difference between a footnote written by the editor and one written by the translator. Warning: unless you know them both well, your guess is wrong.

178-1 The "character name" Rock is based on the fact "Iwata" is written with the two kanji for "rock" and "(rice) farm field." *Dai* is based on Sumiyoshi's first name, Daimaru. Just as Westerners do, Japanese often prefer the sound of an archaic, exotic, or foreign name for a character when they play a fantasy role-playing game. This being *Excel Saga*, of course, these particular names come off as a little awkward.

184-1-1 Original reference is to *Onmitsu* ("those who hide in secret"), short for *Kogi Onmitsu*, the official espionage bureau formed by Ieyasu Tokugawa, founder of the dynasty of shogun that ruled Japan between 1600 and 1868. *Onmitsu* was also a familiar term for the ninja who worked for it; sort of as we might understand a "Fed" to simply mean an agent of the Federal Bureau of Investigation.

186-1 Lord Kabapuu's mighty spring-powered escape capsule is also a modified form of the Yokatopia "Kabapu" mascot. Note the relationship between the small horn and the Kabapuu's "added" crown-dowel.

191 This entire page is a parody of *Nihon Mukashi Banashi* ("Folktales of Old Japan"), an anime series about a super space battleship defending Earth, crewed largely by cute girls of between twelve and nineteen years of age. Actually, it isn't about that; rather, each episode of *Nihon Mukashi Banashi* portrays a folktale of old Japan. I'm not sure which prefecture of ancient Nihon offered the option of those Vermont-style civil unions. And that's izz-out for *Oubliette* this time.

158-2 The *bori bori* sound FX used here is actually a regional variation of the common onomatopoeia for sinking; the translator checked it especially. The editor remarks here he agrees with Adam Corolla that the menace of quicksand, omnipresent in 70s TV shows, is something that needs to be brought back.

163-4-3 The translator notes that those are Buddhist prayer beads, not a Catholic rosary, that Iwata's got in his hands. It's indicative of his character that he would want to cover all bases in his quest overboard to mourn Ropponmatsu I. Some might regard this mix-n'-match as offensive. But you forget that Iwata is an offensive character. Come to think of it, this hasn't been the first offensive thing in *Excel Saga*.

164-2 *Chuugakusei Nikki* ("Junior High School Diary") on NHK, which is known in particular for soap operas targeted at students after school. In one form or another, this show has been on the air for over 41 years in Japan. The actors who play the students are, in fact, real junior high school students (hundreds audition every year) whereas teachers may be played by professional actors (Leo Morimoto, who played Shiro in Gainax's premiere film *Royal Space Force*—and Hiromi's father eleven years later in their live-action film *Love & Pop*—is a veteran of the TV show). *Junior High School Diary* airs on Sunday afternoons, with weekday repeats. It has always been considered as a show whose portrayal of working through "life lessons" is a good influence on kids. Of course, as it is on NHK, Japan's government-run network (see *Excel Saga* Vol. 01, note for 97-5) the show is *a priori* good for you. The official site of the series is: http://www.nhk.or.jp/nikki/pc.html

164-3-3 Matsuya-san means that she isn't sure where to place Ropponmatsu Type II within her own conception of the (vertical and horizontal) relationships she has with other people. This is a more formal problem for Japanese than Americans, with the notion of social hierarchy *per se* both more accepted, and in fact built into personal communication—proper levels of politeness and use of appropriate titles towards others being necessary to correct, well-spoken Japanese. This is particularly a matter of some concern (see her exchange with Momochi, p. 37-39) to someone like Matsuya, who does not intend to be deterred in life, yet whom despite Watanabe's slurs is actually quite formal in manner. The translator remarks this formality is why Matsuya speaks of a "sociogram"—abstracting the issue while making careful note of it— rather than phrasing it something like "place on the totem pole."

169-2-1 By the way, the Minister of Court here is the same dude Hyatt and Excel worked for in Vol. 03, Mission 1. Efficient.

173-4 Now it can be told. Digging ever deeper into the mysterious link between *Excel Saga*'s characters and Fukuoka civic boosterism, Dr. Kabapu's appearance is in fact based on that of, erm, "Kabapu," the mascot of the 1989 Asia-Pacific Expo, held in Fukuoka to celebrate the centennial of the city's official charter in the post-feudal Meiji Era (the locale itself has been active as a center of maritime trade for many centuries). The Expo site was built on Fukuoka's Momochi-hama (ho, ho) ocean front (extensively redeveloped and extended out onto the water for the Expo) and the site dubbed "Yokatopia." It was exactly as you feared; there were people dressed up as Kabapu—indeed,

# If you enjoy
# EXCEL SAGA,
## the editor
## recommends,
## also from VIZ: